Ruling Ideas

Ruling Ideas

How Global Neoliberalism Goes Local

CORNEL BAN

OXFORD
UNIVERSITY PRESS

OXFORD

UNIVERSITY PRESS

Oxford University Press is a department of the University of Oxford. It furthers
the University's objective of excellence in research, scholarship, and education
by publishing worldwide. Oxford is a registered trade mark of Oxford University
Press in the UK and certain other countries.

Published in the United States of America by Oxford University Press
198 Madison Avenue, New York, NY 10016, United States of America.

© Oxford University Press 2016

Library of Congress Cataloging-in-Publication Data
Names: Ban, Cornel, author.
Title: Ruling ideas : how global neoliberalism goes local / Cornel Ban.
Description: New York, NY : Oxford University Press, 2016.
Identifiers: LCCN 2016000682| ISBN 9780190600389 (hardback) | ISBN 9780190600396 (paperback)
Subjects: LCSH: Neoliberalism— Spain. | Neoliberalism—Romania. | Spain—Economic policy.
| Romania—Economic policy. | Spain—Economic conditions—2008- | Spain—Economic
conditions—1975-2008. | Romania—Economic conditions—1989- | BISAC: POLITICAL SCIENCE /
Economic Conditions. | POLITICAL SCIENCE / Political Ideologies / Conservatism & Liberalism.
Classification: LCC HC385.5 .B36 2016 | DDC 330.946—dc23 LC record available at
http://lccn.loc.gov/2016000682

CONTENTS

LIST OF FIGURES

LIST OF INTERVIEWS

Fourteen interviewees not listed below asked that their identity be concealed. They are referenced in the text by their institutional affiliation.

Joaquín Almunia. Former minister of labor in the Spanish government

Moisa Altar. Economics professor, founder of the Doctoral School of Finance and Banking, Bucharest

Emil Boc. Former prime minister of Romania, 2008–2012

Horia Braun. Former research economist at the Research Service of the National Bank of Romania

Daniel Dăianu. Former chief economist of the National Bank of Romania (BNR), 1992–1997, minister of finance, 1997–1998, and board member of the BNR, 2014–

Suzana Dobre. Expert at the Romanian Academic Society (SAR) and member of Expert Forum

Aitor Erce. Economist at the Bank of Spain

Fernando Fernandez. Senior economist with Spain's Center for Monetary and Financial Studies (CEMFI)

Richard Florescu. Economist with the World Bank Delegation in Bucharest

Mircea Geoană. Former chairman of the Social Democratic Party and minister of foreign affairs of Romania

Florin Georgescu. Former minister of finance and deputy governor of the National Bank of Romania

Constantin Gheorghe. Adviser to the Romanian president

Alfred Gusenbauer. Former chancellor of Austria

Anca Harasim. Executive director of the American Chamber of Commerce in Bucharest

Bogdan Hossu. Chairman of Romania's Cartel ALFA labor confederation

Florentin Iancu. Labor expert for Romania's Cartel ALFA labor confederation

Ion Iliescu. Former president of Romania, 1990–1996, 2000–2004

Valeriu Ioan-Franc. Economist at Academia Română (INCE)

Sorin Ioniță. Senior expert at the Romanian Academic Society, chairman of Expert Forum

Ovidiu Jurca. Negotiator for Romania's Blocul Național Sindica labor confederation

Carlos Mulas Granados. Former economic adviser to Spain's prime minister

Álvaro Nadal. Director of the Economic Office of Spain's prime minister

Cătălin Păuna. Senior economist in the World Bank Group office in Romania, Europe, and Central Asia

Romano Prodi. Former president of the European Commission

Petre Roman. Former prime minister of Romania, 1990–1991

Miguel Sebastián. Former head of the Spanish government's Economic Bureau and Minister of Industry, 2004–2011

Adrian Severin. Romania's minister of economic reform, 1990–1991

Cristian Socol. Economic adviser to the prime minister, 2012–2015

Carlos Solchaga. Former minister of finance and economy, 1985–1993

Horia Terpe. Centrul de Analiza si Dezvoltare Institutionala Eleutheria expert

Mugur Tolici. Human resources manager of the National Bank of Romania

Vlad Topan. Economics professor at Academia de Studii Economice, Bucharest

Nicolae Văcăroiu. Former prime minister of Romania, 1992–1996

Javier Vallés. Economist at the Economic Office of the prime minister of Spain

Liviu Voinea. Former Secretary of State at the Ministry of Finance and minister of the budget, Romania 2012–2015

Gheorghe Zaman. Senior economist at Academia Română (INCE)

PART I

VARIETIES OF NEOLIBERALISM

The Ruling Power of Neoliberal Ideas

Ideas are to objects what constellations are to stars.
—Walter Benjamin, *The Origin of German Tragic Drama*

Neo-liberalism is not Adam Smith; neo-liberalism is not market society; neo-liberalism is not the Gulag on the insidious scale of capitalism.
—Michel Foucault, *The Birth of Biopolitics*

Translation is very much like copying paintings.
—Boris Pasternak

Many scholars agree that economic theories are a form of political power because they form the basis of social conventions that provide shared templates and understandings that organize and coordinate actions in the policy arena.[1] There is also an emerging agreement that economic theories with global ambitions such as Keynesianism or neoliberalism exercise this "ruling power" not as rigid scripts to be copied in one location and reproduced in another, but as flexible ideas open to local adaptation and interpretation. As the dominant mode of economic thinking of our time, neoliberalism is not a seamless and steely behemoth, but an evolving hybrid whose every concrete manifestation is imbued with local flavors (Stark and Bruszt 1998; Campbell and Pedersen 2001b; Bockman and Eyal 2002; Kjær and Pedersen 2001; Brenner and Theodore 2002; Pedersen 2007; Brenner, Peck, and Theodore 2010a; 2010b; Peck and Theodore 2012; Mirowski 2013; Ban and Blyth 2013; Schmidt and Thatcher 2013).

The evidence analyzed in this book shows that these local translations are far from being free intellectual exercises or simple projections of local interest group games. Instead, they reflect domestic intellectual history and encapsulate transnational struggles over ideas and resources. The result can be the incorporation of non-neoliberal edits into the texture of neoliberalism.

Broadly speaking, if the policy implications of these alternatives entail the use of the state to buffer the broader society against the dislocations produced by market competition and its associated structures of power and privilege, the resulting local hybrids form a continuum that can be called *embedded neoliberalism*. If, instead, their main implication is not to moderate markets and their effects, but to "set them free" or radicalize them while redistributing resources toward the higher socioeconomic strata, the spectrum of hybrids can be characterized as a form of *disembedded neoliberalism*. These distinctions serve to underscore a more dynamic definition of neoliberalism: as a set of economic ideas and associated policies that have a constant goal (to enlarge the realm of the market) and a variable one (to carry out upwards redistribution).

Should the policy process allow it, embedded neoliberal theories give birth to embedded neoliberal policy frameworks. Similarly, disembedded neoliberal theories beget disembedded neoliberal policy frameworks. It is through these local hybrids and the mobilization of transnational resources and domestic institutions that neoliberalism ultimately becomes a contradictory, yet effectively pervasive and structural, force.

Economic Ideas in Translation

One often hears the argument that while the Keynesian revolution was one of the boldest modern attempts to anchor economic theories in social realities, at the core of the neoliberal "counterrevolution" was "a utopia that, with the help of the economic theory from which it originates, managed to present itself as a scientific description of reality" (Bourdieu 1998, 3). Like all utopian projects, the process of "neoliberalization" has resulted, not in the seamless replication of some neoliberal ideal type, but rather in the creation of a dizzying mosaic of national neoliberal theories and attending policy regimes.

Peter A. Hall's seminal work on the political power of Keynesian ideas began a rich research agenda aimed at understanding how global economic ideas evolved as they were incorporated into domestic academic and policy milieus (Hall 1989). In that volume, Albert O. Hirschman called on scholars to examine this process by looking at such localization processes in both the core and the periphery of global capitalism (Hirschman 1989, 358–359). Subsequently, a rich scholarship addressed the dissemination of neoliberal ideas in localized forms (Campbell and Pedersen 2001b; Bockman and Eyal 2002; Kjaer and Pedersen 2001; Brenner and Theodore 2002; Pedersen 2007; Brenner, Peck, and Theodore 2010a; 2010b; Peck and Theodore 2012; Mirowski 2013; Ban and Blyth 2013; Schmidt and Thatcher 2013). In the pages of the flagship international relations journal (*International Organization*) a study of the spread of legal ideas recently called for embracing a more dynamic view of the spread of social conventions (such as law), whereby scholars focus on diffusion, translation, and repeated transnational exchanges rather than on top-down dissemination (Brake and Katzenstein 2013). The main thrust of this literature was captured by Philip Mirowski's (2013, 13) insight that "Ideas have a nasty habit of transubstantiating as they wend their way throughout the space of discourse; sometimes proponents do greater harm to their integrity than do their opponents. Other times, people seem congenitally incapable of grasping what has been proffered them; and creative misunderstanding drives thought in well-worn grooves."

In short, rather than a mass-produced, slightly shrunk, and off-the-rack ideological suit, neoliberalism is a bespoke outfit made from a dynamic fabric that absorbs local color.

But while this pathbreaking scholarship on the dissemination of neoliberalism has convincingly showed that the existence of ever-evolving domestic hybrids can be taken for granted, it does not tell us how specific hybrids come about or how they survive crises once they become locally dominant. This book seeks to advance the debate by asking why neoliberal hybrids have adopted disembedded (or radicalizing) forms in some countries and embedded (or moderating) forms in others. It also tries to help us understand how these hybrids survived major challenges such as the post-2008 crisis through contingent recalibrations.

To answer these questions, the book focuses on the crafting of neoliberal ideational and policy hybrids in Spain and Romania during critical junctures of their transitions to neoliberalism and then since the Great Recession. In Spain, the transition was fast, but the end result was *embedded neoliberalism*, a hybrid that layered support for macroeconomic orthodoxy, deregulation, and privatization with ideas (and corresponding policies) about the virtues of progressive taxation, robust public services, and broad public investment strategies. After 2008, this hybrid briefly grew even more socially embedded before the recalibration was reversed through a combination of international coercion and domestic consent in 2010. In contrast, Romania had a slower transition, but the end result was disembedded neoliberalism, a hybrid extensively stripped of arguments defending the role of the state in buffering society against market dislocations. Moreover, rather than moderate Romanian neoliberalism, the post-Lehman crisis radicalized it further still, with local policymakers outbidding the International Monetary Fund on austerity and structural reforms.

The book explains these differences using a three-pronged argument that deploys the toolkits of historical, rationalist, and sociological styles of analysis, in line with recent (yet qualified and self-conscious) attempts at "bridging" these perspectives in international relations theory and political economy (Jackson 2004; Nelson and Katzenstein 2014). First, historical legacies shaped the pace of transition to neoliberalism. Neoliberal theories were "domesticated" in different ways because local translators worked with different ideational legacies, having different degrees of familiarity with the fundamentals of the theoretical ancestors of contemporary neoliberalism. While pivotal Spanish policy players had become intimately familiar with these strands of economic thinking and were up to date with the Western economic mainstream, their Romanian counterparts were not. As we will see later on, this difference explains why the embrace of neoliberal theories in Spain occurred much faster than in Romania while buffering subsequent radicalization dynamics. At a deeper level, the argument echoes the "power of associations" thesis in sociology. Spanning the foundational work of late-19th century French sociologist Gabriel Tarde[2] and contemporary actor network theory (Latour 1987) as well as translation studies, this thesis states that the result of ideational diffusion is influenced by ideas that are well anchored in locally institutionalized thought structures.

Second, the timing, depth, and pace of integration of domestic translators into the global neoliberal consensus is critical: early, gradual, and deep integration gave Spanish translators more ample opportunities to interrogate and map out the limits of global neoliberal "scripts." The critical junctures of Spanish neoliberalism during the 1980s were governed by technocrats with international credentials who had been exposed to a variety of international influences during the postwar years: German ordoliberalism, conservative Keynesianism, and Anglo-American neoliberalism.

In contrast, late, fast, and shallow integration in Romania closed such windows of opportunity, resulting in translators who were less inclined to temper the promarket core of neoliberal scripts. In turn, the depth of integration was as much a function of historical contingencies as it was derivative of global structures of power that are best analyzed by a traditional International Relations realist toolkit. Indeed, greater material and professional status resources deepened the Spanish translators' integration into global professional networks, while lesser resources made it more superficial and therefore more experimental (and often quite eccentric) in Romania.

Third, domestic institutions and international coercion mediated the transformation of neoliberal ideas into neoliberal policies. The book suggests that the hybrids that are able to shape policy are those that are advocated from within institutionally cohesive state apparatuses, with minor partisan recalibrations along the way. Institutional cohesion in Spain since 1982 and in Romania during three governments (1992–1996, 2000–2004, 2009–2012) facilitated a smooth transformation of ideas into policies, with minor adjustments due to some initial labor resistance. In contrast, institutional fragmentation during the rest of the democratic period in Romania prevented the adoption of many neoliberal reforms.

Finally, the realpolitik of economic conventions is key to understanding neoliberal rule and crises. Good old bilateral and multilateral coercion understood in a structural realist way (à la Goddard and Nexon 2005) can change the spectrum of domestic translators with policy power by forcibly bringing in sympathetic interlocutors and removing critics. Domestic institutions are limited in their capacity to mediate the transformation of theoretical hybrids into policy hybrids. Even the most cohesive policy apparatuses are no match for the veto power of international financial institutions and financial markets. Between 1992 and 1996, the IMF undermined experiments in neodevelopmentalist translation undertaken by an institutionally cohesive Romanian government. Similarly, European Union governance mechanisms terminated the bold editing of neoliberal fiscal policy with Keynesian ideas carried out by a similarly cohesive government in Spain.

In terms of scope, the book aims to explain how neoliberal hybrids shape policy, not national capitalisms per se. Even after they are adopted, policies are not the end of the story in determining what kind of domestic capitalism one lives in. Whether one looks at this diversity from a varieties-of-capitalism perspective (Hall and Soskice 2001), economic sociology (Stark and Bruszt 1998) or from a neo-Polanyian one (Bohle and Greskovits 2012), national reconfigurations of capitalism appear steeped in a broader cluster of factors than the ideas of policy intellectuals and the policies adopted by governments. To take but one example, to adequately understand the actual outcome of market reforms in Eastern Europe one needs to look not only at what ideas structured the choices of the economic knowledge regimes of the individual countries from that region, or at how much these ideas morphed into policies and institutions. As David Stark and Laszlo Bruszt showed in their classic *Postsocialist Pathways*, one has to go down in the engines rooms of the microeconomic sociology of the transformation and look at firm networks and their embeddedness in complex and hybrid mechanisms of deliberation that defined the aims of the policies and institutions foisted on them from above (Stark and Burszt 1998).

Another self-limitation of the book is that it examines neoliberalism as a body of ideas and policies applicable to a conventional set of policy concerns (macroeconomics, labor economics, etc.) rather than to the totality of human existence, as it is disciplined and punished by structures of power/knowledge (Foucault 2010; Mirowski 2013). While this comprehensive approach is insightful, it is difficult to operationalize empirically in a comparative fashion in a book of conventional length such as this one. The scope of this book should be understood in the light of these caveats.

This introductory chapter begins by providing a particular definition of neoliberalism before delving into an in-depth elaboration of the book's analytical framework. The chapter concludes with remarks on data, methodology, and the organization of the book.

What Do We Talk about When We Talk about Neoliberalism?

The Conceptual Crisis of Neoliberalism

This book proposes a revisionist definition of neoliberalism that aims to remedy some of the weaknesses of existing definitions that some scholars captured more or less polemically (e.g., Ganev 2005; 2015; Boas and Gans-Morse 2009). This definitional endeavor departs from two observations about the state of the art. First, during the late 1990s and early 2000s the deep transformations undertaken by national economies toward a greater role for markets, less regulation, and the erosion of state-enforced social solidarity have made the term "neoliberalism" very popular among social scientists.[3] An insult word deployed by some for economic liberalism and a more analytical term for others, "neoliberalism" was one of the most popular words used in social science during this period. But by the mid to late 2000s conceptual inflation, terminological confusion, and fatigue set in. Many scholars felt that the term had become less analytical, a grab bag of definitions that associate it with a plethora of social facts, from political ideology to a technocratic list of policies and even models of capitalism (Boas and Gans-Morse 2009).

Second, more recent interventions struggle with a different set of issues. The Lehman crisis and its aftermath have revived interest in studying the emergence, consolidation, crises, and resilience of neoliberalism (Ferguson 2010; Brenner, Peck, and Theodore 2010a; 2010b; LeBaron 2010; Duménil, and Lévy 2011; Crouch 2011; Amable 2011; Centeno and Cohen 2012; van Apeldoorn and Overbeek 2012; Bohle and Greskovits 2012; Peck and Theodore 2012; Williamson 2012; Cahill 2013; Manalansan 2013; Hilgers 2013; Jessop 2013; Schmidt and Thatcher 2013; Hall and Lamont 2013). Although there is enormous value added in this new wave of literature, it nevertheless struggles with the tendency to give neoliberalism either a very broad or very narrow definition, generating chains of inconsistencies between policy domains if one goes beyond a single policy area.

Specifically, the dominant policy elites in one country can espouse "Chicago school" orthodoxy when it comes to macroeconomic policy, but they may stick to a view of how income, opportunities, and time should be distributed via taxation, public services, and labor market institutions that may be closer to heterodox economics. In Northern European countries the domestic consensus around orthodox monetary and fiscal policy theories or loosely regulated product markets is textbook neoliberalism. At the same time, their strong welfare state ideologies, tax regimes, and neocorporatist industrial relations are steeped in non-neoliberal traditions (Pedersen 2007). Do the Nordics live under a neoliberal policy regime or a non-neoliberal one? Open any mainstream economics journal and you will note that "core" neoliberal theories such as rational expectations often coexist with Keynesian concepts such as "sticky" wages and prices or "fiscal multipliers." Between 2008 and 2010, the IMF was a supporter of Keynesian demand-side stimulus programs (Ban 2015), and later on it even embraced capital controls and extensive sovereign debt restructuring under certain conditions (Gallagher 2015). Has the enforcer of the Washington Consensus gone Keynesian? How do we make sense of these intellectual and policy mosaics? How do we know that the mosaic is still neoliberal?

Excessively narrow definitions that construe neoliberalism as a contemporary version of laissez-faire liberalism are a partial solution to these issues. Defining neoliberalism as "market fundamentalism" (Bourdieu 1998; Stiglitz 2008; Block and Somers 2014) sits uneasily with the extensive interventions of governments to correct and nudge markets, pay for the financial safety nets for TBTF ("too big to fail") institutions, or institutionalize new forms of economic privilege. This definition also clashes with post-2008 "interventionist" ideas beyond macroprudential regulation and with the espousal of aggressively countercyclical monetary policies by some systemic central banks (Tsingou and Moschella 2013; Baker 2013; Blyth 2013). Similar problems emerge if one reduces neoliberalism to a replay of the Gold Standard liberal economic philosophy and neoclassical economics that had prevailed before World War I. Take the example of an article published in a top-tier political science journal (*International Organization*), in which neoliberalism is defined as

> a revived version of classical liberal economics. Three assumptions are widely shared within the consensus, namely that: the market is the most efficient mechanism for allocating scarce resources; free exchange of goods across borders is welfare improving; and market actors have rational beliefs. Three policy recommendations flow from these assumptions: governments should, in general, pursue fiscal discipline; a country's economic orientation should be outward; and countries should rely on markets for the allocation of goods and resources and for the setting of prices. (Nelson 2014, 308)

Concrete neoliberal theories are certainly steeped in classical liberal and neoclassical economics, but they are not their revived contemporary version. A cursory reading of the current top journals in macroeconomics would reveal that the rational expectations assumption is really not that central to what it means to be a neoliberal today and is not even widely shared among mainstream economists, as it is often assumed. Indeed, once can write papers urging austerity while openly rejecting rational expectations. Likewise, fiscal consolidation is not something everyone—certainly not the IMF economists—would endorse for all countries in times of recession, at least when interest rates are in the zero lower bound and the country in question has fiscal space for a fiscal stimulus (IMF 2008; 2012; Blanchard and Leigh 2013; see Ban 2015 for an overview). Indeed,

> Neoliberals generally do not believe in the comic-book version of laissez-faire sometimes promoted by the economists. They may profess it to the masses; they may even propound it in Economics 101; but it does not characterize their sophisticated internal discussions, and is belied by their political activities. (2013)

To avoid this "too broad / too narrow" definitional problem, this book builds on Mark Blyth's understanding of global neoliberalism as an identifiable set of economic theories such as monetarism, rational expectations, public choice, and supply-side economics, plus the policies and institutions that follow from them (Blyth 2002). But, as the next section shows, unlike Blyth, who analyzes neoliberalism in a single historical snapshot (its emergence during the 1970s and 1980s), this book proposes a definition that travels across time.

Historically Contingent and Intellectually Hybrid

Peter Hall (1993, 278) famously disaggregated economic paradigms into three central variables: "the overarching goals that guide policy in a particular field, the techniques or policy instruments used to attain those goals, and the precise settings of these instruments" (Hall 1993, 278). The book defines global neoliberalism as a set of historically contingent and intellectually hybrid economic ideas and policy regimes derived from specific economic theories whose distinctive and shared goals are the following: make economic policies have credibility with financial markets, ensure trade and financial openness, safeguard internal and external competitiveness.[4]

Elements of competing theories can be edited into local translations only as long as they do not challenge these fundamental goals. No matter how many Keynesian, structuralist, or "populist" impurities are absorbed into these historical hybrids, the end result can still be characterized as neoliberalism if its advocates espouse the need for institutionalized trade/financial openness, public finances benchmarked by financial market credibility, and growth strategies based on the relative competitiveness of the national economy.

This triad is central to neoliberal translations because it disciplines them with market-based devices. As long as translators stick to these targets, they enable the flow of capital across borders, subjecting the epicenter of local tax-and-spend decisions to the perceptions of financial investors. During crises, adherence to these goals pushes states and societies to adjust through market-based competitive strategies such as deregulation, spending cuts, and wage restraint (internal devaluation). These three benchmarks are critical in "litmus test" situations, when local translators address conflicts between the ideational goals of "source" neoliberalism and the policy goals of non-neoliberal ideas used in local translations. For local hybrids to be considered neoliberal hybrids, the translators must always resolve these trade-offs in favor of the three core neoliberal goals.

By taking seriously the intellectual heterogeneity and temporally contingent nature of neoliberalism, this definition takes us beyond the notion of "opposing paradigms" that sows confusion every time a government with impeccable conservative credentials forgets about "Chicago school" economics and launches Keynesian stimulus programs or directs public money toward the country's industrial champions. Instead, this definition focuses our attention on the processes by which different economic theories thought to be antagonistic come to be intertwined over time, forming shifting combinations that nevertheless remain geared around a dominant center constituted by the three goals mentioned above. It is this flexible co-option of competing frameworks that has made neoliberalism more resilient to challenges than classical liberalism ever was (Brenner, Peck, and Theodore 2010a; 2010b; Mirowski 2013).

This definitional strategy also uses specific component parts of neoliberalism that key economic policymakers (and not just other scholars) can understand by virtue of their training or professional experience. The terms "neoliberalism" and "Keynesianism" rarely appear in economic policy reports or economics journals, but rational expectations, real business cycles, and the new neoclassical synthesis do.[5] So too do the concepts of Ricardian equivalence and the Laffer curve. To understand what neoliberalism is, one has to understand what these arcane terms mean, too.

Finally, rather than risk making neoliberalism appear as a seamless and time-invariant construct, this definition is sensitive to the shifting boundaries of neoliberal theories across time. During their postwar marginality, the neoliberal ideas of the Mont Pelerin Society had three strands: "the Austrian-inflected Hayekian legal theory, the Chicago School of neoclassical economics, and the German Ordoliberals" (Mirowski 2013, 42). Then, in the 1970s and early 1980s, monetarism, New Classical macro-, and supply-side economics were the ubiquitous symbols of neoliberal economics (Blyth 2001; Widmaier 2003; Woodford 2009).

But monetarism failed to survive the mid-1980s as a unified body of thought and, from the late 1980s onward, neoliberal theory became characterized by an uneasy compromise between New Classical and New Keynesian macroeconomics dubbed the "new neoclassical synthesis." In practice, this synthesis or

"mature neoliberalism" (Mirowski 2013) was very much unlike "market fundamentalism" à la Friedrich von Hayek or even Robert Lucas. Rather, a reinforced
and increasingly nuanced set of supply-side theories informed conventional
thinking on current account positions, taxation, financial regulation, employment, and industrial policy during this consolidation phase of neoliberalism and
throughout its post-2008 crisis (Widmaier 2003; Woodford 2009; Blanchard
et al. 2010; McCombie and Pike 2013; Cencini 2015).

This definition does not risk muddying the conceptual waters with its
excessive embrace of hybridity, to the point that one no longer knows when a
theory is still neoliberal. In all these theories, a strong preference for credibility-
maintaining low inflation and budget deficits supersedes concerns about unemployment, leaving labor market liberalization (rather than demand-side policies)
to deal with sluggish growth and job performance.

Contrary to conventional thinking, which paints neoliberals as timeless
clones of Reagan and Thatcher, for quite some time mainstream neoliberals have
viewed the welfare state as an "automatic stabilizer" of aggregate demand. What
makes one a neoliberal is that, when push comes to shove, one always chooses
to be guided by the theory of market credibility and therefore choose social
spending cuts even in a recession. Finally, while various forms of open-economy
industrial policy or financial regulation can be accommodated within mainstream neoliberalism, they remain severely hamstrung by the resilience of core
neoliberal theses about comparative advantage and efficient financial markets.

How do these historically variable forms of global neoliberalism "go local"?
The translation approach sketched out earlier suggests that they can acquire
extremely diverse forms that absorb local ideational content. Polanyi's timeless insights can help with the task of keeping these vast translation possibilities
within parsimonious conceptual boundaries.

Real-Existing Local Neoliberalism: Embedded
or Disembedded?

Karl Polanyi (1944) famously argued that the stability of the capitalist system hinges on the extent to which politics can create a balance between market competition and social protection. In international studies, John Ruggie's
term *embedded liberalism* inaugurated a rich research agenda analyzing the rise
and fall of the "tissue of exceptions, expansions and special cases" that circum-
scribed economic liberalism in the context of the postwar class compromise
and its international financial and trade infrastructure (Caporaso and Tarrow
2009, 596). Later, looking at the transformations experienced by the United
States and Sweden during the 1980s and early 1990s, Mark Blyth's *Great
Transformations* (2002) announced the end of embedded neoliberalism and

the advent of *disembedded liberalism* (basically neoliberalism), which aimed at the removal of exactly that "tissue of exceptions, expansions and special cases" which was built during the postwar years. Unlike in postwar social/Christian democratic Keynesianism, the de facto manifestations of embedded liberalism at the domestic level, in the new thinking capital controls and strict financial regulation were judged self-defeating, full employment was no longer the main goal of economic policy, the imperative of demand-side stabilization of economic cycles became a relic and the idea of class compromise receded in the background.

But this was far from being an "end of history" moment. It became clear that liberalism was disembedded at different paces, and in different ways, in different countries and that a considerable part of the tissue in question survived in reconstituted forms.[6] Moreover, the policy and institutional consequences of these different neoliberalisms made a great difference for how people lived under these varied and hybrid regimes. Albeit constrained, redefined, and shrunk by worries about market credibility, vulnerability to an open current account, and concerns about competition across flattened trade barriers, policy regimes as different as social-democracy, progressive liberalism, and the developmental state continued to exist. Consequently, a handful of scholars, also inspired by Polanyi's concept of embeddedness, began to trace the ways in which social protection can be maintained under neoliberalism.

Van Apeldoorn (2001; 2003; 2009, 24–29) broke fresh ground when he argued that, between the Single European Act (1986) and Maastricht (1992), embedded neoliberalism emerged as the successor to embedded liberalism in the EU. This real-existing neoliberalism differed from the US version of neoliberalism, because it was constructed between the ideational and institutional legacy of social democracy and the needs of European capitalist firms facing increasing global competition. Over time, social protection, economic protection, and economic liberalism were addressed via EU integration, with economic liberalism leading the pack by transferring authority over market competition to the supranational EU level. At this transnational level, it was strengthened and extended by *hard* legal and policy instruments, while leaving responsibility for social protection to the individual member states.

A decade or more on, while macroeconomic policies and structural reforms have become the object of hard rules-based supervision and coercion (particularly within the eurozone), employment and human development performance has been protected only by soft EU instruments such as recommendations via the Open Method of Coordination, a view qualified by research on labor rights in the jurisprudence of the European Court of Justice (Caporaso and Tarrow 2009). Although they did not use the term "embedded neoliberalism," other political economists have made similar arguments about what real-existing neoliberalism actually means in the European context (Scharpf 2002; Martin and Ross 2004; Hermann 2007; Jones 2013).

The term "embedded neoliberalism" also diffused into scholarship dealing with semiperipheral contexts such as Eastern Europe and Latin America. Signal here was the work of Dorothee Bohle and Bela Greskovits (Bohle 2006; Bohle and Greskovits 2007, 445–448; 2012), who defined embedded neoliberalism as a state-mediated form of social protection[7] granted through downward social distribution via the welfare state, as well as through "sheltering inherited domestic and new transnational industries by tariffs, subsidies and special regulations." In such regimes, while tensions abound in the space between social demands for equality and corporate demands for efficiency, and between the macrostrategies of governments and the micrologic of firms, politics in the age of neoliberalism is still about what kind of compromises can be negotiated. As Jonathan Hopkin and Mark Blyth put it, after looking at several metrics of embeddedness across core and semiperiphery countries,

> The choice is not simply to embed or not to embed the market. Markets can be embedded in quite different ways and with different consequences for efficiency and equality. In countries where markets are heavily regulated, both efficiency and equality are difficult to achieve because regulatory arrangements entrench privileges and rent-seeking opportunities that systematically favor some groups over others, while burdening the economy with deadweight costs. Where regulation is more market-conforming but markets are embedded through extensive equalizing social transfers, greater efficiency is achieved alongside high equality. (Hopkin and Blyth 2012, 18)

Building upon this work, this book makes a twofold contribution to these contemporary Polanyian perspectives. The first is to underscore the importance of analyzing the redistribution-embeddedness nexus under neoliberalism when we try to identify the nature of different neoliberal projects. At the center of this endeavor is the repurposing of the state, not its destruction. If Polanyi is right and markets must always be embedded to acquire a modicum of stability, the first task of comparative analysis is to focus on acute trade-offs in moments of domestic economic transformations such as crises. Specifically, if in a specific national policy regime those trade-offs are generally resolved using ideas that maximize the policy space for *downward* distribution of income and opportunities to compensate society against market dislocations, then, on balance, we are talking about embedded neoliberalism. The downward distribution of opportunities takes place via public health and education and of income via progressive taxation, labor laws, unemployment, and parental and old age benefits, to name but a few.

A government's espousal of the economic ideas that engender such policies and institutions without abjuring the principles of credibility, openness, and competition is understood in the book as measures of embedded neoliberalism. If, on the other hand, policy trade-offs are generally resolved in favor of *upward* redistribution of income and opportunities (i.e., toward high-income groups and corporations), reshaping the world so as to benefit predominantly their interests while hurting those of lower-income groups, then we are talking about disembedded neoliberalism.[8] Examples include tax cuts that benefit predominantly the higher income percentiles, the political disempowerment of labor union organizations while empowering organized capital, guaranteeing the balance sheets of banks in times of financial crisis, making new markets by privatizing pensions and public services, and so on. Rather than see in social policy a means to compensate society against the adverse effects of the market, the advocates of disembedded neoliberalism see it as just another instrument to stimulate entrepreneurialism by reproducing usable skills. This is an eminently interventionist state, not the minimalist night watchman of libertarian mythology.

Empirical studies show that the hallmarks of neoliberalism (trade liberalization, financial liberalization, and macroeconomic orthodoxy) can coexist alongside protectionist measures for local or new transnational industries (Bohle and Greskovits 2012; Kurz and Brooks 2008). But the existence of such measures is not a marker of embedded neoliberalism unless their social purpose is to redistribute the wealth and opportunities produced by the protected industries in order to ensure social cohesion by generating employment opportunities.

For example, in Nordic countries, neoliberalism was embedded via strong and universal safety nets accompanied by institutionalized inclusion ensured via democratic neocorporatist systems. In pre-2010 Southern Europe, embeddedness mixed universal (albeit not very generous) social welfare systems that benefitted all citizens, state-led corporatism and regulated markets that privileged insiders. In the case of Eastern Europe, the dominant form of embedded neoliberalism is exemplified by the case of the Visegrad countries (Hungary, Poland, Slovakia, Slovenia, and the Czech Republic), where economic protectionism for domestic and new transnational corporate sectors coexisted with relatively encompassing systems of social protection, albeit not institutionalized inclusion for all labor sectors. In Slovenia, economic protectionism for domestic firms was merged with one of the most encompassing social welfare and democratic corporatist systems in Europe. In Romania, however, the ruling ideas tend to be, on balance, of the disembedded neoliberal kind. This is because pivotal policy elites espouse predominantly privatized safety nets and market-based labor relations alongside forms of upward redistribution in favor of new transnational corporate sectors and high-income skilled workers at the expense of lower-income groups.

The second contribution is to explore the more *indirect* possibilities of neo-liberalism's embeddedness, not just the direct ones that the existing literature refers to (economic protectionism and social welfare). In doing so, this book challenges the conventional assumption that neoliberal macroeconomic policy is a form of pure orthodoxy and that embeddedness can only be deployed via direct industrial and social policies. For example, a careful look at real-existing neoliberalism(s) shows that monetary and fiscal policies can provide social and economic protection in indirect ways as well. Regarding monetary policy, the central banks of the United States and some non-eurozone member states (e.g., the UK and Hungary) used economic theories whose implementation shielded their citizens by devaluing currencies and even monetizing state debt. This external devaluation eased pressure on the need to resort to cuts in wages and unemployment benefits as a way to increase exports (i.e., internal devaluation). Conversely, if the export sector is energy intensive, it is currency appreciation that fulfills the same function. When governments face public debt difficulties, national central banks can provide temporary relief by (indirectly) monetizing public debt and acting as a supportive foreign exchange agent for the government, thus preventing the spending cuts that usually fall on social welfare spending (Gabor 2010a; 2014).

Select strands of Keynesian thinking deemed acceptable by mainstream economics today can also embed neoliberal fiscal policy. The new doctrine of the IMF is that during recessions when interest rates are close to zero (making further monetary policy easing irrelevant) and the government has fiscal space (i.e., it does not struggle with high debts and deficits), the government should increase spending on high-employment infrastructure projects, social services, and tax relief for the lower rungs of the income distribution. In the medium term, the objective remains balanced budgets, and therefore as long as one acts within the fiscal space, one remains a neoliberal. If, however, the fiscal space is exhausted, then fiscal austerity has to be adopted to reassure investors (Ban 2015). Again, because the neoliberal emphasis on financial market confidence is the ultimate arbiter of the conditions under which non-Keynesian ideas and policies can be deemed legitimate, such modifications remain within the domain of neoliberalism, albeit a neoliberalism of the embedded kind.

While disembedded neoliberalism is sanguine about the positive effects on growth of spending-based fiscal adjustments introduced immediately (front-loaded), embedded neoliberals reject the expansionary austerity hypothesis and settle for the more jaded (tragic even) kind of perspective that austerity is a contractionary fiscal policy that one needs to adopt in order to avoid being locked out of sovereign bond markets because of the schizophrenia of bond investors.

Furthermore, to cushion the effects of contractions, embedded neoliberals generally attempt to delay (or backload) austerity as much as market sentiment allows, promising medium-term fiscal adjustment frameworks in the meantime.

Even if market sentiment is hostile, embedded neoliberals are recognized for their determination to distribute the costs of adjustments progressively by balancing expenditure cuts with revenue increases, making public wage cuts weigh most heavily upon the highest earners and shielding benefit cuts against the most vulnerable (Blanchard and Leigh 2013). By specifying rules and limits (often of the numerical type) for when and how much fiscal expansion can take place, this approach remains distinctive from Keynesianism, where fiscal interventions are discretionary. At the same time, by endorsing the state's responsibility for its overall level of economic activity, embedded neoliberalism is different from ordoliberalism, where the state's task is to provide stability and predictability (Nedergaard and Snaith 2014).

In short, the book uses a middle-range definition of neoliberalism that overcomes the too broad / too narrow problem of existing approaches by focusing on economic theories and schools of thought as the core of the ideational side of neoliberalism. The following sections combine international and political economy scholarship with an analytical framework for understanding why neoliberalism abets moderating forms in some contexts (embedded neoliberalism) and radicalizing ones in others (disembedded neoliberalism).[9] This theoretical endeavor should be read as an attempt to better specify the insights of the literature focused on translation in international and comparative political economy.

The Political Economy of Neoliberalism in Translation

From Diffusion to Translation: The State of the Art

During the past decade, a rich literature has analyzed economic globalization as a diffusion of liberalizing reforms that has made the economic policies of states look increasingly similar (Simmons and Elkins 2004; Lee and Strang 2006; Simmons, Dobbin, and Garrett 2006; Dobbin, Simmons, and Garrett 2007; Kogut and MacPherson 2008). When combined with interest-based (Culpepper 2010) or historical institutionalist accounts (Hall and Soskice 2001; Mahoney and Thelen 2010; Thelen 2012; Martin and Swank 2012), the literature on diffusion provides crucial insights into why this convergence has failed to eliminate capitalist diversity.

Although some of the contributions in the literature on diffusion have also acknowledged the role of ideas and social construction more generally alongside rationalist and structuralist mechanisms in generating these outcomes (Elkins and Simmons 2005; Simmons et al. 2006; 2008), the main focus has been on the spread of economic policies separate from the economic ideas that constitute their intellectual microfoundations. In contrast, "translation studies" have focused more on ideas and emphasized the domestic agency of local translators alongside the importance of international diffusion structures. Their main insight is that, when new policy ideas diffuse, they are not copied in whole cloth from some (usually external or "foreign") innovator.

A rich interdisciplinary field steeped in organization studies, many of the contemporary translation scholars echo Gabriel Tarde's classic sociology (1890/1903) when they argue that fashions of many kinds—including ideational ones—are re-created as they are being followed, with repetitions re-creating difference. Or, otherwise put, rather than "copy and paste" ideas developed in foreign "labs," receivers tend to actively filter and even reshape these ideas before "adoption" (Campbell and Pedersen 1993; Czarniawska and Sevón 1996; Callon 1998; Sahlin-Andersson 2000; Acharya 2004; 2009; Sahlin and Wedlin 2008; Bockman and Eyal 2002; Pedersen 2007; Fourcade and Savelsberg 2006; Fourcade 2009; Carstensen 2011b; Røvik 2011).

In the context of economic ideas this entails that instead of remaining stable in the process of movement from one institutional setting to another, "new" ideas are translated to "fit" the specific context by economists, civil servants, civil society organizations, corporate holders of techno-scientific knowledge, or even exceptional individuals, going "from fashion to virus" (Røvik 2011), or "from paradigms to bricolage" (Carstensen 2011b). The translators do their translation work either through incremental interventions into policymaking, or by taking advantage of crises that destabilize the existing ideational or policy equilibria.

What exactly shapes the local translations of global economic thinking, however? Peter A. Hall's (1989) pathbreaking book pointed to the critical importance of the political ideology of the dominant political party. For example, ideology explains the adoption of a social democratic version of Keynesianism in Scandinavia and of a militaristic one in interwar Germany and Japan (376–378). The evidence for this argument is overwhelming, but it remains hampered by a tight scope condition (political party hegemony over long periods), which is hard to satisfy when ideologically opposed political forces take over government very frequently.

Another strand of conventional wisdom exhorts us to check if local economic ideas resonate (or can be made to resonate) with neoliberal ones. Peter Hall conditioned the successful adoption of global economic ideas on how well they fit with preexisting "political discourse" (ideas about the role of the state, common

political ideals, collective memories) (Hall 1989, 383). But since discursive legacies are more plastic than conventionally assumed, skilled framers can "sell" new
economic ideas to different constituencies even when they don't fit very well
with local ideas. They often push global ideas' limits of resonance ("goodness of
fit") by redefining what constitutes "widely shared" ideas (Acharya 2004; Jabko
2006; Crespy 2010; Avent-Holt 2012; Schmidt and Woll 2013).

This book builds on this insight by examining the weight of past ideas on the
shoulders of present translators of neoliberalism. However, it interrogates the
assumption made in the framing literature according to which the translators of
neoliberalism are sufficiently familiar with the content of the ideas they are trying
to sell. Such familiarity cannot be taken for granted. Policy experts in many peripheral countries face economic challenges with sparse professional knowledge of what
neoclassical economics was about (let alone neoliberalism) and why they should
buy into its implications. What, then, explains the different supply of familiarity?

The literature on translation also tells us that economic ideas get transformed
as translators adapt them to local context (Hall 1989). However, it does not
tell us about the mechanisms that explain the direction of the transformation.
Sociological approaches making an impact in political economy provide useful
insights in this regard. Bruno Latour, a sociologist of science, found that even the
experts working in the hard sciences such as physics are extremely competitive
and rational in enlisting resources to defeat their competitors. Translation, therefore, is as much a battle of ideas as it is a battle of and for resources (Latour 1987,
30, 37). If this is true of physics, the "hard" science par excellence, it should be
true of economics, a field of inquiry that blends science and moral philosophy.

Tools from the Past

Translation is a bounded form of innovation whereby the translators' credibility depends on their preservation of some "core" of the source text (Freeman
2009, 433). In this case the core is represented by the three main goals (credibility, openness, and competition) that adjudicate trade-offs between the contradictory parts of neoliberal hybrids. Yet how much one can innovate while
staying loyal to the neoliberal theoretical core is not entirely at the translators'
discretion. Indeed, their familiarity with this core is path-dependently determined by the weight of the ideational and institutional past over the present of
translation.

The ideational past is represented by the necessary (albeit not sufficient) conditions for neoliberalism: by its "technical" bedrock (neoclassical economics)
and by its political core (economic liberalism). Certainly, "Neoclassical economics was not intrinsically neoliberal over its entire one-and-a-half-century

history" (Mirowski 2013, 13). Indeed, it even coexisted with constructions as alien to economic liberalism as market socialism (Bockman 2013). In contrast, since the 1920s, the economic libertarianism of the Austrian school always represented a variant of neoliberalism, but its rejection of mathematical methods made it less eligible to serve as a technical core for neoliberalism's postwar push. It can be hypothesized that unsystematic knowledge about the implications of neoclassical economics and economic liberalism caused by the intellectual dominance of interventionist traditions increase the chances of a slower embrace of neoliberalism as well as larger deviations from the neoliberalism du jour. These past traditions should not be understood in methodologically nationalist sense. They can be part of a global or regional past (international dependency theory, continental ordoliberalism, Soviet Marxist-Leninism) that were more broadly seen as legitimate in particular historical moments and whose imbrication in the domestic ideational order cannot be suddenly terminated.

The institutional past refers to the different national institutional traditions governing the economics profession and economic knowledge production in general (Fourcade 2009; Campbell and Pedersen 2014). Open institutions maximize the potential of a fast embrace of neoliberalism, while closed institutions reduce it.

While exposure to neoclassical economics and economic liberalism more generally can be the product of pure historical contingency, the nature of the institutions can be connected to political regime types: more pluralistic regimes foster more open professional institutions than less pluralistic regimes.

In turn, the regime's geopolitical position (isolated, semiopen, open) relative to regional blocs where neoclassical economics is foundational knowledge shapes what constitute past legacies in the first place. Albert Hirschman's (1989) essay on the spread of the neoclassical-Keynesian synthesis made it clear that the geopolitical primacy of the United States during the postwar period was critical for the spread of Keynesian ideas (350–352). According to this insight, economically illiberal authoritarian regimes that are geopolitically part of economically liberal regional blocs are more likely to allow a more permissive institutional environment for local economics by opening them to that bloc's intellectual influence.

Based on these insights it is intuitive to argue that *the domestic translation of neoliberal ideas will be faster if local economists benefited from permissive institutions and geopolitical environments that enabled them to join transnational professional networks where neoclassical ideas circulated.*

For all its horrific political record, Spain's Francoism put only soft constraints on the economics profession, a fact reinforced from the mid-1950s onward by Spain's gradual inclusion in the US-led transatlantic security and economic order and by the significant interventions of the German governments. Although the regime was politically and economically illiberal, local economists could speak and travel relatively freely during the postwar decades and become familiar with the neoclassical bedrock of the dominant postwar school of thought in the Euro-Atlantic area: the neoclassical-Keynesian synthesis. As a result, when oil shocks, democratization in Southern Europe, and the early phases of neoliberalism's dissemination converged during the 1970s, Spain had a critical mass of professional economists deeply familiar with the fundamentals of neoclassical economics. This book shows that this legacy led to the *editing* of neoliberalism with competing ideas, a form of translation that did not displace the goals of this school of thought.

None of these conditions were in place in Romania when geopolitical events and a deep debt crisis put an end to its totalitarian regime. Indeed, national Stalinism had been even more economically illiberal than Francoism. Moreover, it had imposed hard limits on the economics profession and engaged in very limited and inconsistent forms of cooperation with the West. Unlike in Spain, neoclassical economics and its policy implications were somewhat familiar only to a small coterie of entrepreneurial economists. As a result, the first translation of neoliberalism led to the *grafting* of its ideas with interventionist ideas. Grafting was a form of translation that challenged the distinctive goals of neoliberalism and gave birth to neodevelopmentalism. Indeed, it took years of socialization and coercion to build a local elite of translators for neoliberal economics who would not resort to grafting.

Transnational Socialization and Resources

The emerging political economy literature on professional ecologies (Seabrooke and Tsingou 2009; 2014) shows that material, status, and institutional resources heavily affect their professionals' agency, with some research showing that transnational organization and networks are central to the allocation of these resources (Barnett and Finnemore 2004; Fourcade 2009; Seabrooke 2013). As Leonard Seabrooke put it, "Policy networks are ever more centered on those who can demonstrate that their professional skills and professionalization are transnational rather than remaining within a national system" (Seabrooke 2013, 49). Looking at transnational professional linkages between Eastern and Western economists during the Cold War, Gil Eyal and Johanna Bockman also found that "if a certain institutional form is reproduced and disseminated, this is in direct proportion to the amount of resources mobilized through network ties, to the strength of the ties forged, and to the capacity of interested actors to close them in a 'black box'; that is, to hide the work needed to connect together the different elements of the actor-network" (Eyal and Bockman 2002, 314).

Professional status resources have become tied more than ever to international hierarchies (Fourcade 2006; 2009), and the sheer number of high-status international allies one can marshal decides one's capacity to resist critique and "black-box" the problems of one's school of thought (Latour 1987). Similarly, the material sponsorship for diffusion remains key. Marie Djelic's classic study on the dissemination of the ideas and practices of American corporate capitalism and its local adaptation in Europe shows that this outcome would have been impossible absent the sponsorship of the knowledge behind it by the Marshall Plan (Djelic 1998). Philip Mirowski also showed that neoliberal thinking has been resilient since the Great Recession because mainstream economists have had the necessary resources to use "monotonous repetition" to ward off critique (Mirowski 2013).

Building in these insights, the book suggests that *the local distribution of professional and material resources provided by the global disseminators of neoliberalism shapes the local translation of imported neoliberal scripts.* Specifically, the deeper domestic policy elites are enmeshed in resource-rich transnational neoliberal networks and at the expense of enrollment in national and/or transnational networks diffusing alternative ideas, the closer these elites will approximate the global neoliberal doctrines of the day both when the imported ideas seem to confirm economic realities and when they appear disconfirmed by them. When domestic policy intellectuals' training and work entails regular contact with peers or superiors in the "labs" of neoliberalism (globally systemic central banks, international financial institutions, high-prestige academic institutions), translation is more likely to lead to closer approximations of "source" neoliberalism through replicas, framing, or editing.

In line with the literature (see Johnson 2016; Bodea and Hicks 2015 for an overview), one can expect central bank economists (and their collaborators) in both Spain and Romania to embrace the core of neoliberalism the fastest and show the greatest loyalty to its ideas through crises. This is because monetary discipline irrespective of economic cycles and, by extension, pressuring government to embrace fiscal austerity—even at the risk of procyclicality—are part of central banks' credibility portfolios. The same is true of mainstream economists, especially when they seek access to policy influence and international recognition (Fourcade 2009).

However, this book advances the state of the art by showing that central bankers' and other policy economists' professional transnationalization has a greater role than expected in this regard. In Spain central bank economists had high-prestige Anglo-American academic credentials and were often aided by Ministry of Finance staff with a similar profile. Moreover, since Spain joined European monetary integration processes early on, Spanish central bankers (and their academic retinue) were deeply enmeshed in transnational bureaucratic networks for several decades. In contrast, many fewer of their Romanian counterparts could boast such levels of transnational enmeshment in neoliberal networks, making them more experimental in their translation work.

The book also advances the argument that when local policymakers are enmeshed in competing, yet not mutually exclusive, transnational networks, the local translation of global neoliberalism acquires ideas from the competing network. Spain began its economic transition in the late 1970s, when Anglo-American networks competed for shaping the future of Southern Europe with German ordoliberal networks advocating relatively progressive "social market economy" ideas about distribution. Geopolitical concerns with the radicalization of the Left in Southern Europe in particular prompted Germany's intervention in the ideological restructuring of Spain and Portugal's noncommunist Left. The intervention came with resources for "selling" German-style macroeconomic orthodoxy, emphasis on strong technocratic government, and progressive views on redistribution. This transnational flow of resources chimed with American interests while challenging the outright transposition of US monetarist and New Classical economic ideas ascendant at the time.

Finally, much of the diffusion of neoliberalism in Spain took place through technocrats whose professional formation in Anglo-American academia had taken place in the 1960s and early 1970s, a time when neo-Keynesian ideas were still dominant. This created more space for reflexivity vis-à-vis monetarist or New Classical radicalism among these experts and state managers.

This double anchor helps explain why the result of the translation through editing was embedded neoliberalism, a hybrid that had a path-dependent course of its own. This explains why Spanish economists who obtained their PhDs in some of the most intellectually radical ("freshwater") US economics departments (e.g., the University of Minnesota) after embedded neoliberalism took hold embraced more moderate versions of neoliberalism, a transformation process bolstered by New Keynesian ideas becoming more mainstream internationally and these experts' local resocialization via policy careers that did not reward loyalty to their graduate school networks.

In contrast, the fall of communism coincided with the peak of neoliberalism's global diffusion, and there were no transnational networks advocating alternatives to neoliberal theories. During this period, the IMF spun a global network of training institutes for national bureaucrats from economic agencies. Central bankers were the ones who benefited the most. This was also a historical juncture when global neoliberalism was recalibrated to address the context of the East European transition and the editing stressed the market-maximizing ("disembedded") core of mainstream neoliberal theories more than was the case for noncommunist countries. As a result, central bank economists and their associated expert networks in academia and think tanks became the advocates of disembedded neoliberalism. Nevertheless, since transnational socialization was intense only in the case of a handful of individuals, alternative economic and political ideas seeped in, the effects of translation ranging between the moderation and the radicalization of the neoliberal script, depending on context.

Finally, when local policymakers are exclusively, yet loosely, tied to transnational neoliberal networks, the outcome of translation depends on what economic ideas are widely shared domestically and what kind of political projects they are anchored in. One of the implications of the sociology of translation and professions is that "source" economic theories are most likely to be extensively altered with local content where translators are more loosely connected to transnational neoliberal networks and more exposed to swings in the domestic political and professional ideas. This was the case the majority of the Romanian policy experts, other than key central bankers, after the end of communism. At first, neoliberal theories had little traction because the most widely shared ideas were statist and the dominant political project in the country was a postcommunist variety of the developmental state. As a result, neoliberal ideas were grafted with developmentalist ones, resulting in a neodevelopmentalist policy regime that transcended neoliberal theories.

Over time, however, foreign governments, the IMF, and the World Bank funded both professional and "amateur" training programs and local policy advocacy. Foreign aid agencies, international think tanks, and political party networks offered money and professional training opportunities to new domestic proselytizers while actively weakening their opponents. The dissemination infrastructure was a lot more extensive than in Spain, but, critically, it was also less sustained and entailed shallower, less intense, and less consistent forms of socialization. Unlike the central bankers, most policy experts with access to the highest levels of power had experienced at best fast-track socialization in transnational neoliberal networks. The result was a broad diffusion of neoliberal theories as well as the opening up of greater opportunities to layer them with local ideas. From the late 1990s onward, the domestic political tide turned to the right, giving political voice to a mix of conservative political theories, antistate populism, and a homegrown heterodox Austrian school market fundamentalism. Local neoliberalism outbid the market disciplines of "source" neoliberalism, inspiring increasingly radicalized, albeit unevenly implemented, policy programs.

When combined, the legacies of the past, the timing of incorporation in transnational neoliberal networks, and the depth of this incorporation explain the pace of adoption of neoliberal theories as well as why these theories were of the embedded kind in Spain and of the disembedded one in Romania. What they don't explain is why some translations of neoliberal theories shaped policy, whereas others did not.

Institutional Cohesion

Back in 2005 Venelin Ganev challenged ideas-centered accounts of postcommunist transition with the observation that even where shock therapy reforms traceable to neoliberal ideas were implemented, they "were so incoherent, tentative, and contradictory that to depict them as emanations of an ideology that is both comprehensive and radical would amount to committing a grand simplification" (Ganev 2005, 355). This is a nontrivial and very intuitive objection. Ideas do not mechanically shape policy reality simply because they are advocated by some policy players. Instead, they do so through specific actors and under specific domestic and external conditions.

To demonstrate that neoliberal ideas shaped policy, one has to show that powerful actors in the policy sphere actually used those ideas to make concrete policy decisions (Ganev 2005, 362). There is considerable consensus that economists affect policy the most when they occupy "command posts" at the highest levels of the policy process: senior central bankers, economic ministers, heads of state (Hirschman 1989; Babb 2002; Blyth 2002; Chwieroth 2007; Zald and Lounsbury 2010; Montecinos and Markoff 2010; Hirschman and Berman 2014). In turn, economists' presence inside policymaking institutions such as advisory bodies makes for a weaker transmission device, as it does not guarantee more than the fact that the economists' voices will be heard (Hirschman and Berman 2014, 15). Economists can shape policy in more diffuse ways, however, through their professional status or the spreading of their style of reasoning beyond the boundaries of the economics profession (Hirschman and Berman 2014).

While this book provides a broader analysis of how economists' ideas jell into policies, its focus remains on the most direct forms of influence: when the translators become top policymakers and policy advisers. But rather than analyze them strictly as individuals, the book follows them and their ideas as part of broader networks clustered around a few pivotal, high-status players. This does not mean that one "would need a giant crystal Freudian ball to uncover the neoliberal *id* strapped beneath the populist ego" (Ganev 2005, 363). Political scientists do not have a comparative advantage in psychology. What they can establish, however, is that only some ideas and not others shaped the thinking of powerful policymakers across time and in consistent ways, that some ideas were more widespread, more endowed with resources, more entrenched in specific networks than others were, and it is for these reasons that they got to make a difference in the policy arena while their foils withered out.

The other contribution to the literature on diffusion and ideas is to study the institutional constraints that mediate the effects of the ideas advocated by these elite networks on policy. The book hypothesizes that *for these neoliberal hybrids to have any "bite" in policy, their advocates need to be part of institutionally cohesive policy teams that either delegate to them in most cases or simply agree with them.*

Political scientists use the term "cohesion" in the case of political parties (Kitschelt and Smyth 2002; Owens 2003; Hopkin 2001; Hix et al. 2005), cabinets (Kaarbo 2008), and legislatures (Diermeier and Federsen 2008; Caroll and Kim 2010) to refer to the degree to which individuals with political and policy power "stick together" around shared norms, rules, and procedures and avoid fragmentation and strife. By analogy, this concept can travel to the institutional channels with the power to make economic policy or a specific issue area. In most economic policy areas (apart from monetary policy, which tends to be the exclusive province of central banks), democratic states with medium and high levels of bureaucratization need institutional cohesion in the cabinet and in the legislature.

A high level of institutional cohesion means that there are few if any instances in which economists occupying top policy positions are contested in any of those institutions or, if contestation arises, it is effectively suppressed. The highest level of cohesion results from a highly centralized policy process because centralization best minimizes the impact that conflict, an inherent feature of the democratic process, has on the institutionalization of new economic ideas. In contrast, a low level of cohesion is associated with significant and successful contestation and fragmentation.

Spain and Romania offer contrasting cases in this regard. Between 1982 and 2004 Spain was a textbook case of institutional cohesion in the economic policy arena, with the prime minister exercising veto power and unconditionally supporting the finance minister. After 2004, cohesion was weakened somewhat by competition between the Ministry of Finance and the prime minister's council of economic advisers. Nevertheless, conflicts continued to be adjudicated by the prime minister. In contrast, Romania had experienced only two governments with such levels of cohesion (1992–1996, 2008–2012), with the 2000–2004 government achieving medium levels.

Weapons of Coercion, Grounds of Competition

The freedom to hybridize neoliberal ideas is not unlimited, and not all hybrids that have strong domestic institutional support get to morph into stable policy frameworks. Instead, international coercion shapes the translation of neoliberal ideas and ensures their resilience through crises. Together with competition for capital, coercion puts limits on what translations get to shape economic policy.

The classical literature on the diffusion of liberalization sees in socialization, competition, and coercion the main mechanisms structuring what gets diffused and what does not (Simmons and Elkins 2004; Simmons et al. 2008). Also, a rich literature has showed that when transnational socialization fails, familiar forms of transnational coercion and competition such as sovereign bond market pressures, repo market constraints, and international policy conditionality constrain the freedom to mix and match neoliberal and non-neoliberal policies (Mosley 2004; Breen 2012; Torres 2013; Chwieroth 2014; Nelson 2014; Gabor and Ban 2015).

The contribution of this book is the argument that since local policy elites use neoliberal discourse as an exercise in "speaking to the markets" (Schmidt 2014) or to international finance institutions (Nelson 2014) in order to avoid bond market runs or default, this insight can be applied to the economic ideas to which those policies can be traced. For example, looking at 486 IMF loan programs in the years between 1980 and 2000, Stephen Nelson found that IMF loans become less onerous, more generous, and less rigorously enforced when top local policymakers espouse neoliberal ideas. A similarly large study finds that coercion remains a powerful tool for the IMF, but its effects are mediated by the strength of domestic interests opposed to the IMF agenda, such as labor unions (Caraway et al. 2012).

Also, Peter Katzenstein and Stephen Nelson found that central bankers deal with uncertainty by constructing market expectations rather than complacently conforming to textbook rational expectations because they are keen to build "affective trust based on an internally guaranteed sense of security . . . with publics and investors regarding what their expectations should be" (Nelson and Katzenstein 2014, 380). In so doing, they espouse the conventions shared by these economically critical audiences. By putting a high price tag on the public use of some economic ideas by policymakers, these coercive devices can radically constrain domestic translators' freedom to hybridize.

If the translators who matter for the policy process advocate economic ideas whose application would endanger the three specific neoliberal goals (competition, openness, and credibility), coercion kicks in, applying ideational "haircuts" to the resulting hybrids. Even with open financial systems, governments preserved considerable (albeit dwindling) wiggle room for the layering of neoliberal and non-neoliberal theories regarding the distribution of income, opportunities, and time through taxation, the welfare state, or even labor market institutions (Genschel 2002; Swank and Steinmo 2002; Lierse and Selkopf 2016).

However, given their centrality to neoliberalism's programmatic distinction, compromising central bank independence, failure to consolidate budget, and current account deficits or keeping trade open can be hypothesized to entail high costs in term of refinancing one's debt. In this regard, coercion appears as device of both structural power (sovereign bond markets are assumed to be reassured by the local performance of the neoliberal ideas du jour)[10] and institutional action (contemporary IFIs have neoliberal policy doctrines). Policy episodes from Spain in 2010–2011 and Romania between 1992 and 1996 and then again between 2012 and 2014 show that IFIs, sovereign bond investors, and in the case of Romania strategic exporter groups extracted a very high material price for the grafting of orthodox and unorthodox ideas in ways that they judged inappropriate.

While Campbell and Pedersen's "knowledge regimes" (2014) remain critical to understanding who gets to have the legitimate right to shape policy through ideas, in peripheral countries whose governments are exposed to vertical power relationships (such as Spain after 2010 or Romania through most of its democratic history), the very composition of the knowledge regime is shaped by external interventions. Indeed, international coercion shapes not only the outcome of translation, but also the resilience of neoliberal hybrids over time.

The international pruning of local hybrids is most effectively pursued by IFIs when sovereign market vulnerabilities become real or potential balance-of-payments crises. It can be hypothesized that IFIs and systemically important firms (state creditors, key exporters) can use leverage to change the spectrum of actors who can effectively shape the policy process. IFIs can make governments give independence to central banks and other independent agencies such as fiscal councils whose very mandates entail loyalty to the policy doctrines of IFIs. Together with critical private creditors and systemically important firms they can crop translations of neoliberalism that are too different from what their operating frameworks allow.

Conversely, IFIs and important private actors can use leverage by removing (or reducing to ceremonial status) broader societal interests from participating in the local translation of neoliberal ideas. By requiring states to dismantle national or sectoral collective bargaining institutions, alliances between IFIs and systemic firms can remove labor unions from the translation of fiscal theories or ideas about structural reform. The effects of the deregulation of labor markets in Spain and Romania after 2010, the establishment of independent agencies in both countries, and the replacement of tripartite institutions with government-business coordination in Romania after 2013 flesh out this point.

Case Selection

The choice of Spain and Romania is motivated by the excellent variation they show in terms of the critical explanatory factors posited by this book. First, Romania and Spain offer stark contrasts in terms of the depth of the integration of policy elites into international neoliberal networks (gradual and deep in Spain, very shallow in Romania), its timing (ascendance of neoliberalism in Spain and its consolidation in Romania), and its pace (gradual in Spain, fast paced in Romania).

Indeed, some may argue that Slovenia would have been an even stronger case of grafting neoliberalism with democratic neocorporatist ideas during postcommunism (Bohle and Greskovits 2012), but Spain's translation is more interesting because it enables us to examine comparatively the Southern European transition, a process that took place decades ago, when neoliberalism was not as entrenched internationally and when labor unions and the political Left were ideologically and organizationally more vibrant. This choice gives the book not only a cross-country and cross-regional comparison, but a historical one as well, which is critical for emerging interest in the comparative historical analysis of economic crises in Europe.

Second, the stories of Spain's and Romania's translations of neoliberalism are extremely different in terms of the degrees of exposure of their domestic policy processes to conventional forms of international coercion. Romania spent most of the past twenty-five years in some form of loan agreement with the IMF; in contrast, since 1959 Spain has never experienced such agreements. Similarly, when Spain was preparing to join the EU in the early 1980s, beyond trade liberalization the accession process had much looser and specific economic conditionalities relative to the early and mid-2000s, when Romania went through this process. These countries also provide us with the opportunity to compare the different forms of international coercion deployed against a member of the eurozone (Spain) versus a nonmember (Romania).

Third, Spain and Romania create ideal conditions for avoiding selection bias in favor of neoliberal successes and for studying the role of institutions in transforming ideas into actual policies. Indeed, while the transition to neoliberalism succeeded in both countries, Romania also offers a historical case when neoliberalism is effectively rejected as a set of theories as well as a policy program (1992–1996). Also, while all Spanish governments benefited from cohesive policy institutions subject to the unchallenged executive powers of the prime minister, Romania had only short-lived experiences of this kind (1992–1996. 2009–2012).

Finally, this case selection is also relevant for the scope of the book: semiperipheral and postauthoritarian European contexts. Much of the in-depth research on the dissemination of economic ideas focuses on a few critical cases from the developed world such as France, Belgium, Italy, Sweden, and Israel (Schmidt 1998; Blyth 2002; Quaglia 2005; Lindvall 2004; 2009; Maes 2008; Fourcade 2009; Mandelkern and Shalev 2010; Matthijs 2011) or on Chile and Argentina (Silva 1993; Markoff and Montecinos 1993; 2010; Montecinos 1997; 2009; Teichman 2001; Babb 2004; Dezalay and Garth 2002; Biglaiser 2002; MacPherson 2006; Chwieroth 2010).

Yet most of the world is not Sweden or France. And it is even less like the UK, a country that, for better or worse, generates most of the world's ruling economic ideas. Most states are more like Spain and Romania; that is, they are on the receiving end of dominant economic ideas. Latin American states are rather special cases because US geopolitical interests and domestic economic elites were heavily invested in the diffusion process, sending local economists to graduate school in conservative US economics departments. The relevance of such factors extracted from the analysis of the case of Chilean or Argentinean "Chicago Boys" is a lot less clear for the European (semi-) periphery studied in this book.

Data and Methodology

The empirical findings of this book rely on the combination of case studies and the comparative historical analysis of qualitative data between 2006 and 2013 and covering developments between 1938 and 2012. The book uses primary qualitative and quantitative evidence drawn from Romania, Spain, and IFIs.

The qualitative data were collected through archival research, elite interviews, and a focus group. In addition to tens of policy economists from various institutions relevant to the policy process (economic teams of the heads of state, central banks, economic ministries, political parties' economic experts, think tanks, private organizations), I was fortunate to be able to interview actors situated at the highest levels of policymaking. All interviews were carried out in Spanish or Romanian, and the interviewees were selected based on their access to the levers of power in the policy process: heads of state and their economic advisers, ministers of finance, central bankers, and so on. The book also makes extensive use of the memoirs written by senior policy makers such as heads of state and economic ministers.

Some of the book's arguments use an original combination of content and network analysis performed on original data sets in order to visualize complex transnational relationships between the international and domestic advocates of neoliberalism. The main benefit of this methodological combination is that it balances a fine-grained, historically sensitive account with a systematic assessment of the interplay between ideas and the milieus where these theories are crafted and diffused. The data sets and methodological appendixes are available at https://fundprofessionaldataset2013.wordpress.com/.

Organization of the Book

The first part of the book looks at when and how different neoliberal hybrids became the dominant economic thinking among policy elites in Spain and

Romania and shaped policy outcomes in these two countries. Chapter 2 shows that a moderate (or "embedded") variety of neoliberal thinking shaped economic decisions in an institutionally cohesive policy process of democratic Spain. In contrast, chapter 3 shows that after considerable resistance, a more radical ("disembedded") kind of neoliberal economic thinking prevailed among Romanian policy elites. However, unlike in Spain, because of a lack of institutional cohesion for most of the postcommunist period, these ideas were consistently transformed in actual policies with the support of recurrent external coercion.

Part II is about how these hybrids are rooted in different historical legacies. The deep roots of neoliberal ideas in postwar Spain are explored in chapter 4, while chapter 5 shows that these roots were shallow in Romania, with regime type and geopolitical context playing an important role. Both chapters show that, contrary to intuition, depth was inversely correlated with radicalism once neoliberalism became the only game in town.

Part III delves into the mechanisms through which neoliberalism was translated into very different local hybrids in the two countries. Chapter 6 shows that in Spain policy elites were deeply and doubly socialized into Anglo-American and German versions of neoliberalism, with the timing of insertion and the German influence acting as moderating factors. In contrast, chapter 7 shows how coercion played a key role in crushing bold local experiments with non-neoliberal ideas during the early 1990s. Coercion also locked in the eventual shift to neoliberalism experienced by Romanian policy elites after they became enmeshed in transnational neoliberal networks at the peak of neoliberalism's intellectual radicalism and at a time when no competing networks with sufficient resources were available. When combined with homegrown antistate ideologies, shallow socialization in Romania facilitated the radicalization of neoliberalism, not its moderation, as one would expect.

The last part of the book focuses on the resilience of neoliberalism after the Great Recession. Chapter 8 begins by examining the shift in economic thinking in the academic profession and the two institutions that had the most leverage in building a crisis resolution regime in nonbailout peripheral eurozone countries like Spain: the European Commission and the European Central Bank. The rest of the chapter shows how the policy consensus acquired a strong Keynesian flavor and was forced into retrenchment by the combined forces of the bond market and the political interventions of the EU. Chapter 9 begins with an analysis of the change in economic thinking at the IMF (the main external force in the crisis of the noneuro eastern periphery of the EU) and then delves into the confluence of ideational and coercive forces that stabilized neoliberalism in a "disembedded" mode in Romania.

Three caveats are in order before proceeding. Most importantly, the "neoliberals" this book talk about should not be understood as a mass of ideological fanatics. Political scientists do not have the instruments to establish that what people say is the expression of sincerely held beliefs, of career incentives, economic incentives, or coercion. Yet it is of limited relevance that the Spanish and Romanian translators of neoliberalism were ideologues, corrupt operators or merely dedicated public servants or experts who promoted what they understood to be the public good within a given social, political, and economic environment. It is plausible that they were all of the above, depending on individual cases. But if economic ideas do impact economic policymaking, what truly matters is that these actors deployed certain translations of neoliberalism and not others while arguing against alternatives, new and old.

Second, main implication of the findings presented is not to pass judgment on the actual outcomes of Spanish and Romanian capitalisms. This is very much a matter of normative and/or analytical assessment. For example, some would read in Romania's predominantly foreign-owned banking system and pro-FDI industrial policy as the main devices of the country's recent industrial recovery. Others would perhaps point instead to the systemic financial vulnerabilities and the middle-income trap that these features of Romanian capitalism entail. While the book speaks to such debates, it is not meant to adjudicate between their merits.

Finally, the book refrains from discussing the role of corruption and bad governance in terms of poor social cohesion. As a dark form of Polanyian embeddedness, the corruption gnawing away at Spanish democracy and, even more, of the Romanian one have produced non-market forms of social dislocation that are perhaps as important as the market-based forms studied in this book. As one of the critical readers of parts of this manuscript aptly put it, "far away from the corridors of power in Bucharest, bribed judges, sleazy businessmen, corrupt politicians, radical nationalists, revengeful party leaders who seek to exact their vendettas irrespectively of the damage inflicted on public institutions, media manipulators, shady networks straddling the public and the private sphere"[11] wreaked havoc with the lives of millions. I agree. But these are widely documented developments in both countries that a rich literature has mapped out (Villoria et al. 2013; González and González 2014; Hein 2015; Mungiu 2015). The contribution of this book is different and its findings open up the possibility of examining the complex dance of socially emancipating and socially regressive forms embededdness. This is, perhaps, the next challenge that scholars inspired by Polanyi's path-breaking insights should take up in the future.

2

Spain's Embedded Neoliberalism

During Spain's transition to democracy (1975–1982), the country's policy elites layered an accommodative macroeconomic package with progressive taxation, labor market protections, corporatist, and welfare state measures. It was only with the election in 1982 of a socialist government that Spain took a decisive neoliberal turn on many policy issues, from macroeconomic to structural policies. Yet the economic paradigm that undergirded these transformations was not a neoliberalism of the Reagan-Thatcher line. Instead, what emerged was a mix of neoliberal and non-neoliberal policies (Fishman 1989; 2010; Pérez 1998; Boix 1998; Etchemendy 2004; 2011; Royo 2000; 2001) that together represent a case of "embedded neoliberalism," that is, a neoliberalism ensconced within measures that compensate citizens for the dislocating effects of the market.

This chapter provides an explanation of the origins and consolidation of Spain's embedded neoliberalism during the 1980s and 1990s by looking at how key policymakers edited neoliberal macroeconomic ideas with select elements of social democratic thinking on redistribution or heterodox ideas about industrial policy, with euro accession locking in this ideational repertoire and policy regime. First, the chapter maps out the contours of the policies constituting embedded neoliberalism in Spain during the crucial period of the 1980s; next, it traces the channels through which neoliberal ideas were promoted in the policy process and zeroes in on the replication and editing of these ideas by high-profile actors in the revolving doors between the central bank, government, and academia. The following chapters on Spain explain how embedded neoliberalism became entrenched in Spain in the first place and how these ideas morphed into concrete policies and economic institutions whose faults were exposed by the post-Lehman crisis.

The Socialist Road to Embedded Neoliberalism (1982–1996)

A rich scholarship has documented the birth of a new growth model in Spain during the 1980s, with 1982 as the critical juncture of this process (Holman 1993; Boix 1998; Royo 2002; 2008; Maravall 1993; Pérez 1997; 1998; Royo 2000; 2013). Soon after winning the October 1982 elections, the Partido Socialista Obrero Español (PSOE) government led by Prime Minister Felipe González adopted a classic IMF stabilization package based around public expenditure cuts. The central bank joined in, devaluing the peseta, increasing interest rates, and unleashing a wave of financial sector deregulation (Lukauskas 1997; Pérez 1998).

At the cost of two hundred thousand jobs, the Socialist minister of industry, Carlos Solchaga, orchestrated the euthanasia of loss-making state firms, restructuring some and privatizing others while withdrawing subsidies from loss-making private firms (Solchaga 1997, 54–68). Meanwhile, Minister of Labor Joaquín Almunia pushed for the liberalization of the labor market via temporary contracts. Save for some opportunistic backtracking before the 1989 elections, orthodox macroeconomics characterized the rest of González's terms. When Spain was hit by the European recession triggered by Germany's unification and the Danish vote against the Maastricht Treaty, the government essentially reran the 1982 macrostabilization package, with its attendant austerity and labor market liberalization reforms (Royo 2000; Solbes 2013, 151–157).

To bolster the credibility of its macroeconomic orthodoxy, during the mid-1980s and early 1990s, the Socialist government's austerity packages did not spare the welfare state. The cabinet reduced social security spending, tightened eligibility conditions for pension benefits, resisted minimum income schemes at the national level, imposed caps on payments for the injured and the sick, and encouraged subscription to private pension funds (Guillén and Matsaganis 2000; Chuliá 2006). In 1993, in the middle of a recession, the income replacement rate for unemployment benefits was cut and the share of the unemployed population eligible for benefits was halved (Gutiérrez and Guillén 2000; Solchaga 1997, 292–293). It was only in the early 1990s, under electoral and union pressure, that social spending grew from 18 percent of GDP to 24.4 percent, only to be shrunk yet again by the time PSOE left office to 22.4 percent. It was also only under extreme electoral duress and following a general strike that PSOE decided to universalize the coverage of the pension system by introducing noncontributory pensions (Chuliá 2006; Panizo Robles 2006). Most of these measures were adopted without coordination with the labor unions, despite the fact that unions had kept their promise of wage moderation (Royo 1996; 2001).

Some scholars (Maravall, 1993, 156; MacVeigh 1999; Boix 1998) and the policymakers involved (Solchaga 1997; Solbes 2013) credited these reforms with having triggered rapid stabilization, recovery, enhanced competitiveness, and internationalization, while acknowledging that their collateral damage was the implosion of large swaths of Spain's industrial base and the highest unemployment rates among industrialized countries (OECD 1992b, 63–65).

Yet taken as a whole, this neoliberal policy regime was embedded in policies aimed at providing social and economic protection. There was extensive social compensation for the cost of industrial restructuring (Etchemendy 2011), while welfare reforms ended the broadly Bismarckian model inherited from the Franco regime and inaugurated a universalistic social-democratic model in the areas of health, education, child care, and pensions; a model whose increasing budgets often threatened fiscal discipline and pushed finance ministers into fits of despair (Solchaga 1997, 292–303; Solbes 2013, 151–162). While the United States has been struggling to adopt universal healthcare for decades, the Spanish Socialists adopted it in one year and made sure the system was adequately financed through the tripling of healthcare spending.

Public education was guaranteed at all levels, which came at the cost of a fivefold increase in the education budget (Guillén and Matsaganis 2000, 130). By 1995, paid maternity leave covered 100 percent of the last wage stub, universal child care covered all children over three years old, and the eventual introduction of minimum income schemes enabled a reduction in social exclusion rates. After 1990, two million more citizens were included in the public pension system, and the average purchasing power of pensioners increased by 20 percent during the 1990–1996 period. In fact, while in 1982 most pensioners were receiving half of the minimum wage, by 1992 the lowest public pension was level with the minimum wage (Dorado 1993, 68). With adequate funding and professionalization of the public service, Spain experienced very little of the clientelism observable in other Southern European welfare states (Guillén and Matsaganis 2000, 128). The end result of these efforts was a considerable reduction of poverty rates.

The fiscal costs of social protection were paid by increasing the revenue collection capabilities of the state and were distributed in a relatively progressive fashion. The Socialists narrowed the gap with the OECD on taxation by increasing tax revenue as a percentage of GDP from 30.1 percent in 1985 to 34.6 percent in 1985 (de Castro and Hernández de Cos 2008, 1117). Effective tax rates (a measure of how much the government actually collects) increased from 11 percent in 1981 to 16 percent in 1991 (Solchaga 1997, 252–253). Taxes on income and profits increased from 7.6 percent of GDP in 1985 to 10.1 in 1994, with most of the increase weighing on upper income brackets, leading to less reliance on labor taxes in the overall budget and making the bottom 55 percent and the top 1 percent pay the same share of the public budget at roughly

17 percent (de Castro and Hernández de Cos 2008, 1117; Gunther, Montero, and Botella 2004, 357; Solchaga 1997, 251). The contribution of taxable income originating in property and corporate profits almost doubled between 1982 and 1992 (Solchaga 1997, 251–252), so that in less than ten years, Spain converged with European trends in terms of balancing the tax burden between high- and low-income groups.

Faced with mounting unemployment figures, the government did not push for the kind of across-the-board deregulation associated with the Reagan-Thatcher revolution. Instead, in 1984, it negotiated with the unions a middle-of-the-road solution that liberalized short-term employment while sheltering workers with long-term contracts (Royo 2001). There was a very limited labor market deregulation reform in 1994, which eased firing costs to enable firms to improve their competitive position and created more precarious apprenticeship contracts, but left unaltered the core of labor protections, collective bargaining, and the role of the unions (Solbes 2013, 160–161). As youth unemployment was particularly worrying, the government paid for the wages of interns and the training of new workers, while giving tax cuts to employers hiring young people.

The closing of many industrial state-owned enterprises from the heavy industry sector was cushioned by the payment of 80 percent of their gross salaries (nearly their old salary in cash) to the laid-off workers for a period of three years, which in some sectors was extended until early retirement (Etchemendy 2011, 167–174). The government spent 1.14 percent of GDP to compensate the workers via subsidized preretirement, generous severance benefits, employment protection funds, and incentives to firms to relocate in rapidly deindustrializing zones. These measures made possible the rehiring of a fourth of the laid-off workers (Buesa and Molero 1998). Indeed, the former workers of companies under industrial restructuring were, unmistakably, the most compensated working-class segment in neoliberal Spain and in Europe (Etchemendy 2011, 171, 173–174).

The government not only redistributed wealth, but also remained an important player in the economy. It fostered "national champions" via state ownership in competitive sectors (banking, energy, utilities) (Arocena et al. 2006; Montero 2010). Subsidies to sectors like steel or mining, which had high employment but lacked efficiency, were declared wasteful and then withdrawn (Solchaga 1997, 54–63). Meanwhile, subsidies, special credit lines, and even temporary protectionist measures were implemented as necessary features of a modern "competition state" for sectors and firms deemed competitive (telecom, energy, electronics, banking) (Etchemendy 2004a; 2004b). Protectionist barriers set around domestic banks gave Spain a financial system dominated by domestic players with a global reach (Etchemendy 2004; Pérez 1997). As a result, the role of the state in the economy remained strong enough that the "varieties of capitalism" scholarship considers Spain a "state enhanced" type of capitalism, alongside other European Mediterranean countries like France, Portugal, and Italy (Schmidt 1996; 2009; Royo 2008). The tuning of Spain's industrial engines, it seems, was too complex to be left to market forces alone.

In terms of its performance, embedded neoliberalism was a mixed bag. During this period Spain became a modern European country with a sophisticated infrastructure and globally competitive brand names in banking, manufacturing, and energy. Such opportunities for capital were embedded in universal economic rights, continuously improving social services, corporatist industrial relations. At the same time, when adjusted for per capita terms, Spanish purchasing power parity (PPP) and income converged very little with the EU-15 average between 1974 and 1999 (Fishman 2012, 68). Worst of all, double-digit unemployment became the new normal, and the country's manufacturing base could not cope with the pace set by European competitors.

Gaps in Existing Explanations

Neither external coercion nor rational learning can explain the adoption of embedded neoliberalism in Spain under a Socialist government closely tied to the labor union movement. Since Spain has not experienced a balance-of-payments crisis, it has not been subject to IMF conditionality from 1959 onward. Certainly, during the 1980s, EU accession and subsequent membership meant that Spanish governments adopted policies that they did not always want: VAT, extensive trade and financial liberalization, or fishery and farm subsidy reform (Baldwin, Haapararanta, and Kiander 1995; Farrell 2001; Royo 2009; Solbes 2013). But the EU was not in a position to impose hard limits on macroeconomic policy until the adoption of conditions for accession to the European Monetary Union, a process that began almost ten years after the advent of embedded neoliberalism in Spain (Ferrera 2005; Royo 2009). Indeed, the EU was already preaching to the converted in Madrid when it tied EMU accession, a process started in 1990, to the budgetary constraints required by its Maastricht Treaty.

Rational learning is also a problematic fit with the empirics of the Spanish case. Miguel Boyer, PSOE's finance minister between 1982 and 1985 (Boyer 1983; 1984),[1] argued that the attack on the Spanish currency in the fall of 1982 and the faltering French Keynesian reforms initiated in 1981 made the expansionary measures promised by PSOE in the 1982 election manifesto eminently self-defeating. The same view was shared by Minister of Industry Carlos Solchaga (1997) and by Minister of Labor Joaquín Almunia (2001).[2] In interviews with this author, in 2012 and 2015 respectively, both policymakers stressed the centrality of French Socialists' failure.

Political scientists agree. Charles Boix's classic 1998 study of PSOE's economic policies argued that the French "fiasco" in 1981 convinced the PSOE government that expansionary policies could be attempted by one country alone
only at the risk of incurring a high economic and electoral cost (Boix 1998,
108). Similarly, Sophia Pérez argued that the about-face of the French Socialists
in 1982 "seemed to illustrate the impossibility of national Keynesianism," given
the moves toward monetary and fiscal austerity by other national governments
(Pérez 1998, 139).

This conversion or "cognitive updating" thesis is an illuminating but incomplete explanation. Certainly, the failure of French Keynesianism highlighted the
high costs of uncoordinated demand-side stimulus programs and the classical
agenda of the democratic Left. Yet the evidence suggests that the economic team
of the government had made up its mind even before the French government
realized that Keynesianism in one country was extremely difficult to achieve
in Europe's new economic conditions. Finance minister Boyer recently admitted that the decision to enact an orthodox program had been taken before the
French Socialists launched their expansionist economic package and that the
cabinet's technocratic power brokers had seen France as a doomed "textbook
case" of inappropriate economic ideas even before these ideas were tried in practice. Boyer recalls warning González to curb his enthusiasm for French Socialists
and "distance himself from their recipes." The effect of the French experiment,
according to Boyer, was not the conversion of these policymakers, but rather
a way of bringing into line party militants and "vulgar" Keynesians (Boyer
2005, 87).

Carlos Solchaga, Boyer's successor and a man who liked to boast about his
orthodox economic views (Solchaga 1997, 13–29, 150–159), had a detailed
neoliberal macroeconomic and industrial reform policy template carefully laid
out as early as 1981. According to the memoirs of Joaquín Almunia, the former
labor minister, Solchaga reacted to the drafting of an expansionary economic
program by a PSOE team by writing a ninety-page "parallel report" in which
one can find the basic elements of the austerity package adopted in 1982 by the
González government. At PSOE's twenty-ninth convention in 1981, the political program drafters tried to persuade Solchaga to integrate his parallel report
within the boundaries set by their own draft, but he dramatically threw the official program away with the words, "This is rubbish" (Almunia 2001).[3]

The failure of French Keynesianism, then, was in the eye of the beholder, and
the Spanish beholders that mattered for economic policymaking had already
made up their minds before this failure was manifest. Moreover, there was hardly
any "smoking gun" of France's failure until March 1983, well after PSOE decided
on its neoliberal path. It was only then that the internal debate inside party elite
ended and the *politique de rigueur* invoked by PSOE elites and scholarship was

actually adopted (Schmidt 1996, 110–113). Joaquín Almunia also confessed to this author that, by the late 1970s, PSOE's economic thinkers already thought that the French Socialists were ideologically too extreme and that they felt closer to the mix of economic orthodoxy and welfare state represented by the German Social Democrats.[4]

Charles Boix has argued that not only the French, but also the "calamitous Labor administration" of late 1970s Britain was a "strong warning against expansionary strategies" (1998, 109). But if PSOE were aware of British Labour's woes in the late 1970s, then its leadership did not need the French experiment to end in failure in order to turn rightward. It is not entirely clear, however, why PSOE reformers would read in the problems of British Labour a warning against expansionary policies. While popular, this eminently "Thatcherite" reading is controversial. As Colin Hay has recently shown, a Keynesian solution to the 1973 crisis was never really attempted in Britain, and, after 1976, the IMF-imposed economic policy package was anything but Keynesian. Accordingly, the "calamitous Labour administration" and the Winter of Discontent in which it ended was a crisis of "experimental" neoliberalism successfully redefined by the Tories as a crisis of Keynesianism (Hay 2010).

Why did this British Tory story resonate with the PSOE economic team in the first place? Citing central bank reports, Luis Ángel Rojo (1981), and Enrique Fuentes Quintana (1979) as evidence, Boix suggests that such readings of the British and French experiences "were reinforced by an emerging consensus among Spanish economists that the country's persistently poor economic performance derived from structural factors that could not be solved by merely propelling up internal demand" (Boix 1998, 109). Nowhere else is this crucial point systematically explored in the literature. It is to this puzzling interplay between ideational and structural changes in Spain's external environment after the crisis of embedded liberalism but before the adoption of neoliberalism that the next sections turn.

The Revolving Doors

> To understand the Spanish economy is to understand the Research
> Service of the Bank of Spain.[5]

Scholars were right to trace Spanish neoliberalism to the Research Service of the central bank (Lukauskas 1994; Pérez 1997), yet they do not tell us how their ideas gained traction in the corridors of power during the Socialist years. The evidence suggests that the institutional space connecting the central bank, academia, and the cabinet is where the most policy-consequential translation of neoliberal ideas took place through a combination of professional legitimacy and direct access to power.

During the 1970s, Luis Ángel Rojo, the director of the Research Service, and Mariano Rubio, the bank's governor, turned BdE into the country's premier economic research institution. Both were economic liberals with solid transnational connections (Rubio had worked for the OECD), and both thought that economic ideas anchored in internationally certified scientific claims, models, and procedures would triumph in a globalizing world. Already by the late 1970s the Research Service had become the organic intellectual center of the central bank and a pool of talented staff for other critical sites of the economic policy sphere. As one of its prominent economists wrote,

> We had an obsession to make available institutions that were solid, supported by markets and able to ensure their development. . . . Ortega carried this obsession to the Treasury and Martínez Mendez to the National Commission of Stocks and Bonds. The result was that the border between the Research Service and the rest of the Bank of Spain became increasingly blurred.[6]

Since the pay offered to central bank employees was much higher than in academia, the Research Service was in the position to hire young economists with the best research credentials, send them to study in American graduate programs, and encourage them to express themselves in the media as public intellectuals. [7] The enrollment strategy paid off. In a few years the Research Service became one of the country's most prominent research institutions in economics (Aceña 2001). Critically, by the late 1970s it was the main supplier of technocratic talent for political parties and economic policy institutions. Throughout the 1980s and early 1990s, Spanish economic decision-makers "believed that the central bank's view reflected virtually unquestionable expertise" (Pérez 1998, 139).

In addition to professional legitimacy, central bank economists linked to the Research Service had direct access to power under the Socialist government, a development facilitated by the fact that Rojo was perceived to be intellectually closer to social democracy than other central bankers.[8] These economists ensured consistent advice to Prime Minister Felipe González, delegitimized alternative policy views proposed by union-connected MPs, and authoritatively defined what economic choices were possible.

Rojo shaped an entire generation of highly trained policy intellectuals as star central banker, professor, and mentor to key finance ministers and shadow adviser to Felipe González himself. Key ministers of the Socialist governments referred to Rojo as their intellectual master (Solchaga 1997, 14), with one of them accepting a post as finance minister only after Rojo personally called him (Solbes 2013, 264).

Rather than lustration, the Spanish transition ensured the continuity of the Franco-era technocracy, with the Socialists committed to the institutional status quo. Mariano Rubio, the former head of the Research Service during late Francoism and a man who boasted a short period of political exile in 1958 for his involvement with Socialist networks, was appointed governor in 1984. Luis Ángel Rojo himself was confirmed in his post at the Research Service and was subsequently promoted as vice governor (1988) and governor of the bank (1992), receiving the highest state honors for his academic career. No one lost a job in the BdE or economic ministries simply because he or she worked for the authoritarian regime.

The policy czars of the central bank had also secured important beachheads in PSOE. Some observers of Spanish politics during this period argue that Felipe González's access to Spain's captains of industry and banking before 1982 would not have been possible without the contacts of Mariano Rubio, whose family was part of the liberal section of the *madrileño* upper class. And given González's poor competence in economics, Rubio and Rojo had ample opportunities to push their views. As Mariano Rubio's biographer argues, when Rubio and the premier would meet,

> Felipe González listened to the "scolding" given to him by the governor with a mixture of interest and resignation. Mariano Rubio did not have great difficulties in convincing Felipe González, who, hampered by a much more superficial level of economic training, would find himself unable to respond to the torrent of detailed arguments put forth by the governor. (Rivasés 1991, 499)

In addition, Rojo acted as the broker between the old policy establishment and Felipe González's office:

> The entire group of the Franco years was there. Fuentes Quintana, who was once an advisor to the General and who was one of the masters of the group, was there. Others occupied strategic positions in the state administration. . . . The entire team, formed in the Bank of Spain, and whom Mariano Rubio was a perfect epitome of, was an incombustible team tied by great friendships among its members. All were sentimentally social-democrats and ex officio monetarists. . . . Boyer did not matter until he was appointed as PSOE minister. It was upon his appointment that the traditional institutional tension between the Ministry of Finance and the Bank of Spain disappeared. . . . The man who knows economic theory "for real" is Luis Ángel Rojo; he does not like public exposure, but all run for advice to him, including the prime minister, for whom [Rojo] got to write speeches after his election into office.[9]

Rojo's protégées from the university and the Research Service now occupied strategic positions in the PSOE cabinet. Some Research Service economists were simply transferred into the executive. Luis García de Blas took the Social Security portfolio despite not being a PSOE member (Almunia 2001, 150). Guillermo de la Dehesa occupied various top positions in the economic ministries of the first PSOE government. Similarly, Luis Alcaide, a personal friend of both Rubio and Solchaga, became head of External Transactions in the first González government.[10]

Most importantly, both Miguel Boyer, the minister of finance and economy between 1982 and 1985, and his successor, Carlos Solchaga (1985–1993), had graduated from the same economics department at Complutense University, studied with Rojo, and remained wedded to Rojo's economic views.[11] Between 1969 and 1971, both spent their formative postgraduate training in the Research Service. Solchaga in particular had been considered a Rojo protégé and a bit of a wunderkind; both he and Boyer had become close friends with Mariano Rubio during the 1970s (Gutiérrez 1991). In 1972–1974, Rojo appointed Solchaga as a representative of the central bank in the G20 (Muns 1986, 267) and between 1971 and 1974 Boyer and Solchaga received top positions in the research service of the National Institute of Industry (INI), which, despite being part of a public holding, was then trying to replicate the success of the central bank's Research Service at becoming the nation's first think tank (Gutiérrez 1991, 197). As a former Socialist minister put it, "There were no disagreements between the central bank, Boyer, and Solchaga on all aspects of macroeconomic policy."[12]

Deep personal ties cemented the relationship between the ministries and the central bank. Since their youthful activism in a left-leaning student group, Boyer and Rubio had been friends (Gutiérrez 1991), and they welcomed Solchaga into their circle. During the 1970s, both Boyer and Solchaga had been regular contributors to *España Económica*, an elite economic review established and run mostly by Research Service economists who would come to play decisive policy roles under the Union of the Democratic Center (UCD) and the Socialists.

In addition to the contributions of Schwartz, Boyer, and Solchaga, *España Económica* benefited from the work of a veritable who's who of Spanish economic thinking, including "old guard" technocrat-professors prominent in central banking circles, Spanish international civil servants, and future PSOE ministers. Boyer's and Solchaga's tenures in the private sector during the late 1970s and early 1980s did not alienate them from the "Rojo network." Solchaga became the top economist of the research service of Banco Urquijo, an institution known not just for its high-end research but also for its close contacts with Rojo's Research Service.[13]

Given all this, it was unsurprising that during the Socialists' terms in office the identification between the Socialist cadre in the Ministry of Finance and the central bank "was so strong, that one can speak of a veritable colonization by that institution of the upper ranks of the economic policy bureaucracy" (Pérez 1998, 138).

Translating Neoliberalism in Madrid

Using his joint appointments as head of the Research Service of the Bank of Spain and as professor of macroeconomics at the nation's leading university (Complutense), Rojo used the neoclassical synthesis as a platform for building a comprehensive macroeconomic model of the Spanish economy that was the Spanish equivalent of the Samuelson textbook for several generations of economics students. During the late 1960s, he and his collaborators at Complutense and the Research Service (José Pérez, Raimundo Ortega, Raimundo Poveda, Ana Sánchez) began to pay increasing attention to the then controversial monetarist arguments of Milton Friedman, lending them a great deal of respectability at a time when monetarism was still a suspect theory. A right-leaning neo-Keynesian during the 1960s, by the mid-1970s Rojo had become the most authoritative advocate of select neoliberal theories.

By 1971, monetarism found a voice in Spain via Rojo's book *The New Monetarism*, a relatively sympathetic review of the work of Chicago school luminaries such as Milton Friedman, Anna Schwartz, Karl Brunner, and Allan Meltzer. In 1973, acting on their acceptance of the monetarist thesis that the money supply had a fundamental role in the economy, Rojo and his collaborators at the central bank began to advocate the use of aggregate monetary indicators as instrumental variables in the continuous control of liquidity. In contrast with most other capitalist countries gripped by the oil crisis, where the first policy reactions were expansionary (Bermeo and Pontusson 2012), the Research Service advocated for a string of decisions meant to squeeze the money supply, shrink excess demand, and further liberalize the financial system (Rojo 2001, 351). A year later, 1974, Rojo took a step further with his *Income, Prices and Balance of Payments*, a book that employs monetarist arguments to attack the neo-Keynesian macroeconomics (Aceña 1999, 195).

As the stagflation of the 1970s wore on, Rojo applied the final blows to the neo-Keynesian consensus in two studies published in 1976 and 1977 respectively (Rojo 1976; Rojo and Pérez 1977). In this work, Rojo and his Research Service collaborator José Pérez launched an onslaught against decades of neo-Keynesian doctrines and policies. Although Rojo and his "network" resisted being labeled as "monetarists," the central thesis defended in their contributions from the late 1970s onward was an unequivocal reproduction of the classical "quantity of money" thesis, which finds a monetary perturbation behind each bout of inflation (Argandona 1990; Aceña 2001, 536). Such ideas were repeated in a 1978 article coauthored with another Research Service economist.

Increasingly during the early 1980s, monetarism and the ever more influential New Classical school began to dominate thinking in a series of articles published by the same economists in the flagship journal *Papeles de Economía Española*. In these, critical monetarist and New Classical theses were adopted whole cloth: inflation is a monetary phenomenon; demand-side management via fiscal policy is self-defeating; the necessity is to control a monetary aggregate rather than a rate of interest as an intermediate objective; one should fix, announce, and meet monetary targets periodically; a stable monetary supply and demand is central; Lucas's microfoundations critique is accepted, along with a New Classical Ricardian equivalence. In 1984, in what was a succinct translation of the classic "policy irrelevance proposition" advanced by American New Classicals, Rojo argued that

> a drive to advocate continuing public regulations and interventions with a view to correcting market failure and stabilize the economy underestimates the costs of those interventions as well as the limits and risks of stabilizing measures. This, in turn, tends to slow down economic development with strong sources of instability and multiple interventions that escape the criteria of efficiency and fairness as well as with growing degrees of actual insensitivity to discretionary stabilizing policies. (Rojo 1984)

The central bank used its access to the Zapatero government to change the perception of what was economically appropriate within the cabinet and in the broader public sphere. The fulcrum of this conceptual offensive was the selling of "sound finance" and rules-based fiscal policy as a "public good, as something valuable in itself" (Aceña 2001, 542). This led to an almost single-minded focus on inflation as the root of Spain's economic woes, a preoccupation that the Research Service conveyed not only to the executive council of the Bank of Spain, but also to economic ministries and to the Treasury (Aceña 2001, 549; Solchaga 1997, 125–152). For example, during the mid-1980s, Minister of Industry (and then Finance) Carlos Solchaga declared that there was no trade-off between inflation and unemployment in an increasingly globalized economy such as Spain's (Solchaga 1997, 132–133).

The neoliberal replicas churned out by the Rojo network were strengthened during the 1980s by a new wave of Western-trained graduates. They came from or were swiftly incorporated into the professional ecologies where Rojo's network reached. Exemplary in this regard were two students of Rojo: the

Oxford-educated Juan J. Dolado, who became Rojo's successor at the helm of Research Service, and London School of Economics–trained Rafael Repullo, who was the head of CEMFI, the Research Service's think tank and graduate program. Both applied monetarist and rational expectations models to the Spanish economic context from the early 1980s onward (Dolado 1984).

Neoliberal ideas began to make headway outside macroeconomics as well. The Finance and Labor ministries funded studies advocating supply-side interpretations of the causes of unemployment. Socialist finance ministers Miguel Boyer and Carlos Solchaga rejected not only protective labor laws, but democratic corporatism itself by referring to it as "expensive, inefficient and unnecessary" (Maravall 1991, 59). Prominent Spanish labor economists like Luis Toharia and Lluis Fina diagnosed the growth of unemployment in Spain as a symptom of labor laws and institutions legislation, the crowding-out effects of public spending, demographic factors, and changes of relative prices generated by new processes of staff management (Toharia 1983; Fina and Toharia 1987).

A new generation of economists trained in British universities and using the revolving doors between academia, the central bank and the political system then added epistemic weight to these arguments by formalizing them (Dolado 1983; 1984; 1986). Moreover, their research affected government policy more directly; Juan Dolado was the star senior researcher of the Research Service of the Bank of Spain in the 1980s before he became its director in the 1990s. Lluis Fina was a key expert of the Ministry of Labor between 1983. In 1988, a committee of experts chaired by Constantino Lluch, a prominent PSOE intellectual and labor economics expert,[14] largely replicated the same ideas in a report commissioned by one of the chambers of the Spanish parliament.[15] The committee's findings were formalized during the 1990s by a new generation of neoliberal economists and technocrats whose work was published by the Labor Ministry itself, among others (Bentolila 1991a; 1991b; Dolado and López-Salido 1996).[16] Indeed, it was only in the mid-1990s that research began to acknowledge that labor market regulation could not account for the magnitude of unemployment (Blanchard and Jimeno 1995), with neighboring Portugal having better unemployment performance despite more "rigid" labor laws (Fishman 2010; 2012).

Despite the fast replication of monetarism, rational expectations, and supply-side structural reforms, the Spanish translators of neoliberalism did not engage in an exercise of copying and pasting. Indeed, rather than restate all key neoliberal theses, Spanish policy intellectuals edited some of them out. There is no evidence of support for real business cycle theory, the stability of money demand, the exogenous character of the money supply, the intrinsic stability of the private sector, and the intrinsic instability of the public one. Rojo attributed inflation not only to the money supply, as the monetarists did, but to inertia and excess demand in the labor market (Rojo 1976, 130–132). Like a New Keynesian ahead of his times, he endorsed fiscal orthodoxy and monetary Keynesianism (Rojo 1980; 1984; 1986), while remaining openly skeptical of the New Classical thesis on the irrelevance of all countercyclical macroeconomic interventions (Rojo 1993; 2002b, 568).

Moreover, even where neoliberal theses were restated, content was added from extant or competing economic theories. Specifically, more than a decade before the new neoclassical synthesis sealed the compromise between New Keynesians and New Classicalists, Rojo tried to demonstrate the feasibility of a synthesis between Keynesianism, monetarism, and New Classical macro-economics (Rojo 1982, 56–69). The same positions were articulated by the Research Service economists (Aceña 2001), but also by top PSOE ministers like Carlos Solchaga (Solchaga 1997).

This editing of monetarism and rational expectations facilitated the enroll-ment of pivotal policymakers into the New Keynesian camp when the 1980s ushered in the debate between New Classical and New Keynesian macroecon-omists. Carlos Solchaga was very open about his choice. For him, the "old" Keynesianism, based on aggregate demand management via public spending increases, was positively defunct, while New Keynesianism (a mix of demand management, supply-side economics, and moderate doses of monetarism) was not:

> It was obvious that the Keynesian paradigm based on aggregate demand had collapsed, but it was equally obvious to anyone, save for a few monetarist and rational expectations fundamentalists, that the Keynesian paradigm had not been replaced by others. My experience at the Ministry of Industry taught me to factor supply-side factors in mac-roeconomic analysis. . . . Upon seeing the high levels of unemployment combined with inflation, I found it impossible to renounce demand management. On the other hand I was aware that Keynesian policies like public spending increases don't work anywhere, not just in Spain. (Solchaga 1997, 20–21)

Like Rojo, Solchaga did not reduce inflation to a monetary phenomenon; instead, in New Keynesian fashion, he saw it as caused mainly by excessive demand created by menu costs and sticky wages. The strong monetarist thesis that any public interventions such as changing interest rates or manipulating the money supply are not only useless but counterproductive seemed to him "a way to impoverish the analysis of one of the most fascinating aspects of eco-nomics" (Solchaga 1997, 134–135). New Keynesianism provided an acceptable middle ground between neo-Keynesian and social democratic positions on the one hand, and what Solchaga dismissed as the "deification of the market" or the fallacy of confident denunciations of the inefficacy of all macroeconomic policies by monetarists and rational expectations economists (Solchaga 1997, 21–22). Rather than obsess over the money supply, these economists called for more comprehensive anti-inflation policies that included rules-based fiscal policy, social pacts to moderate wage increases, and, in extreme situations, executive "reduction of unemployment insurance, mitigating the negative consequences of the minimum wage, the general elimination of rigidities in the labor market and collective bargaining" (Solchaga 1997, 135).

Similarly, supply-side economics did not unseat key ideas of "old" Keynesian tax economics. Beginning in the early 1970s, the group of economists working with "sound finance" guru Enrique Fuentes Quintana of the Ministry of Commerce began to advocate fiscal policy ideas based in the ideational consensus of "embedded liberalism" (Fernández 2001; Calvo 2004). The resulting "Quintana report" of 1973 blamed regressive taxes and advocated the progressive taxation principles of Britain and Italy, such as income redistribution through taxation and tax incentives for industrial policies. Parts of the report criticized the regressive nature of the extant tax system, claiming it punished the poor and undermined the provision of basic welfare. The authors of the report argued that, since market mechanisms alone were unable to deliver a robust catch-up economic performance, the state had to step in to invest in public infrastructure and services and to subsidize competitive firms that would take Spain into the "First World." They also demanded a steep progressive income tax, taxes on luxury goods, tax breaks for employment creation, the stripping of banking privacy, the criminalization of tax evasion, and the strengthening of tax collection.

The Quintana report became the blueprint for progressive tax reforms adopted by the transition governments and then by the PSOE governments (Calvo 2004, 596–597). The ideas of the report are clearly present, not only in PSOE political programs during the 1980s, but also in the writings of the neoliberal ministers of the González governments. Minister of Finance Carlos Solchaga systematically criticized supply-side ideas about tax cuts on income and profits, such as their role in reducing tax evasion and stimulating investment. After a harsh critique of Reaganite tax ideas and especially of calculative devices associated with the supply-side "revolution" such as the Laffer curve, Solchaga stressed that such reforms benefit the wealthy, demoralize the less wealthy, and are generally inconsistent with Spain's statement of democratic equality between the rich and the poor before the tax collection authorities. As for the supply-side argument that tax cuts increase compliance, he dismissed it as a utopian belief (Solchaga 1997, 258–285).

In addition to their broad acceptance of taxation ideas forged during the Keynesian era, Spain's translators of neoliberalism also appealed to ordoliberalism to embed neoliberalism in society. Against supply-side welfare retrenchment narratives, they supported the building of a social market economy able to generate social peace and support for capitalist competition as the only sustainable form of political economy. As elaborated on at length in chapter 6, during the transition, the German government and the Friedrich Ebert Foundation (the local emissary of the German Social Democratic Party) worked hard to give the real-existing ordoliberalism embedded in the German model a more concrete and accessible face.

As a result, Spanish Socialist policymakers were convinced of the fact that responsible social democracy meant combining fiscal rectitude, central bank independence, corporatist industrial relations, moderately protective labor regulations, and a robust welfare state.[17] The main message was that macroeconomic orthodoxy and the social democratic agenda can go hand in hand (Ortuño Anaya 2005; Sánchez 2008), a proposition that echoed broadly in the writings of the economic ministers of Felipe González (Solchaga 1997; Solbes 2013). As former minister of labor Joaquin Almunia put it in an interview with this author, the model that most inspired Felipe González's policy team was West Germany's, with its compelling balance between the competitive economy of the world's foremost exporter and one of the world's most successful welfare states. "During the 1980s," he said, "with the Swedish model in crisis, Germany showed that you can have an economic order in which the state is the enforcer of capitalist competition, a maker and defender of markets and a guarantor of social solidarity. Germany showed that fiscal and monetary orthodoxy and competitive capitalism are not the enemies of solidarity, but its protective shield."

Industrial policy was another area in which neoliberal arguments about nonintervention did not travel unimpeded. Instead, they were molded on local interventionist ideas that harkened back to the postwar developmentalist years. The neoliberal emphasis on an open economy was edited with the developmentalist argument that fostering national competitiveness in the global marketplace necessitates not just the liquidation or sale of weak state enterprises, but also temporary protectionism for promising ones, the transformation of strong ones into industrial champions, the adoption of incentives for industrial diversification, and the building of legal barriers against mergers and acquisitions that could harm domestic champions (Etchemendy 2004; Arocena, Contín, and Huerta 2002). While being one of the most consistent advocates of competition and while presiding over the shutdown of large swaths of unprofitable publicly owned firms, Minister of Industry Carlos Solchaga nonetheless thought that profitable, tariff-protected industrial firms (such as car plants) should benefit from an extension of Spanish protectionist measures after joining the EU rather than be made "lean and mean" through immediate trade liberalization (Solchaga 1997, 25).

Such ideas were far from an import substitution industrialization theory, however. Instead, they belonged to an open-economy *neo*developmentalist variant of the model that East Asian countries pioneered in the 1980s and deployed extensively decades later (Wade 2003). Rather than shield domestic firms against foreign competitors for the sake of protecting their domestic market niche, Spanish policymakers saw industrial policy as an instrument for enabling the international expansion of Spanish firms (Molina and Rhodes 2007). In this way, Spanish "neoliberals" quietly negotiated the terms of the global transition to the neoliberalization of trade in a more interventionist direction.

Crafting Institutional Cohesion

During their tenure, the Socialists further centralized the policy process by suppressing party democracy, so that by the 1980s "a handful of party bosses could sit down for a cup of coffee and chart the party's course for the next two years" (Gillespie 1989, 363). Indeed, the neoliberal heads of the economic ministries were strongly and consistently supported by an economically amateurish premier who was in turn insulated from the political pressures of the ruling party through baroque, almost Escher-like, formal and informal institutional architectures.

The 1978 constitution ensured executive dominance over the parliament and the prime minister's dominance within the executive (Heywood 1998; Biezen 2003; Biezen and Hopkin 2005). In this system, the cabinet had the dominant role in proposing new legislation and faced low thresholds for ruling by executive decree. Constitutionally speaking, the Spanish executive branch is responsible for introducing the vast majority of the new bills, and the parliament can censure the actions of the premier only by proposing an alternative candidate with a majority vote, an unlikely event given that Spain's electoral institutions favor majoritarian outcomes (Heywood 1999; Biezen 2003). Spain's d'Hondt system of seat allocation and district-level vote thresholds delivers disproportionate seat allocation for large parties (Montero, Llera, and Torcal 1992). Moreover, the cabinet itself is heavily "presidentialized" around the institution of the prime minister (also called "president of the government"). The premier has the authority to dissolve parliament and appoint or sack ministers. In the case of disputes within the cabinet, the premier has the ultimate authority to override all ministers and make the final decision.

The Ministry of Finance was the next most important institution in the cabinet. It controlled the other ministries through the power of the purse and the high status of its meritocratically selected staff (*técnicos de estado*). [18] During the Socialists' first term, its power was magnified following the incorporation of the

Ministry of Economy (Ministerio de Economía y Hacienda, or MEH). Because many of the MEH appointees were intellectually connected with the Research Service of the central bank, the Franco-era conflicts between the central bank and Hacienda effectively ended under the Socialists (Pérez 1997). When labor unions and their party allies challenged the austerity programs of Miguel Boyer and Carlos Solchaga, González always stood by his finance ministers (Iglesias and González 2003; Solchaga 1997; Solbes 2013). Since the prime minister was also the head of PSOE and was successful in imposing internal party discipline, the party's MPs could not stage effective contestations of MEH policies. As Minister of Finance Pedro Solbes recalls, when some cabinet members objected to spending cuts. the prime minister snapped back: "We have two options: we do what the Finance Minister proposes and save time, or we have a debate and approve at the end the proposals of the Finance Minister" (Solbes 2013, 155). As a form of preventive action, PSOE leaders built a highly centralized and authoritarian party structure, making the party unaccountable to its base while suppressing ideological dissent (Lopez Guerra 1984; Gillespie 1989; Share 1998). Although PSOE vice president and vice prime minister Adolfo Guerra held considerable power and was often hostile to liberalizing measures, he served González's economic agenda well when he used his vast intelligence network within the party or cracked down on internal insurgencies (Gillespie 1994, 5). In effect, even though the party's core (Federal Committee and Federal Executive Committee) designed PSOE's electoral platform and other ideological pronouncements, no policy was passed without the consent of the party's secretary general, Felipe González (Hamann 1998, 28).[19] Close to 90 percent of Socialist legislative proposals during González's terms came from the cabinet, and even the 10 percent that were initiated by Socialist MPs had to first be cleared by the prime minister (Hamann 1998, 31).

Inside the party, but removed from executive power and González's inner circle, was the party's left wing (the Socialist Left). Supported by the pro-PSOE Unión General de Trabajadores (UGT) and the PSOE militants, the Socialist Left demanded more expansionary macroeconomic policies and articulated an ideological critique of neoliberalism. But the effects of that vocal critique were muted by the centralization of party institutions and the Socialist Left's own internal problems. The emasculation of the party's Left was locked in through the adoption of a winner-takes-all electoral system for party posts and delegates to party congresses and the use of bloc voting in party congresses (Share 1999). In the only party congress where voting was carried out via secret ballot, the Socialist Left did not get more than 22.5 percent of the delegates' votes for the federal committee that de jure controlled the party executive (Gillespie 1994, 6).

The ability to protect the core executive against the party was further facilitated in Spain by the system of closed lists, which made MPs more dependent on the decisions of the party executive than on the electorate. To top it off, the centralization strategy was bolstered by the entrenched fear of democratic breakdown (Pridham 1990, 115–116). Potential and actual dissidents in this labor-oriented party were haunted by the memory of internal factionalism during the failed Republic of the 1930s, let alone the shockwaves caused by the abortive military coup of 1981 (Field 2011; Share 1998, 98).

In addition to centralization, the party leadership consistently suppressed dissent by co-option via clientelism, the removal of dissidents from party lists, and their demotion (Gillespie 1989, 336–337; Hopkin 2001). González's predecessors, Pablo Castellano and Francisco Bustelo, the Keynesian voices inside the party, were forced out early on. Another Keynesian, UGT leader Nicolás Redondo, was threatened with the resignation of his seat in parliament—an action he was compelled to take anyway in 1987. While some left-wing activists left the party following the resignation of prominent Keynesians, this did not weigh heavily on the top leadership, as PSOE managed to actually boost its membership and activist base to almost a quarter million people by the late 1980s (Share 1999, 98).

Apart from its organizational marginalization, the PSOE left wing had internal weaknesses as well. Its epistemic weakness on economic issues meant that its defense of an expansionary policy alternative was no match for the rebuttals issued by neoliberals, especially after the premature death in 1981 of Manuel Sánchez Ayuso, the only prominent academic Keynesian in the group. Faced with this situation, what was left of the party's left wing focused instead on the cultural and security agenda (abortion, education, NATO membership), rather than on "old" left issues like income redistribution or the role of the state in the economy.

By the late 1980s, the combination of purges and civil service job opportunities left PSOE without an effective left wing (Biezen 2003). After less than three years in office, the party had defanged grassroots criticism by offering activists the chance to take up no less than twenty-five thousand political appointments in the public administration (Gillespie 1989, 131–132). As a result, 70 percent of PSOE's 1988 congress delegates were on government payroll (Share 1999, 98). As one scholar put it, the result was that PSOE "became little more than a vehicle for careerism and personal advancement" (Share 1998, 100) in which "socialist designs seemed to some to have been replaced by designer socialism" (Gillespie 1989, 67). Democracy may have triumphed across Spain's political institutions, but it stopped at the doors of the Socialist Party.

When the "Guerristas" began to weaken in their commitment to protect González and his team during the early 1990s (Lancaster 1994), it turned out that González was such a "sanctified" figure for the party that Guerra focused his critique on the "neoliberal" faction led by Carlos Solchaga (whom he accused of having "kidnapped" González with the aid of bankers and employer organizations) rather than on González (Gillespie 1989).

The prime minister and his economic ministers steeped in the central bank's professional networks continued to constitute an institutionally protected cohesive team even after PSOE lost its majority in the 1992 elections. To secure a parliamentary majority, PSOE had to co-opt the regional Catalan party, Convergencia i Unio (CiU). In Spain, regional parties have a record as reliable partners that tend to "assure national government stability as parliamentary allies during periods of national minority governments" (Field 2013, 294–295). Although the CiU was economically liberal (Gunther 1996, 193), González soon found that its economic agenda was always second to its regional autonomy agenda.[20] As a result, the institutional primacy of the prime minister and his economic team was never subject to serious contestation.

Containing Labor: Seduce and Abandon

Polanyian countermovements struggled against these ideas and their policy consequences in active ways, watering down some of the boldest neoliberal offensives. Student protests and anarchist urban countercultures made an indelible mark on Spanish political culture in the 1980s and 1990s (Kornetis 2014), but by far the most organized and mass form of reaction came from the unions and especially from the pro-PSOE UGT, whose leaders defended social democratic Keynesianism against the cabinet's embedded neoliberalism.

Far from being a "velvet revolution," Spain's political and economic transition was the scene of intense and lengthy worker protests (Fishman 1990; Royo 2001; Ban and Tamames 2015). As long as democracy was not the only game in town, governments gave in, and between 1977 and 1982, Spain's transition was packaged with a democratic corporatism that promised a social democratic future. Peak-level income policy became the new normal in democratic Spain, and both labor and capital got accustomed to it as the years passed (Gunther, Montero, and Botella 2004, 111). Regardless of whether it was state-manipulated (Encarnación 1997) or the result of workers' moderation (Perez-Diaz 1990; Fishman 1990), the institutionalization of cooperation on macroeconomic policy between state, labor, and capital created the institutional infrastructure in which opposing interests would reach consensus (Bermeo 1994; Gunther 1992; Perez-Diaz 1990; Encarnación 1997). The Workers' Statute adopted in 1980 was second only to the country's democratic constitution in terms of its legislative length, and it regulated individual employment conditions, collective bargaining, and union representation at the highest standards available in Germany and Scandinavia.

During González's first term (1982–1986), UGT signed peak-level pacts, accepting the government's demands for wage moderation, expecting that as growth picked up, the government would agree to adopt measures that increased the labor share in total output via wage increases and job programs (Recio and Roca 1998, 149). This clashed with the neoliberal ideas of Boyer and Solchaga, who saw this argument as a plea for fiscal indiscipline and viewed it as a challenge to their theory that Spain's competitiveness on the cusp of its EU membership was best served through wage devaluation.

Therefore, when growth returned in the late 1980s and the government refused to redistribute as much as UGT wanted, the government sacrificed social concertation on the altar of its fiscal and monetary orthodoxy when the union organized a general strike in 1988 (Royo 2000). UGT lost the confrontation, and this effectively broke concertation in Spain for a decade, ushering in costly politics of confrontation for both sides.

The general strike tested the institutional centralization of the policy process that converted neoliberal ideas into neoliberal policies. The UGT had founded PSOE, and PSOE members were also UGT members, so in theory this institutional bond should have posed a strong challenge to the neoliberals in and around the cabinet. In practice, the government was ready to go for broke because the organizational structure of the party defended the party against the demands of unions. In the executive committee of PSOE, the union only had one representative, who was relegated to nonvoting status (Royo 2000, 181). The UGT's institutional access was also weakened by the fact that, in 1987, prominent UGT leaders resigned from their parliamentary seats over a bitter pension debate. As a result, the institutional primacy of the prime minister's close circle and its linkages with the central bank proved resilient even when the UGT managed to coordinate with the communist union (CC.OO) to organize the 1988 general strike. In a show of strength, González called for early elections in 1989 and won them without UGT support.

Moreover, the UGT's Keynesianism was technically "thin." Faced with the barrage of sophisticated projections thrown at them by the minister of finance and the experts of the central bank, the labor union negotiators were unable to put up a fight regarding the numbers at stake. To top it off, the minister of labor himself, a man who once served as the UGT's economist, began to openly share the views of the minister of finance. [21] Labor asserted itself one more time in 1991, when Socialist Left activists, UGT leaders, and a varied assortment of PSOE activists with a communist past organized a broad-based conference that attracted an impressive number of participants.

But the intellectual distance between the Socialist Left academics and UGT unionists, as well as the skepticism toward the Socialist Left among PSOE's regional bosses, combined to wreck PSOE's last internal rebellion against the policies of the neoliberal ministers. A new labor deregulation reform was passed unilaterally by PSOE in 1994, and the general strike called by the unions had even less political effect than the previous one (Espina 1999). Worse still, in the union elections of the same year, the UGT and the CCOE saw a 20 percent increase in successful independent candidates, which "suggested increasing worker exhaustion with the unions' in-fighting" (Dubin and Hopkin 2013, 18). After this strike, organized labor managed to score only minor victories against the emerging alliance between organized business (the Confederation of Employers' Organizations, CEOE) and the users of the revolving doors between the central bank and the cabinet (the right to monitor new labor contracts and introduce amendments in a new draft strike law).

In short, the UGT was no match for the combined forces of the Rojo network and the Guerra party apparatus. The union's moderation and belief in consensus was exposed as dispensable in the new context. Ironically, it took the pressures exercised by euro accession for labor unions to put institutional limits on the policy freedom of the translators of neoliberalism in Spain.

How did this embedded neoliberalism withstand the test of time? The next sections show that while partisanship recalibrated this way of thinking about the economy along partisan lines, overall Spanish neoliberalism remained stable until the Lehman Brothers crisis created new constraints and opened new possibilities. At the epicenter of this policy regime was Spain's accession to and membership in the Europe's monetary arrangements.

Embedded Neoliberalism and European Monetary Integration

"That Load of Irrationality": Joining the European Monetary System

Spain's road to the euro began in 1989, when the Spanish central bank joined the European Monetary System, an agreement between central banks whereby they committed to intervene in coordinated fashion in foreign exchange markets in order to maintain their currencies within a set variation spectrum around an anchor currency: the German mark. The agreement put extremely tight limits on what had been one of the key mechanisms for embedding neoliberal policies: currency devaluation. In effect, a fixed exchange rate mechanism tied Spain to the famously monetarist policies of the German central bank.

Since the EMS was not part of the EU's foundational treaties, joining it was optional. In Spain, the decision to join was taken without a public debate, within the narrow confines of the revolving doors between the central bank and the economic policy mandarins of the cabinet. The prime minister personally played an important role after the German chancellor hurried González to join in exchange for German support for the Social Charter, an EU document embraced by the Spanish presidency of the European Council that balanced market liberalization with an EU-level commitment to economic rights (Marks 1997, 114), a clear reflection of Madrid's embedded neoliberalism and tendency to frame national interests with the most advanced definitions of European integration (Marks 1997).

At first, "superminister" of finance and economy Carlos Solchaga spent a year reluctant to abandon this policy instrument that had served Spain well in the past.[22] But the epistemic firepower of the central bank ironed out Solbes's resistance. For BdE, joining this monetary arrangement fit with its orthodox monetary policy ideas while strengthening its independence, as de facto the EMS made Spanish policymakers answerable to the German central bank. Rojo's researchers changed the conventional wisdom showing that while devaluation had served Spain well in the past, the situation changed after the Spanish economy became more integrated with Europe's. BdE studies showed that the effects of the 1982 devaluation evaporated after a year because Spanish inflation was on average higher than in Spain's European competitors. Therefore, by the 1980s successful devaluations in Spain demanded even more constraining monetary policies, with even more dramatic consequences for output and employment. In contrast, joining the ESM offered less drastic monetary policy contractions in exchange for importing Germany's view that the role of government is not to smooth economic cycles but to defend predictable and stable policies (Solchaga 1997, 107).

An informal meeting in the Moncloa Palace with the prime minister, the BdE governor, Mariano Rubio, and the former minister of finance Miguel Boyer put Solchaga on the defensive. The two central bankers confronted him with the BdE studies and gave him a very particular definition of the meaning of European integration:

> Once inside the EU, we have to follow German directives on monetary and exchange rate policy. Any attempt to evade them would attract harsh sanctions from the market and a costly loss of credibility. If, for example, the *Bundesbank* decided to raise interest rates in Germany, the only space for action left in Spain was to decide by how many minutes and hours later the Spaniards should follow the German lead. Believing that you could act differently meant you did not understand the markets and lived in the past. (Solchaga 1997, 107)

Solbes was impressed but maintained his reservations, defending the embedded neoliberal argument that the wage and price cuts entailed by joining the

EMS in case of recession would not be accepted by society. What eventually convinced Solbes, almost a year later, was his loss of hope that wage moderation can be achieved consensually in Spain: "The general strike of December 1, 1988 and its load of irrationality convinced me of the necessity to take a course of action whose possibilities of success were unknown. Anchoring the peseta in the EMS seemed the best choice" (Solchaga 1997, 108).

As a labor union critic put it in an interview with this author, "If Spaniards could not be Germans, our government thought we could be made to become Germans by tying us to the German mark."

Once inside the EMS, the cabinet tied itself to the mast even as turbulence pushed the stronger economies of Britain and the UK out. In turn, the BdE had such a tight monetary policy that the Spanish currency was the strongest in the European Exchange Rate Mechanism (ERM) between 1989 and 1991 (Pérez 2001, 1213). Between 1992 and 1994 Spain experienced the most severe recession since 1974, bringing unemployment rates to 23 percent, a level not met until the post-Lehman crisis. But rather than drop out of the EMS, the cabinet stayed the course of orthodox macroeconomic management demanded by European monetary integration even as the public opinion was growingly bitter about the Maastricht Treaty that led to the creation of the euro (Powell 2003).

Faced with the recession, Minister of Finance Pedro Solbes reactivated the embedded neoliberalism of its predecessors: public spending and public sector wage freezes, cuts in the supply of public sector jobs, cuts in unemployment benefits, more labor market deregulation. The idea behind the stabilization package was to defend Spain's place in the EMS via confidence and internal devaluation effects. After the failure of corporatist bargaining, these measures were adopted unilaterally against the background of continuing institutional cohesion of centralization (Solbes 2013, 157–162). But failure to strike a social pact with the unions and the attending decentralization of wage bargaining backfired, with decentralized wage growth taking place even in the context of a very tight monetary policy. Neoliberal ideas that tight monetary and fiscal policy in a fixed exchange rate regime combined with labor market deregulation can bring about wage and price restraint proved to be a failure in the context of a decentralized wage-bargaining structure. The same ideas ended up damaging Spain's economic competitiveness because the export sector was repeatedly hit by simultaneous wage increases and currency appreciations, a process that shifted resources toward the service sectors, where firms could pass on easier wage and interest rate costs. Moreover, the interest rate increases meant to moderate wage rises attracted volatile short-term capital inflows that in turn required more interest rate increases, in vicious circles that crippled the central bank's attempt to control domestic liquidity (Pérez 2002, 1213–1215).

Moreover, there was barely any debate in the parliament and the society at large about signing the Maastricht Treaty; unlike in other European legislatures, in Spain the vote was overwhelming: 314 votes in favor, 3 against and 9 abstentions. Indeed, only the ex-communists were keen to challenge the economics behind euro accession.[23] For the prime minister, belonging to EMS was the logical outcome of the single market and of Spain's "return to Europe" and consequently of Spain's shedding of its secular inferior status among European nations. In line with this thinking, Spain became one of the most ardent champions of economic rights, social cohesion, and European citizenship in EU circles (Marks 1997; Solbes 2013, 177–183).

Moving Embedded Neoliberalism to the Right (1996–2004)

Partisan differences are resilient in the economic policies adopted by democracies, and Spain is not an exception (Boix 1998; Huber and Stephens 2012). Beyond doubt, embedded neoliberalism did experience some retrenchment under the conservative PP governments of José María Aznar (1996–2004) regarding issues such as state ownership and distribution, albeit not on macroeconomic issues and labor market regulation. In part, this reflected the profiles of the pivotal players in the cabinet. No longer steeped in the cautious neoliberalism of the BdE, they were a mix of the elite economic bureaucrats of the ruling Partido Popular and economists who came from revolving doors between academia and the private sector. This was also the case with Minister of Finance Rodrigo Rato (Aznar's right-hand man on economic affairs during the PP's opposition years) and Minister of the Economy Cristobal Montoro (finance professor at a provincial university and economist for the employers' association).

Overall, the economic ideas of the Aznar policy team reinforced the macroeconomic orthodoxy of their predecessors, with euro accession and membership strengthening their resolve. The BdE continued to be the unassailable bastion of expertise that it was under the Socialists, its prestige further magnified by the fact that Rojo and his closest associates had acquired what a Ministry of Finance economist interviewed by this author called a "mythical status," due to their high profile in the design of the euro. The central bankers' ideas about the importance of low inflation, balanced budgets, and labor market deregulation were also the cabinet's ideas, and, accordingly, Spain was among the star pupils of the euro accession. Ironically, however, the extremely tight monetary policy of the central bank failed to rein in inflation, a fact that motivated the government to restart centralized collective bargaining to centrally obtain wage moderation, an event that proved crucial in the taming of inflation in Spain from the mid-1990s onward (Pérez 2002, 1214).

While in Italy euro accession was seen as an external anchor for the beleaguered domestic advocates of macroeconomic conservatism, in Spain it was seen merely as a process that recognized the dominant thinking among the country's policy elite.[24] On fiscal policy, Minister of Finance Rodrigo Rato (future managing director of the IMF) admitted in private that he "had largely followed the policies that Solbes had started" (Royo 2009, 64). Moreover, a year after the euro was adopted, the two parties stood together when their leaders signed a balanced budget objective, one of the few instances in which PP and PSOE agreed in public on anything.

The political resilience of macroeconomic orthodoxy within the euro was tested over the following years. In 2003, while Germany and France blinked when faced with the fiscal constraints of the Stability and Growth Pact soon after the euro was inaugurated, Aznar's government did not. For technocrat Luis de Guindos, the euro accession was not an ideational straitjacket, but merely the international recognition of Spain's road to economic liberalism that began with the 1959 Stabilization Plan (De Guindos 2005, 112). The policy intellectuals of the Aznar policy team were keen to disembed the neoliberal project from such social objectives as providing high-quality employment in competitive state firms, providing patient finance to employment-sensitive sectors, or striking a more progressive balance between low- and high-income groups via the tax system. They inveighed against state ownership and proclaimed the inherent superiority of the private sector, while anticipating an economic miracle driven by lower corporate taxes and deregulation of the real estate and construction sector, which they judged to be one of Spain's main sources of comparative advantage in the eurozone. In their judgment, the private sector could not be wrong, and the very idea that their policies created a real estate bubble was rejected. As Cristobal Montoro put it, "The concept of the real estate bubble is a speculation made by the opposition politicians who talk unwisely about the brick-and-mortar economy, forgetting that construction is a fundamental sector for the economy of this country."[25]

In line with these ideas, in a few years Aznar's group demanded (and obtained) the privatization of all major state-owned firms in telecom (Telefónica), fuels (Repsol, Enagás), infrastructure (Endesa), and banking (Argentaria). The government's share of the stock market went down from 10.87 percent in 1996 to just 0.52 percent in 2004. Although they did not challenge progressive taxation per se, they gave tax cuts to the top of the social pyramid and, after deregulating land use and construction, they unleashed Europe's greatest real estate bubbles funded by liquidity from core eurozone countries. The Socialists' legacy of the investor state was effectively a memory by the time they took office again in 2004. However, the rest of their legacy was far from being in tatters.

At the same time, although Minister Montoro had written ominously about the transition "from the welfare state to welfare society," in reality his voice was isolated, and the technocratic inner circle was never gripped by Thatcherite enthusiasm for challenging the Socialists' conventional wisdom on the welfare state. Although social spending was modestly trimmed, the cuts were far from dramatic and were justified as an unpleasant cost of euro accession rather than as valuable in their own right. Massive government spending on employment-intensive public works continued, and government revenues were increased as a share of GDP from 37.3 percent in 1996 to 39 percent in 2004. In a prime ministerial speech in the parliament made in 1998 it is hard to find evidence of anti-welfare state rhetoric.[26]

Similarly, in his 1996 campaign, Aznar stressed his intention to reboot the dialogue with the unions, while critiquing the Socialists for failing to do so (Hamann 2011, 175–179). Although Rato pushed for a comprehensive deregulation of the labor market following the 2000 elections, the team as a whole was not entirely convinced of the ideas behind it, so when the unions went on general strike, the government backed off. Finally, the principle of progressive taxation remained deeply entrenched in the writings of Aznar's economists, which helps explain why the tax reforms they proposed were hardly a Reaganite revolution: the tax brackets were cut from five to four and the marginal rate was cut by barely two percentage points. Even while in opposition, the party's main economist's view of tax reform was only a recalibration of the existing tax system (Nadal 2006).

Moving Embedded Neoliberalism to the Left (2004–2008)

In 2004, after eight years in opposition, the Socialist Party had become one of the most progressive center-left parties in the world on gender parity, gay rights, the environment, and other postmaterial policy issues as part of a strategy to rebrand socialism and incorporate new constituencies (Encarnación 2009). Yet as far as its economic ideas were concerned, the party reaffirmed embedded neoliberalism while pushing its fringes to the left. PSOE's unexpected victory in the 2004 elections opened up space for such progressive recalibrations of embedded neoliberalism.

On the one hand, euro membership and technocratic elite continuity reinforced macroeconomic orthodoxy. The top of the finance ministry (Minister Pedro Solbes, his deputy, Miguel Ángel Fernández Ordóñez, directors Enrique Martinez Robles, Juana Lazaro, Soledad Abad) had staffed the very top positions in economic ministries during Felipe González years (Solbes 2013, 263–267). They held similarly orthodox views with the economists of the prime minister's Economic Bureau (Domenech, Estrada, and González-Calbet 2007) held similar views. For Zapatero himself, sound finance was "the guarantee of maintaining public services" (Solbes 2013, 263).

Budgetary stability as defined by the fiscal rules of the euro was a key objective. To lock it in, in 2006 the government translated its commitment into law even as France and Germany had just broken the common currency's fiscal rules. The law stipulated that if GDP grew by more than 3 percent, the government would book surpluses; if it grew between 2 and 3 percent, the budget would be balanced; and if growth was below 2 percent, the government would be allowed to run a 1 percent deficit, two points below the threshold demanded by the Stability and Growth Pact (Solbes 2013, 296–298).

Rather than relax at the sight of the declining interest rates brought by the euro, the loosening of the fiscal rules of the eurozone in 2005, the influx of immigrant labor, and the massive infrastructure spending financed by EU funds, the technocrats tightened the fiscal belts and made a drastic cut in public debt their principal objective (Solbes 2013, 279).

In terms of distribution, radical proposals to balance more welfare spending with a libertarian flat tax "revolution"[27] never made it into doctrine or policy practice, having been deemed outlandish by the finance ministry. Instead, the 2007 tax reform was informed by more moderate embedded neoliberal ideas about balancing equity and growth incentives. On the left side of the ledger, the reform reduced the tax burden on labor and gave tax cuts for challenging family or personal situations; on its right side, it reduced the marginal income tax and gave a neutral treatment to income from savings and capital (Solbes 2013, 273, 293–294).

Zapatero's technocrats also embraced supply-side economics embedded in the competitiveness agenda of the EU. Minister of Finance Solbes and his team, along with the Economic Bureau, were keen on supporting a blitzkrieg of structural reforms designed to make the economy more flexible and more open by defending economic competition, stimulating innovation, and further liberalizing telecom, transportation, service, and retail markets (Solbes 2013, 292–345). The economists recruited by Zapatero from the revolving door between academia and the BdE had taken a dim view of some of the aspects of embedded neoliberalism, such as the relatively high protection afforded to workers with long-term contracts and the unemployed (Segura 2001).

Some PSOE technocrats also made the case for orthodox pension reforms, such as increases in the retirement age and the number of hours worked (Balmaseda, Sebastián, and Tello 2002). For the finance ministry economists, the solution to the injustices of duality was a "big bang" reform that would reduce severance pay costs while stimulating long-term contracts and pegging wages to productivity levels (Solbes 2013, 301–302). The prime minister's Economic Bureau built on the EU's interest in stimulating more innovation among its member states and pushed for a comprehensive policy to shift Spain's economic model away from its traditional brick-and-mortar path and toward higher value-added sectors and a high-skill labor force (Solbes 2013, 263). To reach this goal within the existing limits allowed by the EU, they proposed doubling public spending on research and development by 2008 while also increasing funding for student fellowships.[28]

At the same time, local policymakers sought room for maneuvering in both macroeconomic and welfare state terms. Javier Vallés, a former Research Service economist who went on to work for the Economic Bureau of Prime Minister Zapatero, coauthored a study alongside world-famous academic Jordi Galí and David López-Sallido (an ex–Research Service economist and Federal Reserve Board researcher) that replaced strong neoclassical assumptions (e.g., Ricardian consumers) with Keynesian ones (rule-of-thumb consumers, sticky prices) and found that increases in government spending during recessions lead to increases in consumption. They argued that fiscal expansion can be successful because "the combined effect of higher real wages and higher employment raises current labor income and hence stimulates the consumption of rule-of-thumb households" (Galí, López-Salido, and Vallés 2007, 260). For the prime minister himself, once fiscal rectitude was in place, the government should engage in further wealth redistribution by increasing minimum pensions, providing more affordable housing, and increasing spending on education (Solbes 2013, 263).

Other Research Service economists who would go on to serve in Zapatero's Economic Bureau found that, in the EMU, there is no direct effect of money upon inflation and output, a refutation of the monetarist core of some versions of neoliberal theory (Andrés, López-Salido, and Vallés 2001). Economists from the same bureau also contested the comparative advantage thesis advocated by EMU growth theory, showing that the euro's financing of the construction sector bubble and the stagnation in public spending on innovation meant a worrying slowdown in the country's productivity performance (Domenech, Estrada, and González-Calbet 2007). Finally, despite bowing to orthodox pension reforms ideas, these economists did not go so far as to accept radical neoliberal ideas such as pension privatization (Balmaseda, Sebastián, and Tello 2002). As chapter 9 shows, this intellectual openness close to the prime minister's office helped to inspire the adoption of a strong fiscal stimulus in 2008–2010.

During the early 2000s, PSOE economists strengthened the embedded character of Spanish neoliberalism by proposing new ideas about the welfare state. Within the limits of fiscal orthodoxy, they advanced the argument that a higher minimum wage and minimum pension, more spending on affordable housing, and the establishment of a new social program for dependent persons would distribute the windfall revenues from the boom more evenly, while also representing a social investment in the country's labor force (Zapatero 2013). Moreover, on labor market reforms, the economic team of the first Zapatero government was ambivalent about the virtues of deregulation espoused by the central bank and academic economists. While the minister of finance was ready for the option to use executive power to loosen up the labor market institutions that locked in Spain's famous dual labor market curse that protected insiders, the rest of the team felt less strongly about it. Moreover, from the first months of his term, the prime minister signed a social pact whereby he agreed not to push through the parliament any social reforms without the consent of organized labor and capital (Solbes 2013, 281).

The same institutional conditions that favored the transition to neoliberalism under Felipe González also favored its consolidation under Aznar and Zapatero. The prime minister's office and the cabinet continued to "dominate the policy process to the exclusion of parliament, interest group participation and even smaller, supporting parties when policies are made by minority governments" (Chari and Heywood 2009, 49). Moreover, power concentration and executive dominance (rather than consensus) have become more deeply embedded over time (Chari and Heywood 2009, 32).

This was especially true under Zapatero, who centralized relevant economic expertise in his Economic Bureau, an institution that effectively became a "shadow Finance Ministry" (Solbes 2013, 274). Moreover, the intellectual coherence of Zapatero's policy team was deepened by the fact that some of his key advisers and ministers had done their PhDs at the University of Minnesota during the early 1980s. Moreover, finance minister and vice president of the cabinet Pedro Solbes, an old hand of the González governments, was picked for the job from his post as vice president of the European Commission, where he developed a reputation as the chief enforcer of the Stability and Growth Pact.[29] In effect, neither PP nor PSOE had to go to great lengths to control dissenters within the party's ranks. Rather, for institutional cohesion to endure, consensus was only necessary within a core executive group.

As for coalitional dynamics, the PP governments (1996–2004) and the minority government of Socialist Zapatero's first term (2004–2008) had no major ideological disagreements with their supporting partners (Field 2009, 48).[30] The PP did not have a parliamentary majority in the 1996 elections and had to get support from both the center-right Catalan Convergence and Union (CiU) and the more centrist Basque Nationalist Party (PNV). However, as center-right parties, neither ally was a real obstacle to the government's economic agenda.

The Euro Road to Lehman

The neoliberal ideas underpinning the euro and European financial integration combined with domestic dynamics to prepare the grounds for a financial and fiscal crisis of epic proportions once the unthinkable (no sudden stops inside the eurozone) became a reality in 2008.

With currency risk gone, Spain experienced a quick convergence of its interest rates to German ones during the 2000s (real interest rates dropped by ten points by 2005) just as credit and collateral conditions loosened up. As we saw, the PP and PSOE governments maintained their "sound finances" record on public debt and deficits but were complacent with high levels of private debt and a remarkable property bubble via easy consumer credit, mortgage loans, and loans to property developers intermediated by Spanish banks. A critical vulnerability of this development was that much of this intermediation was serviced by the *cajas*, savings banks over whom regional governments had regulatory authority. Prudently, the BdE had limited their operations within the region, but the 1992 EU Directive on Banking removed this regulation, allowing these parochial institutions to go national and even resort to euro-denominated wholesale funding sources on a large scale. Most of the funding thus intermediated went to real estate developers, with the significant exception of the high-productivity research sector.

The combination of large capital inflows and domestic institutional characteristics created one of the world's largest asset bubbles, as cheap money met the loosening of zoning regulations. As a result, by 2005 lending for construction reached 29 percent of GDP, consumer credit was half of GDP, six hundred thousand new housing units were built every year, and real estate price increases were larger than in the United States and the UK. The asset bubble created fiscal illusions for the government as well. By 2007 Spanish tax revenue was two percentage points of output higher because of additional real estate transactions (Fernandez-Villaverde and Rubio-Ramirez 2009, 11–15).

By the mid-2000s Spain caught the "Dutch disease." Human capital moved from the export sector toward real estate, with increasing wages in construction increasing the dropout rate from the education system (Fernandez-Villaverde, Garicano, and Santos 2013). As labor productivity failed to catch up and with construction absorbing more and more labor and investment, Spain's gaping current account imbalances demanded 520 billion euros in external financing between 2000 and 2009, a gap financed via portfolio debt securities and bank loans unleashed by financial integration in the eurozone (Quaglia and Royo 2013, 496). The problem with this growth model was that Spanish banks depended on international wholesale interbank funding in what had become a pan-European market thanks to political decisions made by the European Commission and European Central Bank (Gabor and Ban 2015).

The construction boom concealed the inability of Spain's growth model to reduce high levels of unemployment while locking a large part of the young males into low-productivity construction jobs. It also fed a triumphalist discourse about Spain's economic performance that obfuscated the mediocre record of Spain's relative income per capita within the OECD. It was only after the crisis triggered harsh introspection that mainstream economists admitted that in this regard Spain was in 2008 exactly in the same position it was in 1975: twenty percent points below the OECD average (De la Fuente and Doménech 2009, 191).

The counterfactual represented by the high-employment Basque country provides an interesting counterfactual. Here, the *cajas* functioned as development banks for local export-oriented industrial firms, thus preventing an asset bubble from forming in their region and enabling a coordinated capitalism that generated high productivity, high exports, and high incomes (Fishman 2012, 71–72; Royo 2008, 145–179). In contrast, large Spanish banks and *cajas* in other regions that did not have the "developmentalist" political mandate of the Basque *cajas* refrained from lending to nonconstruction firms and small and medium enterprises, being responsible for Spain's structural unemployment (Pérez 1997; 1998). Since Spain's version of embedded neoliberalism had delegitimated the role of public development banks, the easy money and deregulated zoning turned the Spanish economy as whole into a time bomb rather than into an economically balanced export powerhouse.

While the central bank did not sound the alarm bell, the government's technocrats and international financial organizations did. As early as 2004 the IMF alerted the finance ministry that credit growth and the real estate bubble were extremely sensitive to increases in interest rates. Yet the government failed to withdraw tax subsidies for real estate purchases—a key device of the bubble— citing lack of political support and the neoliberal idea that the twin bubbles would moderate themselves by virtue of market rationality (Solbes 2013, 276). These were not some local pathologies, but the reflection of what was the conventional wisdom at the time. As a Spanish banker told this author, "Before Lehman the European message was that Spain should make the most of its comparative advantage in land availability and splendid weather by letting cheap German liquidity fund a construction boom."

Moreover, Spanish central bankers and private banks facilitated the financialization of the state via EU policies. Between 2002 and 2008 they endorsed the EC's and the ECB's push to make government bonds from all over the eurozone the most important collateral used by banks to borrow from each other. As a result of the implementation of this idea as policy, government debt became the fuel of the European financial engine, creating a buildup of greater and greater risk in the years before 2008 (Gabor and Ban 2015). In effect, these EU decisions pushed the realm of the market to the point that the societies' promise to pay (after all, this is what government bonds are) became a mere appendage to the decisions of financial actors. As chapter 9 shows, the consequences of the ideas with which Spanish authorities dealt with the euro would come to haunt them after 2008.

Conclusions

Spain's embedded neoliberalism became institutionalized during the fourteen years of rule of the Spanish Socialists and survived their defeat at the polls in 1996. But this policy regime had deeper roots. It originated in the specific translation of neoliberalism during the 1970s and early 1980s by a group of Spanish economists who used the revolving door between the central bank, academia, and the state. Select strands of monetarism and a particular synthesis of New Classical and New Keynesian macroeconomics became the new mainstream in Madrid. But rather than replicate these ideas out of whole cloth, they edited them with select Keynesian ideas about the distribution of the tax burden in society, progressive readings of ordoliberal ideas about the "social market economy," social democratic ideas about economic rights, and structuralist ideas about "industrial champions." With some partisan recalibration, successive governments reproduced this dominant view throughout booms, busts, and strains of European monetary integration.

A cohesive and centralized policy process giving pride of place to the central bank and the economic ministries in the cabinet institutionalized these ideas in policy. Central bankers and economists connected to the central bank who later became ministers of finance ensured consistent advice to the prime minister, crowding out alternative economic ideas. Critically, their translation work was sheltered from broader party and societal pressures by a high degree of institutional centralism enforced by the Socialist Party in power. Once institutionalized, technocratic elite continuity and continuing institutional cohesion reproduced these ideas over the following decades' booms and busts and the strains of European monetary integration.

3

Romania's Disembedded Neoliberalism

Late but Radical

Policy elites in postcommunist Romania embraced neoliberalism late, but when they did, most went all the way down, giving birth to a policy regime and economic system that leaves few tools to embed markets into progressive societal demands. Indeed, Romania's policy regime went from a synthesis of neoliberalism and the developmental state in the early 1990s to a neoliberalism with marked libertarian tendencies during the 2000s mainly because this is how the elites du jour understood the conventional economic wisdom of the day. Specifically, during the first half of the 1990s electoral outcomes brought to power political elites who had a large conflict-prone relationship with the advocates of neoliberal ideas and policies. This changed after 1996 when the levers of power went to the domestic advocates of various flavors of neoliberalism. By the mid- 2000s it became clear that both the left and the right of the political spectrum were keen to advocate and institutionalize a disembedded neoliberal policy regime in Romania. Although external coercive and competitive pressures played an important role, they struggle to explain this radicalization.

As we saw, in Spain the economic transition and EU accession ended with the country's institutionalization of a more balanced relationship between market and society. By the time Romania joined the EU in 2007 its default policy regime was heavily unbalanced in favor of supporting market rationality over social cohesion while income, opportunities, and time were redistributed away from labor and toward capital. As a result, the country's representatives supported economically liberal coalitions in Brussels on a whole raft of issues, from taxation to working time regulation, (Copeland 2014, 159). Overall, as chapter 9 shows, the Great Recession and the post-2010 austerity programs consolidated this outcome.

A cursory view at the literature and the figures of the EU statistics office Eurostat shows that there was very little in the way of social cohesion on offer in Romania from the early stages of market reforms during the 1990s, through its EU accession process and, finally, the eve of its EU membership in 2007. After twenty years of transition, the case for Romania being a low-wage, low benefits country is compelling. Statistically, it compared unfavorably with almost all East European member states in terms of socioeconomic rights, inching closer to Baltic-style capitalism (Bohle and Greskovits 2012; Ban 2013). According to Eurostat, while Spain spent 20 percent of its GDP on social services in 2007, Romania spent just 13 percent, the lowest rate of social protection expenditure per inhabitant (PPP) in the EU. The figures were roughly similar in late 1980s Spain and late 1990s Romania. Critically, while twenty years of transition in Spain institutionalized social policies that were largely based on universal access, Romania's were highly targeted to specific vulnerable groups and conditional on (mostly) workfare requirements. A UN survey of the economic situation of the Romanian population found that

> The fact that Romania ranks at, or near, the very bottom on almost all measures of poverty and social exclusion within the European Union has been exhaustively documented by the European Union, the World Bank, UNICEF and a host of other observers. In addition to the 40% who are at risk of poverty or social exclusion, 29% are estimated to be severely materially deprived, which is almost three times more than the EU average. A new composite Social Justice Index, which scores EU countries based on poverty prevention, equitable education, labor market access, and other factors ranks Romania 27th.[1]

Moreover, in the late 2000s Romania still vied for the last place in the Eurostat's economic indicator rankings for the national minimum wage, while competing with Bulgaria for the lowest spot regarding the levels of poverty and severe material deprivation (including among children), the number of working poor, and the share of labor in the wealth being produced (Popa 2012; Bodea and Herman 2014), with some scholars identifying the increasing racialization of poverty in Roma "ghettos" (Vinze and Raț 2013). In contrast, during the 1980s Spain started a fast convergence with the EU on social spending and outcomes and, over time, came close to the EU average for all these measures, at least until drastic austerity measures imposed by the governance of the Eurozone crisis in the 2010s began to bite (Moreno 2013; Moya et al. 2013).

Throughout the 1990s and the 2000s, deindustrialization combined thin safety nets in Romania kept the reservation wage low and personal dependence on the labor market high. Before 2008, only labor market protections for the public sector and some parts of manufacturing remained relatively strong (Bohle and Greskovits 2012; Trif 2007; 2008). Nevertheless, as chapter 9 shows, even this remaining form of embeddedness of the Romanian political economy did not survive the Great Recession, when reforms drastically scaled back employment protections and replaced statutory corporatism at the national, sectoral and firm level to a liberal "voluntary" system that "made it almost impossible to negotiate new national and sectoral collective agreements between 2011 to 2014" (see Adăscăliței, and Guga 2015). Unsurprisingly, no less than a third of the labor force emigrated from the late 1990s onwards, the largest migration wave inside the EU in decades (Ban 2012), making some scholars observe that migrant work abroad became a safety valve for extreme and extensive social dislocations. Indeed, through the remittance flows it generated, massive migration became a structural aspect of the Romanian welfare system (Meeus 2013).

How did this happen? This chapter shows that after considerable initial obstacles in the early 1990s, during the late 1990s and well into the EU accession years (2000–2007), Romanian governments unleashed market forces through market-maximization policies while institutionalizing generous regulatory and tax rents for both foreign and domestic capital. In the background, a weak bureaucratic state often reluctant to enforce constraining tax laws on a systematic basis passed the burden of adjustment onto the least fortunate wage earners and consumers.

Specifically, beginning with the second half of the 1990s the country's policy regime began to offer investors a "competition state." One side of this competition state was of the market-based variety. During the late 1990s and through the late 2000s successive governments adopted extensive privatizations at below-market values, the longest weekly work schedules in the EU, very low flat-rate taxes, even lower effective tax rates, and sparse regulation. A study found that "since 1992 the average company tax burden of the underlying model company has dropped by almost 65 percent; as a result, Romania holds second position among the group of Central and Eastern European EU member states" (Spengel et al. 2012). According to the Romanian central bank, although the profit margins of Romanian firms are among the highest in the EU, their willingness to pay tax already very low statutory tax rates is among the lowest (Georgescu 2015).

Romania also offered "soft" enforcement of labor regulations and loosely regulated finance (Voinea 2009), driving local levels of labor productivity to competitive regional levels.[2] While in 2000, Romania attracted almost half of the total foreign direct investment for the Balkan region, between 2004 and 2008 it was overtaken only by Estonia and Bulgaria in terms of FDI inflows. Fourteen billion dollars entered the economy in 2008 alone, and on the eve of the debt crisis Romania attracted a share of FDI inflows (35 percent) that was similar with the region's engineering powerhouses (Slovakia, Poland, the Czech Republic) (Estrin and Uvalic 2014). The inflows were associated with a significant increase in export complexity (Bajgar and Javorcik 2015) and, according to some, job quality (Javorcik 2014). This industrial recovery seemed to vindicate the EU and domestic promoters of the country's growth strategy (Medve-Bálint 2014).

The financial sector was also deeply transformed. Successive governments and the central bank created a banking system that was almost wholly foreign-owned, with the subsidiaries of West European banks making up 89 percent of the market.[3] The system was driven by carry trade and backed by a central bank whose policy tied financial sector stability to the business calculations of foreign owned banks (Gabor 2010a). To boost the local financial sector and marketize old-age insurance, the government transferred a part of mandatory social security payments into private pension funds (Orenstein 2008). When coupled with the arrival of nonresident investors, this financial system fed a consumption bubble that paved the way for yet another wave of neoliberal transformations after the Lehman crisis (see chapter 9).

As shown in the introduction, disembedded neoliberalism is not market fundamentalism. Instead, it is a set of ideas (and associated policies) that balance strategies that maximize the role of markets with forms of state intervention that redistribute income, opportunities, and time in ways that benefit capital and high-income earners disproportionately. As elsewhere in the region, the purpose of this redistribution is to boost the country's competitiveness in international supply and financial chains in parallel with the maintenance of a political support base (Bohle and Greskovits 2012). In the case of Romania, this meant a strong willingness to subsidize the internationalization of Romania's productive base through uncompetitive privatizations carried out at large discounts, subsidized energy produced by state firms or credit guarantees and other forms of state aid for new transnational industries. In the manufacturing sector, large domestic and multinational firms also received large subsidies, loan guarantees, and tax breaks. Finally, upwards redistribution also came in the form of publicly subsidized housing for young middle-income families and a flat income tax system that benefited disproportionately the upper runs of the income pyramid.

These decisions came at the expense of the social cohesion and state investment in education, research and other key enablers of sustainable development. As a result, the competitiveness of the country was narrowed down to low-wage, low-benefits work for the assembly of increasingly complex, yet overall semistandardized goods transported on an improving road infrastructure within (mostly) German, French, and Italian manufacturing supply chains (Ban 2013b).[4]

The price tag was high and multi-faceted. Public utilities were privatized, and private operators took the almost guaranteed profits that utilities generate. However, according to the government auditor (the Court of Accounts), they raised prices close to EU levels while not making the promised billions of euros investments.[5] Both in this case and in many others, such findings entailed no follow-up. The other price tag is in the form of neoliberal populism, an electoral strategy whereby incumbents ease the tax burden while increasing pensions and public sector wages on an ad hoc basis (usually right before elections) while refraining from less reversible strategies of embeddedness such as strong public services and comprehensive social policies.

To find out where disembedded neoliberalism came from, this chapter begins by mapping the limits of conventional approaches emphasizing a combination of external coercion, market competition and domestic institutions. To fill in the unexplained gaps, it explores the role of market reformers, their ideas and the institutions in which they were embedded. The analysis focuses on how central bank economists, influential academics and think tanks hybridized the global neoliberalism du jour with more radical (and marginal) varieties, including select ideas from the quill of economic libertarianism.[6]

The Limits of Conventional Explanations

The existing literature dealing with the causes of this systemic transformation of Romania's policy regime points to a combination of external coercion, market competition, and domestic institutions. For some (Gabor 2010a) the driving force of neoliberal reforms has been the alliance between the IMF and the central banks. For others the explanation can be found in the way in which this conditionality was mediated by coalitional politics (Pop-Eleches 2008) and the ways in which domestic elites coped with their inferior status and weak capacity while negotiating wiggle room with the Fund (Pop 2006). Other scholars have made similar arguments about the interplay between EU conditionality and domestic institutional structures (Cernat 2006; Vachudova 2005; Papadimitriou and Phinnemore 2004; 2008; Pridham 2007; Epstein 2008a; 2008b; Trif 2008). Finally, some comparative work on Romania focused on transnational advocacy coalitions linking IOs and nonstate actors such as think tanks (Orenstein 2008a; 2008b; Appel and Orenstein 2013)

A distinct strand of literature focusing on capitalist diversity in the region attributed these transformations to a broad range of transnational mechanisms, from competition (Nölke and Vliegenthart 2009) to nudging (Medve-Bálint 2014). Dorothee Bohle and Bela Greskovits's (2012) emblematic work found that the answer to the puzzle of how different policy regimes dealt with the tensions between market mechanisms and protective social arrangements is in the interplay between such transnational forces and the initial choices of transformation strategies, which were in turn constrained by the socialist past and Polanyian movements and countermovements (Bohle and Greskovits 2012).

These are powerful accounts that inform this book's attention to the role of external conditionality and its linkages with domestic processes. However, this literature has important gaps. Most of these studies give the greatest causal weight to material structures and incentives-based political contention, relegating ideational explanations to a residual function. Indeed, the diversity of policy regimes that emerge from the brew of transition is seen as derivative of the ways in which domestic economic, institutional, and political processes filtered transnational demands for neoliberal policies. Economic ideas matter only as a background variable, usually in the form of the steady external supply of neoliberal theories.

The main gap in this literature is that it does not explain the radicalization of Romanian neoliberalism. In other words, why did local translators go beyond expressing conformity with what was demanded by the IMF, the World Bank, the EU and other actors on whom governments relied for funding, membership and other benefits. Why, for example, scrap the World Bank-designed progressive income tax system and replace it with a libertarian low flat tax? Why go beyond calls to have a predominantly privately-owned banking sector and privatize all state banks of any significance and turn them into subsidiaries of West European banks? Why challenge the EU from the economic right on issues as diverse as pension reform and public service privatization?

Some of the existing research dealing with Romania's neoliberal transformation directly (Pop 2006; Epstein 2008; Gabor 2010a) or indirectly (Orenstein 2008; Appel and Orenstein 2013) do focus on economic ideas as principal causal factors, showing how the IMF, the World Bank, or the EU (re)socialized local elites into global neoliberal economic thinking through long-run, regular, and intensive interactions. These are compelling explanations, but they tend to reduce the transnational advocacy for neoliberal ideas to one or two international organizations, leaving the systematic analysis of other diffusion agents (academia, nonprofits, corporate sector) to future research. Hillary Appel and Mitchell Orenstein's work is a notable exception, but their findings on complex advocacy coalitions are issue-specific (tax and pension policy) rather than integrative and pitched at the level of the national policy regime as such. Most importantly, all these idea-centered explanations do not specify the relationship between ideas and coercion or between ideas and resources while assuming that global neoliberal theories are either rejected or adopted, with no attention to the hybridity of their locally autonomous adaptation by domestic translators. The following chapters on Romania take up this task.

Finally, Romania's high levels of poverty (including working poverty) and social exclusion caused by these policies were not a simple reflection of the country's GDP or the structure of the labor market, with its high share of low-skill subsistence farm employment (see Bodea and Herman 2014 for an overview).

Neither can they be attributed solely to the poor technical capacity of the state, racism or rampant corruption (World Bank 2005; Vincze and Rat 2013; Mungiu 2015). The same is true of the upwards redistribution outcomes via taxation, low wages and state aid. These are important factors but the country's social disloca-tions are also the result of policy choices steeped in a widely shared economic ideology that subordinates social cohesion to the main goals of neoliberalism without agonizing over the attending trade-offs, as it was the case in Spain. A UN mission to Bucharest described this situation in the following way:

> Government services, especially, but not only for the poorest, are gen-erally the worst in Europe, based on indicator after indicator. I was often told [by government officials, author's note] that poverty is a choice . . . Even the International Monetary Fund told me that Romania has enough fiscal space to increase spending on poverty eradication. But the resources have instead been used to finance even better conditions for the relatively well off. Not only does the Government refuse to increase spending, it has the most regressive tax system in Europe [. . .] It has made the deliberate political choice not to make its tax system more progressive, missing yet another chance to help the poorer groups in society [. . .] Some of my interlocutors spoke of neo-liberal assump-tions aimed at minimizing both taxation rates and social protection, while facilitating wealth generation without regard to redistribution. Instead of social or citizenship rights, the dominant discourse was one of equality of opportunity, as opposed to affirmative action[7]

Neoliberalism and the Postcommunist Transition

The timing of economic transition relative to the specific form of neoliberal orthodoxy is critical in explaining why Romanian neoliberalism was more dis-embedded than its Spanish counterpart. Specifically, Eastern Europe as a whole became exposed to a version of neoliberalism that was much more market radi-cal than Western neoliberalism was at the time when Spain began its economic transition.

A good starting point in exploring this hypothesis is the literature showing that the collapse of East European communism proved to be an opportunity for the advocacy of radical neoliberal theories, often with the support of local econ-omists (Bohle and Neunhöffer 2009; Bockman and Eyal 2002; Bockman 2011). The result of this advocacy was an East European version of the Washington Consensus, yet a stronger aversion to discretionary macroeconomic policies, state-led industrialization, progressive income redistribution, and mass politics.

At its core, neoliberal transition economics as a whole rested on the IMF's traditional macrostabilization model, which linked balance of payments problems to "excessive domestic expansion." According to the IMF's official historian, its logic was as follows: a sustained reduction in nominal domestic credit and government spending would reduce the growth of real demand in the short run, producing a short-run downturn; but if the measure was accompanied by a devaluation, the effect of declining inflation, after one year, on real credit growth and growth of external competitiveness would push up the growth rates. The virtuous effect that this macroeconomic intervention would have on growth would be boosted by supply-side policies such as tax cuts and deregulation that encourage investment. If growth occurred too slowly, then blame could be targeted at imperfect implementation or local problems with human capital (Boughton 2004).

This was an off-the-shelf the IMF applied to all countries experiencing balance-of-payments difficulties, including capitalist ones. But transition economics went further than IMF-style macrostabilization or mainstream economics more generally regarding three main issues: the role of the state as owner and investor, industrial policy and distribution.

First, transition economics also had a theory about why and how to eradicate the state as owner and investor and, to this end, it measured the "success" of transitions in terms of how countries compared to an idealized market economy model, rather than to real-existing varieties of capitalism (Stark 1994, 63–82). Innovations in economics in the 1980s such as incomplete contract theory argued that state enterprises had to be privatized immediately rather than gradually or not at all because in *all* economic systems private ownership is superior to public ownership because it provides better incentives to invest, innovate, and reduce costs. Even if one had, say, Scandinavian state institutions, public ownership was a second-best option and, accordingly, the mixed economy was regarded as inappropriate. While Southern European elites did not faced external advocacy or coercion pushing for these ideas, the East European ones did.

Second, when the Spanish Socialists came to power in 1982, the idea that there was no alternative to eliminating industrial policy was in its infancy, with the Reagan-Thatcher couple being its vanguard. The opposite was the case in the 1990s, when this idea sat at the core of the Washington Consensus. To weaken the basis of industrial policy, public banks were seen as institutions programmed to misallocate credit and were put at the top of privatization lists even as they continued to exist in many advanced capitalist economies (Demekas and Khan 1991; Roland 2002; Boughton 2004; Cernat 2006; Gabor 2010a).

The third dimension of radicalization regarded distribution. Universal safety nets and extensive public services were still part of mainstream economic thinking during the mid-to-late 1970s and early 1980s, when Spain laid the foundations of its post-authoritarian political economy. As we saw in chapter 6, the model was Germany and Sweden. The context was completely different twenty years later in the context of postcommunist transition. The advocates of neoliberal transition economics were aware that their model entailed extensive unemployment, large increases in inequality and downward mobility for large masses of people. Accordingly, they feared that the citizens would use the new democratic institutions to demand protection against economic dislocation (Sachs and Lipton 1990; Lipton et al. 1990). But, unlike in 1970s Southern Europe, when one could reasonably anticipate that such dislocations would benefit the communists (see chapter 6), this was no longer the case when communism was, to put it politely, a political threat of severely diminished probability in the region. The result was advocacy for basic, means-tested safety nets and progressive taxation systems and warnings against more generous West European–style welfare states (Kornai 1997; Deacon and Hulse 1997).

Finally, while the Spanish economic transition took place at a historical juncture when postwar (neo)Keynesian economists were challenged by monetarists and New Classical economists, yet were still a force to be reckoned with, the 1990s were a very different game. This was the time of the "New neoclassical Synthesis," a time when neo-Keynesians had been beaten and the new normal was a compromise between 1970s New Classical radicalism and a stripped down version of Keynesianism (the New Keynesians) who had bought into the main assumptions of the former. Relatively optimistic towards monetary policy as a means of macroeconomic stabilization, this consensus view was very skeptical of the usefulness of fiscal policy outside very limited contexts because the expected "rational expectations" of economic agents beat the Keynesian (or expansionary) effects of fiscal policy: when the government tries to stimulate the economy, households and firms expect tax increases in the future and therefore cut spending and investment (Ricardian equivalence). It was only in the late 1990s that this conventional wisdom began to be challenged by some mainstream economists who argued that not all fiscal stimulus programs are doomed and that it makes sense to consider demand-side policies to defeat recessions (see Arestis 2007 and Ban 2015b for overviews).

Unlike in other East European countries, this view of postcommunist economic transformations met with a great deal of ambivalence in Romania during the early transition years. Between 1990 and 1996, the dominant economic ideas in the state were a hybrid of neoliberal transition economics and developmentalist ideas that harkened back to the 1990 *Blueprint* discussed in chapter 5. One elopmentalist faction ("liberal elopmentalism") was overall positive toward the liberal economics that constitute the bedrock of neoliberal transition economics while having strong reservations regarding some of its major postulates The other side of neodelopmentalism ("populist neodevelopmentalism") was more statist, left-populist, and explicitly anti-neoliberal. Give this late starting point, it took years to populate the Romanian state with sympathetic interlocutors for neoliberalism.

The Neodevelopmentalist Interregnum
Liberal Neodevelopmentalism (1990–1992)

The advocates of liberal neodevelopmentalism were the most reform-minded and pro-Western elite of communist-era technocracy and academia. These academics, technocrats, and government ministers had attended university in the 1960s and 1970s and joined the socialist elite against the backdrop of Ceaușescu's move toward liberalization after 1968 (prime minister Petre Roman himself had studied engineering in rance in the early 1970s). Following the May 1990 elections and the landslide victory of the National Salvation Front (FSN), many of them occupied leading positions in the economic ministries of the first post-1989 governments.

On the one hand, the liberal neodevelopmentalists agreed with the mainstream transition economics view of the IFIs and private consultants that excess demand, the credit overhang, multiple exchange rates, and price controls were the main obstacles to a successful transformation and growth strategy. The prime minister and his economic ministers believed that price liberalization would "get the prices right," eliminate supply gluts, and reduce corruption.[8] Minister of Finance (and future prime minister) Theodor Stolojan even outbid the IMF by advocating near-zero deficits in the middle of the worst recession since the 1930s (Severin 1995, 96).

It would be unwise to use this as evidence that this was a neoliberal cabinet. When faced with a trade-off between neoliberal objectives and developmentalist ones (industrial policy, progressive taxation, public ownership over utilities), they did not need to be forced by domestic opposition to choose the latter. In spite of their proliberalization rhetorics, these pivotal policy players had a weak commitment to the comprehensive price liberalization stipulated in neoliberal scripts. Faced with inflationary pressures triggered by the first wave of price liberalization in an economy with strong monopolistic and oligopolistic structures, the cabinet adopted targeted price controls. They also did not agree that the Romanian industry should be sacrificed on the altar of exchange rate unification.[9]

Government ministers defended financial repression using negative real interest rates and envisaged at best a gradual phasing out of the two-tiered exchange rate system. Support for privatization stopped at the door of energy, public transport, and utility companies, which were turned into French-style state-owned firms that could not be privatized because of their public service status. Finally, while neoliberals favored moderate marginal tax rates, the premier and the economic ministries wanted a steeply progressive income tax system for both individuals and corporations and adopted income tax brackets ranging between 6 and 45 percent.

Institutional discord hampered the translation of all liberal elopmentalist ideas into policy. Although the FSN had won the elections by a landslide and had a comfortable majority in the parliament, the cabinet had to contend with nearly constant opposition to its economic agenda coming from the president, the ruling party, and their sympathizers in the state bureaucracy. Indeed, important part of the FSN's left wing was wedded to economic theories close to market socialism and punched above its weight in terms of political influence. The market socialists felt that a reformed version of the planned economy never had a chance in Romania and felt that scrapping socialism altogether was suicidal.[10] They diagnosed the country's economic failures in Ceauşescu's mismanagement and abandonment of the technoscientific core of socialism, not in state socialism per se (Siani-Davies 2007, 196–197). Rather than scrap planning altogether, they endorsed a variant of it that factored in market signals and aimed to break down giant state-owned firms into smaller, worker-controlled units as in Yugoslavia. Finally, they wanted state ownership over most of the industry and agriculture for the foreseeable future and pleaded for the institutionalization of equal relations between private, public, and cooperative forms of property (Constantinescu 1991; Dumitrescu 1993; Manolescu 1995).

The market socialists controlled the presidency of the Senate, the leadership of the Chamber of Deputies, and the Economic Commission of that chamber. They also had the ear of the presidency, and key secretaries of state in the economic ministries were sympathizers. These positions were strong enough to inflict heavy damage on liberalizing reforms and eventually dilute them, which is what happened (Severin 1995; Betea 2008). President Iliescu first tried to mediate the conflict between the market socialists and the liberal developmentalists, but by the winter of 1990–1991 he began to openly side with the former.[11]

Faced with this three-pronged resistance, Roman pushed for a political resolution of the conflict inside party structures at its extraordinary convention in March 1991. The party endorsed the premier's economic program, but the political victory was short-lived. The market socialist contingent continued to hamper further liberalizing reforms, particularly the cabinet's legislation for privatization. Critically, after coal miners rioted in Bucharest and placed the government building under siege in the fall of 1991, FSN's internecine warfare reached a new climax. The president asked the cabinet to resign, and at the March 1992 party convention, the party split. Roman's team maintained control over FSN, and the party's left wing formed the Democratic Front of National Salvation (FDSN).

A new administration ushered in by the 1992 elections rolled out a more state-led version of elopmentalism to address the country's macroeconomic, structural, and social challenges. This new hybrid ultimately tampered not only with the instruments and settings of neoliberalism, but also with its goals. Far from proposing a conformist embedded neoliberal agenda, its economics entailed the construction of a mixed-economy developmental state.

Populist Neodevelopmentalism (1992–1996)

Populist neodevelopmentalism attacked both neoliberal transition economics and liberal neo-developmentalism with a mix of nationalism and pro-labor rhetoric that promised to defend national sovereignty, the large parts of the industrial legacy of communism and ordinary people against pre-communist elites and foreign interests—depicted as attempting to deprive workers and domestic capital of their political and economic rights.[12]

In more technical terms, this was an intellectual hybrid fraught with tensions between select structuralist, neo-Keynesian, and neoliberal thinking. Its main premise echoed structuralist economics, not neoliberalism: since the economy had the most centralized structure in east central Europe and an unusually high percentage of single-company towns, a gradualist and flexible transition strategy to a mixed economy was politically and economically more desirable than shock therapy. Echoing the postwar mix of neo-Keynesianism and statism particular to countries such as France, its main goal was to save industrial employment via the maintenance of a mixed economy in which the state would remain a key banker and owner of strategic industrial firms (Iliescu 1994; Văcăroiu 1998).[13] Fiscal orthodoxy and the promotion of foreign direct investment were subordinated to industrial policy ideas stressing domestic industrial recovery and industrial upgrading.

The premier and the president's economic advisers sang the praises of low budget deficits, exchange rate liberalization, and disinflation[14] but consistently subordinated them to the goal of arresting the deindustrialization process and the collapse of domestic demand. They also pleased for doubling public investment, public purchases of domestic industrial goods, subsidized credit to industry, and the automatic indexation of the minimum wage.[15] Rather than embrace untrammeled trade openness via comparative advantage, they adopted a view that stressed industrial policy as an instrument to achieve competitive advantage, a classic heterodox position.

On the issue of trade and financial openness, the thinking of the most powerful policymakers (president, premier, economic ministers) was shaped by the fear that extensive trade liberalization would dismantle the country's industrial base and relegate it to the status of an exporter of raw materials and low-value-added goods (Iliescu 1994; Văcăroiu 1998; Georgescu 2002). Echoing structuralist arguments, Prime Minister Văcăroiu defended fixed prices, considered strategic for industrial policy (energy, rail transport), and wanted substantial capital controls to manage a dual exchange rate. More heterodox than the authors of the Blueprint, he also resisted demands for full exchange rate liberalization with the argument that the export industry was dependent on the import of intermediary goods for which there were no locally produced substitutes.[16] In a show of force signaling commitment to industrial policy, the new cabinet drafted fifty-three strategy papers for all industrial sectors[17] and gave state-owned banks a critical role in funding industry and shoring up state companies. As the premier argued,

> Given the conservative policies of the central bank, the unraveling of interenterprise networks, and the lack of a modern financial sector in Romania where enterprises could go and raise finance like they do in the developed economies, the only way to provide finance to firms that hired most of the labor force was through the banks owned by the state.[18]

Finally, both left-leaning and right-leaning populist ideas shaped policymakers' view of how the state should deal with distribution problems. On the left, officials expressed commitment to progressive taxation, the universal character of health, education, and pensions, as well as the subsidization of basic needs (heating, electricity, medicine). Similarly, tax policy became more progressive. Left-leaning populist calls for saving industrial employment and nationalist calls for creating a domestic capitalist class cohabited in the same doctrinal "big tent."[19]

Such economic ideas faced few domestic political obstacles to become economic policies. Unlike Roman's cabinet, Văcăroiu's benefited from a high level of institutional cohesion. Indeed, this government was the most stable in Romania's democratic history, and its reshuffling barely affected the economic ministries. Although they often espoused more liberal views than the premier and the president, the economic ministers generally toed the cabinet's official line. Their memoirs also suggest that there was also nearly seamless convergence of views on economic reform between the president and the premier (Iliescu 1994; Văcăroiu 1998). Moreover, Văcăroiu had no political ambitions and therefore acted as little more than the projection of the president in the cabinet (Abraham 2006, 122; Văcăroiu 1998). The president, in turn, delivered consistent support when the premier was challenged (Boda 1999, 105–129). The premier was allowed to appoint his own ministers, although only one (the minister of tourism) was a member of the governing party.[20]

To top it off, following the split with Roman's faction, party whips made sure that factional strife would be kept under control until after the next elections.[21] The governing party thus became almost the presidential party and was so tightly controlled by Ion Iliescu that party insiders went as far as labeling this period a "presidential regime" (Abraham 2006, 98). The president, the premier, and the chairmen of the two chambers of the parliament met on a weekly basis and consensually settled policy disputes, thus removing possible political struggle in relations between the executive power and the legislative.[22] In the light of all this, there were no significant clashes within the top economic policy team.

While cohesive at the top, the populist neodevelopmentalists failed to ensure political cohesion at the grassroots level. For all its rhetoric about workers' rights and success at reducing unemployment between 1994 and 1996, they not only failed to coopt labor, but also were on a collision course with the country's vocal labor unions, with labor unrest peaking in 1993 and 1994. This showed the limits of top-down neodevelopmentalism in a wobbly democracy and, once macroeconomic stabilization was secured and growth returned, the government signed the first tripartite social pact with the unions in 1995 (Zic 1998; Kideckel 2002), a move that halved the number of strikes. In exchange for wage indexation, the government obtained social peace, although not necessarily broad electoral support.[23] Critically, this co-option exercise included the miners' union, the militant arm of the Romanian working class that had brought down the liberal neodevelopmentalists (Vasi 2004).

Endogenous tensions and transnational constraints undermined the ambitions of the liberal neodevelopmentalist project. Failure to develop strong line ministries and nodal agencies with long-term development horizons and embedded state autonomy vis-à-vis the public sector management elite bred a number of pathologies.[24] An important corollary of development agencies without embedded autonomy was that just as it neglected to adequately fund research institutes staffed by thousands of highly trained PhDs, in effect letting them fall apart, the government asked state banks to extend subsidized credit to sectors that did not produce high-value-added output (steel, animal husbandry, coal-powered electricity plants).[25] Most importantly, the domestic capitalist class was allowed to emerge using highly predatory strategies at a time when the loss of purchasing power that had occurred between 1990 and 1992 persisted. Many who managed state companies set up private companies that made profits that their privileged access to valuable information awarded. The closer a person was to the nomenklatura networks that constituted the government's power base, the greater were the chances of getting rich in this way (Stoica 2004).

Finally, tax collection capacity, a fundamental feature of successful developmental states, remained dismal even by the region's low standards. Government agencies tasked with industrial policy were poorly coordinated. Nonmeritocratic personnel policy and mediocre wages invalidated their promise to develop complex indicative planning strategies and were responsible for the bureaucracy's enduring weakness in terms of technical and administrative capacity.[26] Policy czars like the premier and the president were aware that this system crated practices that hemorrhaged the most valuable industrial assets,[27] but they did little to curb them. In doing so, they missed a unique opportunity to build an effective state and broad social coalition, supportive of democratic developmentalism. In a country where social inequalities exploded, corruption scandal abounded and the purchase power of most remained stubbornly low, this was not received well in the broader society. This failure ushered in a different relationship with neoliberal transition economics and neoliberalism more generally.

Crafting Disembedded Neoliberalism

The Translators of Neoliberalism

Chapter 2 has shown that in Spain the main translators of neoliberal ideas formed a tight network centered in the research service of the central bank and elite academic institutions. While the main translators frequented a more diverse and more loosely connected set of professional environments, in Romania they too clustered around the revolving door between academia and the central bank.

Throughout the 1990s, the central bank's governor, Mugur Isărescu, and his senior economic team had their day jobs at the central bank while remaining tied to academia. Moisa Altar, the man who kept alight local interest in mainstream Western economics during the 1980s, stuck to academia but enjoyed considerable informal influence in the central bank.[28] Some took up leading positions in center-right parties and academic institutions (Radu Vasile, Mircea Ciumara) or moved through the revolving doors between the economic institutes of the Romanian Academy, the central bank, and consulting in policy think tanks connected to BNR (Lucian Croitoru, Liviu Albu). Like their Spanish counterparts, they lived off of their public sector jobs and did not use their strategic positions to get wealthy. They were united by a sense of distinction created by the fact that they were part of the informal elite of researchers and technocrats who had studied developments in Western economics during communism and, as chapter 7 shows, became the sympathetic interlocutors of international financial institutions. As central bankers and sympathizers of the center-right, they sought to distance themselves from the elopmentalist economists, then accused of being a "neocommunist" extension of the old regime (Pop 2006).

After 1997, these economists took charge of economic ministries (Daniel Dăianu, Ilie Şerbănescu, Mircea Ciumara) or became prime ministers (Radu Vasile, Mugur Isărescu). BNR chief economist Daniel Dăianu became minister of finance, Lucian Croitoru worked as economic adviser to the prime minister, and Mugur Isărescu served as premier in 1999 and 2000. As a close observer of the Romanian central bank noted, the coincidence between Isărescu premiership and the avoidance of default in 1999 "reinforced the neoliberal idea that the central bank was the locus of economic competence and that irremediably incompetent politicians had to be constrained to make decisions consistent with the policy priorities established by the central bank" (Gabor 2010a, 34).

The annual reports of the central bank and the publications of its top economists during this period are little more than pious replicas of the neoliberal transition economics. In flagship journals (*Oeconomica*) and prestigious paper series, leading economists using the revolving door between academia, the central bank, and the post-1996 governments translated for various local expert publics the main tenets of the new neoclassical synthesis and supply-side theories about taxation and labor markets. At the same time, this evangelizing effort was accompanied by introducing local innovations into the imported scripts. Most of the time, the result was the radicalization of the policy implications of neoliberal transition economics.

As chapters 5 and 7 show, these technocrats were embedded in broader political milieus of the opposition against the ex-communist ruling party, FSN. In these environments, neoliberalism's message appealed to the antistatist ideologies that were shaping domestic politics in the region. In this ideological climate, the "great conflation" of neoliberalism and democracy gave neoliberalism a powerful advantage over its heterodox competitors. This conflation relegated demands for economic democracy or protection from the displacements of the market to the dustbin of unfeasible and dangerous radical projects. The casting of the politics of 1989 in a "state versus society" mold allowed neoliberal technocrats to argue that the state had to be continuously shrunk and put in the service of a "market society."

Beyond the Washington Consensus

At a time when Romania had a state-dominated economy and an incoherent and untested institutional infrastructure for the market, local neoliberals spent a great deal of time replaying the fights between neo-Keynesian and New Classical economists, except with few to man the neo-Keynesian ramparts (Ban 2011, 421–425).

The main foil of Romanian neoliberals was neo-Keynesian theory. They repeated Milton Friedman's message that there was no trade-off between unemployment and inflation and declared the self-defeating nature of activist fiscal policy via an oversimplified version of the neoliberal narrative about the "failure of Keynesianism" during the 1970s (Croitoru 1994; Isărescu 1991).

This translation enabled them to black-box the collapse of aggregate demand and blame high unemployment on the unions and "rigid" labor regulations (Croitoru 1993; Ţurlea 1999). A decade after monetarism's star had eclipsed in mainstream macroeconomics (DeLong 2000), Romanian neoliberals gave monetarism a new lease on life (Gabor 2010a).[29]

Although they lived in a country gripped by extensive disorganization in industrial relations, local technocrats replicated the neoliberal argument that the biggest risk for macroeconomic policy was that rational workers demand even higher wages/subsidies to compensate the expected loss of purchasing power caused by the price liberalizations announced by the government. Given this argument, the only acceptable option was sudden and comprehensive price liberalization accompanied by extensive privatization (Croitoru 1993, 34; Isărescu 1990; 1992; 1996; Dăianu 1991; 1992; Negriţoiu 1995, 48–49, 207). Echoing Washington Consensus thinking (Deacon and Hulse 1997), many paid lip service to the need to have basic safety nets for the unemployed, the elderly, and the socially marginal, while decisively replacing the commitment to universalism and equality of outcomes that we saw in the case of Spanish neoliberals, with means-tested benefits and equality of opportunity (Croitoru 1993, 169–170; Dijmărescu 1994, 83–85).

Rather than examine the relative effects on unemployment of a politically engineered collapse in public demand, Romanian neoliberals simply embraced the standard OECD diagnosis of unemployment in developed capitalist countries: rigid hire-and-fire rules and insider-outsider labor markets (Croitoru 1993). In line with the dominant view in Western economics at the time, others detected disincentives for employment in the minimum wage itself (see Ban 2011, 445–448 for an overview).

Also, by the mid-1990s the technocrats, civil society leaders, and center-right parties shared the view of transition economics advocate that the longer the institutions of state interventionism were maintained by heterodox strategies, the more the antiliberal social forces would mobilize to increase the social costs of economic and political transition. In their view, they would do so through rent seeking, spoilage, and the threat of regression to statist authoritarianism. In other words, the closer one was to neoliberalism, the further from the specter of the authoritarian state. Even though some leaders of the center-right (especially the Peasants' Party or PNTCD) were closer to Christian Democracy and social liberalism, their economists framed evolutionary-institutionalist perspectives on transition as producing, at best, delays in reform and at worst a democratic collapse. In this narrative, inspired by liberal political theory, the only opponents to market reforms were the already privileged and the widely despised members of the communist elite, while the rest of civil society was assumed to have an interest in a neoliberal transformation (Ban 2014). On the margins of the economics profession, by the late 1990s think tank experts also introduced in the broader Romanian policy debate the "public choice" argument that governments have an innate propensity to expand unless checked by new public management "best practices" (Ban 2011, 496–498).

A good proxy for the level of incorporation of neoliberal macroeconomics and financial theory in the academic environment closest to the central bank by the late 1990s and early 2000s are the dissertations defended by the graduates of the Doctoral School of Finance and Banking, the country's elite graduate program in economics that supplied top experts to the central bank. From Robert Lucas's positions on fiscal policy and the human capital factor, to Merton Miller's and Ross Levine's arguments about the role of deregulated finance for growth, the repertoire of Western orthodoxy became part of postgraduate training for Romania's economists. Overall, one can note a high level of support for the tenets of mainstream transition economics, with a major tilt towards its shock-therapy version.

Similarly, orthodox ideas about the extent of central bank independence, social security financing, the most "progrowth" levels of taxation, and the low likelihood of economic growth even at very low levels of inflation became familiar and "indigenized" with local data. New concepts (shareholder value) and methodologies (value at risk) were applied and recalibrated in graduates' dissertations regarding the situation of the Romanian economy (Ban 2011). Finally, complex models and longitudinal data series for EU countries were marshaled in support of supply-side taxation policies. These theses argued that Europe's high tax rates have a negative effect on economic growth, that the relationship between government expenditures and economic growth is negative, that there is a consistent negative relation between budget deficits and growth, and that government consumption has a much larger negative effect on growth than total government expenditure.[30]

Although the dominant mode of the 1990s was that of replicating international neoliberal scripts in a scramble to catch up with the capitalist core, the kernels of local radicalization are already there.

First, on fiscal policy and structural reforms by the mid-1990s there was a tendency to outbid the implications of the Washington Consensus and mainstream macro. For the central bank's chief economist, the emergence of late payments between firms (arrears) was a form of money, and to the extent that it affected state firms, this money had to be factored into the calculation of inflation and deficit figures (Dăianu 1994a, b; 1996). In practice, this meant that the spending cuts that mainstream economists and the IMF demanded in times of recession would have to be even deeper and privatization even faster and more extensive. Similarly, Cristian Popa, Dăianu's successor as head of the central bank's chief economist office proposed a microeconomic theory about the rise of interfirm debt, a factor that prevented successful macrostabilization through the buildup of arrears. Because profit-making could only be conceived as a peripheral concern to public firms, Popa argued that such suboptimal behavior was bound to continue as long as the economy remained predominantly state-owned. In practice, workers controlled the factories, and their utility-maximizing behavior could be no other than preserving employment and wages despite a fall in output. In order to be efficient and rational, the microeconomic world of postcommunism had to perform according to the assumptions of rational expectations theory: "Any important progress towards market-conforming rationality will not occur until considerable segments of economic agents will behave in an economically optimal manner rather than in a rent-seeking one" (Popa 1994, 134).

The second dimension of radicalization concerned redistribution via taxation. Here, the dominant view layered standard Washington Consensus ideas about expanding the tax base with Reaganite conservative "revival" arguments. Although the first postcommunist Romanian tax code had been drafted by the World Bank,[31] it soon came under fire from economists who used supply-side tax theory and a good dose of the Ronald Reagan cult to demand changes that would make it less progressive and more corporate friendly (Croitoru 1993, 105–106, 161). Croitoru suggested that dinsinflation should be followed by tax cuts for higher income brackets, a general reduction of the progressive nature of the tax system, the termination of taxes meant to stimulate certain kinds of behaviors deemed good for the economy, greater reliance on consumption taxes, the expansion of the tax base. The high progressivity of personal income tax was blamed as one of the causes of weak job creation (Croitoru 1993: 105–106; 161).

This radicalization tendency seemed to draw less on economics than on international pop-academic tracts complemented by local antistate sentiment. In this context, another marker of radicalization strategy was the treatment of a controversial idea or figure from the fringes of the neoliberal universe as if it were part of the mainstream "scientific" core of Western neoliberalism. Lucian Albu, an academic economist close to the central bank, did this with the "Laffer curve" and the supply-side argument that tax cuts for corporations pay for themselves (Albu 1994, 37, 41–43). Albu did this despite the fact that few mainstream Western economists or the IMF took such arguments seriously.[32] Indeed, while supply-side economics was just one of the contestants in the field of Western orthodox economics during the 1990s, in Bucharest, Albu declared it "the core of modern tax policy" (Albu 1994, 41). Attacks against progressive taxation continued in the second half of the 1990s, when the emerging "experts" of politically influential think tanks such as the Romanian Academic Society (SAR) began to put progressive taxation in their crosshairs (Ban 2011).

Third, the radicalization of the imported neoliberal script manifested itself on the issue of redistribution via spending. As we saw, the advocates of neoliberal transition economics warned against premature welfare states and advocated for targeted and conditional benefits. In a country that experts saw as having little more than a "residual" welfare state (Deacon 2000), some went as far as arguing that capital accumulation, economic growth and redistribution could not be pursued simultaneously and that the historical record suggested that the first should take priority (Dijmarescu 1994: 80). SAR's experts-most of whom lacked professional credentials in economics- revealed that Romanians did not appear aware of the "prohibitive" tax costs they paid for social spending and suggested that the gratuitous access to university education created perverse incentives for students, pleading for the introduction of student fees.

Neoliberal Transition Economics in Power

After 1996, a political shift to the right ushered into power the key translators of neoliberal theories in Romania. The ex-communists lost the 1996 elections, giving both the presidency and the cabinet to the Democratic Convention (CDR), an ideologically mixed coalition whose core members (the Peasants' Party and the Liberal Party) had run on a combination of neoliberal transition economics and social cohesion. Since this was the first election in which the incumbents were defeated, the Convention's victory de facto ended the political transition in Romania and bestowed the greatest degree of political legitimacy known by a political formation in Romania's history (Pop-Eleches 2001).

The new policies were a Romanian version of "shock therapy." Soon after taking office, the coalition began to enact an economic reform program designed by the IMF and Leszek Balcerowitz, the "father" of Polish shock therapy. The reform program's main thrust was a dramatic squeeze of credit combined with drastic austerity measures and extensive neoliberal structural reforms. According to the *Economist*, this was the most radical shock therapy package tried anywhere in the region.[33]

Total credit fell by more than 50 percent, and multiple exchange rates were terminated and replaced with a float. The government halved spending on public services, completed price liberalization, imposed extensive wage devaluation, terminated export and import quotas, and reduced tariffs on imports of agricultural and industrial products. All of this was followed by supply-side tax reforms: corporate tax cuts, marginal income tax cuts, fewer tax income brackets. A big chunk of the country's industrial base was privatized or liquidated, and the public ownership funds that managed state firms were converted into simple investment funds. In effect, the government sold almost 40 percent of its enterprises for a paltry 2.1 billion dollars through an opaque process in which the state's inspectors were forbidden to investigate the sales. Public service outsourcing and "new public management" procedures entered the government's agenda (Pop 2006).

Contrary to the expectations of its designers, the shock therapy sent the economy into a prolonged tailspin that triggered not just a social tragedy, but also a macroeconomic quagmire. In a second wave of deindustrialization, industrial output in 2000 fell by 20 percent relative to 1996, shifting the country's trade profile toward lower-value-added exports. Those who remained unemployed saw a doubling of the poverty rate (Tesliuc, Pop, and Panduru 2003). A quarter of a million small businesses went bankrupt as a result of a large contraction of real credit and the abrupt cessation of state subsidies to agriculture. Simultaneously, a sudden reduction of import duties on food led many large state farms to file for bankruptcy.

As privately owned subsistence farms failed to spontaneously increase their productivity and foreign capital did not rush in to establish large agribusiness, the result was an immediate collapse of agricultural output and a permanent balance-of-trade deficit for agriculture. The collapse of large state farms led to the collapse of large public development banks that had provided them with credit (Banca Agricolă and Bancorex). In the absence of viable welfare or employment options, significant numbers of the unemployed became subsistence farmers in rural pockets of poverty where basic services had been gutted by austerity. This process was so extreme that it led to the first urban-rural migration in modern European history (Zamfir 2001) and marked the beginnings of the largest migration wave from Eastern to Western Europe (Ban 2012). After three years of harsh reforms that brought the government to the brink of defaulting on its foreign debt and declaring a state of emergency in face of mounting labor struggles, the signs of recovery remained weak. The government went through three changes of prime minister (Victor Ciorbea, Radu Vasile, and Mugur Isărescu), and, faced with rioting miners in the Jiu Valley, it put tanks on the streets outside Bucharest to prevent a repeat of the 1990–1991 "miner raids."

The electoral cost of the economic collapse was immense. The once triumphant center-right Democratic Convention experienced an electoral disaster in the 2000 elections. The conservative Farmers' Party, the center of gravity within the coalition, did not even reach the electoral threshold necessary to enter the parliament. Other Convention members lost two thirds of their 1996 votes. Ex-communist Iliescu defeated the radical right-wing populist Vadim Tudor in the second round of the presidential elections, with the former's party winning the second-highest number of seats in the fourth parliament (Pop-Eleches 2001).

The 2000 elections were won by the ex-FSN of Ion Iliescu, now rebaptized the Social Democratic Party (PSD). Adrian Năstase, the new party and government boss, saw himself as a Third Way reformer who thought that the era of the class politics of "old" social democracy was definitively over. In contrast with the arrival of the shock therapy government in 1997, the winning of the 2000 elections by the ex-communists (now (re)baptized Social democrats) was the other critical juncture of the translation of neoliberalism in Romania (2000– 2004)—one that remains uncovered in the literature—has been characterized by a similar degree of centralization in the policy sphere as during the González government in Spain.

Dodging Embedded Neoliberalism
Translating the Brussels Consensus

From Korea to Brazil, the late 1990s were years of extreme social dislocation, financial crises, and macroeconomic turbulence, while the 2000s were the years when neoliberal ideas and reforms came under the hammer in many developing regions. Moreover, EU enlargement created opportunities for engaging with embedded neoliberalism, an evolving ideational terrain where neoliberal, ordoliberal, and social democratic ideas make orthodox neoliberalism "stop short of fully disembedding the European market economy from its postwar social and political institutions" via attempts to maintain the social consensus around the need to restructure the "European social model" (van Appeldoorn 1998, 32).

This brand of neoliberalism, upheld at the EU level by a broad coalition of bureaucrats and globally minded private sector owners, appealed to broader societal interests by stressing the continuing importance of the state as provider of investment-oriented macroeconomic policies, infrastructure, state aid, a skilled and healthy labor force, and social stability. While social cohesion and the state provision of public social goods survived, they were nevertheless increasingly subordinated to the overriding objective of competitiveness (van Appeldoorn 1998).

But by the time the EU began its eastward enlargement, the "embedded" part of this doctrine began to flag, and consequently the prospective member states were treated with a more market-oriented approach meant to support the competitiveness of West European capital (Bohle 2006; Medve-Bálint 2013). Even so, Romanian neoliberals faced deindustrialization, unemployment levels at record highs, and the beginning of Romania's largest emigration wave in its history, with calls to circle the wagons of an even more radical brand of neoliberalism. Indeed, while most of the 1990s were spent on replicating imported scripts, the social countermovements stirred by the complications of the post-1996 reforms triggered a process of marked ideological radicalization. The aim was no longer some yet to be defined version of real-existing Western capitalism, but a narrower spectrum of choices, that ranged from liberal ("Anglo-American") varieties of capitalism and visions of a market society completely disembedded from popular demands. Ironically, Romania's EU integration process coincided with the local rejection of all forms of coordinated and social democratic continental capitalism and the aspiration for more market-based templates.

The rallying cry was that more and deeper neoliberal reforms would bring about a robust recovery (Croitoru and Târhoacă 1999; Albu and Pelinescu 2000; Drăgulin and Rădulescu 2000; Croitoru and Schaffer 2002; Isărescu 2003; 2005; Isărescu, Croitoru, and Tarhoaca 2003; Croitoru 2003a; 2003b; Altar 2003). Internal events like the recovery from early 2000 and external events like the crisis in Argentina in 2002 served to reinforce calls for more fiscal austerity, credible commitments to structural reforms,[34] inflation targeting, the partial privatization of the pension system, flexible hire-and-fire rules, and the deregulation of temporary employment. Tax cuts were advanced as the solution to a whole slew of issues, from the weak capacity of the state to collect taxes, to the disappointing flows of FDI. Some defended the virtues of current account liberalization and expressed no awareness of the growing rifts in international circles over this issue in the aftermath of the East Asian crisis (Croitoru, Dolţu, and Târhoacă 2001). Others renewed attacks against the indirect financing of budget deficits through the practice of central banking funds for banks pledging government bonds as collateral (Vrânceanu and Dăianu 2001).

The radicalization of neoliberal economics by some of the leading translators gained pace as different social groups sought in the "old" EU different sources of policy inspiration (Jacoby 2006; Trif 2008). Even as the World Bank began to reevaluate its development doctrine and signal more sensitivity to inequality and poverty (Cammack 2004; Woods 2006), many Romanian economists began to frame the very idea of wealth redistribution as a cause of the crisis. They made bold statements that "budget transfers sustain unviable social insurance systems and ineffective social insurance schemes" (Croitoru and Târhoacă 1999, 13). In a society that was experiencing a dizzying pace of growth in social inequality and had one of the lowest social protection expenditures in Europe (Milanović 1999), the neoliberal camp demanded not just tax cuts at the top end of the income distribution, but also increases at the bottom and more reliance on regressive value-added taxes (Croitoru and Schaffer 2002; Albu 2001).

The Group for Social Dialogue, the bastion of elite civil society and intellectual anchor of the center-right since 1990s formulated such ideas even more explicitly and fewer caveats. Beginning with the late 1990s, in their flagship weekly *Revista 22*, prominent intellectuals interpreted the failure of shock therapy as a failure of political will rather than of the neoliberal transition model itself. Against this background of disappointment with the CDR government they had supported and even gave top names to, these intellectuals cautioned against continental capitalism (and social-democracy in particular) as paternalist and praised the liberal (Anglo-American) model[35]. As a result, the pages of *Revista 22* are filled with tirades against collective bargaining and the role of labor unions[36]. Others went further, even. Some denounced any role of the state as provider of social protection by sounding alarms about its potential to morph into authoritarian socialism (Patapievici 2002) or at least violate the republican principle of "equality before the market."[37] In some cases, calls for radical reform were clothed in anti-democratic proposals about depriving pensioners and citizens with little education of the right to vote,[38] or in language about racial hierarchies among European nations, with Romanians, both "Latin" and contaminated by communism sitting at the bottom of the pile.[39]

It was also during this period that the local translation of neoliberalism began to mix libertarian and interventionist elements. These interventions were meant to make new markets and transfer wealth upward rather than embed neoliberalism, their aim being to shore up a local middle class and integrate the country into West European financial and supply chains. Select ideas associated with the Austrian school began to move from the fringes of academia to the summits of centrist parties like the Liberals and the Democrats.[40] The radical idea that drastic tax cuts are good in themselves, as an instrument of reforming the state by starving it, began to emerge. The reasoning behind this thinking was steeped in both classic libertarian ideas about the state and in widely resonating local understandings of the state as a damaging structure oscillating between being object of the predatory behavior of interest groups steeped in the communist past and the source of random, ill-timed, and often repressive interventions in the economy.

A cacophony of libertarian and interventionist ideas cohabited in select niches of academia, civil society, political parties, and organized business. In these milieus, the state was both unfixable and dangerous, and therefore all economic policies that depleted its resources were advantageous. But there was one big qualification for all this: the state can be a positive actor if it can be repurposed to recreate the world in the interest of modernizing liberal social forces such as local and foreign entrepreneurs. In this spirit, in 2003 a neoliberal think tank (SAR) and its supporters pioneered the idea of a "flat tax" on all income and capital, in effect demanding the termination of progressive taxation (Evans 2006). Although the progressive tax system had been designed by the World Bank in the early 1990s and had experienced several waves of reforms that dramatically reduced its progressivity, neoliberals still labeled it "socialist" and an obstacle in Romania's economic modernization path.

For mainstream global neoliberal approaches, cutting taxes in times of high economic growth—let alone making them "flat"—was likely to trigger economic imbalances through their negative effects on government fiscal sustainability (Keen, Kim, and Varsano 2006). In the region, Hungary and the Czech Republic responded to competitive pressures not by adopting a flat tax, but by lowering their taxation rates. Furthermore, competition in a world with open capital markets would predict that what matters is taxation levels rather than a particular kind of fiscal reform (Baturo and Gray 2009). It takes a radical neo-liberal view of state-society relations and of what states can do to attract invest-ment in order to take such a bold step. By the mid-2000s that view was widely shared in Romania, as evidenced by the fact that rather than remain part of the neoliberal fringe, this idea enjoyed high support in the mainstream, having been embraced by the Social Democrats' prime minister and minister of finance, by the center-right Justice and Truth coalition that came to power in 2004, and by the governor of the central bank.[41] What is more, the flat tax received support from foreign-trained experts in the Ministry of Finance.[42]

It was also in 2003 and 2004 that a coalition of multinational capital organi-zations, their law and accounting firms, international consultancies, think tanks, and politicians opened a new front: labor market deregulation.[43] Labor unions may have delivered the social peace needed for smoothing EU negotiations, but it soon turned out that they did not have a role in Romania's European path beyond delivering short-term social peace. Inspired by the prospect of EU membership, local labor law professors, labor union experts, and representatives of domestic capital started working on a new labor code within the corporatist Economic and Social Council as early as 1998, with West European labor union experts offering feedback.[44] The code was adopted in 2003. What mattered the most in its adop-tion was not neoliberal labor economics but local legal traditions, and given that French legal culture was closest to Romania's, the code had a distinctly French template.[45] It seemed to be the first sign that EU integration could entrench a more socially progressive brand of neoliberalism in this part of the EU periphery.

This was a short-lived victory for labor. The IMF quickly made the reversal of the French-inspired labor code part of its conditionality and asked the World Bank to foot the bill for an expert report on "best practices."[46] The European Commission also gave its blessing to this antilabor offensive in its 2004 and 2005 reports on Romania's accession. Given the IMF/World Bank/EC doctrine regarding labor market issues, this move was predictable, particularly in a coun-try that adopted precisely the kind of labor protections that the EU was fighting against in Western Europe; what was more surprising was that think-tankers, the economic experts of centrist parties, and the emerging voice of foreign capital went beyond IMF doctrine and demanded no less than the complete destruc-tion of institutions that protected any form of collective bargaining. International coercion and local advocacy for neoliberal ideas worked in tandem, blocking out legal experts in the labor ministry and academia whose training in French law doctrine clashed with the neoliberal economics. For local advocates steeped in think tanks and linked to the local USAID office and US-funded think tanks like CHF Romania, such institutions were mere relics of national Stalinism, time capsules that trapped the freedom of individuals to be entrepreneurs on the labor market or in business. The generalization of the economic form of the market through the idea that labor was just something to be traded in the market and that any institutions mediating the relationship to protect the social body against monetary exchanges began to put down roots.[47]

Some of the exceptions from this trend came from among those academic and central bank economists who had had the most extensive professional socialization abroad. The trigger was the emerging controversy over capital controls in the aftermath of the East Asian crisis. While some defended full current account liberalization (Croitoru, Dolțu, and Târhoacă 2001), others made the case for soft capital controls, as advanced by Paul Krugman in the aftermath of the East Asian crisis (Dăianu and Vrânceanu 2002). For the latter, this controversy opened the first cracks in orthodox transition economics, and they showed increasing awareness of the criticism made of this school of thought by critical economists like Dani Rodrik and Joseph Stiglitz (Dăianu and Vrânceanu 2002). To this end, Dăianu produced research showing that reliance on capital flows as a source of development was associated with exposure to the risk of the sudden reversal of those flows (Dăianu and Vrânceanu 2002).

The doctrine that prevailed in the Ministry of Finance[48] and the central bank[49] was a neoliberal view radicalized by the idea that double-digit current account deficits that might emerge from liberalization were unproblematic as long as they were financed by private rather than public money. At the heart of this radicalization was the local enthusiasm for a fringe neoliberal argument advanced by Nigel Lawson, Margaret Thatcher's Chancellor of the Exchequer, who had made the case that an increase in the current account deficit determined by increasing private sector exposure was harmless and, in fact, a way of signaling investor credibility (Voinea 2013, 989–990).

The Ebb and Flow of Institutional Cohesion

The paucity of institutional cohesion exposed the neoliberal project conducted by the 1996–2000 CDR government to important challenges that are well documented in the literature. Grigore Pop-Eleches's (2008) work has showed that bickering in the center-right coalition that governed Romania between 1996 and 2000 contributed to diluting neoliberal reforms. Liliana Pop's (2006) and Daniela Gabor's (2010a) research has showed that despite this, policy changes driven by international conditionality accumulated to deeply transform market-society relations in Romania anyway.

Arguably, what saved the neoliberal project from complete implosion was the beginning of Romania's EU accession integration in 2000, a process that brought investment, migration opportunities, and, critically, stronger support for neoliberalism's translators across the entire ideological spectrum. In contrast to the CDR cabinets, the Năstase government was as quietly disciplined as the Văcăroiu government, and its economic ministries were not affected by reshuffles. By contrast to the "presidentialized" cabinet of the 1992–1996 period, however, Năstase's term was marked by a weak presidency and a strong cabinet, a shift that was formally ratified in the new constitution passed in 2003.

The institutional cohesion characterizing the policy process was facilitated by three main factors. The first was Năstase's successful centralization of power in the party executive and the "pacification" of regional bosses through a complex system of favors and rents that ensured the autonomy of the executive. Despite the adoption of primaries in the fall of 2004, the party executive remained untouched. Second, for the first time in the party's history, the cabinet developed mechanisms to completely control the rank and file and to buffer the pressures on President Iliescu. Thus, Năstase was head of both the cabinet and the party, key ministers occupied strong party positions (two vice presidents and the party's chief strategist), and some of the new technocratic recruits who were not even party members in 2000 (finance minister Mihai Tănăsescu and foreign affairs minister Mircea Geoană) ascended to vice presidential positions. Buffeted, Iliescu and his more left-leaning economic advisers (Gheorghe Zaman and Florin Georgescu) generally supported the economic policy course of the cabinet and opposed the cabinet only on the issue of the flat tax in 2003.[50]

Third, with the party under his control, Năstase appointed a US-trained technocrat at the Ministry of Finance and replaced the Democratic Convention's state secretaries in all economic ministries with technocrats still in their late twenties and early thirties (Năstase 2004). The same reshuffle happened in the special economic agencies (privatization, foreign investment, capital markets). This was a different breed of technocrat: most had studied economics abroad, and many had worked for private consultancies. In the hiring process the premier privileged Western education and theoretical over practical training, as he saw socialization in the traditions of the Romanian public service to be a major disadvantage (Năstase 2004, 89). The commerce ministry was now controlled by an experienced foreign-trained neoliberal economist (Eugen Dijmărescu) whose professional trajectories, affiliations, and reputation were connected with the technocrats of the previous government.

In contrast, the center-right coalition that governed between 2004 and 2008 benefited from less than a year of institutional cohesion, enough to pass the flat tax. With few exceptions (pension privatization), after 2005 the adoption of neoliberal reforms stagnated as a result of conflicts within the coalition and between the prime minister and the president. In 2007 the coalition was effectively dismantled. It was not until late 2009 that Romania got another institutionally cohesive government, right in time for the further radicalization of Romanian neoliberalism on the eve of the European sovereign debt crisis.

Labor and employer organizations intervened in this institutional dynamics. In 2003 the government adopted a labor code meant to buy "social peace" for the duration of EU membership accession (Trif 2008).[51] The new government was keen to throw out the code, but the weakness of the minority government and the shrinking of the labor force due to migration made the adoption of these reforms difficult, with a local World Bank representative telling this author in 2009 that the issue was no longer on his institution's agenda in Romania.[52] It took extensive privatization and the crisis of 2009–2010 for multinational capital to successfully push for labor market deregulation.

With the Social Democrats in office, the adoption of EU-mandated economic institutions, the privatization of the "jewels in the crown" (banks, utilities, energy, large manufacturing), the deregulation of the current account, and the business confidence brought about by the expected membership combined to attract over one hundred billion euros to the Romanian economy and enable some of the highest growth rates in the EU. The bulge in industrial investment quadrupled the country's exports and slowed down the process of deindustrialization.

Critically, EU integration strengthened the hand of neoliberal reformers in all parties (including the ex-communists) and crowded the neodevelopmentalists out of the policy sphere. Unfortunately for the advocates of this strategy, the massive inflows of speculative financial investment combined with the effects of a flat tax to fund a surge in imports. This led, in turn, to a large current account deficit that paved the way for a financial crisis after Lehman created dramatically different conditions for funding the current account deficit, making the country "go subprime" (Gabor 2010a).

Radicalizing Disembedded Neoliberalism (2004–2008)

Under the Tăriceanu government (2004–2008) the neoliberal transformation of Romania grew in the direction of the libertarian experimentalism pioneered by the Baltic countries in the late 1990s. By achieving growth rates higher than those of the trailblazers of liberalization (Poland, Hungary, and the Czech Republic) between 2004 and 2008, Romania's "dependent market economy" model (Ban 2013) seemed vindicated. Yet the Great Recession called this model into question as shrinking capital inflows and external demand combined with compressed domestic demand, leaving policymakers without robust means of intervention (Ban 2013).

The influx of consumer credit that accompanied the sale of most of the banking sector to transnational banks based in the eurozone supplied governments with a strong economic source of domestic legitimacy. Consumption levels depressed during the early transition by restrictive macroeconomic policies of dubious benefit for the economy as a whole recovered as a result of credit (Gabor 2012). Between 2001 and 2008 an unprecedented number of Romanians making claims to middle class status reveled in the long-promised Western-style consumption whose financing was done mostly through easy credit and tax cuts at the top. While the state cut debt, individuals and firms throughout Romania increased it. From a paltry five billion euros in 1999, Romanian private debt went up to two hundred billion euros in 2009. As a result, overall debt increased five times, from ten billion in 2000 to nearly fifty billion in 2008. When combined with the pent-up demand for credit due to very restrictive monetary policies during the 1990s, this led to a sudden increase in private debt in general.

Dependent banking was a quick fix for the sociopolitical crisis of Romanian postcommunism, yet it failed to serve the Romanian economy well. As in the other dependent market economies, while foreign ownership in the financial industry blew a huge consumer credit bubble, it made only a marginal contribution to industrial investment, whose growth was largely connected to the integration of Romanian industry into Western supply chains (Ban 2013b). Second, since easy credit benefited mostly an emerging middle class (about 20 percent of the population by most estimates) whose consumption patterns revolved around imports, the local subsidiaries of foreign banks assembled together the main engine of the East European crisis: gaping current account deficits (Voinea 2009; Voinea and Mihăescu 2012). Third, owing to the importance that the favorable interest rate differential played in the profit strategies of the foreign-owned banking sector, foreign banks funded a massive increase in construction expenditures by becoming the originators of a mortgage lending in euros and other "hard" currencies. Romanian governments did not act forcefully against mounting external deficits, and even when they did act, the poor EU governance of transnational banking left enough loopholes for banks to take full advantage (Bohle and Greskovits 2012, 227).

Libertarian tax policy and deregulatory enthusiasm in financial matters combined with neoliberal populism to transform the Romanian economy into a ticking bomb. The deregulation of consumer credit, lax zoning regulation, and the light-touch taxation of real estate transactions fueled a consumer and real estate bubble fueled by massive capital flows. The adoption of a 16 percent flat tax on personal income and corporate profits distributed 40 percent of the gains to the top 10 percent of formal sector employees and business owners. Given the wage-led nature of the Romanian economy, the flat tax reform stimulated demand in an upswing cycle, with 74 percent of the flat-tax gains going into consumption.

Since a large part of this consumption benefited imported goods, the country spent on current consumption goods, with imports accounting for a large portion of the increase in consumption spending (Voinea and Mihăescu 2009; Voinea 2013).

By 2008, the situation was further worsened by the decision of the incumbents to increase wages in the public sector in ways that worsened income inequality and increased the consumption of imported durables. The result of these decisions was that the current account deficit spiraled upward, entering a double-digit territory where a balance-of-payments crisis would become the predictable result of a sudden stop in capital flows.

All of this would come back to haunt policy elites after the Lehman crisis seemed to challenge fundamental assumptions of the neoliberal script. But while the post-2010 crisis in the eurozone originated in an overdeveloped financial sector marked by the merger of collateral and sovereign debt markets (Gabor and Ban 2013), Romania's economy was ravaged by a different kind of dynamic. In late 2008, the country had a low degree of financial intermediation, thin financial markets, and an undeveloped market for derivatives (Voinea 2009, 35–49). As in Hungary and the Baltic countries, what fueled the flames of the crisis was the combination of central bank-led financialization and the incentives of systemically important Western European banks that controlled Romania's financial sector (Gabor 2013; Ban 2013). Moreover, the favorable interest rate differentials between Romania and the eurozone or Switzerland created a housing bubble financed in hard currency, a development that increased the costs of external devaluation in hard times.[53]

If, during the 2000s, banks from the EU "core" made fortunes in Southern Europe largely through wholesale markets that boomed under the impetus of euro convergence (Gabor and Ban 2013), in Romania and Eastern Europe they generally simply bought existing state-owned institutions (Voinea 2013; Gabor 2013). As a result, over 80 percent of credit originated from the eurozone, a development that was tantamount to the privatization of these countries' money supply (Blyth 2013, 220). This transformation supplied East European governments with an additional economic source of domestic legitimacy as consumption levels that had been depressed during the early transition by restrictive macroeconomic policies of dubious benefit for the economy as a whole recovered as a result of credit (Bohle and Greskovits 2012).

There were few wrinkles in these rather uniform neoliberal developments. One was the granting of generous parental leave and benefits in order to counteract the looming demographic problem. The other was the emergence during the late 2000s of pro-FDI industrial policy ideas that argued in favor of state intervention to nudge private investment up the ladder of complexity. This resulted in tax breaks for the emerging (and quite successful) IT sector and the government's credit guarantees for the building of research and development facilities attached to multinational investments in manufacturing (Ban 2013b). Finally, the neoliberal arguments for labor market deregulation were successfully resisted by legal experts, ministerial staff and labor unions. In 2003 Romania adopted of strong collective bargaining institutions and a proworker labor codes in 2003, asa quid pro quo for the social peace needed to polish Romania's EU accession dossier.[54] The advent of a conservative government in 2005 whose economic ideology stressed economically liberal and even libertarian themes also pushed for labor market deregulation. Yet the immediate coordination of labor unions, their capacity to mobilize external support from West European unions, and particularly the credibility of union threats delivered by the memory of extensive labor militancy during the 1990s made the government adopt a much more moderate labor reform in 2006, with union consent (Trif 2008; Adăscăliței and Guga 2015). The mass migration of the labor force in EU member states in the late 2000s and the subsequent drying up of excess labor further weakened the case for the kind of "big bang" deregulation that the liberal coalition of domestic and external interests wanted.

Conclusions

Unlike Spain, neoliberal ideas found few sympathetic interlocutors after the end of the authoritarian regime in 1989. Indeed, the first transition years were dominated by technocrats who advocated and implemented various degrees of neodvelopmentalist approaches to the challenges of postcommunism. However, by the late 1990s, international financial institutions, transnational academic and civil society networks, and Western-licensed yet domestically organized graduate programs provided the cause of neoliberalism in Romania with a critical mass of sympathetic interlocutors in the revolving doors between the central bank, government, academia, and think tanks.

Like their Spanish counterparts, Romania's translators of neoliberalism scrutinized some of the aspects of this body of thought and wove together a network of localized conceptual relations between neoliberalism and other schools of thought (institutionalism, structuralism, the Austrian school). These relations radicalized some of the "classic" neoliberal positions on macroeconomic management, distribution, investment flows, and industrial policy. On balance, the result of this translation was a variant of neoliberalism that was generally less statist and less redistributive than Spain's. Even as the policy prescriptions of these ideas wreaked havoc with the lives of millions of Romanians, a perverse circular logic saw its proponents continue to double down on their ideas with every crisis that challenged the wisdom of their approach.

Finally, unlike in Spain, the Romanian carriers of these economic ideas did not always benefit from levels of institutional cohesion high enough to enable a smooth implementation of ideas in policy. Indeed, only half of the transition period benefited from such favorable institutional conditions, with internal attrition and labor contestation weakening policy implementation. As a result, Romania's neoliberal transformation depended more on external forms of coercion than Spain's.

PART II

THE WEIGHT OF THE PAST

4

The Deep Roots
of Spanish Neoliberalism

When Francisco Franco's authoritarian state ended in 1975, neoclassical economics had a strong foothold among Spanish policy intellectuals. Cold War geopolitics and the regime's internal dynamics had enabled many of them to internationalize their professional lives and enjoy relative intellectual freedom. In these conditions, economic liberalism survived and even prospered, bringing into its fold economists trained by British and German professors.

This chapter tells us that, after World War II, Spain's relatively liberal regulation of the economic profession, increasing opportunities for Western training, and the high status attached to Western education within economics enabled the gradual spread of neoclassical economic ideas in both the central bank and academia. This occurred even as Spain's official policy paradigm was leaning heavily toward a local version of developmentalism. Critically, these ideas were not steeped in radical economic liberalism. Instead, the precursors of neoliberal ideas that took hold in this country had a particular German flavor, a fact that gave Spanish neoliberalism a distinct identity from the 1970s onward.

From Autarchy to Liberalization

Until the Nazi military disaster became apparent in 1943, the Spanish political order was that of a single-party state with powerful totalitarian tendencies of fascist inspiration (Linz 1964; Anderson 1970; Gunther 1980; Miley 2011). After 1943, Francoism reacted to the Nazi military collapse by slowly morphing into a bureaucratic (as oppose to sultanistic, as in Romania) authoritarian state with a rubber-stamp parliament and a strong, yet pluralistic, executive.

The political economy of this regime changed over time. During early Francoism (1939–1959) Spain pursued an import substitution industrialization (ISI) strategy (Anderson 1970; Pérez 1997). The government ran high budget deficits to pay for industrialization, though without the corresponding increase in fiscal revenue that took place elsewhere in postwar Europe. Not surprisingly, this resulted in unsustainable foreign currency debt, transforming this development model into a ticking time bomb. The unavoidable explosion came in 1956, when Spain's citrus crop, an export staple, dropped to half of its 1955 level, leading to a major balance-of-payments crisis. Effectively bankrupt and contested by student protests, miners' strikes, and an emerging clerical opposition, Franco operated a cabinet reshuffle in 1957 that brought into the government a handful of liberal economists.[1]

The new economic ministers ushered in by the crisis convinced Franco that an IMF-style economic macroeconomic stabilization program could stabilize public finances, reduce social unrest, and make the average Spaniard wealthier—all while avoiding the progressive tax hikes that the regime's wealthy backers disliked (Anderson 1970). After seven months of preparation, Spain unveiled it as an orthodox Stabilization Plan on June 30, 1959, that was aimed at liberalizing trade, inviting foreign investment, and taking the necessary fiscal and monetary measures required to restrict demand and contain inflation. The "mixed banking" of the ISI era was terminated, commercial and investment banking were separated, and the central bank was nationalized.

But orthodox macroeconomics had to cohabit with developmentalist industrial policy. Rather than scrapping industrial policy, the government took a more selective approach to industrial development. While most industrial firms had been considered of national interest after 1939, now only select sectors and subsectors judged by technocrats to have a "pull" effect on the rest of the economy were to receive extensive government support. Critically, French-style "indicative" planning was introduced and maintained for more than a decade. This was not the end of the developmental state. It was only its recalibration.

The combination of macrostabilization and developmental state worked. After a year of stagnation in 1960, Spain's economy experienced a decade-long growth spurt. Industrial output grew at double-digit rates every year, and industrial employment saw unprecedented increases. Despite a myriad of problems, by the time Franco died in 1975 Spain had become an upper-middle-income industrial economy and had meritocratic sectors of its technocracy that were ready to push the country toward more economic liberalism once Franco's conservative regime met its demise.

This much is well documented in the literature. What is less known is where this local support for liberalization came from in the first place in a country known for an authoritarian-corporatist version of "big government" and for one of Europe's weakest liberal traditions in economics. It is to this question the analysis turns to next.

The Rise and Fall of Spain's Developmentalism

For most of its modern history, Spanish economics was remarkable for the virtual absence of any influence of neoclassical economics (Almenar Palau 1999; Ban 2012), with state interventionism inspired by German neohistoricism being dominant until Franco came to power (Velarde Fuertes 2001).[2] The influence of the neohistoricists waned after General Francisco Franco's rebel army won the Civil War in 1938, killing, imprisoning, or pushing into exile a large part of the country's population that had anything to do with the Spanish Republic. Some of the Republican-leaning neohistoricists exiled themselves, while others perished. Those who had passably conservative credentials became gradually institutionalized in the economics departments and research institutes of the new regime, where they carried on some form of developmentalism (Velarde Fuertes 2001, 354).

During World War II, the country's long tradition of economic interventionism transitioned into a brand of fascist developmentalism layered with Nazi and fascist economics. The pillars of the regime also saw in Nazi Germany a powerful example of how to prosper while the economies of many liberal countries were in crisis (Pérez 1998). The result was a hybrid policy paradigm in which large public works were financed by deficits and executed by public-private cooperative ventures that excluded organized independent labor. As a result, the central pillar of Spain's developmental state during the 1940s was the power of the public sector in the drive for industrialization, continued protectionism, and deficit spending as a means to finance industrialization (Velarde 2001, 353–354; Cavalieri 2014). This corporatist brand of import substitution industrialization was relatively short-lived. Corporatism's association with fascist politics and the intervention of United States and the IMF in the economic crisis of 1956 facilitated a general liberalization in economic policy and, critically, bolstered the influence of professional economists in the policy sphere (Cavalieri 2014).

As fascist developmentalists' influence receded after the 1956 crisis, Spain became a battleground between economic liberals and developmentalists. While the former looked for inspiration in the classics of German ordoliberalism and Anglo-American neoclassical economics, the latter modeled their ideas on French developmentalism. Geopolitical openings were important in this regard. The former felt empowered by the increasing American influence in Spain after the Korean War, with the attending withering of the isolation imposed on the regime after the Civil War.

The turn to France prevailed during the 1960s and early 1970s and was facilitated by France's success and its governments' share in the surveillance of communist networks. During the late 1940s and early 1950s French governments had perfected the economics of Europe's most successful developmental state: a combination of Keynesian macroeconomics and coordinated government-corporate relations known as "indicative planning." This made France one of the most spectacular cases of industrial development during the postwar period while delivering more and more French citizens with substantial economic rights, from full employment to an extensive safety net (Loriaux 1991).

This combination of state-led industrialization and social inclusion caught the attention of a group of Spanish technocrats with access to the levers of power for whom the nationalist objective of industrial modernization and the social-Catholic doctrine of providing for the poor went hand in hand. For them, indicative planning was a way to salvage the state-led development project from the critiques formulated by a rising chorus of pure neoclassical and neoclassical-Keynesian synthesis economists empowered by the 1959 stabilization and liberalization reforms (Rodó 1992; Pérez 1997, 73; Parache 2004; Zabalza 2013).

Like their French counterparts, Spanish indicative planners were neo-Keynesians. They argued that the 1959 Stabilization Plan led the economy into a liquidity trap that was responsible for severe disinvestment in the private sector (Anderson 1970, 103–117; Pérez 1997, 68–73; Cavalieri 2014). Consequently, the planners advocated (and implemented) bold state stimulation of internal demand and showed only moderate concern for the inflationary costs of this strategy (Anderson 1970, 164–167; Pérez 1997, 70–75). They also tried to embed liberalized trade principles in nationalist interventionist ideas by increasing the level of industrial specialization in the private sector and by developing industrial champions (Pérez 1997, 70–72; Loriaux 1991). This technocratic economic ideology was subordinated to a wider economic nationalist one that depended on the state's rationalization of market relations and on appeasing the social tensions that social-Catholic beliefs found to be inherent in capitalism and threatening to Spain's conservative social status quo (Ramos-Gorostiza and Pires-Jimenez 2009; Cavalieri 2014; Zabalza 2013).

But the survival of the policy regime hinged on its sponsorship by key regime figures and the international support granted by French indicative planners, not on a robust epistemic network protected by claims to science. The assassination in 1973 of their patron (Admiral Carrero Blanco, Franco's right-hand man) and the abandonment of indicative planning in France itself after the 1973 oil shock deprived Spanish developmentalists of the external anchor they had benefited from for over a decade, making them virtually irrelevant during the transition period.

Mandarin Economists and the State

Although the dominant policy paradigm in Spain during Franco was antiliberal, the regime did not suppress intellectual pluralism in the economics profession and watched as economic liberalism put deeper roots in postwar Spain while incentivizing epistemic arbitrage in the profession.

Despite its authoritarianism and centralism, the Franco regime was not particularly strict about suppressing economic ideas that were critical for its predominantly developmentalist policy. Although Franco was adamant about forbidding the existence of formal factions inside official organizations, groups organized to pursue "nonpolitical" objectives were allowed to exist autonomously from state control (Gunther 1980). Most importantly, academics, and even the national media, were allowed to engage in debates that offered opinion dissenting from the regime's economic orthodoxy. Perhaps the strongest piece of evidence that the regime was implicitly supportive of intellectual experimentation in the ranks of liberal-minded economists was that the economic mouthpiece of the Franco's regime, the *De Economía* review, hosted key debates on the uses of Keynes's *General Theory*.

Indeed, the policing of economic ideas was so soft in Spain that the endorsement of ideas antithetical to Francoism (such as Hayek's famous "road to serfdom") by some economists had little consequence. When future celebrity economic theorist Valentín Andrés Álvarez was reviewed for tenure at the economics department of the University of Madrid in 1945 after having published a selective endorsement of this Hayekian argument in an economics review, the challenge to his candidacy by a Falange hardliner caused no backlash (Sánchez 2002, 170 n. 13). Also, by the mid-1960s, the regime authorized the publication of almost the entirety of Marx and Engels (Almunia 2001, 35). In this climate of intellectual pluralism, corporatist autarchists, ordoliberals, classic liberals, and neohistoricist institutionalists were all free to publish, teach, travel abroad, and offer their advice to the regime. Unlike in Stalinist systems like postwar Romania, where prewar education in Western universities was likely to lead to exclusion from the profession, in Spain, Western-trained pre–Civil War economists who had not been active on the side of the Republic maintained and even enhanced their professional status. To incur punishment, challenges had to be open and explicit.[3] This "nonpolitical" pluralism enabled the formation of a diverse spectrum of ideas in which economic liberalism would grow in importance over time (Linz 1965; Gunther 1980; Fuentes-Quintana 2001).

In addition to tolerating a certain degree of pluralism, the regime incentivized epistemic arbitrage. The establishment in 1943 of Spain's first economics department (The Faculty of Political and Economic Sciences at the University of Madrid, or FPSE) and two government think tanks (the Sancho de Moncada Economic Institute and the Economic Section of the Political Studies Institute) bolstered the economics profession (Fuentes Quintana 1999). Critically, the heads of these institutes served as economic advisers to Franco, and, later, some of the most prominent names of the post-1959 governments were selected from the ranks of the researchers based at these institutes. FPSE faculty routinely taught advanced classes or supervised projects in these public think tanks. All of this was happening as prominent foreign-trained economists taught at FPSE while simultaneously holding administrative positions in the highest advisory bodies of the government. Holding such dual positions became the new marker of the highest form of professional authority.[4]

As the state adopted a more bureaucratic (as opposed to personalistic) authoritarian character during the 1960s and early 1970s, more and more intellectuals moved between academia and the economic bureaucracy. Holding joint appointments in academia and an economic ministry or the central bank continued to be a mark of professional prominence,[5] with elite sectors of the bureaucratic corps emerging as critical sites of applied economics research via their flagship economics journals.[6] For new economic ideas to have a high impact, they would have to be advocated by economists using these revolving doors.

Current and future academic celebrities divided their time between FPSE and research for economic ministries or for the central bank (Velarde Fuertes 2001). After 1956, younger professors and civil servants like E. F. Quintana or L. A. Rojo, the future architects of Spain's neoliberalism, collaborated with those technocrats in the finance and trade ministries who had a direct impact on the policy templates adopted by the ministers themselves. Moreover, by the early 1970s, Quintana headed the research service of the Ministry of Finance, while Rojo held the same position at the central bank—the institution where he would later serve as governor throughout the critical economic reforms of the 1980s. Spanish technocracy was producing its cadre reserve, and unfortunately for the regime, there was no love lost for the developmental state on the reserves' bench.

When Franco's regime ended in 1975, the economics profession was at the height of its political and cultural influence. Academic economists (especially those with "mandarin" status) came to exert remarkable influence in the state. The rest of the chapter shows that the neoliberal seeds had been planted many years before, against the background of the crisis of fascist developmentalism and thanks to an open dialogue with the British and German neoclassical traditions that began in the 1930s and was intensified during World War II. Yet it was truly the revolving doors between academia and the state that allowed a neoclassical group to establish growing influence.

The Seeds of Neoliberalism

The diffusion of neoclassical economics to Spain dates back only as far as the 1930s and was the result of a transnationalization of graduate education that proceeded, ironically, with state support. The neoclassical "young Turks" studied abroad and returned to Spain with a sense of mission, a professional pedigree, and, as it turned out, a lot of luck. Lucas Beltrán, the towering figure of postwar Spanish economic liberalism, studied with Hayek at the London School of Economics (LSE) and then returned to Spain to teach economics. A member of the Mont Pelerin Society for two decades, he also popularized the latest neoclassical fashions in public finance as editor of *Moneda y crédito*, the flagship review of the discipline that remained for decades a safe outlet for advocates of liberal economics and was one of the earliest sites of Spanish monetarism (Almenar Palau 2002). Beltrán was also instrumental in writing the first massive introductions to Röpke, a founder of ordoliberalism and Hayek, the luminary of the Austrian school (Huerta de Soto 2007).

Another British-educated economist, Luis Olariaga, edited *Economía Española*, a review that often employed Hayekian ideas to debunk Keynes, the New Deal, and other interventionist ideas while advocating the cause of the limited liberal state. The leader of the anti-Keynesian reaction was Olariaga himself (Fradejas 2015). José María Zumalcárregui, the founder of Spain's first economics department (established in 1943) and a strong advocate of neoclassical marginalism, had studied with Pareto at Lausanne during the 1920s (Sánchez 1996). Joan Sardà, the chief architect of the 1959 Stabilization Plan and the head of the Research Service of the central bank during the 1960s, had studied economics at LSE before the Civil War, where he was drawn to T. E. Gregory's militant anti-Keynesianism. During his later studies in Munich, he became receptive to the influence of Carl Manger, the founder of the Austrian school, and his disciple, Böhm Bawerk. Sardà's international career during the 1940s and 1950s further consolidated his professional cosmopolitanism and offered his Spanish colleagues access to the latest debates in the field during a time of international isolation for Spain (Velarde Fuertes 2001; Estapé 2000).[7]

By the late 1930s, these Spanish neoclassical economists trained at British and German universities began to attack the Historical school consensus and its prescriptions for economic policy. They proposed a new narrative to explain Spanish economic development that would become influential beginning in the 1950s. The central tenet of this narrative was that whatever Spain had achieved in economic terms was not due to government intervention but rather despite it, with FDI and export-led growth playing a pivotal part (Aceña 2000; Sánchez 1996; Love 2004; Fernandez Blanco 2007).

What gave the Spanish neoclassical tradition its strongest push during the 1940s and early 1950s was sheer historical contingency: the arrival in Madrid of German economist Heinrich von Stackelberg, one of the "greats" of ordoliberalism, the German offshoot of midcentury neoliberalism. Immediately after his arrival, the German economist began to teach in the very core of Spanish official economics: the Institute for Political Studies, as well as the newly founded Department of Economics at the University of Madrid (the Complutense). After von Stackelberg, Spanish economic thinking would be deeply ensconced within the transnational neoliberal network constructed by Western liberal economists spooked by the success of Keynesianism after World War II.

Neoliberalism, German Style[8]

Built between the 1930s and 1950s by luminaries of German social science—such as Walter Eucken, Wilhelm Röpke, Franz Bohm, and Alfred Muller-Armack—ordoliberalism sought a middle path between socialism and laissez-faire liberalism while bolstering the claims made by neoclassical economics. It did so by developing microeconomics and promoting the use of a strong state in order to build and guarantee an institutional environment in which the free market could produce results close to its theoretical potential (Watrin 1979; Ptak 2009; Vanberg 2011).

Ordoliberal theory holds that public policy should be guided by the creation of a competitive market economy using a set of credible rules and institutions. Considered a form of "liberal conservatism" by one of its founding fathers, ordoliberal theory was slightly different from laissez-faire liberalism, and its similarities with aspects of Austrian school and Historical school economics should prevent its complete conflation with the neoclassical tradition. Unlike other intellectual traditions closer to laissez-faire liberalism, ordoliberalism was selectively skeptical of unfettered markets, pointing to markets' natural propensity to give birth to oligopolies, monopolies, and worrisome social disruption. Consequently ordoliberals pleaded for "liberal interventionism," a hybrid framework that blended collective bargaining, antimonopoly/-oligopoly institutions, centralized coordination among firms, minimal social safety nets, low inflation, independent central banks, balanced budgets, and free trade. Thus, the state was not merely a neutral aggregator of individual interests, but also a meritocratic agent entrusted to advance the economic welfare of the nation through increasing economic competitiveness.

The existing scholarship on ordoliberalism considers this school of thought to be specific to Germany. Yet the manner in which ordoliberal ideas traveled southward during the mid-1940s left a deep mark on Spain's mainstream economics and helps us understand the roots of embedded neoliberalism. The main agent of its diffusion was Heinrich Freiherr von Stackelberg, a German microeconomist of world renown with ties to the Nazi regime.[9] During the reclusive 1940s, Spanish economists' access to great Western economics professors was made difficult by a combination of insufficient funds and the isolation of Franco's regime. In the midst of this upheaval, von Stackelberg offered his Spanish admirers an opportunity to be connected with Western economics and to change the parameters of "mainstream" economic thinking in Spain.

In the early 1940s, von Stackelberg settled in Madrid. Increasingly estranged from Nazism and fearing that his life was in danger, he searched for a way out of Germany.[10] In 1943, while teaching economics at Bonn University, von Stackelberg was offered a visiting professorship in Madrid, where the economics profession was being reorganized by the fascist government. As he had returned ill from the Russian front, von Stackelberg received permission to leave for Spain.

Von Stackelberg was one of the first participants in the Freiburg Circle, a dissident group of preeminent ordoliberals (Senn 2012, 568),[11] and he became known as an ardent proponent of the use of econometric methods for expressing ordoliberal arguments (Eucken and Schmölders 1948). During the 1930s and 1940s, he became internationally famous for pivotal innovations in microeconomics, and today the use of his ideas is as widespread as those of Pareto, Walras, and Nash (Senn 1996; 2012). A Nazi he may have been, but his work was reviewed favorably in US academic journals.

Von Stackelberg's relocation had long-lasting and perhaps unexpected consequences for economic debates in midcentury Spain, the only non-German-speaking country where ordoliberalism proved to be an important intellectual vector for influential economists.

The most important of these consequences was the adoption of von Stackelberg's microeconomic critique of Keynesianism, with devastating consequences for activist fiscal policy.

Von Stackelberg's sojourn in Madrid was facilitated the fact that his ideas made sense in Spanish elite circles in this particular historical moment. He arrived in Madrid at a time when the economics section of the recently established Institute of Political Studies sought to boost its reputation by hiring a prestigious international scholar. The search ended following the decisive intervention of Miguel Paredes Marcos, a Falange-affiliated finance professor who had studied economics with von Stackelberg in Germany. In addition to his professional admiration for the German professor, the Spanish economist also noted von Stackelberg's penchant for the brand of authoritarian nationalism espoused by the Francoist regime at the time (Velarde 1999). Moreover, from the perspective of Nazi-wary fascists, von Stackelberg's political credentials were impeccable. Although he had defected from Nazi ideology, he remained nevertheless a committed right-wing nationalist. This unique combination of qualifications had great appeal in Madrid's post–Civil War sociopolitical order.

Von Stackelberg's ordoliberalism resonated particularly well with economists already steeped in the neoclassical tradition who supported the Franco regime for its conservatism despite their critiques of its economic policy. Friendly toward the nationalism espoused by the regime, these Spanish economists sought an economic framework that left room for a promarket sentiment while still allowing for a strong state to act on behalf of national interests. Ordoliberalism fulfilled these requirements. It stressed the importance of a strong state, and according to some interpretations, in its early form it was permeated by a conservative religious concern with the "moral crisis" of modern societies (Ptak 2009). It is therefore not surprising that this mode of politics was attractive to the conservative Catholic intellectuals influential in Spanish economics at the time. Furthermore, like many Catholic policymakers who formed the backbone of the regime (Velarde Fuertes 2002, 353), the ordoliberals were critical of the social injustices created by unfettered markets, but stopped short of advocating income redistribution bold enough to upset the status quo (Watrin 1979). Theirs was a patriarchal vision of redistribution, anchored in respect for the stability, security, and "natural order" of the estate model of social stratification (Ptak 2009).

Soon after his arrival, von Stackelberg befriended luminaries of the older generation of neoclassicists (Perpina i Grau, Zumalacárregui, Olariaga) (Velarde Fuertes 2002, 361–362). According to Juan Velarde, a Spanish economist trained in the early postwar years, Stackelberg not only became part of the teaching and research apparatus of the discipline, but also supported the group of economists who had initiated an implacable direct and indirect critical enterprise targeted at a radical transformation of Spanish economic policy (1999).

Critically, the German economist provided not just knowledge, but also access for Spanish economists to what would become Germany's postwar ordoliberal networks. One particularly consequential contact was Walter Eucken, the leader of the ordoliberal group and an influential architect of Germany's postwar economic model. After von Stackelberg introduced Eucken's work to his Spanish colleagues, a growing number of Spanish economists began using it to critique the economic policies of their own regime—without challenging the regime's political ideology. In 1949 von Stackelberg's followers used his reputation with the ordoliberal group, then dominant in post-Nazi Germany, to bring Eucken himself to lecture in Madrid. Eucken's lectures were then edited and published in Spanish. The Spanish state itself bankrolled the ordoliberal strand. In 1948 and 1949, Spain's World Economy Institute organized research trips to Kiel, Geneva, and Brussels to study the policy implications of European economic liberalization. Joan Sardà, the future chief economist of the central bank, was a part of these delegations, and his travels inspired the ordoliberal-Keynesian synthesis that later became central to his successful Spanish economics textbook (Velarde Fuertes 2002, 363–364; Lissen and Política, unpublished manuscript, 16).

Von Stackelberg died prematurely of cancer in 1946, but his impact on Spanish economics continued long after his death, building coalitions with potential sympathizers, sharing his contacts in German economics, training a group of young followers selected from Spain's leading economists, and publishing his last contributions to world economics as a "naturalized" Spanish economist. [12] Critically, von Stackelberg educated an elite group of six young economists who would go on to gradually shift Spain's economic discourses and policy toward economic liberalism and neoclassical economics. Valentín Andrés Álvarez, José Castaneda, Miguel Paredes, José Antonio Piera, Alberto Ullastres, and José Vergara Doncel took advanced seminars with von Stackelberg and, as translators of his work into Spanish, they socialized with him frequently (Fuentes Quintana 2002, 52; Sánchez Hormigo 2002, 169; Segura Sánchez 2002, 391).

After von Stackelberg's passing, almost all of these economists assumed prominent positions in academic and bureaucratic fields, thus contributing to the entrenchment of ordoliberal economics—in particular—the mathematical methodological imperative advocated by von Stackelberg. Alberto Ullastres was appointed minister of commerce in 1956, where he was one of the architects of the 1959 Stabilization Plan. After this appointment, he went on to serve as the top economic minister for relations with the European Economic Community. Miguel Paredes became the editor of the economics section of the influential Aguilar publishing house (Segura Sánchez 2002, 391).

During the 1950s and 1960s, Álvarez and Casteneda, the most respected names in early postwar Spanish economic theory and microeconomics (Segura Sánchez 2002), reproduced the microeconomic and quantitative focus of von Stackelberg in their research and especially in their popular economics text-books (Fuentes Quintana 2002, 73–74; Almenar Palau 2002, 458–459). They also grew to be internationally visible. Álvarez was the only midcentury Spanish economist to have been published in English, which brought him much fame and influence at home (Álvarez Coruguedo 2001, 236–237) and Castaneda, for his part, developed a good reputation among French liberal econometricians, which enabled him to travel abroad extensively (Villar Saraillet 1999, 256).

The "von Stackelberg network" also shaped the professional training of impor-tant policymakers during the post-Franco transition. Most notably, Álvarez, Castaneda, and Vergara Doncel mentored both Luis Ángel Rojo and Enrique Fuentes Quintana, who, during the 1970s and 1980s, came to occupy top posi-tions in the elite economics department at Complutense, the finance ministry, and the central bank (Rojo 1999). Von Stackelberg's arrival in Spain was thus a dramatically important event. At a time when Keynesianism ruled abroad and the Spanish policy was dominated by interventionism, von Stackelberg's neo-classicism changed the course of Spain's future economy.

Ordoliberalism and the Dilution of Spanish Neo-Keynesianism

In discussions that took place in 1943 within the Freiburg Circle, von Stackelberg is on record as opposing not only state planning—which he critiqued in mathematical form (Eucken and Schmölders 1948, 134)—but also of other forms of Keynesian state activism that were then being attempted in North America and Britain. Yet such criticisms remained within the normative positions of the ordoliberal group, where the critique of state intervention was not of the market fundamentalist type. Although in his opus he openly expressed his allegiance to the neoclassical theory of Manger and Walras, von Stackelberg advocated forms of intervention he found consistent with the market economy, such as limited forms of price intervention, income policies, and extensive forms of taxation (Backhaus 1996).

Von Stackelberg brought this anti-Keynesian animus with him to Spain. Immediately after his arrival in Madrid in 1943, the German professor embarked on an attack of Keynes's ideas. In a lecture he gave in Madrid to the crème de la crème of Spanish economics, he used Hayek's arguments about the low levels of calculus capacity in human minds to contest Keynesians' claims that the government can calculate adequate levels of aggregate demand and intervene in the economic cycle through activist macroeconomic policies. This critique legitimized Spanish liberals' subsequent push to make balanced budgets the norm of fiscal policy. After undercutting the centerpiece of Keynesianism, von Stackelberg exhorted Spanish economists to question the very scientific character of Keynes's iconic work (Velarde Fuertes 1996).

To drive this argument home, von Stackelberg posited that microeconomics be the benchmark for evaluating the scientific character of macroeconomic arguments, concluding that these foundations were missing in the *General Theory*. Based on these considerations, von Stackelberg called for continuing commitment to the neoclassical core in general and the microeconomic benchmark in particular. Soon, this principle shaped the teaching of economics in Spain; economic departments began to equate "good economics" with the rigorous application of standard microeconomic theory to macroeconomics (Fuentes Quintana 2002, 72–73; Segura Sánchez 2002, 390–391). In other words, he advocated the neoliberal "microfoundations critique" more than twenty years before this argument became the main weapon of the neoliberals in Anglo-American circles.

In his Spanish publications, von Stackelberg tried to eviscerate many of the Keynesians' claims to novelty by asserting that most of them could already be explained using a neoclassical vocabulary (Palau 2002, 453–455). Yet, unlike the Austrians, he wanted a strong state able to stimulate and guarantee economic competition, as well as allow for measures to modestly redistribute income (Palau 2002, 461–462). Moreover, unlike economists closer to the laissez-faire end of the liberal economic tradition, von Stackelberg appealed for extended forms of taxation, price interventions, and income policies (Backhaus 1996), a position that moderated the market fundamentalism held by some Spanish liberals on these issues.

Von Stackelberg's critique of Keynes's macroeconomics was powerful enough to shape Spain's own nascent Keynesian tradition in economics. Beginning in the 1950s, many Spanish economists who espoused the ideas of the neoclassical-Keynesian synthesis (the mathematized face of Keynes's *General Theory*) joined the ruling elite of the top economic departments in Madrid and Barcelona. By the end of the decade, these economists also secured top positions in the state as advisers, government ministers, and central bankers (Quintana 1999; Aceña 2001).

But this was not the same Keynesianism that shaped policy in Western Europe at the time. Spanish historians agree that between the mid-1950s and mid-1970s, very conservative interpretations of neo-Keynesianism dominated economics departments and, at critical junctures, key institutions of the state as well (Palau 1999; Velarde Fuertes 2001). A crucial trend was that Spanish Keynesians broke with the core policy implication of the Western neo-Keynesian consensus—not to mention Keynes's general theory—in their use of demand-side policies to stabilize economic cycles and foster full employment. Instead of countercyclical intervention backed by an expanded fiscal power of the state, the Spanish Keynesians were primarily concerned with inflation and the dangers of fiscal activism. Moreover, as early as the 1950s, these economists turned inflation into the central pillar of macroeconomic analysis. As historian Salvador Almenar Palau put it, "With regard to what was customary in other European countries, the main difference was that Keynesian macroeconomics [in Spain] was used to cool the economy and abandon inflationary fiscal activism" (1999, 495).

This conservative reading of Keynesianism can be traced to von Stackelberg. Indeed, engaging with his microfoundations critique of Keynes was something of a rite of passage in Spanish economics (Velarde 2001, 363). Most importantly, the prominence of the "von Stackelberg critique" created incentives for prominent Keynesians in academia and the state to graft Keynesian ideas onto Spain's newly acquired ordoliberal legacy. During the late 1940s and throughout the 1950s, the ordoliberal concern with the inflationary risks associated with demand-side interventionism became paramount in the writings of mandarin

economist Torres Martínez, then government adviser, mentor to many postwar top economists, and dean of the newly founded economics department at
the University in Madrid. Although he is remembered as the prime exponent
of the Keynesian tradition, Torres emulated von Stackelberg's apprehension
over the demand-side policies of postwar neo-Keynesians on the grounds of its
poor microfoundations. Rather than focusing on boosting domestic aggregate
demand, as was de rigueur among neo-Keynesians elsewhere, Torres saw exports
as the real engine of growth for a country like Spain (Palau 1999, 467–472).

The scholarly and policy work of Bank of Spain research director Juan Sardà is
equally illustrative of von Stackelberg's legacy. While accepting the basic tenets
of the *General Theory*, Sardà insisted that the contributions of Keynes should
be balanced with ordoliberal insights. While controversially declaring that
Keynesian thinking was "not absolutely incompatible with the general ideas that
dominated the Ordo group" (Palau 1999, 476), he vehemently rejected compat-
ibility between Keynesianism and the planning posited at the time by orthodox
neo-Keynesians.

Similar attempts to mix Keynesianism with ordoliberalism can be seen in the
work of Fuentes Quintana, the doyen of Spanish neo-Keynesianism and one of
the most prominent policymakers of postwar Spain. In a touchstone article published in 1951, Fuentes Quintana introduced Spanish economics to the most
up-to-date presentation of the neo-Keynesianism (Palau 1999, 479). Beyond
putting forth his own ideas, Fuentes Quintana also proved instrumental in popularizing the research materials of the Ordo group shortly after their publication
in Germany.[13]

Conclusions

Neoliberal theories had deep roots in postwar Spain due to permissive institutions and the geopolitical environment in which the authoritarian regime was
embedded. During Franco's authoritarian regime, the flame of economic liberalism and neoclassical economics was kept alight in this Iberian country by the
public servants who benefited from a considerable degree of intellectual diversity and professional internationalization facilitated by Spain's integration into
the American security sphere of interest.

Intriguingly, the flame was fanned by the integration of an actively anti-
Keynesian brand of German ordoliberalism brought to Spain during World War
II by Friedrich von Stackelberg, a Nazi apostate and high-profile member of the
Freiburg School. As celebrity professors, policymakers, and editors, his follow-
ers facilitated the professional advancement of a generation of Spanish econo-
mists who pursued their advanced degrees in economics in the 1950s and 1960s

and who came to play leading roles in academia and the state well into the 1990s. Even the Spanish economists that were relatively sympathetic to Keynes were influenced by these views.

While Spanish ordoliberals had gained access to transnational networks and acquired strong international credentials and an embedded autonomy vis-à-vis the authoritarian regime, the authority of their Keynesian counterparts hinged on the protection of regime insiders and connections with French planners. In the mid-1970s French indicative planning and Francisco Franco died at roughly the same time. The association with Franco's regime tainted Spanish indicative planning, while the ordoliberal Spaniards gained respectability by virtue of their relative outsider status. The contemporaneous demise of Franco and French planning thus paved the way for the neoclassical counterrevolution, while the chances of alternatives to neoliberalism originating from Spanish economists were minimal.

The political transition that began in 1975 terminated Spain's authoritarian regime, handing the levers of policy power to the promulgators of the neoclassical-ordoliberal synthesis that developed under Franco. As a result, a preference for the institutionalization of a rule-bound and market-oriented order constituted the normative universe of Spain's economic transition during the 1970s and 1980s.

5

The Shallow Roots
of Romanian Neoliberalism

Global economic thinking does not disseminate in a historical vacuum. To be translated as close to the "original" as possible, economic ideas need a complex set of favorable circumstances. Most importantly, they need a critical mass of policy intellectuals embedded in their transnational dissemination networks. Even in a country as traumatized by the combination of political despotism and centrally planned austerity as Romania was during the early 1990s, the absence of these policy intellectuals meant that neoliberal economic ideas did not immediately and systematically shape local economic ideas, let alone policy choices. Indeed, as chapter 7 shows, a full-fledged domestic neoliberal coalition took years to build. When transition toward democracy allowed economists and policymakers to openly express their opinions about the problems and prospects of their country's economy, it became obvious that the most they could articulate was a local version of neodevelopmentalism, an economic doctrine that was predominantly heterodox and (quietly) anti-neoliberal at the core.

In countries like Romania, Bulgaria, East Germany, and Albania, authoritarian rule was considerably tighter, and the precommunist acceptance of the ideational bedrock of neoliberalism had been much weaker than in the Czech Republic, Hungary, and Poland (Bockman and Eyal 2002; Evans and Aligică 2008; Cerna 2011; Bockman 2011). Moreover, Romania had developed a strong antiliberal tradition even before the communists took over in 1949. Moreover, the Romanian brand of communism was hostile to market socialism, a hybrid developed by Yugoslav and Hungarian economists that attempted to reconcile socialist economics with neoclassical economics (Bockman 2011). To top it off, unlike Franco's Spain, the Romanian regime did not reward social networks formed between Romanian and Western economists during the detente years, and, by the 1980s, it even repressed them. This made communist Romania a particularly infertile breeding ground for the growth of a local neoliberal epistemic network before the regime collapsed.

The poor state of international exchanges of economic ideas under Ceaușescu serves to underscore how limited Romania's exposure was to Western neoclassical economic ideas. This comparatively less internationalized state of the Romanian economics profession means that its members were both slower to pick up on the neoliberal message and ultimately more vulnerable to radicalization than the more international Spanish one.

These arguments are based largely on primary evidence obtained through archival research, interviews with top policy intellectuals and high-level policymakers, as well as a careful reading of economics literature published in Romanian over several decades.

A Barren Land for Economic Liberalism

After the 1990s, many Romanian academics, politicians, and policy leaders sought to renew connections with the precommunist past and the interwar period in particular. The newly established central banks (re)published the work of *interbellum* economists, and public nostalgia for the ebullient intellectual life of the 1930s became almost compulsory. Yet the object of this nostalgia had little to offer to the prospective neoliberal reformer. If neoclassical economics is neoliberalism's historical locus classicus, there was little of it even in the thinking of the cosmopolitan interbellum luminaries so revered in postcommunist Romania. Indeed, beginning in the second half of the nineteenth century, all leading Romanian economists advocated development strategies based on protectionism, state intervention, and a mixed economy. These dominant figures of Romanian economics came from a generation of economists who had been thoroughly influenced by the ideas of French neomercantilism and of the German Historical school (Murgescu 1990).

The most dramatic manifestation of the Romanian interventionist tradition during the *interbellum* years was the corporatist import substitution industrialization theory of Mihail Manoilescu, an economist whose work enjoyed worldwide notice and even policy impact in Latin America (Love 2004, 114–120). According to Manoilescu, industrialization was the only way out of underdevelopment for agrarian economies, and to this end he made a forceful case for autarkic industrial development as the sole way to counter the structural constraints on Romanian attempts to break out of the periphery. With Manoilescu, the interventionism of Romanian economics reached its apex and transitioned into a form of heterodoxy shaped by a state-dominated authoritarian corporatism, a regime to whose construction he contributed as a minister between 1938 and 1940 (Schmitter 1978).

In contrast, economic historians have not detected any strong push for a liberal economic program during this period. Well educated abroad, the great

Romanian economists of the first half of the twentieth century were very familiar with neoclassical marginalism, yet they never developed systematic research
agendas based in this tradition, and, overall, they resented it (Love 1996, 14;
Kirițescu 1992; Stoenescu 1998). But while the mastery of marginalist economics and particularly of its neoclassical variant was being rewarded in some quar-
ters in postwar Western Europe and North America, in Romania these traditions
were soon to be "blacklisted" by the advent of Stalinism in 1949.

Economists and the State under National Stalinism

Romanian national Stalinism was much more aggressive than Spanish Francoism
in its repression of free thought, a fact that would diminish local familiarity with
economic liberalism in Romania and prevent any affinity toward liberal ideas
from emerging once the regime's time was up. In one of the many examples of
political violence carried out after the ascension of the new regime in 1949, the
faculty of the Bucharest Academy of Economic Sciences (Academia de Studii
Economice, or ASE), the country's elite economics department, was decimated
by waves of demotion, marginalization, and even imprisonment.[1] These forcibly
emptied positions made room for new faculty hastily trained in Soviet economics. Similarly, in 1952, the economists of the central bank (Banca Națională a
României, or BNR) and its prestigious Research Service, a refuge for Western-
trained economists, experienced imprisonment and demotion to clerical jobs.

However, this authoritarian repression of free thought in the economic profession did not necessarily lead to its demodernization, let alone its destruction.
First, after decades of largely qualitative economics, the profession followed the
general Western and Eastern quantitative turn. While a large part of Romanian
academic economics was relegated to regurgitating Soviet economic textbooks,
the stringent needs of the planning apparatus for extensive quantitative skills
created a professional environment that rewarded economists well trained in
analytical methods. The result was a professional community whose skills were
useful to the state[2] and whose sophistication in mathematics granted both status
and political protection (Tiberiu Schatteles, cited in Aligică and Terpe 2007, 20).

Furthermore, the institutional infrastructure and the resources of the profession saw unprecedented expansions. The epicenter of the profession was still the
Bucharest-based Academy of Economic Sciences, but, over time, new academic
institutions appeared where advanced mathematics kept ideological policing at
bay. Critically, the regime set up a number of large economics "institutes" within
the Romanian Academy (Academia Romana), a research body inherited from
the liberal era (1866–1938). These institutes, whose staff saw massive expansion,
served as a kind of government think tank. Elite economists routinely taught at

ASE, did research for the Academy's institutes, and, in some cases, served for the Planning Commission (Bălaş 2000). During these decades, some institute researchers also worked part-time for the Ministry of Finance (Kiriţescu 1992, 339). These institutions all rewarded formal mathematical techniques above all other forms of professional knowledge.[3]

It was in the cracks opened by East-West exchanges during the Cold War that technocratic insiders who later became the Romanian translators of neoliberalism acquired the knowledge to form epistemic networks that would service the deep ideological and economic transformations of postcommunism. Critical in this regard was the fact that the expanded infrastructure of the profession allowed for infrequent yet sustained opportunities for those who had an intellectual interest and no political dossier weighing them down to stay abreast of Western economics. The Institute of Economic Research (IER) of the Academy (a government think tank specialized in advanced research), Cybernetics Institute (an elite academic department), the Romanian Communist Party Academy (the communist cadre university), and the Chamber of Commerce, or the American Library, began to develop basic collections of Western economic reviews and books starting with the 1960s (Bălaş 2000, 329; Severin 2000).[4] During the 1960s and 1970s, the Foreign Trade Institute of the Foreign Chamber of Commerce, an institution that drafted reports on the dynamics of international trade, also provided similar research resources (Aligică and Terpe 2007, 11–13).

In these spaces of technical neutrality, transnational linkages with Western economists could be forged and the seeds of economic thinking critical of central planning began to grow, aided by favorable geopolitical events such as the detente and the "special relationship" between Romania and the United States. Although this did not turn a significant number of local economists into recruits for the neoliberal cause, it did allow a few of them to gain a sense of the mainstream debates unfolding in Western economics.

Detente and Professional Transnationalization

The "thaw" of Romanian Stalinism during the 1960s and 1970s was slower and more superficial than the reforms adopted by the Polish, Hungarian, and (for a brief period) Czechoslovak elites (Tismăneanu 2003). Nevertheless, it put an end to the more extreme forms of parochialism within the economics profession enforced by the "hard" Stalinist regime of the 1950s.[5] After almost three decades of isolation, detente and an anti-Soviet pivot in Romanian foreign policy made possible the renewal of academic exchanges between Romanian and Western economists.

In 1962, the Ford Foundation began to fund study trips for Romanian economists to US economics departments. By 1979, several English-speaking Romanian economists were enrolled in exchange programs coordinated by the US National Academy of Sciences, and several mathematical economists began to attend Kondratieff's Russia Center at Harvard.[6] In 1971, a year after Ceaușescu's presidential visit to the United States, this cooperation was so extensive that the Ford Foundation and a deferral program for academic exchanges (IREX) began funding a management studies exchange program in Bucharest (Byrnes 1976; Bockman and Eyal 2002, 325).

Such opportunities allowed a handful of Romanian economists to conduct research in top American and British universities and develop professional relations with their Western peers.[7] Many used the opportunity to acquire data, skills in input-output modeling, and access to the basic books and journal subscriptions of Western economics. Above all, they received direct access to the state-of-the-art theories and analytical methods of Western economics. Even more telling, during the late 1960s, Western economists interested in the strengths and limits of socialist economics began to lecture in Bucharest. Such was the case of Wassily Leontief, the neoclassical input-output (IO) modeler from Harvard, who lectured at the Romanian Academy of Economic Sciences in June 1968.

The economists who capitalized most on these exchange opportunities were a group of linear programmers who had access to both the technocracy at the State Planning Committee and the elite research institutes that had been established by the regime within the confines of the Romanian Academy. Between 1970 and 1971, Aurel Iancu, then a senior researcher at the Academy and one of the earliest advocates of mathematical economics, used an IREX fellowship to do research at Harvard, MIT, and Berkeley and to participate in the seminars of such luminaries as Leontief, Samuelson, Solow, and Debreu. As a result, the work he published after his return from the United States showed a significant degree of integration of select methodological approaches current in mainstream US economics[8]. While in the United States, Iancu also struck up a long-term relationship with Nicholas Georgescu-Roegen, the most famous Romanian economist in exile, who had become a radical critic of the neoclassical-Keynesian synthesis.[9] Leveraging this experience, during the 1970s Iancu frequently had the opportunity to present his work at professional conferences in Italy and France.

Other scholars embarked on research trips to Western Europe, with or without American funding. In 1969, Gheorghe Zaman, then a young researcher at the Institute of Economic Research (Institutul de Cercetări Economice, or ICE), spent a few months at Cambridge University. During his stay, he trained in the mathematical modeling of consumption and took classes with leading heterodox (post-Keynesian) economists of the day (Richard Stone, Nicholas Kaldor, Joan Robinson). While in the UK, he learned modeling techniques for IO, consumption, and forecasting in capitalist economies.[10] A year later, he was a guest scholar at the American Studies Seminar in Salzburg (Austria), one of the US-sponsored venues of the detente.[11] In 1970, Zaman was appointed by ICE as the scientific secretary and co-organizer of Franco-Romanian colloquia on economic efficiency and planning organized in Paris during that time (Zaman 1970).

A direct conduit of professional access to applied mainstream Western economics was the IMF's training center (called the IMF Institute) in Washington, DC. This author's research in the IMF archives reveals that, following Romania's induction as an IMF member state in 1975, seven economists from the Ministry of Finance enrolled in courses on applied topics such as macroeconomics, balance-of-payments methodology, financial analysis, and public finance.[12] In 1976, IMF Institute director Gerard Teyssier spent five days in Romania and received the request of the Romanian minister of finance to have as many economists as possible trained in Washington. The director also met with the IMF Institute's alumni from Romania as part of a visit to the training facilities in the Ministry of Finance.[13]

Thus, the internal loosening of Romania's national Stalinism and the external opportunities granted by detente enabled a handful of Romanian economists to tap into the resources and professional networks of Western economics. However, this opening did not spread the seeds of neoclassical economics in Romania. None of the Romanian economists who benefited extensively from direct East-West exchanges followed the Eastern/Central European path of joining the neoclassical circles that some of their peers in east central Europe did (Bockman and Eyal 2002; Bockman 2012), and the few who did emigrated during the 1970s.

A clear example of the influential, yet limited, exchange of ideas between Romania and the West can be observed in the experiences of three mathematical economists: Emilian Dobrescu, Aurel Iancu, and Gheorghe Zaman. Their study trips to the West enabled them not only to appreciate the dynamics of capitalist economies and Western academic freedom,[14] but also to publish several studies on economic growth modeling based on the IO models used by Wassily Leontief at Harvard. Since input-output analysis was as consistent with central planning as it was with Keynesian demand management, the end result was the development of an input-output model for Romania's communist economy, an enterprise that demanded considerable local innovation in the translation process. Zaman, an economist who served as the economic adviser for two presidential administrations after 1989, built an IO model for the Romanian economy in 1970 based on Western models developed by Leontief, L. Johansen, and François Perroux.[15] Similarly, Iancu edited the IO model he studied at MIT and Harvard by reframing the theory of the price mechanism in a command economy. Particularly interesting in this reframing was a methodological innovation that made input-output modeling "travel" in a nonmarket economy where prices did not reflect supply and demand factors: the use of all forms of energy as an indicator for the real level of prices.

From the perspective of the regime, IO was harmless. It was mathematically sophisticated but ideologically acceptable. Therefore, far from triggering the regime's ire, this Romanian editing of IO into the country's economic plan was temporarily welcomed and even integrated into the planning techno-structure as a tool for dealing with an increasingly complex industrial and agricultural modernization program. As Zaman said about the IO techniques he learned in the UK:

> Upon my return to Romania, these techniques and ideas were well received, as communist planning methods were not enough. The real economy demanded refinement and sophistication in the models being used. They were unable to follow upstream and downstream flows in the national economy, the buildup of interdependencies. I was personally in charge with inserting trade flows in a Romanian IO intersectoral model, which helped us figure out what the production levels should be given domestic and external demand.

The same was true for popularizations of the latest debates in Western economics, as long as they were embedded in ideologically conformist frameworks. For example, after his return from the United States, Iancu suffered no professional punishment after he popularized some of the latest developments in Western economic debates in his books on economic growth and international finance.

A few Romanian mathematical economists engaged more systematically with Western economics and confused ideological censors by shrouding their arguments in abstract math (Ban 2011). Tiberiu Schatteles, Ihor Lemnij, and Egon Bălaş became familiar with Hungarian, Polish, and Yugoslav syntheses of neoclassical and socialist economics ("market socialism"), while testing the boundaries of socialist economics by engaging with neo-Keynesian macroeconomics. Yet, since their subfield (operations research) was a small niche in microeconomics and was far removed from the more systemic questions that macroeconomists asked, they had little to say about the merits of the debates between neoclassical, (post-)Keynesian, and market socialist economists that marked the history of the Cold War.

The Limits of Repression and Resistance

The last decade of the Spanish authoritarian regime coincided with the rapid professional reconnection of Spanish economists to world economics and especially to Anglo-American universities. The opposite was true in Romania, where the international professional networking opportunities initiated during the detente years came to a virtual halt during the 1980s. During this time, the regime tightened its authoritarian rule over society, and, after the 1982 debt crisis, it decisively turned inward, effectively cutting its connections with the West (Ban 2013).[16] This included an end to scientific exchanges and cuts in funding for subscriptions to scientific journals (Grigorescu 1993, 102–135). The abrupt severance of direct ties between Romanian and foreign economists came right at a time when Hungarian, Czech, and Polish economists who were more deeply embedded in Western networks were gradually growing skeptical of the idea that market socialism could solve the economic crisis of the Eastern bloc (Bockmann and Eyal 2002; Babb 2012).

While the closure was not airtight, it did not allow for systematic forms of transnational professional socialization. Training at the IMF Institute in DC continued, keeping some of the key future technocrats of postauthoritarian governments plugged into contemporary economic debates. However, the cooling of Romania's relations with the IMF in the aftermath of the 1982 debt crisis was unmistakably apparent. While Hungary and China organized workshops with policymakers to explore alternatives to central planning, Romania did not attend, despite being the first communist country to join the Fund.[17]

The archives of the IMF Institute reveal that, between 1982 and 1987—even as Romanians were absent from most IMF conventions—communist Romania sent as many economists to be trained there as it did during the 1970s.[18] Here they became exposed not only to statistics training but also to public finance classes that reflected the Fund's monetarist views. Eleven economists from the Ministry of Finance and one from the central bank took classes in financial programming policy, economic analysis, and public finance.[19] Nevertheless, these were very short training programs usually lasting only a few weeks and, of the eleven economists, only one (Theodor Stolojan) put his skills to political use after 1990 as minister of finance (1990–1991), prime minister (1991–1992), architect of a conservative coalition in the 2000s, and presidential adviser during the adoption of post-2008 austerity programs.

Some of the critically minded economists continued to read Western economics literature at the American Library or in the library reserves of their own departments and institutes. As Daniel Dăianu remembers: "I learned the 'technical' language [for my critique], when I found in the American Library my own alma mater; here I found P. Samuelson, M. Friedman, Hayek, W. Baumol, R. Okun, and others."[20]

Attempts to stay abreast of Western economics continued in the Romanian Academy (Academia Română), the state's large think tank and the graduate school of the communist party (Academia Ştefan Gheorghiu, informally known as the "Party School"). In the World Economy Institute of Academia Română, economists still received Western journals in exchange for their own institution's review published in English. It was from this institute that the crème de la crème of the post-1989 elite emerged, including Mugur Isărescu, the central bank's governor.[21] The same was true of the Communist Party Academy, the multilingual faculty specialized in international political economy within a dedicated division (Severin 2000). Unlike institutes and the ISE, the level of the economic debate was less technical and more interested in intellectual frameworks and politics than in mathematical modeling.[22]

While the incentives for conformity with the "party line" increased, not all economists folded, and some went as far as voicing dissent and accepting the consequences. In October 1982, the US-trained Emilian Dobrescu, the most capable planner in the country, was fired over his opposition to Ceaușescu's early debt repayment and austerity program. Five years later, three leading economists (Constantin Ionete, Tudor Bugnariu, and Mircea Stoica) wrote a critical study of the economy that suggested the adoption of Hungarian-style reform socialism (Ionete 1993, 193 n. X, 203).

Although isolated, these acts of intellectual resistance suggest that the regime's grasp on the profession was not total and that some economists were able to carve out spaces of critical discourse where unorthodox readings, studies, and talks could take place. After all, reading and discussing developments in Western economic scholarship was not punishable as long as it did not lead to open endorsements of Western critiques of the policy status quo in communist Romania. Many economists who had professional aspirations but were reluctant to play the easy game of ideological comformity sought and found protection in the Cybernetics Institute established in 1972 by Manea Mănescu, Ceaușescu's premier and a second-rate economist infatuated with cybernetics, a field that he understood very little (Ban 2011). Here they had the freedom and the resources to keep up to date with Western literature and even maintain correspondence with leading US economists.[23]

Under the thin cover of "know your enemy" pretenses and arcane technical language, Professor Moisa Altar quietly organized seminars with the "who's who" of the post-1989 economic technocracy in the central bank and various government agencies that discussed the latest debates in Western economics and especially the rise of monetarism and new neoclassical economics.[24] The requirements for membership in this elite and informal professional network included proven competence in the latest debates of the American Economic Association. This entailed proficiency in English and the capacity to survive Moisa Altar's intense grilling sessions. As Altar remembers,

> Only those who knew economics for real felt at ease in the group. And in order to know economics, you had to be up to date, read American

journals with a pencil in hand, and get hold of Russian translations of the latest names in the US economics departments. These books cost around ten lei. It was nothing—a couple of coffees. . . . For most of my colleagues, this toil was not worth it. It just made no sense from the point of view of one's career. One could advance in the ranks simply by aping Ceaușescu's babble.[25]

As the 1980s wore on, some economists of the Altar group were confident enough that their dissimulation techniques would get their criticism past censorship. Between 1984 and 1987, Vasile Pillat and Daniel Dăianu published a string of articles in a Romanian review meant for English and French speakers that made subtle critiques of the traditional socialist development model and suggested what was, in effect, a market socialist model (Dăianu 1984; Pilat and Dăianu 1984; 1985). Later on, Dăianu published a critique (in English) of the economic status quo in Romania using the radical positions of Janos Kornai, a Hungarian economist known in the West for his neoclassical attacks against socialism and his evidence that the former could not be fixed with market reforms. Kornai had critiqued Soviet orthodoxy since 1953, but it was within his 1980 book that Dăianu found inspiration. In it, the Hungarian economist argued that chronic shortages were not the result of planners' mistakes, but rather systemic problems inherent to socialist economies (Kornai 1980; Bockman 2011).[26]

Nevertheless, the lack of a significant transnational social component to these efforts meant that, even as neoliberal ideas became mainstream in Western economics by the end of the 1980s, these ideas were not exactly internalized by even the most Western-minded Romanian economists. The next section provides evidence for this claim.

From National Stalinism to Neodevelopmentalism

The traumas of austerity and extreme repression that marked the last few years of Nicolae Ceaușescu's national Stalinism did not lead Romanian economists and policymakers to throw the economic role of the state out the window. Instead, during the first half of the 1990s, the most influential among them sought a development paradigm that balanced industrial recovery with the transition to a market economy. In so doing, they negotiated a place for a small corpus of neoliberal policy ideas to be woven into local developmentalist traditions, a process that more often than not made the resulting hybrid appear predominantly developmentalist, not neoliberal. I call this hybrid "neodevelopmentalism."

Like their "classical" developmentalist ancestors, neodevelopmentalists assume that the world economy consists primarily of nation-states that
compete with each other through their companies. Yet unlike the protectionism of the former, the latter entails extensive (albeit selective and gradual)
engagement with the world economy via the state-led stimulation of foreign
direct investment and export-led strategies, as well as increasing the share of
medium and high-value-added, domestically produced products and services.
During the 1990s, postcommunist countries as different as Slovenia, Slovakia,
Romania, Ukraine, and Belarus all sought to deal with the particular challenges of postsocialism with various local versions of this neodevelopmentalist compromise.

While some Romanian neodevelopmentalists were more open to hybridiz-
ing developmentalist and neoliberal ideas than others, memoirs by top policymakers[27] and my interviews with them (Iliescu 1994; Roman 1994; Văcăroiu
1998) traced their thinking to a report commissioned by the state in early 1990.
Entitled *The Blueprint for Romania's Transition to a Market Economy*, the research
that gave birth to the report involved some twelve hundred academic and policy
economists tasked with diagnosing the country's economic problems and proposing solutions. The *Blueprint* (or *Schiță* in Romanian) is the researcher's dream,
as it captures the thinking of the ensemble of the profession a few months after
the revolution of 1989, a period well before substantial professional (re)social-
ization took place.[28]

The commission that wrote the *Blueprint* was coordinated by Tudorel
Postolache, the doyen of the economic profession and a francophone technocrat
with heterodox views who had served for years on the Planning Commission. His
reputation as a mild-mannered consensus builder and specialist on "advanced
capitalist economies" got him the top job.[29] The commission included a handful
of economists whose views had been shaped by experiences in Western universities. Yet the dominant and most numerous voices were those of economists
whose training and work was geared around domestic professional experiences.[30]
Moreover, according to one of its former members, this commission drew on
the extensive macroeconomic and industrial policy expertise of communist-era
planners whose expertise in complex and cross-national analyses in all industrial
branches was highly appreciated by Postolache.[31]

The commission was driven by a professional ambition to find a local,
tailor-made answer to the challenges of transition, rather than copy and paste
off-the-shelf templates. The key concern was that regular citizens should ben-
fit from transition rather than be its passive subjects, and therefore the issue
of the "social bearability" of reforms remained at the core of the commission's
works. This ambition was further amplified by the enouragement received from
heterodox Romanian economists who had gained world fame in American

universities (Nicholas Georgescu-Roegen) or in the French planning agencies (Ioan Stoleru).[32]

The *Blueprint* proposed a neodevelopmentalist compromise for a postcommunist economy.[33] On the one hand, it advised the irreversible adoption of what were, in its view, the basic infrastructures of a market economy. Some of these encompassed liberalization measures (price liberalization, demonopolization, management independence and hard budget constraints for state firms, positive interest rates, market-based allocation of credit, privatization, no monetary financing of deficits), while others dealt with the establishment of its basic institutions (the capital market, financial supervision, the tax system, antimonopoly laws, and labor market institutions).

But beyond these fundamentals, its drafters feared that a neoliberal transition strategy would lead to the serially correlated bankruptcies of integrated industrial complexes, and thus to massive unemployment and social turmoil.[34] To hedge against such scenarios, they erected three main defenses. First, in terms of the pace of transition, the neodevelopmentalists rejected the choice between shock therapy and gradual transition to the market economy and proposed instead a "fast paced gradualism" and "an opening to a spectrum of varieties of market economy that would be as wide as possible and fit the needs, capacities, traditions and interests of Romanian people, while adopting what fits organically from the practice of advanced economies" (*Schiță* 1990, 11–12). The second critical difference was that they targeted as the end point of transition the achievement of a mixed economy with a large public sector (30–40 percent of the economy) (*Schiță* 1990, 15). To underscore this objective, the commission demanded the adoption of French-style indicative planning (20–21), having received the contributions of none other than Ioan Stoleru, then head of the French Commisariat du Plan.[35] This was a very different endgame than the liberal market economy envisaged by neoliberal transition economics, either in its gradualist or shock therapy versions.

Sequencing was key in this regard. Although ambiguities remained, industrial recovery in sync with social protection came first, while macroeconomic stabilization and price liberalization came second. The first goal was to be achieved mostly through credit to industrial firms via state-owned development banks, managerial retraining, and indicative planning à la postwar France, with the last item receiving the most attention by far in the document.[36] It seemed as if the neodevelopmentalists rejected the market reforms versus social protection, accumulation-before-redistribution categories used by neoliberals.[37]

The neodevelopmentalism of the *Blueprint* was most evident in its position on privatization, the hallmark of transition economics. The authors of the *Blueprint* did not see this process as valuable in itself or as a form of credible commitment to international financial markets. Instead, they regarded it as a complex developmental tool that accommodated both liberal and developmentalist opinions. State-owned companies deemed to serve strategic objectives were simply declared unprivatizable. Public development banks and cooperative banks played a major role in the financing of export competitiveness and social objectives. While the authors attributed a key role to foreign direct investment, they stressed that the state should channel these investments toward high-value-added sectors.

The neodevelopmentalist spirit of the *Blueprint* was also manifest in the other hallmark of transition economics: price liberalization. The authors shied away from adopting a single strategy on this front, leaving policymakers to choose between a liberal agenda, which entailed completing price liberalization over the next three years, and a neodevelopmentalist one, which called for a more gradual and selective liberalization by maintaining price controls for raw materials, fuels, electricity, and basic necessities. This gradualist approach also called for a delay in the liberalization of prices for goods and services produced by monopolies until after the monopoly situation was terminated.

Macroeconomic objectives were subordinated to the goal of industrial recovery. To this end, the authors of the *Blueprint* attempted to forge a compromise between the orthodox objective of price stability and developmentalist objectives such as minimizing job loses and external competitiveness achieved via currency manipulation. Finally, Romanian neodevelopmentalists were aware that, in a democratic system, it would be difficult to develop an accumulation strategy that was tailored solely to the interests of state and the private capital soon to be born.[38] To this end they committed to a left-of-center vision of society-market relations. To pay for the social costs of the incoming economic transformation, they demanded that public investments be reduced from 30 percent of GDP to 20 percent and defended the universal provision of healthcare, education, and social welfare. The *Blueprint* also had a "social clause" that stipulated that the transition program should be carried out in consensual ways and with social policy ensuring the feasibility of its execution. (*Schiță*, 1990, 11–12; INCE 1991, 13). It also set quantitative social metrics and indicated what policy measures should be adopted to meet them: minimum wages tied to decent living standards, price controls for basic staples, early retirement packages for the unemployed, transportation subsidies, universal unemployment insurance schemes, universal healthcare, universal education, and the balancing of pro-FDI measures with state credit for employees who wished to buy shares in their own enterprises (INCE 1991, 10).

This was certainly a left-of-center view of market-society relations, but unlike the social democratic neodevelopmentalism of Slovenia (Bohle and Greskovits 2012), the Romanian neodevelopmentalists professed more commitment to the interests of state and private capital. It was a policy paradigm that was more nationalist and developmentalist than it was socially egalitarian. The idea was that salvaging industrial employment was the best social policy, and therefore the establishment of a robust system of income redistribution took a backseat to industrial policy. To save employment, small and medium state enterprises were to be privatized immediately, while those large state-owned enterprises that were large employers were to be maintained as public enterprises and receive targeted subsidies.[39] Critically, the *Blueprint* proposed cuts in current spending in order to have funds available for public investment in "strategic industries" and in firms experiencing temporary difficulties. The authors also envisaged a corporatist contributions-based welfare state in which firms shared in the provision of social benefits.

While a dozen of the commission's members had been on short research trips to the West during the 1970s, only two had studied in the United States or Britain for more than a few months (Aurel Iancu and Gheorghe Zaman). Still, both Zaman and Iancu had been trained by British and American Keynesians in the heyday of Keynesianism before being cut off from the Western economic profession by the politics of the Ceauşescu regime. There was little peer pressure from what was by now a US-centric economics profession (Fourcade 2006; 2009) that could be exercised on pivotal members of the commission. Indeed, some economists who would later become some of the most influential translators of neoliberalism as central bankers (Mugur Isărescu, Lucian Croitoru) or top policy researchers for the central bank and IFIs (Alexandru Albu, Aurelian Dochia) were active members of the Postolache Commission. For better or worse, its deliberations were shaped by domestic rather than international considerations.

Conclusions

While neoliberalism had deep roots in Spain, it had shallow ones in Romania. The main reason for this difference was the fact that Romanian economists did not benefit from permissive institutions and sustainably favorable geopolitical openings. There were fewer professional exchanges with Western academia and IFIs, and even when they took place, they were short and highly irregular. Only a handful of Romanian economists studied in the United States and Britain at the graduate level. In contrast, dozens of Spanish economists had done so. While the Romanians studied for an academic year at most, their Spanish counterparts did their full PhDs at top Western universities. Indeed, no Romanian got a PhD in institutions where neoclassical economists were active and returned home to a top-level job, as was the case in Spain. In short, after more than ten years of detente, dissident thinking in Romanian economics remained circumspect—at least publicly—toward Western economics in general and neoclassical thinking in particular.

Moreover, Franco's regime allowed a much more extensive degree of intellectual pluralism in the profession than the Ceauşescu regime did. Economists with economically liberal views worked in academia and the central bank in Franco's Spain, while, in Romania, they faced severe professional (and even penal) punishment for much more modest deviations from the official economics of the state. With its 1980s closure, the regime tightened its control of the profession and, with it, decimated opportunities for transnational professional networking. Indeed, as neoliberal theories became dominant in Western economics during the 1980s, Romanian economists faced such levels of professional isolation that keeping up to date with professional debates was an act of political bravery. Finally, while, in Spain, the regime did not change the professional norm that awarded high professional status to local economists with Western training and professional networks, the opposite happened in Romania.

The result was that this intellectual bedrock of neoliberalism was explored unsystematically and was never openly upheld in this southeast European country. Even when they were confronted with intense pressures to engage in a regional "race to shock therapy," at the beginning of transition Romanian policymakers took neoliberal transition economics with more than a grain of salt. Instead of replicating this policy paradigm, these economists hybridized it with heterodox economic ideas commonly associated with the developmental state tradition. This legacy meant that the transition to democracy was associated with much more intellectual contestation of neoliberalism in the initial phase and its radicalization later on, with no "classics" to defend a moderate version of neoliberalism, as in Spain.

PART III

NEOLIBERALISM ACROSS BORDERS

6

Spain

Intensive Transnational Socialization

The Anglo-German Origins of Spanish Neoliberalism

Resources mobilized by both Anglo neoliberalism and German ordoliberalism helped to shape Spain's economic policy after the transition to democracy. Chapter 4 showed that the deep transformations of the Spanish economics profession during the postwar decades were influenced as much by British-trained neoclassical economists as they were by the local followers of ordoliberalism. This chapter argues that the trend of transformation continued after the end of Franco's regime and its developmental state in 1975. Indeed, policymakers trained by and/or heavily exposed to American, British, and German diffusers of economic ideas propelled Spain away from authoritarian developmentalism and toward embedded liberalism, a policy regime where neoliberal and non-neoliberal ideas formed an influential, resilient, and sometimes tensely contradictory cluster of economic perspectives.

Unlike their relatively isolated Romanian peers, from the mid-1960s onward Spanish economists were able to access and engage with the emerging neoliberal tide via economics PhDs at elite British universities, central bank-funded research stints at top US economics departments, long professional appointments in international economic organizations, and the broader inclusion of Spanish academia and policy institutions in dense transnational exchanges. External and domestic funding kept the wheels of this transnational socialization turning faster over time, so that by the 1980s many Spanish economists were not just spectators of, but instead active participants in, the global turn to neoliberalism.

This gradual yet intense transnational professional socialization of Spanish economists does not tell the whole story, however. During the 1970s, Germany's

Social Democratic government invested considerable resources into pushing back a radical socialist turn in Spain, while also giving Spanish policy experts a clear sense of how social cohesion and competitive capitalism could be reconciled. The result of these twin socialization processes was the emergence of Spain's distinctive brand of embedded neoliberalism.

Geopolitics and Anglo Pedigree

Even before Spain organized its first free and fair elections after Franco's death, the country's leading economists had become active participants in the transnational professional networks of economists clustered around high-prestige British and American academic institutions. This was primarily the result of three factors: the pre–Civil War tradition of studying economics in Britain; the institutional entrepreneurialism of the Spanish central bank's Research Service; and the funding opportunities awarded as part of American overtures toward Franco after the change in America's European security strategy following the Korean War.

Beginning in 1951, Spain enjoyed a period of international opening, first toward the United States with the signing of the Treaty of Madrid (1953), and then toward Western Europe. This opening was triggered by a geopolitical shift in Asia (the rise of Maoist China and the outbreak of the Korean War), and also by the toughening of anticommunist campaigns in US domestic politics (Lopez 2000; Calvo-Gonzales 2007; Cavalieri 2014). In exchange for setting up American military bases in Spain, the United States granted the regime substantial economic aid and began to liberalize student exchange programs with Spain, though it stopped short of putting too much pressure on Franco to embrace American "embedded liberal" economic ideas. When Senator J. William Fulbright, chair of the Senate Foreign Relations Committee, traveled to the American bases in Spain, he was appalled to discover that the scenario approved for the annual joint American-Spanish military maneuvers was "a domestic insurrection in which the American military intervened to save the Spanish government" (Calvo-Gonzales 2007, 745).

During the early 1960s, American grants enabled future central bank economists like L. A. Rojo and Pedro Schwartz to pursue graduate studies in economics at the LSE, where they were mentored by Karl Popper and Lionel Robbins, two economic liberals known for their critiques of Keynesianism (Blaug 1990; Henry 2010). The LSE is where Joaquín Muns, another influential economist of the period, pursued his graduate studies during this period. While Rojo's and Muns's LSE experiences led them toward the editing of neoliberal theories with select Keynesian ones (see chapter 2), Schwartz moved closer to radical neoliberalism.

Soon after their return to Spain's academic and bureaucratic meritocracy, Rojo and Schwartz occupied top positions in the economics department of Complutense (FPSE) and in the central bank, where they remained for decades. During the 1970s and 1980s, the two men were regarded as the country's most respected names in macroeconomics and economic theory respectively, while remaining internationally connected (Almenar 2001). Thus, Rojo was Spain's representative in the United Nations Development Programme, the financial committees of G-20, and the European Economic Community's monetary union expert committees. In turn, Schwartz became an associate fellow at University College London and an active member in the Mont Pelerin Society.

By the late 1960s and early 1970s, the United States had emerged as a competing source of new economic ideas for Spain's emerging technocratic elite that would play key roles in the state during transition and well into the 1980s and 1990s. Grants offered by the central bank's Research Service enabled young economists to study in American graduate programs—an opportunity that allowed Carlos Solchaga, the future Socialist "superminister" of finance and economics during the 1980s, to spend one year at MIT at a time when Keynesianism was in decline, albeit not terminated.

In 1969, José Toribio finished his PhD on repressed inflation in the UK and Spain at the University of Chicago with Milton Friedman as his adviser, returning to Spain a "hard" monetarist. After graduation, he was hired by the Research Service and later by the Ministry of Finance before moving to the research service of Banco Urquijo in the late 1970s, where he was a colleague of Solchaga's. Toribio was also credited with converting Pedro Schwartz and José Argandona—often described as leaders of the right wing of Spanish neoliberalism in the 1970s and 1980s—to the Chicago school of economics (Argandona 1972; 1976; 1977; 1985; Díaz 1983; Argandona 1990).

In the late 1960s and early 1970s, the Spaniards' LSE connection to the neoclassical economists continued to thrive. For example, Tomas Esteve, the importer of public choice theory to Spain, took classes at the LSE with neoclassical mandarin Harry Johnson.[1] The same period of time is also associated with a new phenomenon: the growing international prestige of Spanish economists, who were now being recruited by top American and British economics departments while still remaining relatively involved with debates in Spanish economics.

Thus, by the late 1970s Andreu Mas-Colell, Rojo's teaching assistant at Complutense, was appointed as a full professor of microeconomics at Berkeley and then at Harvard; rather than stay completely immersed in American economics, Mas-Collell intervened in Spanish economics reviews with articles announcing the shift away from Keynesianism in economics (Mas-Colell 1983) and secured a joint appointment in Barcelona's Pompeu Fabra University.

In 1986, the LSE gave Oxford-trained Rafael Repullo a tenured position, but after spending one year (1985–1986) teaching at LSE and working as a Research Service economist, Rojo's former protégé chose the Service.

During the late 1970s and throughout the 1980s and 1990s, the internationalization of the Spanish economic profession continued. Many Spanish economists remained abroad and became global academic celebrities (e.g., Xavier Sala-i-Martin, Jordi Galí), while others returned home and elevated the Rojo network to new heights of professionalism. After his graduate studies in economics at Essex and a visiting professorship at the University of California, Berkeley, Carlos Sebastian, another neoclassical-monetarist synthesizer, joined the finance ministry as an economist for the first González government. In addition, two of Rojo's students, who clothed their master's ideas in the latest econometric models, returned to Spain with British PhDs to further consolidate the epistemic authority of the Research Service.

Juan J. Dolado shuffled back and forth between graduate studies at the LSE, visiting positions at France's *écoles* and the Bank of England, and his job as senior economist at the Service until he became Rojo's successor at the helm of that institution in 1992. Meanwhile, the Oxford-trained Rafel Repullo was offered tenure at Oxford but was eventually lured back to Spain in 1987 by Rojo to establish and head CEMFI, an institute of the Research Service specializing in monetary and fiscal policy. At CEMFI, Repullo was joined by fellow Oxford PhD and (subsequently) Nuffield College and LSE research fellow Manuel Arellano.

As a result of increasingly dense transnational ties, by the late 1970s Spanish economics was far removed from the epistemic periphery it had been in the 1940s and 1950s. This tradition continued in the 2000s, when the main economic advisers of the Zapatero governments (2004–2011) had all received their doctorates in economics from leading US and British economics departments (see chapter 8). As one Spanish economist put it in an interview with this author, "By the late 1970s and early 1980s Spain no longer had an inferiority complex in economics, and by the 1990s we were becoming one of the big players in global economics in terms of how many Spaniards were now on the covers of books and articles published at the top of the discipline."[2] The network displayed in figure 6.1 links some of the key Spanish economists discussed above with their coauthors, showing how extensively international their research was between 1979 and 1993.

By contrast, the intellectual adversaries of the neoliberals had a much thinner dossier to stand behind. The structuralists had no foreign graduate degrees, with the exception of the academically inactive and politically isolated Oxford-trained Luis Gamir, the minister of commerce from 1980 to 1981. Gamir had an Oxford PhD in economics who studied with T. Balogh, W. M. Corden, and other British Keynesians (Diaz 1983, 826). He was still an unreformed neo-Keynesian

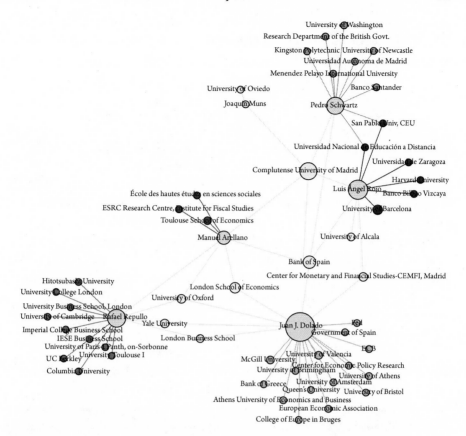

Figure 6.1 Institutional affiliations of the coauthors of top Spanish economists.

during his tenure as minister of commerce, but his official position in the UCD and his loyalty to the center-right barred him from influencing the Socialists. Similarly, his sparse research record did not lend him a great deal of real influence in academic economics.

By the early 1980s, the largely French-speaking "diehard" Keynesian camp (A. Fernandez Diaz, Emilio de Figueroa, Sánchez Ayuso) could not marshal any foreign-trained PhDs in their struggle against the neoliberals. Also, with the exception of Sánchez Ayuso's continuous correspondence with Nicholas Kaldor, the Keynesians' alternative forms of professional transnationalization were reduced to sporadic academic cooperation with a small group of interdisciplinary French Keynesians (Diaz 1983, 826–827). This was the case with Emiliano de Figueoas's constant presence in François Perroux's heterodox seminar at the College de France during the late 1970s and A. Fernandez Diaz's cooperation with the French development economists (Diaz 1983, 825). In 1982, with the premature passing of the consistent Keynesian Sánchez Ayuso[3] and with Gamir's entry into the neoconservative Alianza Popular (the ancestor of today's Partido Popular), Keynesianism disappeared from Spanish academic economics and was upheld only by amateur economists affiliated with the labor union movement.

International Organizations and Diffusion

Graduate education in British and American universities was not the only diffusion channel for economic ideas, however. With the support of Washington, Spain joined the IMF, the World Bank, and the OECD in the late 1950s. The IMF's intervention in the post-1957 crisis weakened the leverage of ISI economists and strengthened the hand of the synthesizers of neoclassical and ordo-liberal economics in government and the central bank (Ullastres, Rubio, Sarda, Varela, Quintana, Sanpedro). But IOs changed the boundaries of economic debate in less direct and more gradual ways as well when they retrained key sectors of the local technocratic elite via long-term appointments in the domestic policy sphere.

In total, thirty-one Spanish civil servants were posted with the OECD and twenty with the IMF between 1960 and 1982, and most of them returned home to join economic policy institutions (Muns 1986, 224–226, 261–266, 433–436). As one prominent example, economist Mariano Rubio worked for the OECD before embarking on a spectacular career at the central bank of Spain, where he would eventually become governor. At the suggestion of Research Service director Juan Sarda, Rubio worked as an economist for OECD's Southern Europe Division in Paris between 1959 and 1962. There he furthered his economics education and, upon his return, was hired as the general director of financial policy in Spain's Ministry of Finance before quickly advancing through the ranks of the central bank, going from deputy general director to governor in just a few years (Rivasés 1991). In addition, some of the most important translators of the neoliberal ideas and reforms espoused and implemented under the Socialists spent years of their professional lives in Brussels. For example, Pedro Solbes, a key architect of Spain's accession to the EU, worked for Spain's office in the European Commission between 1973 and 1978. Before becoming finance minister in the fourth Socialist government (2004–2008), Solbes served as the head of the Directorate-General for Economic and Financial Affairs (DG ECFIN), the main economic policy body of the European Commission, from 1999 to 2004. Indeed, Solbes was one of the key designers and enforcers of the eurozone rules (Solbes 2013, 201–254).

Another foreign-educated economist, Joaquín Muns, used his extensive epistemic authority, gained from years of service at the IMF and World Bank, to help induce a neoclassical shift in Spanish economic debates during the 1980s. Muns, an LSE-trained economist and professor at the elite economics department of Universitat Autònoma de Barcelona (UAB), served in the IMF at the heights of the (neo-)Keynesian era (1965–1968) before becoming an executive director during the IMF's turn to orthodoxy (1978–1981). Between 1980 and 1982, Muns also enjoyed a stint as an executive director in the World Bank. During this time, Muns wrote frequently in the influential economic review *Papeles de Economía Española*, where he advocated price stability over full employment, using his authority as both an academic and an adviser to the government (Muns 1981, 8). Another famous Spanish economist who went on to work for the IMF was Rodrigo Rato, the architect of the economic reforms adopted by Spain's conservative governments between 1996 and 2004, who went on to become the managing director of the IMF.

Fast-track socialization via IO training was less important (and necessary) than in Romania, however. Between 1964 and 1982, no Spanish economist participated in the seminars of the IMF Institute, and only three Spaniards took part in its training programs. Moreover, only twenty-eight Spaniards enrolled in the Institute's classes, a level that a historian of IMF-Spanish relations regarded as rather low (Muns 1986, 225). Similarly, although it doubled between 1970 and 1972 (from six to twelve), the IMF staff of Spanish origin in 1982 (fourteen people) was still well below Spain's IMF quota. Further, only half of them worked as economists, a situation that IMF staff of Spanish origin attributed to the scarcity of US-trained Spanish economists and to the Spanish government's low level of interest in promoting Spain's representatives (Muns 1986, 262–263, 265 n. 50). Finally, only two economists were selected to participate in the IMF's two-year training program for young economists, a program that was regarded as an antechamber for full employment with the IMF.

Beginning in the 1970s, staff from the OECD and the IMF's Europe and Research division chose the Research Service of the Bank of Spain as the main platform for "technical cooperation" with the Spanish authorities. Experts based out of the research department of the IMF gave talks in the central bank, while other Fund experts organized their seminars in the same institution (Aceña 2001). OECD reports also routinely cited the central bank and remained silent on other sources. These forms of external validation proved important for consolidating the prestige of the Service as the country's most authoritative guardian of economic orthodoxy (Muns 1986).

Domestic Debates and International Classics

Despite the importance of international experience, Western graduate education and professional socialization via long stints in IOs were not the sole engines of transnationalization. The 1970s also marked the beginning of the direct involve-ment of neoliberalism's leading Western advocates in Spanish debates, as well as the integration of Spanish economists into prestigious international conference and publishing networks. For example, in 1972, Milton Friedman gave talks in Madrid and debated monetary policy with Richard Musgrave, a Harvard-based Keynesian, in an international seminar organized by a local newspaper and attended by top-level bureaucrats of the Franco regime (Friedman and Musgrave 1972). Friedman warned Spanish authorities against using increases in the quantity of money for economic development purposes and instead advo-cated central bank independence and robust deregulatory reforms of the finan-cial sector. He also suggested that inflation targeting by the Spanish central bank was the only guarantee of stable economic growth, while also making the case for a floating regime for the peseta.

Key parts of the state bureaucracy controlled by liberals actively sponsored professional socialization. The Research Service of BdE and the trade ministry's Institute of Fiscal Studies funded regular forms of consultation with British, American, and Italian economics departments and fellow technocrats (Calvo Lagares 2001). In 1971, several senior researchers at the Institute for Fiscal Studies traveled to Britain to seek advice on reforming the Spanish tax system via special seminars and interviews with British economists active in policy. A similar research visit was organized in Italy the following year, although this time the focus was seeking the counsel of Italian tax experts in the Ministry of Finance. The Institute invited a number of Italian and British tax economists to lecture or to accept visiting fellowships. The ideas generated by the transnation-alized research activities of the Institute during the early 1970s gave an emerging elite of Spanish technocrats concrete and actionable policy ideas about taxation and regulation that were a mix of Keynesianism and neoclassical economics. Elite continuity after the end of the Franco regime gave these transnationalized technocrats the power to put this synthesis into practice and ward off the radical-ism of a rising libertarian chorus.

Indeed, at the margins of the profession, libertarian economists also drew upon the influence of international networks. Friedrich von Hayek, a leading member of the Austrian school of economics, traveled to Spain a few times dur-ing the 1970s and attended the Austrian school seminar organized by a local libertarian think tank (Villalonga Foundation),[4] all the while keeping a regular correspondence with its members throughout the decade (Huerta de Soto 2008, 264, 266). During the 1970s, its representatives organized informal, yet regu-lar, libertarian seminars for influential academic elites and young economists (Pascual y Vicente 1980). Throughout the 1960s and early 1970s, the founda-tion embarked on a systematic process of translating the essential contributions of the Austrian school.

By the early 1980s, the Villalonga seminar was no longer a prime site of encounter for the elite of Spanish neoliberalism's libertarian wing. In this respect, it had been eclipsed by the Institute for the Market Economy (IEM), an organization established in 1978 by Pedro Schwartz, one of Villalonga's leading members. Schwartz wanted to take "pure" neoliberalism beyond the "talking shop" stage and give it a stronger policy orientation. To this end, he invited prominent liberal economists into his circle and attracted a number of young economists to coauthor policy reports and academic materials for IEM. The IEM's executive committee was chaired by Juan Sarda himself, and, in addition to Schwartz, it included prominent British liberal economist Lord Robbins and two Spanish economists who were members of the Royal Academy.

IEM provided a public policy critique platform for young American- and British-trained conservative academic economists, who began attacking government policies from a monetarist perspective in a string of systematic studies generated by IEM-affiliated researchers. The most prominent among IEM's studies was *Money and Economic Freedom*, a book-length monetarist critique of the financial policy of the central bank authored by Francisco Cabrillo and Fredric Segura. The study argued for a complete liberalization of exchange rates and for the freedom of international capital movements by deploying the theses of Chicago monetarists.

Yet despite their international connections Villalonga and the IEM failed to effectively challenge embedded neoliberalism, which was becoming increasingly entrenched in the central bank, academia, and the state technocracy. The main reason was their inferior resources, as a function of a different age in the global diffusion of neoliberalism. Unlike in 1990s Romania, there was little, if any, transnational material support for radical neoliberalism in the 1970s and early 1980s, as advocacy for such ideas was largely relegated to US and British political life at the time. Moreover, Spanish capital did not see in think tanks a platform for advancing its interests; on the contrary, as Socialist ministers Carlos Solchaga and Joaquín Almunia testified in their memoirs (Almunia 2001; Solchaga 1997), business often opposed neoliberal macroeconomic measures and saw that its most important demands (labor market deregulation and wage compression) were already consistently advocated for from within the economic ministries and the central bank.

Without a doubt, by the 1970s, Spanish economists in general and the economists who played important roles in government in particular were deeply enmeshed in the transnational networks of the economics profession through which neoliberal ideas began to flow during the late 1970s and early 1980s. Moreover, the moderation of mainstream neoliberalism in the Spanish context was bolstered by Spain's exposure to a second wave of external advocacy for ordoliberal ideas closer to Germany's brand of social democracy. Combined, these transnational processes facilitated the diffusion of "mainstream" neoliberal theories while warding off radical neoliberalism.

Moderating Neoliberalism with German Ideas
German Interests and Southern Socialism

The strong support for embedded neoliberalism in Spain under a Socialist government whose leaders had been openly Marxist just four years before getting elected can, in large part, be attributed to the power-political dimension of Germany as the guarantor of the liberal order in Europe and defender of a monetarist view of crisis management.

Even before the neoliberal movement began to emerge in late 1960s America, in Germany ordoliberalism had established itself as a steadfast defender of some of the fundamentals associated with neoliberalism today: orthodox and rule-based monetary and fiscal policies, central bank independence, economic openness, and the maximization of internal and external market competition. At the same time, this German "liberalism with rules" did not share the antistate impetus of neoliberal doctrine. For proponents of ordoliberalism, a strong but only selectively interventionist competition-oriented state was the very guarantor of a robust market economy. Moreover, to neoliberals' great irritation, most ordoliberals thought that social cohesion via shared prosperity and democratic corporatism was the life insurance of capitalist systems. By turning these ideas into policy actions, postwar Germany became not only one of the most competitive economies in the world, but also one in which the aspirations and objectives of the political Left had advanced very far by the time neoliberalism entered the mainstream during the 1970s.

Soon after the oil crisis of 1973, the German model of capitalism became the envy of virtually all stagflation-stricken countries. As everyone else was experiencing extreme economic and social challenges, with Britain enduring the humiliation of an IMF bailout in 1976, Germany's export prowess was unchallenged and its combination of low unemployment, well-funded social services, and undisturbed growth performance made many national leaders wonder if the country's orthodox monetary and fiscal policies were, in fact, at the root of all this success. Kathleen McNamara (1998) showed that it was at this decisive moment that many European nations began to emulate German economic ideologies and tried to help their economies by creating pan-European currency-stabilization schemes anchored in the German currency. The result was the diffusion of German anti-inflationary ideologies and the end of searches for a progressive and viable set of answers to stagflation.

More recent research has showed that there was more to the story behind Germany's rising power. Julian Germann (2014) found that, during the mid- and late 1970s, Germany's Social Democrats worked to disembed the liberal economic order to keep the world economy open for its exports and shore up its competitive position, and, critically, to defeat the interventionist and expansionary responses of the European Left. Germann's archival research finds that

> German state managers sought to use their financial influence in order to shift the social balance of power in favor of those forces willing to follow German stabilization and away from those forces that were held to endanger access to this vital zone economically or politically. . . . The disciplining of labor and the left wing of the SPD in the early 1970s thus found its external extension in attempts to keep radical forces out of government in Britain, Italy, and France. . . . Concerned about an electoral victory of the French left . . . which had adopted a far-reaching Common Program based on nationalization, welfare expansion, and worker control in 1972 the German government had sought to support the Barre government (1976–1981) and its technocratic state bureaucracy in its efforts to imitate the German success. (Germann 2014, 709)

It is this strategy, and not Germany's postwar model per se, that stabilized the social consensus inside Germany while undermining it in states whose economies could not, by virtue of their structure, benefit from austerity measures and tight monetary policy. Germany's "particularistic way of coping with the crisis thus contributed decisively, though not deliberately, to the 'disembedding' of the liberal international economic order" (Germann 2014, 706).

Bringing the Iberian Socialists into the fold was part of this strategy. German money, experts, and ideas flowed south toward Madrid to shore up a template of social democracy with *Modelldeutchland* characteristics. The inclusion of PSOE in bilateral partnerships with German Social Democrats in the mid-1970s made an important contribution to clarifying the economic policy identity of the PSOE elite. Through frequent bilateral visits, participation in each other's party congresses, logistical or expert support, and even friendships among top party leaders, PSOE soon became the Iberian "pupil" of the SPD.

This had three main consequences for Spanish political life: the definitive elimination of a potent source of leftist radicalization in a French-style socialist-communist alliance; the emergence of West German social market economy, rather than French socialism, as the idealized model of state-market-society relations; and the normalization of monetarism, central bank autonomy, and fiscal rigor as the standard response to Spain's macroeconomic challenges. It is against this shift in the sphere of political ideology in their main external sponsor that Spanish Socialists carved out space for embedded neoliberalism in the economic sphere.

Geopolitical factors specific to the dynamics of the Cold War and the internal politics of the Socialist International played a considerable role in giving the ideologically moderate German Social Democrats greater influence than the radical French Socialists, whose economic ideas threatened the liberal order that Germany was determined to defend (Pilar-Atunyo 2005). Following the October 1973 oil shock, the United States and West Germany became acutely concerned that the succession problem of the ailing Franco regime, the threats to political stability posed by Basque independence militancy, and the social unrest caused by unemployment and decreasing consumption could strengthen the hand of the Spanish Communist Party (PCE) relative to other leftist socialist organizations.[5] Given the high political investment of continental and Nordic social democratic parties and labor unions in the anticommunist agenda of the Cold War, parties like the SPD had strong incentives to preempt a strong communist-dominated Left in Southern Europe.

This dynamic was strengthened by the internal politics of the Socialist International, where the French-backed idea that center-left parties should establish alliances with communist parties was being taken seriously by many socialist parties in Europe at the time (Atunyo 2005). This internal rift within the International was magnified by the strength of communist parties in Iberia and Greece, whose ailing authoritarian regimes were being most actively combated by communists, and where weak socialist or social democratic organizations were expected to be tempted to form "popular front" alliances with the communists. Moreover, since the end of the Civil War, France rather than Central or Northern Europe had been PSOE's main base of external operations. French was the preferred foreign language of Socialist elites, and González himself had been elected as party president at a PSOE congress organized in the French town of Suresnes with the help of the French Socialist Party.

Yet, in the end, it was German Social Democrats rather than the French Socialists who came to exert the most influence over the struggling PSOE. There were several reasons for this outcome. First, as the richest and most politically successful party in the SI, the SPD was better positioned to affect the orientation of PSOE. Its party foundation (Friedrich Ebert Stiftung) had decades of experience with transnational party assistance, and while the French Socialists came to power only in 1981, the SPD had been in government from 1966 until 1982. This gave the SPD the benefit of using West German embassy contacts and other government privileges to intervene inside Spain. Furthermore, the SPD was the only member of the Socialist International that channeled resources toward PSOE before the end of Francoism, and was the only party that had a real understanding of the situation of the opposition inside Spain.

The SPD's unique experience in forming transnational party contacts with the Spanish center-left enabled it to play a decisive role in averting a socialist-communist front in Spain, and, in the long run, it laid the basis for normalizing PSOE's economic agenda. The SPD overcame its skepticism that the ideologically more radical yet only superficially Marxist PSOE[6] had the potential to replicate German social democracy following the perceived danger of a euro-communist Portugal in 1975 and the PSI's decision to openly cooperate with the Spanish Communist Party at the same time. This convinced the SPD that the PSOE's Felipe González and his team were a preferable alternative because, by this time, González was adamantly opposed to a political front with the communists, a choice he framed rather strategically and dramatically as conducive to a repeat of the Spanish Civil War (Ortuño-Anaya 2005, 204–205).

What mattered for the SPD was the organizational strength of PSOE outside of Madrid. Ebert Foundation fieldwork conducted in 1975 had revealed that, in contrast to the largely Madrid-based PSI, PSOE had a real (albeit sparse) organizational basis throughout Spain and had the potential to get more than 25 percent of the vote. As a result, the SPD decided to throw its full weight behind PSOE. To this end, it opened an official Ebert office in Madrid, led by its experienced Mexico director Dieter Koniecki, and also pushed the Socialist International (then chaired by Willy Brandt) to recognize the executive team of Felipe González as the legitimate representatives of socialism in Spain.

At the cost of DM 15 million over the 1975–1980 period, the SPD then tasked Ebert with the direct financing and training of a PSOE cadre (Konicki 1986). SPD chairman Willy Brandt became González's mentor and invited the young Spanish party leader to the Mannheim convention of the SPD in late 1975, a moment that was tantamount to launching González internationally (Ortuño Anaya 2005, 204). With SPD as facilitator and sponsor, González was received by the leaders of the European Commission in Brussels, welcomed into the European Parliament, and asked to give interviews to European newspapers. Also, at the SPD's behest, the SPD-affiliated union IG Metall became intensely involved with the PSOE-affiliated labor union UGT. Its funds and technical assistance helped the UGT resist the entreaties of much stronger communist unions (Comissiones Obreras) to form one big labor union confederation in Spain.

The most important result of this personalized new partnership was that the "French" scenario of a communist-socialist front in Spain was preempted as long as the González team under siege from the Madrid PSOE faction—then open to a socialist-communist alliance—was able to control the party. To this end, the SPD was ready to tolerate the fact that, in the 1977 elections, PSOE competed with an economic program that was in many regards to the left of the communists. Indeed, the Germans' antipathy toward the communists was so deep that, when Brandt visited Madrid in December 1976 to attend the PSOE convention, he advised PSOE leaders to take part in the first elections regardless of whether the PCE would be legalized or not (Whitehead 1992, 304). This intervention had enduring effects, because PSOE maintained its distance from the communists even after the Cold War ended. Critically, Germany's intervention prevented not just a socialist-communist alliance in Spain, but also the kind of Keynesian policy scenario that PSOE's rank and file and the labor unions wanted.

Ordnungspolitik with Vitalpolitik

During the late 1970s and early 1980s the German model was based on collective bargaining and progressive positions on the welfare state and taxation, not just on some neoclassical purism (Young 2013). Moreover, even the ordoliberal core of this hybrid was not particularly hostile to the state and progressive distribution concerns, as "the establishment of the social market economy, and the measures to generalize the enterprise form through society, were accompanied by what Ropke referred to as a vitalpolitik, or a 'politics of life,' a highly activist social program to 'shift the center of gravity of governmental action downwards" (Flew 2012, 56). In short, what Germany exported was not Anglo-American neoliberalism, but an embedded neoliberalism whose core was a synthesis of ordoliberal and social democratic ideology.

During Spain's transition, the Ebert Foundation (the local emissary of the German Social Democratic Party) invested important resources in giving its particular social democratic reading of ordoliberalism—the prevailing economic ideology of German center-left governments during the 1970s (Hagemann 2013)—a more concrete and accessible face. In what amounted to a classic case of transnational advocacy, Ebert helped the establishment of a PSOE political foundation (Fundación Pablo Iglesias) to serve as a platform for its organization of more than two thousand seminars and symposia (Koniecki 2007). Ebert also published various studies meant to demonstrate the virtues of combining fiscal rectitude, central bank independence, corporatist industrial relations, progressive labor regulations, and a robust welfare state.[7] To this end, the foundation organized no less than twelve international conventions of constitutional law professors to advise the Spanish constitutional convention in 1977, enabling the adoption of German institutions such as collective bargaining.[8] In 1978, the foundation went so far as to bring together Spanish and German unions and employer organizations to learn about collective bargaining (Documentos Ebert 1978; Koniecki 2007). Their main message was that macroeconomic orthodoxy and the social democratic agenda can go hand in hand, rather than act as the foes they were assumed to be in other national capitalisms, a proposition that echoed broadly in the writings of the economic ministers under Felipe González (Solchaga 1997; Solbes 2013).

In the late 1970s, the German embassy, in collaboration with the Ebert Foundation, put together several seminars on the implementation of a "social market economy" in Spain, bringing together the top German and Spanish academic economists of the time. For example, a 1979 conference brought to Spain German economists from the Universities of Nürnberg, Marburg, and Würtburg and representatives of the federal government. In these seminars, the "social market economy" was defined in the social democratic Muller-Armack tradition as "free markets with social compensation." This was in contrast with the conservative interpretation, stressing strictly laissez-faire economics, monetarism, prohibition of cartels and anticompetition practices, monitoring of companies with large economic power, eliminating barriers to entry, monetary stability, and central bank independence.

Ebert also paid for the conference expenses of economics professors from various German universities as well as those of middle- and high-level German government bureaucrats. It also invested in the strengthening of democratic neocorporatist relations in Spain by training representatives from the Socialist labor union UGT and the main employer confederation CEOE, as well as leading labor law experts from Spanish universities. Between 1978 and 1988, Ebert ran six regular meetings among the labor, capital, and academic experts every year. The twenty working papers that resulted from the permanent workshop testify to the aim of institutionalizing German-style corporatist ideas and norms about the labor market in conditions of coordinated capitalism.

As former minister of labor Joaquín Almunia put it, the model that inspired Felipe González's policy team the most was West Germany, with its compelling balance between the competitive economy of the world's top exporter and the welfare state that ranked as the most successful in the world. "During the 1980s," he said, "with the Swedish model in crisis, Germany showed that you can have an economic order in which the state is the enforcer of capitalist competition, a maker and defender of markets, and a guarantor of social solidarity. Germany showed that fiscal and monetary orthodoxy or competitive capitalism are not the enemies of solidarity, but its protective shield."[9]

Conclusions

On the eve of the neoliberal shift in Western economics, Spain's leading economists had become active participants in the transnational networks of British and American academia. This was primarily the result of three factors: the pre–Civil War tradition of studying economics in Britain; the institutional entrepreneurialism of the central bank's Research Service; and, most importantly, the substantial external professional and material resources invested in professional transnationalization as part of American overtures toward Franco's regime. Most of the economists who studied abroad returned home and built spectacular careers at the helm of top policy and academic institutions. Moreover, some of the key players in Spain's neoliberal shift spent years working for international economic organizations, with fast-track forms of professional training playing a minor role in local elite (re)building. By the 1980s, their work was conducted in highly internationalized ways.

The timing of extensive professional socialization was critical. These Spanish economists obtained advanced degrees or worked for IFIs at a time when professional training entailed exposure to both Keynesian and anti-Keynesian ideas and knowledge. This contributed to more nuanced translations of neoliberal ideas at the critical juncture of Spain's economic transition. Competing, but nonantagonistic, diffusion processes shaped the final outcome as well. A critical factor in the moderation of Spanish neoliberalism was Germany's intervention in the formation and ideological clarification of the political party that ruled over Spain's economic transition: the Socialists. German involvement prevented not just a socialist-communist alliance in Spain, but also the kind of Keynesian policy scenario that the majority of PSOE members and labor unions so desperately longed for. At the same time, the version of ordoliberalism "sold" reinforced a center-left editing of neoliberalism with ideas that upheld the value of collective bargaining and progressive positions with respect to the welfare state and taxation.

Domestic professional institutions played an important role in this regard. Unlike in Romania, Spain's market fundamentalists tried to gain a foothold in the policy sphere at the time when there was little, if any, transnational support for such an initiative, and when corporate interests were not yet socialized into bankrolling such ideas. As a result, their resources bled dry, and the radicals were locked out of the policy sphere during the critical decade of Spain's transition to neoliberalism.

7

Romania

Recurrent Coercion and Fast-Track Socialization

Ruling by Force and by Force of Thought

With their ability to extract drastic economic policy changes, the actions of international financial institutions can explain a great deal of the deep economic policy changes experienced by Romania since the early 1990s. They account for both the gradual chipping away of unorthodox neodevelopmentalism between 1990 and 1996 and the embrace of disembedded neoliberalism after 1996. Nevertheless, the interference of IFIs in the domestic policy space cannot explain how local policymakers themselves became advocates of disembedded neoliberalism, nor can it explain why the policy prescriptions implemented in Romania were often more orthodox than those that the IFIs pushed for.

This chapter shows that, while the joint efforts of IFIs have been effective in gradually pushing Romanian elites towards neoliberal policies, the dissemination of status and material resources by IFIs, Western governments, and foundations have also been instrumental in creating what Ngaire Woods (2006, 73–74) called "domestic interlocutors" for neoliberalism. However, this is not another story about "Chicago Boys" remaking a national economy in the image of an orthodox economic script they learned in graduate school. Instead, Romanian neoliberalism was a project undertaken via short-term and nonlinear episodes of professional transnationalization, open to competing and more radical projects that resonated with increasingly influential local political theories of state-society relations.

The contrast with Spain provides some important insights in this regard. While, in Madrid, professional economists had a tight grip on the policy process, in Bucharest credentialed economists shared the spaces of the policy process with amateur ones, self-appointed "policy experts" based in elite and transnational sectors of the nonprofit sector. Aided by a supportive international environment and bolstered by the cultural and political robustness of local anticommunism, the relatively shallow transnational socialization of this network of domestic translators facilitated the eventual radicalization of neoliberalism in Romania.[1]

Neoliberalism by Force
Trimming Neodevelopmentalism (1990–1996)

Between 1990 and 1996, the main outcome of international lending agreements was to set hard limits on Romanian neodevelopmentalism. In this regard, both the IMF (and the World Bank) had the necessary leverage. First, the importation of consumer goods to address pent-up demand after a decade of harsh neo-Stalinist austerity coincided with the war in Iraq (the main oil provider for Romania's oil-intensive economy). Second, the collapse of the trade agreements among former communist countries just as central planning was being dismantled meant that the supply chains of Romania's particularly centralized industry unraveled. These converging processes led to a sharp deterioration in the country's current account. However, due to the long-run effects of the conflict with creditors triggered by Nicolae Ceausescu's debt repayment schedule (Ban 2012) and political uncertainties, neither the national Treasury nor the central bank could access international private markets, leaving the IMF and the World Bank as the only available creditors (World Bank 1991, 7).

The neodevelopmentalists in power needed the IMF because there were alternatives to financing the deficit, not because they bought its economics wholesale. Indeed, they saw it as a "single trick" monetarist actor unwilling to acknowledge the extremely interconnected nature of firms in postcommunist Romania and, accordingly, they tried to resist its demands as much as they could within the boundaries of dependence on the IMF's lending decisions.[2]

Specifically, the local authorities' view of recovery clashed with the "excess demand" view of the IMF and the central bank (Gabor 2012). The IMF and its domestic ally, the Romanian central bank (BNR), saw stabilization as the main challenge of transition and argued that sustainable recovery and disciplined macroeconomic policy could only be achieved by imposing complete market discipline on SOEs.[3] The IMF-BNR couple therefore treated neodevelopmentalists' use of unconventional monetary and exchange rate policies as inappropriate quasi-fiscal expansionary and industrial policies and, consequently, targeted the subsidized credits, arrears and outright subsidies to the export sector and high-employment firms that the government allowed. Simultaneously, they pushed the government to force SOEs to turn to market-driven sources of financing,[4] a request that critical economists found particularly unrealistic considering that such a market simply did not exist at the time (Gabor 2010a).

The first stand-by agreement with the IMF in April 1991 identified the monetary overhang—not recovery from the worst depression since the 1930s—as the main policy priority. Using a monetarist theory of prices, IMF experts linked prices to the broad money supply and inflation to excess demand. Therefore, the Fund asked the government to liberalize industrial prices and to cheapen imports by devaluing the currency (IMF 1991; Demekas and Khan 1991). Unfortunately for the IMF, the attempt to "make markets" via the resulting convergence between an inflationary shock and a systemic credit crunch rendered firms unable to pay their suppliers, sending the level of intercompany arrears to 40 percent of their turnover, leading to more inflation (Gabor 2010).[5]

To prevent a meltdown of the economy, the Roman cabinet orchestrated a systemic bailout of state firms through the monetization of intercompany debt. This led the IMF to suspend the agreement, but not before advising the central bank to neutralize the effects of the bailout by enforcing credit repayments before maturity and passing reserve requirements on bank liabilities (Gabor 2010a). As a result of this intervention, the government's compensation scheme was largely sterilized by the first months of 1992 (IMF 1992),[6] credit contracted in both nominal and real terms, drying up liquidity, destroying close to a third of the country's extensive manufacturing sector, and leading to the loss of one million jobs (Ban 2011, 201–207). With this economic and social disaster in the background, the government had little political capital left.

Similarly, the World Bank's loan program from June 1991 provided financing for a list of critical imports in exchange for the Romanian government's agreement to use the bank's technical assistance in its privatization and social safety net programs, a relatively modest constraint on the government's independence (World Bank 1991). However, these conditions suddenly multiplied in subsequent programs, forcing the government to adopt a laundry list of macroeconomic and structural reforms (World Bank 2005). Accordingly, some of the cabinet's neodevelopmentalist reforms such as markup caps, export restrictions, and nonprivatizable state firms were sent to the chopping block (Pop 2006, 129–131).

Again, the BNR acted as the reliable domestic interlocutor of the IMF and the World Bank throughout from the 1990s onwards.[7] This role was critical during the neodevelopmentalist governments. Backed by the two IMF programs signed during the Văcăroiu government (1992–1996), the central bank blamed recent policy failures on the monetarist expansion forced by the previous government and consequently employed contractionary monetary policies (Isarescu 2006, 43–86). Empirical research shows that these policies "created liquidity shortages where policy discourse saw excess liquidity, produced repeated payment blockages where it was supposed to liberate a 'repressed' financial system, contracted industrial production instead of producing growth, and fed exchange-rate devaluations into inflationary pressures" (Gabor 2010a, 107). The government rebelled against such constraints whenever its external position improved, and on two occasions it forced the not-yet-independent BNR to extend preferential credit to specific SOEs and monetize government debt (IMF 1994; 1995; 1996; Isarescu 2006, 25–26).

At first, the BNR played along but soon it struck back with IMF support and imposed very high rates on the preferential credits, thus frustrating one of the government's chief policy goals (Gabor 2010a). Faced with these defeats, the cabinet held fast on issues where the central bank had no power. For example, it rejected the Fund's demand that domestic energy prices be aligned with international ones— despite the fact that Romania's domestic production was cheaper. The same happened to requests for privatization campaigns intended to shrink state ownership regardless of sale price or profitability (Văcăroiu and Smeoreanu 1998).

The IMF's decision to suspend its fourth stand-by agreement and pull the plug on this grafting exercise came just four months before the 1996 general elections.[8] When the opposition (which was generally aligned with the neoliberal transition economics of the IMF) took power, it inherited an economy that was still predominantly state-owned, a reflection of the Văcăroiu government's successful fight against some of the Fund's demands. However, even before 1996, the BNR-IMF alliance had helped to block the very heart of the neodevelopmentalist strategy: the ability to use the exchange rate to boost industrial competitiveness and create a financial system orientated toward recapitalizing the country's industrial base.

Locking In Neoliberalism (1996–2006)

The 1997 stand-by agreement with the IMF helped to clarify the goals of the new government coalition, an ideological mosaic known as the Democratic Convention. While the previous agreement had been codesigned by the IMF and the BNR, this time Prime Minister Ciorbea insisted this should be strictly an IMF job, "to validate the claims that they had held throughout the 1990s that they were the true—and thus neo-liberal—reformers" (Pop 2006, 130). His successors also never doubted the economic philosophy behind the IMF's policy design for the Romanian economy (Vasile 2002; Isărescu 2006).

The coalition concluded that the BNR's attempts to use monetary policy to stabilize prices had been systematically compromised by developments endogenous to the political economy of neodevelopmentalism: the lack of central bank independence, government pressures for BNR credit facilities targeted at specific sectors, and the demands of energy-intensive industrial sectors that exchange rate management be subordinated to their own import needs. This meant that the agreement effectively banned the monetization of state debt by setting up a market mechanism for auctioning government securities (Gabor 2010a). It also banned neodevelopmentalist scenarios by requesting that disinflation trump the industrial recovery stimulus, an objective to be reached by transferring the funding needs of high-employment SOEs from the central bank's lending portfolios to the government's fiscal policy. Based on the same characterization of the disinflation-industrial recovery trade-off, the Fund gave the central bank what it had long been clamoring for: a managed exchange rate policy. Finally, the BNR's theories about "strain" and bank-insider loops (detailed in chapter 3) were fleshed out into hard targets for the number of systemically unviable SOEs to be closed down and the number of state-owned banks to be privatized. World Bank lending and technical assistance lubricated the more detailed aspects of structural reforms (privatization, liberalization) while also pushing the government to adopt measures meant to embed the neoliberal project such as the strengthening of state capacity, reducing urban-rural as well as ethnic divides in the provision of safety nets or the establishment of compulsory health insurance funded through payroll taxes (World Bank 2005, 18–22).

Due to a combination of the IMF's own doctrinal changes, labor strife, and the pre-election neoliberal populism and poor institutional cohesion mapped out in chapter 3, the agreement was not fully observed (IMF 2000). Nevertheless, despite some of the most violent episodes of labor contention, ranging from "occupied" factories to epic and violent marches on Bucharest by the miners' union, this agreement (and its 2001 successor) has been extremely effective in engineering nothing less than a Great Transformation of the Romanian political economy. By 2000 Romania was on its way to becoming an economy dominated by the private sector, whose current account deficit was financed through volatile capital inflows and firesales of valuable state owned firms and whose policy regime stressed export competitiveness through internal deflation at the expense of domestic demand and in the absence of industrial policy (Pop 2006; 2007; Ban 2011; 2013a).

Institutionally, the central bank became the main pillar of the policy process, its disinflation strategy through exchange rate appreciations that fueled current account deficits taking precedence over more accommodative solutions. To prevent exchange rate volatility when hot inflows threated to reverse, BNR restricted banks' access to the domestic liquidity. The defense, also used by East Asian countries throughout the 1997 crisis, and sanctioned by the IMF in that context, sought to raise the costs for speculators by making it more expensive to borrow domestic currency.

In 1998, the collapse of two state-owned banks, once a critical component of the neodevelopmentalist project, was used as evidence that the state cannot be a banker (World Bank 2005; Cernat 2006). It also boosted the case for the privatization of all public banks, with the state's development bank being quickly sold off to Société Générale. In this environment, the high interest rates used to curb inflation further increased uncertainty in the financial sector (then still dominated by public banks), incentivizing them to extend credits with short-term maturities to firms, effectively sending adrift a large part of the state-owned industrial sector and some of the SME sector as well.

In 1998 the costs of financial restructuring put pressure on government balance sheets and attracted further speculation, and the Asian crisis made access to international sovereign bond markets all but impossible. In these conditions, the IMF conditioned disbursement of the next tranches of the loan on the Treasury's issuance of T-bills on the private market through its short-lived "burden sharing" doctrine (Pop 2006). As the new government gave BNR more independence, the central bank put into practice its theory that monetizing government debt should not be attempted. With 120 percent rates for three-month bonds, the government had to tighten its belt further while simultaneously covering its foreign exchange needs through more fire sales. Such feedback loops locked in drastic austerity, extensive deindustrialization, and privatization, while also depriving the state of public banks that could be deployed as part of industrial policy strategies in the future (Gabor 2010a). Prime Minister Radu Vasile's memoirs noted that everything that BNR did throughout this period expressed its complete support for the IMF's policy line (Vasile 2002).

The twin conditionality deployed by the Bretton Woods and EU institutions proved critical in speeding the transformation process. Once Romania was invited to begin the EU accession negotiations in 2000 and successful completion of agreements with the IMF was effectively a condition of membership, the EC pushed IMF leverage to its highest levels, and, as a result, for the first time since 1990 the Romanian government completed an IMF agreement in 2004 (Papadimitriou and Phinnemore 2008).

This deep transformation of the domestic policy regime was further consolidated by local consensus that EU membership was a strategic and popular objective (Snagov Declaration 1995; Pop 2006). As chapter 3 showed, for neodevelopmentalists, European integration was understood as an opportunity to moderate the dislocations produced by the market via social legislation, development funds, and opportunities for labor solidarity.[9] However, for neoliberals, one of the functions of the "return to Europe" narrative was to conflate Europeanization with more neoliberalism.

Dorothee Bohle (2006, 57) observed that, during the early 2000s, the EU "exported a more 'market-radical' variant of neoliberalism to its new member states," an outcome this author attributed to the intent to keep pressure on embedded neoliberalism in Western Europe. A close reading of the European Commission's regular reports on Romania's accession between 1997 and 2006 confirms this insight.[10] Basically in its yearly accession reports the European Commission backed all IMF and World Bank programs to the point that the Commission's accession reports dealing with macroeconomic and structural reforms are little more than mirror images of the IMF's Article IV consultations and loan programs with Romania.[11] Neoliberal ideas contested within the EU-15, such as the thesis that privatizing utility companies and state-owned banks delivers better public goods than the state, became metrics for assessing whether Romania could formally be considered a "functioning market economy." Finally, in 2004, the EC joined the IMF and the World Bank in issuing a strong critique of the new Romanian labor code, which itself had been designed by Romanian experts and corporatist institutions keen to see EU accession as leverage to transplanting ideas from French and Italian labor codes.[12]

Critically, the radicalization of local neoliberalism in the 2000s beyond the limits stipulated in the Commission's reports did not receive a riposte from the EU, the supposed guardian of embedded neoliberalism. While rigorous and fast in its condemnation of privatization delays or flagging fiscal policy discipline, EC reports (and for that matter, any EU sources) remained silent when Romania changed its taxation paradigm in 2005 and adopted a flat tax. This was a controversial libertarian policy idea with little resonance in the EU-15 or in the Bretton Woods institutions and mainstream economics for that matter. The same was true of the idea that pension would become more sustainable if the government mandated that a part of pension contributions should go to private pension funds. [13]

Moreover, while some EU heads of state and Commission economists were irked by the flat tax "revolution" in Eastern Europe, prominent ECB economists cheered the reforms. In 2004, Tommaso Padoa-Schioppa, a member of the ECB executive board, stated that if such competitive tax pressures coming from Eastern Europe "were to put pressure for tax reform in the euro area, as the lower tax rates in Ireland have already done, this could only be for our benefit. Arguments about unfair tax competition should not be used as a smokescreen to distract attention from what every citizen in the euro area knows: that tax regimes need to change, and fiscal pressure has to fall" (cited in Vliegenthart and Overbeek 2009, 156).

These findings highlight not only the importance of joint (EU and IMF) conditionality as a critical coercive mechanism for the dissemination of neoliberalism, but also the experimental character of East European transitions from the standpoint of the EU. They bolster the argument that, contrary to conventional wisdom, the net effect of EU-level coordination on taxation has been to accelerate tax competition, with EU enlargement acting as one of the causes of this phenomenon (Genschel et al. 2011).

Finally, EU accession-related transnational political processes facilitated the removal of neodevelopmentalism as a domestic project by shifting the political identity of the main ex-communist party (formerly the National Salvation Front [FSN], the Democratic Front of National Salvation [FDSN], and the Party of Social Democracy in Romania [PDSR]). As chapter 3 showed, during most of the 1990s, the party had been quick to shed its economists who had moved too close toward mainstream neoliberal views of transition economics. As in Spain, geopolitical shifts that put Romania on the list of countries eligible for EU accession have made even ex-communists join the neoliberal chorus. The critical event in this regard is that the Kosovo war convinced West European elites that Romania had the potential to go from a country at risk of falling prey to ethnic violence to a pole of Atlanticist stability in the region (Phinnemore 2010; Papadimitriou and Phinnemore 2008).

EU accession conditionalities and bilateral quid pro quos (such as selling premium state-owned firms to investors from countries that supported Romania's accession) proved to be critical in the systemic transformation of the Romanian economy after 2000. Indeed, the promise of membership was too tempting even for the party's old guard.[14] Although Ion Iliescu was reelected in 2000 and his economic ideas were far from being a translation of neoliberalism, he and his numerous supporters in the party were strong supporters of EU integration and were ready to pay the ideological price in part because they thought that "the aggressive self-sufficiency of the market radicalism we have seen after '96 will find it hard to survive inside the EU because the EU also means Social Europe, not just Market Europe."[15]

But as Adrian Severin, one of the architects of the party's transformation, told this author in 2006, "In 2000 EU accession put a high price tag on the party's traditional statism represented by Ion Iliescu; being for Europe meant being against the economic philosophies that dominated the party in the early and mid-1990s." The effect was signaling credibility via personnel changes. As Severin put it, "Integration also meant promoting economists closely connected with Western institutions in economic ministries alongside a wholesale restructuring of the party's ideology."[16] It is for this reason that leadership of the Ministry of Finance was given to a technocrat trained by the Bretton Woods institutions rather than to the respected but openly Keynesian economist Florin Georgescu, the economic éminence grise of the party. To inspire confidence that the economic policy of the PSD was no longer captive to unorthodox economists, the new party executive invited Adrian Severin, the most economically liberal minister in the 1990–1991 Roman government and the scourge of heterodox economists, to join the program-rewriting effort.

But these incentives do not explain why the new party elite centered around Prime Minister Adrian Năstase has been so consistent in advocating a shift to neoliberalism inside Romania's economic Left even after they left government in 2004 (or, indeed, after they were removed from politics by anticorruption campaigns ten years later) (Năstase 2007). The former head of the European Commission who negotiated Romania's membership told this author, "We had the feeling that the Năstase cabinet was both competent and convinced of the thinking behind the economic conditions of membership. . . . We did not have to convince them; it was like preaching to the converted on economic issues."[17] In public, at least, Năstase and his team impressed their harshest critics on the neoliberal right with their unwavering commitment to Europe's ruling ideas, and in 2003 they went as far as advocating a flat-tax system, a proposal shut down through Florin Georgescu's extraordinary intervention and President Iliescu's angry rebuttal.[18]

As in the case of PSOE almost three decades earlier, the PDSR's international recognition and embrace of 1990s European social democracy stemmed from the EU enlargement incentives that ushered in the influence of West European center-left parties. As a result of these transformations, in 2003 the (now rebaptized) PSD was allowed to join the Socialist International, and, during the early 1990s, Năstase also became a regular at the Progressive Governance conferences of Third Way party leaders such as Tony Blair, Peter Mendelson, Dominique Strauss-Kahn, and Gerhard Schroeder.[19] The era of the class politics of "old" social democracy was definitively buried, and the ideas proposed by the intellectual entrepreneurs of this transnational party network were being sold to enthusiastic East European converts "tired of being treated as poorly reformed communists."[20] Critically, unlike in Spain, this transformation took place at a time when German social-democrats were experiencing their own Blairite moment (Brettschneider 2008) and did not face a battle for the soul of European social-democracy, as they did in the 1970s (Paterson and Sloam 2006). As a result, during the early 2000s there was less of a concerted effort to socialize their Romanian peers in the virtues of the social-democratic reading of the German ordoliberal policy consensus. Simply out, this time around West European social democracy did not oppose neoliberalism in a peripheral country with competing economic ideas.

To sum up, cooperation between Washington and Brussels generally had the effect of locking in a neoliberal policy regime in Romania so that, by the early 2000s, even the ex-communists folded and "social Europe" could go only as far as the Third Way. As the next sections illustrate, this deep transformation was not just a story of coercion. Staffing the political, administrative, and policy apparatuses of postcommunist states with sympathetic and skilled interlocutors was a task that lent itself to socialization. But, unlike in Spain, Romania's historical conditions required that this socialization be fast and targeted at both professional economists and enthusiastic amateurs alike. As chapter 3 showed, the result was that sometimes the students of neoliberal theories outbid the teachers. Both the EU and the World Bank conditionality introduced not only neoliberalism, but also non-neoliberal ideas closer to social-democracy into the policy sphere. They included the ideas behind a tax-financed universal health care system, a progressive income tax system, adequate child protection or anti-poverty and anti-discrimination programs and so on. Certainly, the policy relevance of these ideas was constrained by the neoliberal macroeconomic regime that Washington and Brussels promoted, but during the 2000s all these nuances in the imported neoliberal script would be lost in the evolving translation of neoliberalism in Romania.

Neoliberalism by Force of Thought
The Power of International Status Hierarchies

One of the striking patterns in this author's interviews with policy intellectuals in Bucharest was their reference to "serious Western economists" and the near-complete lack awareness of the existence of Western heterodox perspectives on the East European economic transition (see also Pop 2006). The reason, it turned out, had to do with the high status enjoyed by neoliberal economists, which, in turn, was a function of their access to professional and material resources.

The international advocates of neoliberalism benefited not only from the support of Western resources and a better ideological fit with the new political and civil elites of Eastern Europe. In addition to these considerable advantages, they could also leverage overwhelming professional resources to weaken their adversaries. Neoliberals occupied pivotal positions in government, worked as advisers to heads of government, and sat on the boards of flagship economics journals. Others were senior staff in IFIs, were recognized as international academics, established schools of economics with international pedigree in Eastern Europe, and circulated through the revolving door between all these institutional settings.

The high salience of neoliberal economists in debates over the East European transition was often asserted but never demonstrated empirically on a systematic basis. A combination of network and content analysis can address this gap. The network can be read using the following rule of thumb: the thicker and shorter are the linkages, the higher the number of economists associated with a school of thought. The comparison brings to the fore several dimensions of the superior resources of the neoliberal (or orthodox) camp. First off, figure 7.1 shows that the orthodox were more closely tied to economists with PhDs obtained in top economics departments like Harvard, MIT, Minnesota, or Chicago than the revisionists were. In contrast, while top departments like the LSE and Yale appear in the revisionist network, their contribution is comparatively a lot weaker. Given the status position awarded by one's PhD in the hierarchies of the profession (Fourcade 2006; 2009), this asymmetry helped tilt the playing field in favor of the orthodox.

The difference is even more striking if we go beyond one's graduate school experience and look at the actual professional experiences of the orthodox and the revisionists during the late 1980s and early 1990s, the critical juncture of transition. As figure 7.1 shows, the neoliberals' institutional bases cluster strongly around the top of the academic hierarchy: Harvard, MIT, Chicago. Their appointments also include the IMF and the World Bank as well as "real world" posts such as consultancies or policymaking positions in Eastern Europe and Latin America, with Russia and Poland looming large in the distribution. Contrary to conventional wisdom, EU institutions and the US government are rather insignificant providers of professional affiliations for the intellectuals of neoliberal transition economics. Other usual suspects such as central banks, private financial institutions, and global players in the consulting market are also peripheral. In short, the core of the neoliberal network was a US-based epistemic community situated at the apex of academia and institutional financial institutions.

In contrast to this neoliberal network, the revisionist one is almost purely academic and less connected in the top economic departments (see figure 7.2). While it may include Harvard and MIT, they are a lot less important than the University of Washington, University of Maryland, Columbia, and Stanford. Unlike the neoliberal network, here continental European universities and heterodox US schools like the University of Massachusetts at Amherst play an important, albeit not central, role. The World Bank looms large, but this is a consequence of hosting such prominent critics of neoclassical transition economics as Joseph Stiglitz, David Ellerman, and Branko Milanović. The "great absentees" in this network are the IMF and advisory positions for national governments, which meant that the revisionists were not invited to advise the governments of postcommunist countries (see figure 7.3).

In sum, the revisionist network was a US-based epistemic community situated largely on the middle and lower rungs of the academic profession, with

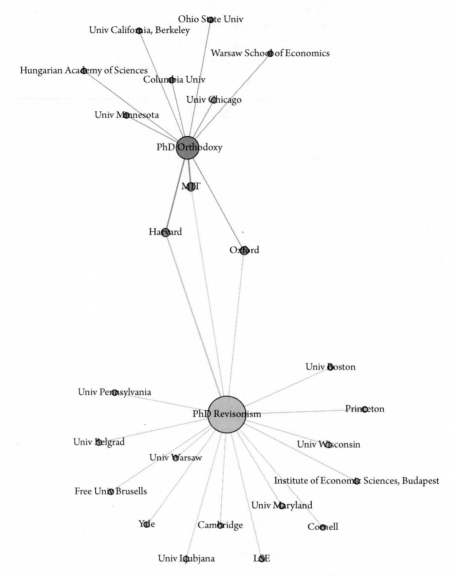

Figure 7.1 PhD-granting institutions of economists involved in the economic transition debate. *Source*: LinkedIn and institutional bios.

a weak membership in international financial institutions, whose members seemed to have been excluded from the government consulting opportunities opened up by the end of the Cold War. While neoliberals spoke from the centers of political and academic power, the revisionists could make their view known only in academic debates or in the dissident but politically weak milieus of the World Bank.

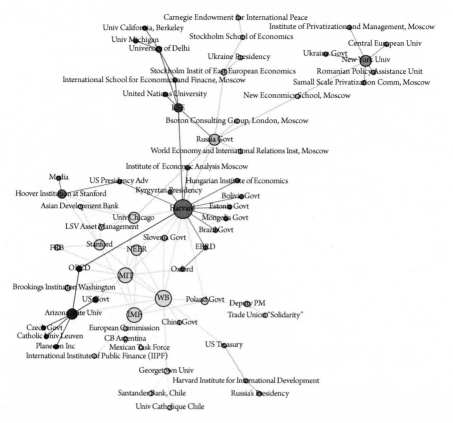

Figure 7.2 Institutional affiliations of the proponents of neoliberal transition economics.
Source: LinkedIn and institutional bios.

The Chicago Boys Did Not Go to Bucharest

A critical mass of economists whose status and professional market value hinges on being conversant in the ideas, models, and skills that constitute international mainstream economics does not arise naturally in countries with erratic exposure to neoliberalism. Only external sponsorship can facilitate this process, as was the case in Spain, where central bankers and economic ministers received substantial graduate school experience in the United States and the UK. Some had these experiences in the 1960s, at the height of postwar Keynesianism, while others had them during the 1970s, when the monetarists and New Classicalists challenged the establishment. Chapter 2 showed that these gradual and intense socialization experiences, which took place before neoliberalism became the only game in town, helped to facilitate the emergence of an embedded neoliberal policy regime in Spain.

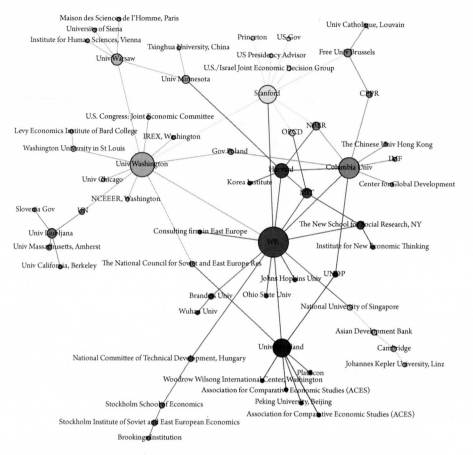

Figure 7.3 Institutional affiliations of the proponents of revisionist transition economics.
Source: LinkedIn and institutional bios.

The opposite was the case in Romania, where central bankers and other top policy makers experienced fast-track socialization during Fukuyama's "end of history" moment, when mainstream economic thinking about the postcommunist economic transition had purged many of the compromises forged between neoliberal and Keynesian thinking:

> During the Cold War, the economics profession was growing more exclusive, but was not completely intransigently intolerant of rival doctrines, for reasons of ideological appearances. For instance, evidence from the Paul Samuelson archives suggests he really did nominate Joan Robinson for the Bank of Sweden economics "Nobel." Things really ratcheted upward in terms of imposed conformity only after the Fall of the Wall, for equally obvious political reasons. (Mirowski 2013, 22)

Even so, since fast-track socialization did not take place on a substantial scale until the late 1990s, the heavy lifting of translation during the critical moment of neoliberal transition (1996–2006) was left to domestically trained economists and political appointees whose lack of economic sophistication in the technical aspects of neoliberal economics was matched by their self-confident espousal of neoliberal folk theories.

Once the threat of communism abated in 1991, European and American donors ceased to focus on funding advanced degrees at American and European universities, a typical investment in professional socialization during the postwar decades. Instead, they deployed much less systematic forms of professional (re)socialization, such as short-term training programs in international financial institutions, academic exchange programs, and IFI-subsidized local replicas of US-style graduate programs. Romania's economic policy elite was therefore trained in such programs, and, even as late as 2012, the country's central bank did not have a single economist with a Western PhD.[21] The only local policy economists who had substantial overseas experience (a one-year postdoc at Harvard) were two central bankers, and (as chapter 3 showed) they were not among the radicalizers of neoliberalism.

Some of the most important conduits for professional (re)socialization was the training programs of the IMF and employment in the Bretton Woods institutions. Of these, the longest ones were in the form of employment. Thus, in 1993, central bank chief economist Daniel Dăianu became a visiting fellow at the IMF, and, years later, the future adviser of the central bank governor (Lucian Croitoru) followed into his footsteps. Similarly, the chief technocrat of the country's most powerful political party between 2000 and 2004 (Mihai Tănăsescu) cut his teeth on transition economics at the Joint Vienna Institute before he spending several years in Washington as a member of the IMF and World Bank staff. Finally, Theodor Stolojan, an old hand within the technocratic center-right governments of the 2000s and often considered the first "reformist" prime minister of Romania between 1991 and 1992, trained at the IMF Institute during the communist era before joining the World Bank staff in 1992. In short, some of the key minds behind Romanian neoliberal reforms from 1996 onward had been IMF or World Bank employees.

While stints in Washington lasted for at least a year and benefited a handful of technocrats, the critical mass of transnationalized economists trained by the IMF was achieved via fast-track socialization. Of special relevance in this regard was the establishment of a joint initiative between the IMF, World Bank, OECD, Bank for International Settlements, European Bank for Reconstruction and Development, and the Austrian government: the Joint Vienna Institute (JVI). With its formation, the JVI became an extension of the IMF's main training program for postcommunist countries. As part of an organized effort of reconstruction in 1992, the JVI's main mandate was revised to prioritize the training of midlevel technocrats from postcommunist central banks and ministries of finance. Together with the IMF Institute in Washington, DC (the Fund's main training institution), the JVI taught applied economic policy courses to 3,795 technocrats from east-central Europe and the former Soviet Union (Broome 2010; Broome and Seabrooke 2015).

The JVI aimed to build "new skills, new knowledge and new habits of mind."[22] According to Andre Broome, its common cognitive framework had three foci: "(1) how market economies ought to work; (2) what are the appropriate instruments and goals of economic policy; and (3) where the line should be drawn with respect to the limits of state intervention in the economy" (Broome 2010, 611). At first, this meant teaching basic concepts and calculative devices about capitalism (such as the role of money in a market economy, treasury management, balance of payments, and bankruptcy statistics), or the fundamentals of the classic IMF macroeconomic stabilization package (the identification of imbalances, the quantification of proposals for coordinated financial programming, and the monitoring of adjustment programs).[23]

Over time, however, the range of classes was expanded to cover the full spectrum of neoliberal theories, including areas as diverse as financial supervision, taxation, labor market reforms, and human resource management in central banks. Already by 1995, the JVI was teaching "second-generation reforms" that simultaneously targeted the deepening of neoliberal policy programs and improving the institutional capacity of governments.[24] It also taught technically more advanced classes focused on the diffusion of advanced macroeconomic models used by the IMF and Western central banks.[25] Moreover, during the 2000s, the educational effects of the JVI were further buttressed by the incorporation of Romanian central bankers into transnational central bank networks centered around the Fed and the Bundesbank.[26] As figure 7.4 shows, Romania's technocracy benefited extensively from this opportunity, especially from the mid-1990s onward.

In the view of senior staff in the BNR and the ministry interviewed by this author in 2014, JVI graduates who had become regular JVI attendees became a high-prestige group, and they constituted the technocratic backbone of the modernized Romanian policy process.[27] They also indicated that since the students were in low- to mid-ranking positions in their institutions, this systematic effort to create a new technocratic elite did not have a noticeable impact until the late 1990s and benefited the Romanian central bank more than it benefited the economic ministries. Indeed, it was only in the mid-2000s that a JVI-trained economist took a senior position in the Ministry of Finance.[28]

Moreover, even when they did have a measurable impact, JVI graduates did not always play off the IMF script. In 2003, JVI graduates in junior and midlevel

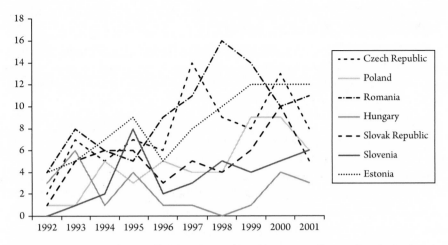

Figure 7.4 Number of central bank and Ministry of Finance staff trained at the IMF Institute and the Joint Vienna Institute. *Source*: IMF Institute; Joint Vienna Institute.

positions in this ministry proved to be the sympathetic interlocutors of radical neoliberals in the world of think tanks, international accounting firms, and organized multinational interest who advocated a flat tax on personal and corporate income against the IMF's cautionary remarks.[29]

A focus group organized by this author with Ministry of Finance staff who had experienced JVI from the 1990s onward revealed that JVI training was primarily a channel of diffusion of technical skills and knowledge. After returning home, the graduates used JVI models doing macro forecasting and fiscal risk evaluations. While some of these models were simply replicated, others were recalibrated to fit domestic priorities, data, and economic conditions. Nevertheless, none of the fourteen staff interviewed showed interest or satisfactory knowledge of macroeconomic policy controversies taking place in international economics and had a very instrumental view of their JVI education. When asked to state their views on internationally controversial issues like the flat tax or pension privatization, they were generally favorable to them and used journalistic and "common sense" arguments rather than professional ones.

Chicago on a Budget

Western PhDs and other forms of graduate training in economics were the hallmarks of the Spanish policy elite. This has not been the case in Romania, where institutional inertia and uncompetitive wages hampered an intense transnationalization scenario via the academic channel. Even as late as the 2000s, Western PhDs were formally recognized only after some considerable bureaucratic hassle, and the organizational culture of many policy institutions did not always attribute high status to Western training.[30]

Moreover, reforming domestic economics departments to quickly churn out sympathetic interlocutors was a difficult task. Institutional inertia and legal considerations made the existing faculty hard to dislodge,[31] and, as one Western researcher noted, apart from "a few highly motivated individuals who sought out and taught themselves substantial parts of Western economics," Western academics that arrived in the region soon after 1990 realized "that there was a virtual absence of any exposure to the neoclassical theories and empirical methods standard at that time in the West" (Earle 2007, 278). In these conditions, US and European government funding as well as philanthropic funds enabled willing Romanian economists to study, do research, or lecture in Western economics departments. For a generation of economists whose basic freedoms of movement and speech had been limited by decades of national Stalinism, training and working in international economic institutions and Western universities were exciting prospects, indeed.

As the central bank's competitive pay policy attracted some of the best-trained and internationally minded economists in the country, it was BNR that benefited the most from the more substantial disbursements. While neodevelopmentalist economists lingered in local universities and institutes,[32] a few leading central bank economists like Daniel Dăianu and Cristian Popa benefited from yearlong Fulbright fellowships at Harvard in 1990–1991 and 1994–1995, respectively. Both were visiting scholars at the University of Michigan, and occasionally gave lectures on transition economics at the LSE and US Ivy League economics departments. Similarly, a few economists from the econometrics-heavy Institute for Economic Forecasting, a branch of Academia Română, also benefited from similar, albeit shorter opportunities of this kind. As shown in chapter 3, some of them (e.g., Lucian Albu) coauthored with central bankers some of the most important research that embedded neoliberal theories in the domestic context.

In contrast to central bankers, staff at low-paying, lower-status economic ministries had neither the English skills nor the training to benefit from such substantial professional socialization experiences. Indeed, among the economic ministers of the "shock therapy" governments (1996–2000), only three were economists (Daniel Dăianu, Mircea Ciumara, and Ilie Șerbănescu), and of these only Dăianu had a serious international professional portfolio. In fact, one of the most resolute neoliberal ministers of finance had been a mere provincial-level accountant (Decebal Traian Remeș), while one of the reform ministers had been an engineer trained in East Germany and China (Ulm Spineanu).

Moreover, it was only toward the end of the 1990s that the EU and the World Bank spent hundreds of thousands of euros restructuring economics education in public universities. This endeavor was supported by the United States, whose

Fulbright fellowships were specifically intended to fund one-year teaching stints in Eastern Europe for American and Western European academics. Even with this, the results have been uneven at best.[33] Interviews conducted by this author in 2006 and 2009 revealed that institutional inertia in top economics departments lasted well into the late 2000s, so that the intellectual landscape of the faculty covered a broad spectrum, from neo-Keynesian to Austrian school orientation. Nevertheless, it was only the Austrians and the orthodox BNR faculty that enjoyed high prestige and had a consistent following, with attractive BNR employment representing an important incentive.

Given this institutional inertia, delayed funding, and the fact that none of the Romanian economists who did PhDs in Western universities seemed tempted to return home, the establishment of new Western-style graduate programs that would bypass existing institutions became critical to the dissemination process. But, again, it was the fast-track mode that dominated this form of professional socialization, and the main beneficiary was the central bank.

Specifically, during the 1990s USAID, the Mellon Foundation, and George Soros's Open Society Institute funded the establishment of a US-grade PhD program in Prague (CERGE) with a faculty populated by Western academics. In addition, the Open Society Institute established an MA-level program attended by many Romanian students at Budapest's Central European University. The same organization also paid for the fellowships of hundreds of graduate students from the former Eastern bloc. Over time, Western-funded business schools teaching mainstream economics began to spring up throughout the region, sometimes as subsidiaries of Western institutions (e.g., the Stockholm School of Economics in Riga). By the mid-1990s, transnational MA programs began to better address this supply problem. The mainstream-heavy economics MA program at Budapest's Central European University (CEU) became a supplier of new staff for BNR and particularly for its Research Service.[34] But more than any other international program, it was a local elite MA in economics that had the greatest impact.

It was a tuition-free graduate program jointly funded by the EU and the World Bank and entitled the Doctoral School of Finance and Banking (or DOFIN), whose academic mandarin and founder was Moisa Altar, the same person whom chapter 5 identified as having fostered interest in Western orthodox economics during communism. Now, he single-handedly worked to make DOFIN one of the four centers of excellence in economics of the European Union.[35] Known as the most "Westernized" of the ASE faculty, Altar set up DOFIN as a surrogate Western graduate program and demanded high standards from the very beginning.[36]

Altar turned DOFIN into a premium program whose graduates would become the country's economic policy elite in the 2000s. Dissertation committees had to be chaired by economists from leading Western European and American economics departments, with local academics playing a very marginal role over-all.[37] Additionally, the program offered course modules taught by faculty from such cradles of orthodox economic thinking as the Sorbonne (Paris), European University Institute (Italy), Universidad Autónoma de Barcelona (Spain), Erasmus University (Holland), Reading (UK), Chicago, and Rutgers (United States). The coursework covered the whole spectrum of advanced finance degrees, from theory, international financial economics, and monetary policy institutions to derivatives, value-at-risk models, and capital asset pricing. The level of the students' work was unusually high, even by international standards. Carol Alexander, a professor of risk management at one of DOFIN's partner universities (University of Reading), declared:

> The DOFIN MSc students rank amongst the best in the world. In my opinion the general level of DOFIN students is actually better than most of the large and famous American and European business schools. Two of my most talented PhD students came from DOFIN and I am hoping to take more in the future.[38]

For the second time in fifty tears, Altar's intellectual and organizational entrepreneurship was de facto bringing Western graduate education home to Romania. Economists who had assumed key positions in the central bank, the government, and the country's top private banks went through DOFIN.[39]

In short, it took almost a decade to build a critical mass of internationally trained economists for Romania's main policy institutions, with the central bank getting the lion's share of this transfer of resources. The main consequence of this asymmetry was that the central bank became the obligatory passage point for the IMF and for the executive. Indeed, by the mid to late 1990s senior economists who had benefited the most from international professional networking before 1989 (Mugur Isărescu, Napoleon Pop, Constantin Kirițescu) and the younger central bankers who studied abroad after 1990 (Daniel Dăianu, Cristian Popa, Lucian Croitoru) had a virtual monopoly over the kind of knowledge that the IFIs needed and that constituted the bedrock of applied neoliberal theories. In effect, they constituted a reserve of cadre for governments, as demonstrated by the appointment of Daniel Dăianu as minister of finance in the shock therapy government and of Mugur Isărescu as the last premier of the same government.

Indeed, the advocacy for relatively technical versions of neoliberal theories in Romania during the transition to neoliberalism came either via IFI staff or through the central bank's elite corps or their networks in academia and elite research institutes. That said, it is important to point out that, as in Spain, economists with substantial academic experiences in Western Europe were not the main contributors to the radicalization of neoliberal ideas in Romania, especially after Romania's economic transition was completed and economic problems could no longer be blamed on the socialist legacy. US-trained Florin Georgescu was the fiscal architect of neodevelopmentalism, and he used his skills to block the adoption of the flat tax by the center-left government in 2004. Daniel Dăianu's critiques of neoliberal radicalism that began during his term in office as minister of Finance[40] increased in intensity during the mid to late 2000s. As chapter 9 shows, a top macroeconomist trained in Sweden whose skills landed him a job at one of the research centers of the European Commission became the country's most outspoken Keynesian. As opposed to fast-track socialization with international networks, intense professional socialization facilitated a more moderated perspective on neoliberal ideas.

However, the next sections show that, unlike in Spain, neoliberal theories had not only a purportedly apolitical, technical form, but also an openly political, indeed "folk" one, and it was the latter that contributed the most to the growing radicalization of neoliberalism during the 2000s. Indeed, in addition to the difficulty of having enough neoliberal economists with technical skills, advocacy for neoliberal ideas also suffered from a short supply of smart policy entrepreneurs, secondhand dealers, and popularizers. This supply problem, however, would eventually find a potent solution: the think tank.

From Civil Society to Capital

Democratization, Civil Society, and the Localization of Neoliberal Thinking

During the early 1990s, the promotion of democracy and neoliberalism often went hand in hand. This "Great Conflation" of political liberalism and radicalized economic liberalism resonated with local antistate sentiment after the end of communism as well as with the agenda of multinational vested interests. This proved to be a boon for entrepreneurial (and often deeply convinced) civic activists for whom shrinking the state was a democratic objective, indeed a guarantee that the return to authoritarian socialism would become impossible for economic reasons. As a US-based scholar and consultant advocating neoliberalism in Eastern European capitals put it at the time, "The transition process is dependent on how well developed civil society is, because the better developed it is, the sooner other, more representative forces will defeat the state managers" (Aslund 1992, 63).

Rather than leave the development of these pro-neoliberal civil society actors to the market, Western governments and private foundations bankrolled fellowships and graduate programs in hopes of cultivating an alternative cache of elites prepared to take on, or even replace, the state managers. Although primarily aimed at creating a strong domestic elite of democracy advocates, this transnational socialization endeavor was also successful in converting the widespread but economically vague anticommunism of the local intelligentsia into a support base for neoliberal ideas.

In its early stages, this strategy had two unanticipated consequences. First, the (real or imagined) dissidents who benefited from these opportunities to train abroad experienced West European or North American realities through the filter of the elitist and frequently antiprogressive readings that fed communist-era "resistance through high culture" strategies (Tănăsoiu 2008). As a discourse analysis of some of the canonical texts produced by these intellectuals shows, there was a great deal of rhetoric "against feminism, 'political correctness,' multiculturalist and affirmative policies as manifestations of 'American communism,' or of a new type of 'Leninist-Nazi racism.' . . . There was an allegiance to economic neoliberalism with a conservative defense of tradition, particularly Christianity and the tradition of Western 'high,' canonical culture, as well as with a political conservatism" (Preoteasa 2002, 275).

Through such filters, "big government," the welfare state, unions, and labor parties themselves were often portrayed as forms of "socialism," domesticated projections of dangerous forms of collectivism held at bay by mass consumption. By the mid-1990s, for the reformist intelligentsia based around the Group for Social Dialogue (GDS) the endpoint of transition was not some generic form of "Western market economy," but instead a market society liberated from popular demands for redistribution and subject to the enlightened guidance of "civic intellectuals." Even the standard welfare institutions of Western social democracy were viewed as political pathologies whose implementation in Eastern Europe would hamper the desired "decommunization" of economy and society. Indeed, by the mid-1990s it was this radical "folk" neoliberalism that gradually became the dominant strain within civil society and the emerging elite of the center-right parties (the National Liberals and Farmers' Party) that formed the core of the Democratic Convention government in 1996.

The other challenge for the promoters of neoliberalism was that while there was no shortage of generically promarket civil society actors in early 1990s Romania, these actors showed little appetite for getting specific about the policy implications or the empirical grounding of their claims. Indeed, for these elites, support for the market economy was not about adhering to a concrete set of economic theories or policy programs. Rather, it was simply one of the side effects of their ideological positioning against the detested "neocommunist" government and their aspiration to morally cleanse the state after decades of authoritarianism (Pop 1998). But by the mid-1990s, this gap was filled by the emergence of local economic policy think tanks staffed by those from the best and the brightest of the emerging transnationalized elite that was able to start an educated conversation about economic reforms.

Rather than be a part of a coherent strategy for elite reconstitution, the think tank was an unintended outcome of funding shortages. Following the formal consolidation of democracy in Romania after the victory of the opposition in the 1996 elections, the prodemocracy NGOs faced funding shortfalls and were forced to diversify their expertise portfolios. During the early 1990s, many within the Western security establishment had feared a post-Yugoslav-style civil war in Romania. Reflecting these concerns, John Mearsheimer wrote in *Atlantic Monthly* in 1990 that "absent the Soviet occupation of Eastern Europe, Romania and Hungary might have gone to war over this [ethnic] issue by now, and it might bring them to war in the future" (Mearsheimer 1990).

Against this backdrop, human rights, judicial reform, civic education, and political party institutionalization were agenda issues that garnered funding for civil society organizations. In so doing, these organizations became obligatory conduits between Western interests and the transformation of the domestic political scene. Once the wars in Bosnia and Croatia died down and the liberal coalition seized power in 1996, Romania became a less compelling case for Western donors. Immediately after 1996, this bête noire of transitology (Linz and Stepan 1996) was now regarded as a consolidated democracy (Spendzharova and Vachudova 2012), and Western funding started flowing instead to public policy advocacy. In 1996, the well-respected democratization scholar Thomas Carothers was dispatched to Romania by the Carnegie Endowment. He noted that American funding

> has been concentrated on what I will call civic society organizations— small nonprofit NGOs seeking to affect governmental policy. Up to 1995, US civil society assistance concentrated on the more political types of such NGOs. . . . With the recent establishment of the Democracy Network program, socio-economic NGOs now also fall within the US civil society assistance effort, provided they are policy-oriented NGOs. . . . These local NGOs no longer have only politics-related themes such as human rights and civic education as their main area of work; they now sometimes focus on more economic-related concerns. . . . In short, assistance programs involving NGOs increasingly relate explicitly to both democracy promotion and economic reform. (Carothers 1996, 65, 107)

In the new context, there was also continued investment in institutional development and, increasingly, in willing antigraft activists (Sampson 2005). Yet the game changer was the increasing demand for local expertise about the quality of domestic institutions. The demand came from IFI and state experts in the EU who were frustrated with the half-successful reforms adopted in the region at a time when institutionalist arguments were ascendant in transition economics (Roland 2000). Into this gap, the prodemocracy NGOs of the early 1990s stepped in as public policy think tanks, just as their favored political parties were building the post-1996 conservative government.

Scholarship has showed that the main function of neoliberal think tanks was the interpretation and legitimation of neoliberal measures adopted through IFI conditionality (Stone 2003, 54). Often, their nongovernmental status lent them the image of nonpartiality, allowing them to serve as a "transmission belt into civil society"—into schools and into public consciousness (Stone 2001, 347). In this way, the depoliticization of economic policy could be framed as a reaction to democratic demand from civil society.[41]

"Russian Doll" Neoliberalism

"The Russian doll structure of the Neoliberal Thought Collective," wrote Mirowski, "would tend to amplify and distribute the voice of any one member throughout a series of seemingly different organizations, personas, and broadcast settings, lending it resonance and gravitas, not to mention fronting an echo chamber for ideas right at the time when hearing them was most propitious" (2013, 49). Romania's transnationalized think tanks plugged into political parties, the corporate world, academia, and elite civil society illustrate this point.

Staffed by professional economists who used the revolving doors between academia and the central bank, some think tanks translated technical neoliberal theories and models into domestic professional language and research. On balance, these actors were the carriers of the relatively moderate version of technocratic neoliberalism. The second function was the translation of what cab be termed "folk neoliberalism." As opposed to technocratic neoliberalism, this is an ideational constriction that dwells less on the econometric modeling and universal technical languages specific to mainstream economics and more on descriptive, media-friendly and conventional public policy approaches. Folk neoliberalism was performed first by "dual use" NGOs (half democracy and good governance promoters, half economic think tanks) and later on by specialized business think tanks. Staffed mostly by amateur economists and a diverse array of intellectuals, the portfolios of these organizations boast some of the most radical and successful neoliberal innovations (flat taxes, pension privatization) alongside more conventional neoliberal ideas. Finally, the third function was to socialize and familiarize an emerging generation of journalists, activists, and academics with the theoretical fundamentals of economic theories that challenged neoliberalism from the libertarian right.

The economic think tank that enjoyed the greatest prestige in the eyes of the IFIs during the late 1990s and early 2000s[42] was the Romanian Center for Economic Policies (CEROPE). Established in 1998 by the Soros Foundation and two associations of local liberal economists (The Romanian Economics Society and the Foundation for Economic Reform), this think tank projected a quieter form of epistemic power than policy advocacy think tanks by focusing on the production of macroeconomic research for powerful international audiences. In essence, CEROPE functioned as an interface between the central bank and high-prestige research institutions.[43] During BNR governor Isărescu's premiership (1999–2000), many CEROPE members served in pivotal positions within the government, and between 1998 and 2007, its website was the go-to source for economists in the central government who worked on EU accession issues.[44] The CEROPE reports reflected the policy orthodoxy of the EU's accession reports and offered IFIs (and the European Commission in particular) detailed domestic confirmations of their diagnoses of the Romanian economy. Its working papers, academic articles, and books cemented its international status and facilitated its inclusion in the World Bank's Global Development Network, while also earning it "policy reviewer" status from the OECD.[45] Finally, during the late 1990s and early 2000s, CEROPE enjoyed the sponsorship of a variety of Western actors invested in the East European economic reform agenda (USAID, World Bank, Bertelsman Foundation, OECD) whose continuing support raised its professional status in the domestic policy process.

Unlike CEROPE, policy think tanks both reinforced and extended the economic orthodoxy of the IFIs in more experimental directions. The first to break the ground of nonprofit neoliberalism with radicalizing tendencies in Romania and set the example for others was the Romanian Academic Society (Societatea Academică din România, or SAR). Established in 1995, SAR was one of the political development NGOs established with EU and Soros Foundation funding. The timing of its establishment could not have been better, as international economic institutions were just then growing impatient with the poor capacity of Romanian shock therapists to sell and implement neoliberal reforms. As the SAR director noted,

> After the enthusiastic start in 1997, it had become clear for local and foreign experts that Romanian governments lacked both the staff and the experience to deal with the complex problems of the Romanian economy. Furthermore, it lacked a general philosophy of transformation of the command economy, centralized state and their long enduring institutions into a real market and competitive society able to apply successfully for the European Union. For this huge task the Romanian political class . . . had obviously no models and no methods: it needed think-tanks to clear the way.[46]

For the next twenty years, SAR was actively engaged in specific policy issues, prepared to take sides in the political system, and able to monitor the economic sustainability of the public advocacy process. The profile of its think tankers was a unique hybrid: many acted as academics, editorialists, activists, consultants for international organizations, political advisers to center-right parties, and even civil servants during the Democratic Convention's spell in government. It was these credentials that awarded them what Leonard Seabrooke called "epistemic arbitrage" (Seabrooke 2014), rather than narrow epistemic proficiency in economics, that made them attractive to foreign donors and domestic political entrepreneurs alike. Most were social scientists and had studied in Western graduate programs, where they acquired systematic knowledge about what was viewed in the West as "best practice" economic and political liberalization. Seeing themselves as the ambassadors of a renewed Romanian liberal project meant to bring the country "back into Europe," they bitterly resented the perceived stagnation of Romania under the neodevelopmentalist project of the ex-communists (Mungiu-Pippidi 2002).

Embracing a political development agenda was both a choice (reflecting their liberal democratic values) and a rational material strategy during the period in which Western organizations were generous in funding those who articulated a prodemocracy agenda. Indeed, SAR was the poster child of the Great Conflation between democratization and neoliberal reforms. Its initial activities consisted of liberal-democratic education, grant-writing training for NGOs, and political training for MPs. Following its success in shaping the government program of the Democratic Convention and subsequent judicial reforms, SAR decided to mix a liberal-democratic political agenda (characterized by the improvement of central and municipal government and better citizen access to government) with an economically neoliberal one.

SAR's members had credentials that were modest by international standards—no PhDs from Western universities—but which seemed stellar in the Romanian context, where Western professional experiences were scarce after many years of isolation. SAR's research director was a former journalist and the recent graduate of an MA program in comparative politics from Central European University. Others boasted work experience in the US corporate sector, a very rare professional commodity in the local job market at the time. In addition, SAR's economic collaborators (Daniel Dăianu, Lucian Albu, and Paul Dragoş Aligică) all had short-term postgraduate experiences in IFIs or European or US academia.

SAR's story was part of a bigger international development. Unlike in countries such as Spain, where the hard boundaries of the economic profession kept think tankers outside the gates of the policy process, in the politically fluid Eastern Europe of the 1990s and 2000s, amateur economists from these institutions took a seat at the table almost as equals. Economic transition consultants based in Western think tanks and known as "reformologists" brokered policy transfers across borders by providing ready-made policy templates and often financial resources to East European think tanks (Hemment 2004). They sponsored conferences and specific research projects targeted at Eastern European think tanks that had the political connections necessary to move ideas and polices from deliberation and design to adoption and implementation (Stone 2001, 350; 2000, 66).

Dual-use think tanks such as SAR and professional research think tanks such as CEROPE served as the trailblazers of the effort to transform neoliberalism from a resonating yet ultimately foreign theory into the new language of an emerging generation of politicians, policymakers, and journalists. This collaborative nature of neoliberalism via local NGOs was consolidated after the achievement of macrostabilization and basic market reforms during the 2000s. Yet new forms of advocacy actors and advocacy resources entered the stage during this period, pushing the agenda beyond what the IFIs demanded, and promoting libertarian theories about low-flat-tax systems that took even the IMF (Keen, Kim, and Varsano 2006) and local central bankers by surprise.[47]

This shift was reflective of the systemic changes produced by neoliberal reforms, and the European integration of the Romanian economy became a link in West European financial, supply, and wealth chains (Ban 2013; Gabor 2013), helping to develop a substantial domestic entrepreneurial and investor class. These transformations brought into the policy process consultancies, business law firms, business think tanks, and task forces of foreign investors' councils and chambers of commerce. Staffed by nonprofit professionals, lawyers, and economic consultants with international clout, organizations such as Romania Think-Tank, Academia de Advocacy, and CHF International Romania had no qualms about engaging with the cabinet to forge linkages with the private sector and especially with its multinational end.

Closely connected with the increasingly visible transnational capital and development aid structures of large donors, these organizations translated the agenda, advocacy language, and advocacy repertoire of US probusiness think tanks. At the same time, they "edited" the latter's agenda by placing a strong emphasis on the further development of liberal-democratic institutions and "good governance" concurrent with the advancement of an economic agenda. Democracy, good governance, and market reforms have remained a joint project ever since. In this way, they replicated SAR's prided Janus-faced identity: promoter of political virtue and partial advocate of a neoliberal economic agenda.

Academia de Advocacy (AA) is illustrative as a case where the supply of translators was changed as a direct result of external intervention in a climate of growing business presence in the policy arena. Established in 2002 by a provincial Romanian businessman from one the country's first export-processing zones and bankrolled by five domestic employer organizations, AA was the first professional probusiness think tank. By the end of the decade, it provided a critical linkage between the business world, public policy debates, and the corridors of the policy process. Accordingly, during the battle over the deregulation of the labor market in 2004, it was recognized as the most articulate voice of the procorporate side.[48]

Its founders partnered with the Bucharest chapters of USAID and with one of the institutes of the US-based National Endowment for Democracy (the Center for International Private Enterprise, or CIPE) to benefit from the Americans' organizational and advocacy expertise. With the aid of a CIPE-provided American advocacy consultant, AA began training a new profession (advocacy consultants), and, most importantly, it began a systematic effort to catalog the "best practices" on taxation and the labor market advocated at home by US business organizations. Brought together in booklets and guidelines, these "best practices" were then systematically disseminated to government ministries and media outlets. To ensure that governments would not ignore them, AA organized public hearings and carried out a systematic monitoring of parliamentary debates on its issues of interest.

All along, AA received CIPE "coaching." The passing of the strict 2003 labor code and the debates surrounding the flat tax during the same year gave AA the opportunity to become a competent and media-savvy player whose experts brought together employers and probusiness tax and labor experts in a dozen workshops that were publicized and managed to receive extensive media coverage. During its seminars, AA disseminated supply-side arguments against labor unions and proworker hire-and-fire regulations among journalists, academics, and business leaders. Until AA became involved, employment protection legislation had largely been a nonissue, and the employer organizations that had advocated for deregulation had no cross-national data or economic conceptual repertoire with which to press for reforms.

In this new context, advocacy for neoliberal affairs by nonprofits became a more complex affair that required the establishment of policy coalitions as well as effective coordination to maximize resource use. For example, before center-right parties picked up the labor market deregulation topic in 2004, the local chapter of the American Chamber of Commerce (AmCham) teamed up with new think tanks (Academia de Advocacy, CHF Romania) to put the issue on the agenda year earlier.[49] Similarly, in the case of the flat-tax campaign of 2003, Price Waterhouse Coopers paid for expensive downtown locations and sent their own experts, while SAR and the experts of a private law company specializing in tax optimization worked a high-prestige group of politicians and journalists in the room.[50] PWC also sponsored sessions on advocacy techniques taught by Slovakia's neoliberal Hayek Institute to SAR staff.[51] It was the econometrically sophisticated "Big Five" consultancies serving private investors that did the forecasting models purporting to show that there were no losers with the adoption of the flat tax, not SAR's policy popularizers. Indeed, the increasingly transnational pattern of neoliberal advocacy bringing together think tanks and other policy actors was an East Europe-wide phenomenon:

> Fiscal specialists came together in conferences devoted to the flat tax, involving both government technocrats and liberal policy advocates from local think tanks, such as the Center for Economics and Politics in the Czech Republic, the Institute for a Market Economy in Bulgaria, the Romania Think Tank, and the Free Markets Institute. Regional meetings of the Mont Pelerin Society also focused on the flat tax concept. (Appel and Orenstein 2013, 139)

The Austrian School's Revolving Doors

The flat-tax "revolution" in Eastern Europe served the agenda of neoliberal think tanks in the United States and the UK (Rabushka 2003; Mitchell 2007; Evans and Aligică 2008; Grecu 2004), reaching as far as the economic team of future chancellor Angela Merkel (Fuest, Peichl, and Schaefer 2008). It also highlighted the fact that libertarian ideas nurtured in relatively small niches in Western Europe had gone mainstream in Eastern Europe.

Alongside think tanks that spread different versions of actionable neoliberal ideas, other civil society organizations challenged mainstream neoliberalism with Austrian school economic thinking, ranging from anarcho-capitalism to Hayekian "centrism." The local translation of the Austrian school had begun in the early 1990s among a few marginal philosophers and young, maverick economists who offered free seminars to an emerging generation of journalists, academics, and politicians.[52] Ensconced in academia and publishing—the founder was the editor of the country's most respected private publishing house (Humanitas)—they turned the Austrian school into a high-profile school of thought by the late 1990s, and by the 2000s the main courses on comparative economics at the leading economics departments in Bucharest were taught by economic libertarians. To this day, the bulk of neoliberal thinking takes place in high-prestige academia.[53]

For a while, the libertarians were mostly on their own, a grass-roots movement operating on volunteering. The US-based Ludwig von Mises Institute and other American libertarian organizations also chipped in with resources during the 1990s, but these were far from significant,[54] and most of the diffusion work was done on a volunteer basis by exceptional individuals such as Paul Dragos Aligică, a senior fellow at the F. A. Hayek Program of the notoriously libertarian Mercatus Center of George Mason University.

For a while, it seemed that like in Spain, economic libertarians would remain on the fringes of the policy process and, when interviewed, they complain about their ideas having little traction. This situation began to change towards the mid-2000s, however. Then, the establishment of a policy-oriented think tank (Centrul de Analiza si Dezvoltare Institutionala Eleutheria, CADI) with funding and institutional support from a local capital as well as a litany of US and European libertarian think tanks (including the Cato Institute, Heritage Foundation, Atlas Foundation, Timbro and the Taxpayers Alliance)[55] took libertarian ideas into the policy world.[56] Their international profile was heightened when an international libertarian convention organized by CADI brought to Bucharest not only a Who's Who of the American and European libertarian movement (including Grover Norquist and Jose Pinera), but also guests whose professional affiliations included mainstream Western institutions such as the European Commission's diplomatic office in Romania, OECD, USAID, or the European Investment Bank.[57] In the light of the fact that EU enlargement was supposed to also entail the strengthening of EU social policy standards in countries like Romania, the presence of the European Commission delegate at a convention where European-style tax and welfare systems were pilloried as manifestations of "socialism" was particularly intriguing.

The migration of this part of the Romanian libertarian movement from its academic and civil society recesses to the policy process was facilitated by the fact that even though they did not receive as much support from organized domestic capital as they hoped for, local libertarians began to receive the patronage of key economic advisers within the Băsescu administrations (Theodor Stolojan, Andrea Paul Vass, and Cristian Preda). A presidential adviser and head of the Liberal-Democratic Party, Theodor Stolojan even became an official CADI collaborator. President Băsescu himself expressed its support when he accepted an invitation to address an international libertarian convention hosted by CADI.[58] Critically, in 2008, the head of CADI coauthored the economic program of the center-right party (the Democrat-Liberals, PDL) that would govern Romania during its difficult post-Lehman years.[59] In the central bank, the economic counsel of the governor was perceived in libertarian circles as a fellow traveler.[60]

Conclusions

International coercion played a key part in trimming the unorthodox readings of neoliberal policy programs adopted by Romanian governments while locking in the commitments of its sympathetic interlocutors. Accordingly, it constrained the local freedom to hybridize and ensured the adoption of neoliberal reforms in the absence of the institutional cohesion of governments whose policy czars had embraced neoliberal ideas.

For more than twenty years, the leverage of the IMF, the World Bank, and the European Union ensured the neoliberal transformation of the dominant policy regime in Bucharest, irrespective of the partisan shifts unleashed by the country's political cycles. Critically, coercion turned the central bank into a pivotal player in the policy process. But, compelling as it is, the policy coercion explanation is incomplete. It overlooks the importance of the transnational socialization processes through which Romanian policy elites eventually adopted the ideas behind neoliberal policies. This made agreements with IFIs a mere external anchor and insurance policy for translating shared ideas into policies. Moreover, coercion does not explain why domestic translators who controlled the commanding posts of the policy process pushed beyond the limits of the IFIs' conventional neoliberalism du jour.

During the 1990s, neoliberal economic theories lacked qualified professional economists with extensive exposure to international economic networking and who were ready and willing to staff the top offices of the state or advocate for neoliberalism from outside the state. International professional and material resources invested in fast-track socialization changed this dynamic and turned the country's economic knowledge regime into a central bank-centric set of institutions. However, it took years before a critical mass of technocrats of this kind began to emerge, and even then not a single recipient of a prestigious Western PhD held any position of power. Until then, the translation of neoliberalism had to make do with a handful of central bankers and top-level bureaucrats with international professional experience, leaving the rest of the job to less internationally networked political appointess. As chapter 3 showed, in the specific conditions of postcommunist Romania this facilitated the emergence of disembedded neoliberalism.

The poor supply of neoliberal technocrats with international credentials was compensated for by the success of nonprofits at capturing international resources, popularizing neoliberal ideas, articulating them in policy formats, and organizing advocacy coalitions around specific issues. Some of these issues reinforced the agenda of the IFIs, but others went beyond it to create an increasingly radicalized form of disembedded neoliberalism. Given the porous nature of the policy process, many of their ideas now constitute the reality of the low-tax, low-wage, low-benefits Romanian policy regime.

PART IV

NEOLIBERALISM'S RESILIENCE
SINCE THE GREAT RECESSION

8

Recalibrating Embedded Neoliberalism in Spain

Before the Lehman crisis struck, Spain was a model member state of the eurozone: a spectacular growth rate, massive expansion of job opportunities, rising incomes, and governments that had been not only more fiscally orthodox than Germany's, but also paragons of debt reduction through a prudent fiscal policy on the upswing. When financial turbulence pulled the plug on its enormous real estate bubble, the government had budget surpluses and one of the lowest public debt levels in the eurozone. Along with Ireland, Spain was the star performer of the Stability and Growth Pact.

But unlike Ireland, Spain faced the Great Recession with Europe's largest fiscal stimulus, turning Zapatero into an FDR-like figure. In 2008 the government launched (largely) spending-based stimulus plans worth ninety billion euros (8 percent of GDP), a fiscal effort that was three times greater than Germany's and almost twice as big as the United States' as a share of total output.[1] The largest of them was adopted in November and received clearance from Brussels (Zapatero 2013, 164; Solbes 2013). The measures balanced progressive redistribution with supply-side measures meant to wean the economy off its dependence on construction and other brownfield sectors: large-scale solar power projects, more public spending on research, and development activities and projects that gave Spain the longest high-speed rail infrastructure in Europe.[2] For low-income households there were minimum pension increases and mortgage payment moratoria while for small and medium enterprises the government provided access to subsidized credit lines. A large part of the construction sector's former labor force was employed in thirty thousand municipal projects designed to improve infrastructure and restore heritage sites, a sensible move for a country with a large tourism sector.

According to one estimate, the stimulus plans created 410,000 jobs, temporarily arresting the dramatic increase in unemployment.[3] In December 2008, Zapatero announced a new twenty-two-billion-euro stimulus program based largely on infrastructure spending to be launched in 2009. Even after the shift to austerity under external duress in 2010, the government tried to salvage core services and spread the costs more evenly through tax, spending, and labor market policies. Indeed, it was only after the election of the conservative Rajoy government that Spain's embedded neoliberalism was ground to pulp through a combination of external coercion and domestic conviction.

Based on comparative research and a careful analysis of primary documents and interviews with pivotal decision-makers, this chapter shows how Spanish embedded neoliberalism survived the crisis through two government terms. The main claim is that the different translations of neoliberal ideas by the Socialist government (2008–2011) and the PP government (2011–2015) were critical factors in shaping the local crisis management regime. At the same time, the external coercion exercised after 2010 through an understudied version of the banking-sovereign loop and the politics of EU institutions drastically curtailed the translation space available to local policy elites, ensuring the resilience of embedded neoliberalism in a retrenched version relative to the precrisis years.

Gaps in Conventional Explanations

It is tempting to reduce Spain's stimulus program from 2008 to 2010 to a knee-jerk economic reaction to the recession triggered by the financial crisis. Granted, the country had a surplus and low debt, and monetary policy in the eurozone quickly entered the zero-lower-bound zone, so why not use the fiscal space to address the collapse in domestic and external demand, with the attendant sky-rocketing unemployment and depressed public investment?

Careful comparative analysis suggests that the decision to adopt this stimulus cannot be abstracted simply from the fact that the government's prudent pre-crisis fiscal policies had left the Spanish government with a fiscal surplus and a very low public debt. Not all EU member states with low debt and low deficits met the Great Recession with a fiscal stimulus. Countries like Ireland and Estonia frontloaded harsh fiscal consolidation packages immediately after the Lehman crisis despite having large fiscal surpluses and very low levels of government debt. Moreover, they frontloaded spending cuts, defending their low flat taxes and stating publicly that austerity was not only a reassuring mechanism for investors, but also the "bitter medicine" needed to get back to growth (Blyth 2013; Kinsella 2011; Sommers and Woolfson 2014).

The contrast between "Keynesian" Spain and "austerian" Ireland suggests that the adoption of stimulus policies by Spain needs to be explained rather than assumed as a natural reaction to a deep downturn. Rather than use the "fiscal space" as an opportunity to stimulate its battered economy, even before the sovereign debt crisis became a reality in the eurozone in late 2009, the Irish government frontloaded spending cuts (Hardiman and Regan 2013; Robbins and Lapsley 2014). Indeed, in the fall of 2008 austerity was used by local elites as a means to signal Ireland's credible commitment to markets in the hope that this would stabilize private investment (Kinsella and Leddin 2010). It was a sample of New Classical economics unreconstructed by the New Keynesian nuances of recalibrated neoliberalism analyzed in the previous chapter.

Spain's stimulus programs are also intriguing because of their composition. Mainstream economists would struggle to explain why the stimulus was spent largely on public works, green energy projects, and redistributive measures, rather than on tax cuts, the default mode of stimulating the economy in mainstream accounts. This choice is puzzling because in applied macroeconomics, public investment was deemed to have a much lower effect on output than tax cuts, and it was not until 2012–2013 that this conventional wisdom was challenged in academia and the IMF (Ban 2015).

A strictly materialist approach would also struggle to explain the reason why stimulus programs were withdrawn so long after the fiscal space had been lost in mid-2009 or, more importantly, why Zapatero's combination of austerity and structural reforms from 2010 was accompanied by a series of resolute (albeit eventually defeated) attempts to shield the welfare state and labor legislation.

Again, comparative analysis is useful. The importance of the Spanish attempt to salvage embedded neoliberalism in Spain in conditions of external duress is underscored by the different ways in which the Romanian governments analyzed in the previous chapter responded to sovereign bond market and EU-IMF pressures during the same spring. In May 2010, the Spanish governments made top income earners contribute a lot more than their Romanian counterparts did. The tax on capital income in Spain was increased from 18 percent to two tax bands of 19 percent for up to six thousand euros a year and 21 percent over that limit. While high-income groups' tax rate went up, low-income Spanish taxpayers received tax credits and experienced no increase in their income tax rate. In contrast, the income taxes for the wealthiest individuals (over 120,000 euros a year) went up to 44 percent.

Spanish policymakers cut far less from benefits and social services and made cuts more progressively than did the Romanians. Cuts to public sector wages did not average more than 7 percent in total even at the peak of the conservative government's austerity drive. In contrast, their Romanian counterparts endured a flat 25 percent cut at the outset of the crisis. This "flat tax"-style spending cut was so harsh that IMF managing director Dominique Strauss Kahn flew to Bucharest and delivered a speech in the Romanian parliament asking for cuts that shifted a greater part of the burden onto those more able to pay. Moreover, while Spanish governments hesitated to cut unemployment benefits until 2012, the government in Bucharest the government did not. The unemployed saw their allowances slashed by 15 percent and made harder to access, despite the much lower (official) unemployment rate in Romania. Spain's healthcare system executed spending cuts mainly through pricing pressure on drug suppliers and the introduction of small copays. In Romania this essential public service was decimated by extensive hospital closures, deep cuts, and creeping privatization, leading to a mass exodus of physicians from the country.

Third, the onslaught on unions and workers' rights was both more reluctant and more limited in Spain. In 2010, the Zapatero government tried to defend embedded neoliberalism through labor market reforms that balanced security and flexibility that was consistent with the embedded neoliberal principle of negotiating a compromise between credibility with the markets and society's demand from protection against the market. As Zapatero's economic adviser put it, "The prime minister tried to do a balancing act between signaling to financial markets that Spain was serious about structural reforms while expressing his belief that the precariousness of those on short-term contracts, most of them young people, was a national tragedy."[4] In contrast, the Romanian governments used an emergency procedure in the parliament to undertake the most extensive deregulation of Romanian industrial relations on record. National-level bargaining was simply eliminated, labor-capital relations were reduced to the firm level, union representatives lost their protections, firing became easy, and temporary contracts and work conditions were freed from union intervention and court procedures (Domnisoru 2012; Trif 2013; Ban 2014). Moreover, the new law on social dialogue adopted in 2011 was so restrictive of unionization that it was deemed by the International Labour Organization to be in breach of one of its core conventions.[5] Such measures were not adopted in Spain even after the conservatives came to power in 2011.

To better understand Spain's policy decisions during the crisis we need to look closer at how neoliberal theories and policy programs were recalibrated around 2008–2009, at the politics shaping the resilience of embedded neoliberalism that characterized to varying degrees the thinking of pivotal elites in the second Zapatero government (2008–2011) and then to examine their partisan recalibration during the conservative government of Mariano Rajoy (2011–2015).

The Recalibration of Neoliberalism

The year 2008 was not a bad one for well-read and well-trained economic technocrats serving left-leaning governments ruling over recession-struck countries with high unemployment rates, such as Spain. When the Great Recession struck, mainstream macro was not a single dish of anti-Keynesian ingredients, but a much broader menu of choices. One could swing to the left or to the right depending on one's intellectual preferences and affiliation. Mainstream arguments for using demand management during recessions began to emerge during the early 2000s, but it was only after 2009 that modern macro was effectively taken by storm by economists from the left New Keynesian side of the new neoclassical synthesis. The spearheads of change were economists from Berkeley (Christina Romer, Alan Auerbach, Brad DeLong, Yuriy Gorodnichenko), Northwestern (Martin Eichenbaum, Larry Christiano, Sergio Rebelo), and the Fed (Gauti Eggertson) who argued that fiscal policy activism was needed to counter the Great Recession; their prestigious academic affiliation and publications as well as their sophisticated use of complex models that approximate the conditions of the crisis (tight microeconomic fundamentals, zero-lower-bound interest rates) enabled them to make a strong case against austerity. As the sections below show, Zapatero's economic team made the most of this opening.

The terrain where the battle took place was the fiscal multiplier, or the impact that a rise or fall in government spending or tax collection has on a country's economic output. If fiscal multipliers are small, countries can cut spending faster or raise more in taxes without much short-term damage. If they are large, then the process can become self-defeating, with each dollar of spending cuts costing the economy more than a dollar in lost output and thus actually increasing debt-to-GDP ratios.

A stream of studies found consistently high fiscal multipliers that urged at least caution regarding contractionary fiscal policies.[6] For example, a recalibrated model with financial frictions found that increases in government expenditure can be a more powerful stimulus in the short run than tax cuts (Fernandez-Villaverde 2010). Using New Keynesian models, fiscal policy "mandarin" Michael Woodford further boosted the case for countercyclical government spending, arguing that with sticky prices and wages, fiscal multipliers can be larger than one and can lead to an increase in welfare (Woodford 2011). Lawrence Christiano and Martin Eichenbaum's supported his findings with an article showing that when nominal interest rates are bound at zero, the fiscal multiplier is significantly larger than predicted under standard New Classical macroeconomics models. To this end, they provided empirical evidence for a new prostimulus argument: multipliers are large because the rise in government spending increases output, marginal cost, and expected inflation. Since nominal rates are at zero, a rise in inflation causes a decrease in real interest rates, which leads to a rise in private spending. This initiates the process of rising output levels again, and the net result becomes a large increase in output.

New Classical and right New Keynesian economists struck back, finding very low and negative multipliers (Cogan et al. 2010), showing that higher debt cancels the effects of higher spending multipliers (Uhlig 2010) or arguing that the debate over fiscal policy cannot be settled because of the indeterminacy of research on multipliers, thus suggesting that policy should err on the side of conservatism (Ramey 2011; see Ban 2015b for an overview).

In short, the claim that the transatlantic technocratic elite was homogenously "neoclassical" or that one would have to "go heterodox" to be against austerity should be reconsidered. By 2009, it was no longer possible for policymakers to claim that most economists agree with the counterproductive nature of expansionary fiscal policies when interest rates are close to zero or there are significant financial frictions in the economy.

For a while, the European Commission opened up to these insights. Between 2008 and 2010 the EC and the summits of the EU heads of state supported a strong and coordinated fiscal stimulus for countries with fiscal space, such as Spain. In the fall of 2008 the Commission had its own "Keynesian moment," having championed coordinated deficit spending when it implemented the European Economic Recovery Plan (EERP). However, at closer inspection it became obvious that this Keynesianism was but a series of edits on the neoliberal script, because the sovereign market was deemed to be the ultimate judge of whether a state had "fiscal space" and therefore could stimulate the economy or not. Keynes's work may have been dusted off for about eight months (Blyth 2013), but only within the limits allowed by the credibility principle that sits at the heart of neoliberal economic theories:

> In countries with high deficits and debt levels, a stimulus could prove less effective as it raises sustainability concerns. In countries with poor competitiveness and large current account deficits, a large fiscal stimulus would worsen competitiveness problems and slow down necessary adjustment. Countries with large current account as well as public deficits may have no room for fiscal stimulus. In contrast, countries with current account surpluses could reduce their imbalances through a significant domestic expansion. Here, a larger fiscal expansion would be of significant domestic as well as euro-area benefit. Countries in intermediate situations should consider combinations of fiscal stimulus and structural reforms that maintain growth in the short run and improve sustainability in the medium term. (European Commission Quarterly Report, December 2008, 4)

The Institutions and Ideas of Spain's Recalibrated Neoliberalism

The Resilience of Institutional Centralization

Zapatero's team made the most of the prostimulus ideas promoted from late 2008 through late 2009 by the IMF, the European Commission, the G-20, and leading academic macroeconomists. In his memoirs, Zapatero stresses that he saw the stimulus as much a local project as the reflection of the Keynesian ideas upheld by these institutions (Zapatero 2013, 162), including the European Commission's redefinition of structural reforms as including more public spending on SMEs, education, vocational training, infrastructure, and research (Zapatero 2013, 163).

Re-elected in the spring of 2008, Zapatero's new government benefited from the smooth executive-party relations and a centralization of the policy process in the prime minister's office that characterized the prime ministership of Felipe González, his long-serving Socialist predecessor in the Moncloa Palace between 1982 and 1996. PSOE was as disciplined as ever, and the small left parties that gave the cabinet solid parliamentary support were more than thrilled to support the stimulus (Field 2013).

The macroeconomic orthodoxy sanctioned by Brussels was safe and sound in the hands of the minister of finance, Pedro Solbes, Felipe González's last minister of finance, who went on to serve as vice president of the European Commission during the building of the European monetary union (Solbes 2002; 2013). The traditional alliance between the central bank and the Ministry of Finance was safe as well.

A Moderate Keynesian Revival

Fernández Ordóñez, Solbes's former deputy, was now the governor of the central bank. An economist in the Research Service of the Bank of Spain described the relationship between the senior management of the two institutions as a "love fest."[7] Everyone was in agreement with the supply-side measures of the embedded neoliberalism represented by the EU's Lisbon Agenda.

Just like Felipe González, Zapatero was trained as a lawyer and entered politics as a young man. Not only was his economic expertise very thin, but he had also showed little interest in economic policy before 2008.[8] When he appointed Pedro Solbes, the former vice president of the European Commission and enforcer of the Stability and Growth Pact, as his finance minister, Zapatero effectively farmed out fiscal policy to the guardians of the Brussels-Frankfurt Consensus. But the expansion of this consensus in the form of the broader microeconomic reforms of the Lisbon Agenda meant the prime minister needed advice on a greater set of economic issues than finance ministers and central bankers are typically tasked to address. It is out of this increasing demand for more complex expertise that he set up his own Economic Bureau (Oficina Economica) and staffed it with some thirty economists with advanced degrees.

At first, the Economic Bureau was entrusted to local defenders of fiscal orthodoxy. The first head of the bureau was Miguel Sebastián, an academic who earned his PhD in the heartland of US mainstream economics, the University of Minnesota. By the late 2000s, after years of serving in the government, Sebastián's views on fiscal policy had become more revisionist. Although the domestically trained David Taguas, his successor at the helm of the Bureau, had more orthodox views (Taguas 2012), in April 2008 the directorship of the Economic Bureau passed to Javier Vallés, an economist who, Minnesota PhD notwithstanding, had been at the forefront at the Keynesian shift on the multiplier debate presented in the previous chapter (Galí et al. 2007).

The Keynesian team at the Economic Bureau had a strong ally in the new PSOE think tank Fundacion Ideas. The most prominent of the economists at Ideas was Carlos Mulas Granados. He was very close to Zapatero, involved in drafting the PSOE electoral program in 2008, and boasted a PhD in economics from Cambridge. From his position as minister of industry and close adviser to Zapatero, Miguel Sebastián was a loyal supporter of these two voices in the cabinet.[9] In his memoirs, Zapatero makes it clear that they were his chief source of economic advice (Zapatero 2013, 83–93, 106, 142–143, 167–178) and that the Economic Office provided him with close to fifteen hundred reports and memos (Zapatero 2013, 179).

At Fundacion Ideas, Mulas Granados coordinated with Jesus Calderas, a pro-labor sociologist who served as minister of labor in the first Zapatero government, to produce economic policy reports for the government. Such activities enrolled New Keynesians of global fame such as Andre Sapir and Jean Pisan-Ferri, who had been known for their critique of conservative interpretations of mainstream economics. They were later joined by two of the most prominent critiques of austerity from a Keynesian perspective (Joseph Stiglitz and Paul Krugman), who advised Zapatero during the Great Recession. Stiglitz traveled several times to Madrid to advise Zapatero and encourage him to stay the course through 2008 and 2009,[10] declaring once that his fiscal package was superior to Obama's stimulus.[11]

The economic ideas of the Economic Office–Ideas cooperation were an experiment in fiscal revisionism. What is of critical importance in this regard is that Sebastián, Nunez, and Vallés (*los minesottos*) abandoned the New Classical orthodoxy of their youth and moved toward a more left-leaning interpretation of New Keynesian macroeconomics. In 1993 Sebastián and Vallés authored an orthodox real-business-cycles article critiquing discretionary fiscal policy and upholding rules-based monetary policy (Dolado et al. 1993), but by the mid-2000s they had shifted their views. Indeed, Vallés coauthored one of the most iconic articles of the New Keynesian resurgence of fiscal activism in the mid-2000s, which confirmed that, contra New Classical fiscal policy pessimism, increases in government spending do generate a positive, significant, and lengthy (about four years) response in output (Galí, López-Salido, and Vallés 2005;

2007). Together with Angel Estrada, another Oficina Economica researcher, he had advised the cabinet to shift Spain's economic model away from construction and into sectors with higher productivity through higher public spending on R&D as well as liberalizing labor and product market reforms (Estrada García, Pons, and Vallés 2006).

Mulas Granados was a moderately orthodox macroeconomist, and his pre-2008 research shows that he found empirical evidence for fiscally sustainable social-democracy in a monetary union: balanced budgets plus supply-side policies of capital formation and public employment maintenance, even at the cost of cuts in public consumption and transfers (Mulas Granados 2003; 2006). For him, austerity could be expansionary only when supported by devaluation, an impossible condition within the euro (Mulas Granados 2005). At the same time, his research during the first stages of the crisis shows that given financial frictions and near-zero interest rates, these policy fundamentals must change. As a research consultant for the IMF, he contributed to the Fund's revisionist drive (Ban 2013). In 2009, he coauthored with senior management articles that rejected the expansionary austerity thesis and advanced the argument that in recessions produced by financial crises, increases in government consumption reduce the duration of downturns, while increases in government investment improve medium-term output performance (Baldacci, Mulas Granados, and Gupta 2009). Through Mulas Granados, the IMF's Keynesian door opened in the very office of the Spanish prime minister.

Based on such professional ideas, both Vallés and Mulas Granados's advised the prime minister to implement a large stimulus based on a balance between public investment and consumption, with a focus on the latter. They insisted that the quality of these investments was paramount and insisted that shovel-ready projects run through municipalities should be balanced with supply-side investments in research, rail infrastructure and green energy (Mulas Granados and Sanz 2008; Mulas Granados 2010). While they envisaged fiscal consolidation in the medium term, they thought that public investments and automatic stabilizers should be the last items on the chopping block because of their critical role in stabilizing demand in an environment with financial frictions and close to zero interest rates.[12] When the finance minister voiced concerns about higher deficits, Zapatero and his team continued to argue that the return to growth should precede fiscal retrenchment and that Spain had the margin to use public spending to stimulate growth even after Plan E went into high gear (Solbes 2013).

The Economic Bureau–Ideas collaboration also meant that the prime minister got a crash course in macroeconomics. A team of five economists from these institutions supplied him with accessible macroeconomic readings authored by Paul Krugman and the early work of Ben Bernanke on the Great Depression,[13] so that in his memoirs he nominates Paul Krugman, Joseph Stiglitz, Dani Rodrik, and Jeffrey Sachs as the economists that informed his views the most (Zapatero 2013, 320–327, 377).

Not everyone was on board with Spain's "Keynesian" recalibration of the country's embedded neoliberalism. In addition to the conservative opposition spearheaded by PP's Mariano Rajoy, Spain's traditional alliance between the central bank and the Ministry of Finance pushed for a rejection of Keynesian innovations and a restatement of orthodoxy within embedded neoliberalism.

Although the euro weakened its role in the Spanish policy process and the head of BdE did not have the same high reputation among economists that Luis Angel Rojo once did, the onset of the crisis found BdE in a solid position. The G-20 summit from November 2008 essentially used off-the-shelf ideas about macroprudential regulation used by Spain's central bank (Solbes 2013, 396). Its reports therefore still weighed heavily in public policy debates.[14] Early on in the crisis, BdE took a sanguine view of the emerging consensus in the macro-economics of recessions and the stimulus, albeit one trimmed down to a more modest scale. Its *Annual Report* for 2008 finds that given the scale and predicted duration of recession as well as the moderation of inflation expectations, the implementation of expansionary demand-side fiscal and monetary policies was "warranted." In line with the calibrated neoliberalism discussed in the previous chapter, the BdE cautioned that actions should address medium-term sustainability concerns and be focused on direct income transfers to low-income groups and increases in government purchases and productive public investment because of their higher fiscal multiplier effect relative to tax cuts (BdE 2008; 37–39; box 1.3).

Defeating the Orthodox Resistance

The central bankers' support for the stimulus was weak and fleeting, however. Although the BdE's reports acknowledged that these "Keynesian" measures would in fact contribute to recovery and the reduction of unemployment, in practice it worked to convince the government to reduce their size.[15] Moreover, the support was both short-lived and conditional upon the adoption of neoliberal structural reforms and the continuing availability of "fiscal space," meaning budget deficits within the 3 percent limit stipulated by the eurozone's rules. When the government exceeded that limit soon after Plan E was adopted, the BdE voiced its opposition at regular intervals.

As soon as January 2009 BdE, in lockstep with the ECB's call to austerity, demanded that the government announce a framework for "substantial consolidation" to meet the 3 percent deficit limit by 2012 (BdE 2009, 37). A year later, the BdE annual report demanded an immediate withdrawal of expansionary policies while stressing that austerity should be based more on spending cuts than tax increases (BdE 2010, 7). In the view of BdE, if there was any space for growth stimulation, this could be found in supply-side structural reforms that enhanced competition, lowered wages, and restored profits (BdE 2010, 20). Critically, the references to the fiscal multiplier from the 2008 report wither out over the following years.

In line with the tenets of the new neoclassical synthesis, the BdE blamed both the contraction of demand and labor market "rigidities" for the dramatic increase of unemployment, demanding extensive deregulation of collective bargaining arrangements and employment legislation in addition to more active job search programs and training for the unemployed (BdE 2009, 39–40). Additionally, the BdE framed the crisis as an opportunity to carry out an extensive deregulation of the service sector, the liberalization of energy prices, and the redesign of incentives for a greater accumulation of technological capital (BdE 2010, 24, 41–42). The only editing of the ECB line was that Spain's central bankers never subscribed to the ECB's expansionary austerity thesis. Instead, they saw seeing austerity as a contractionary measure made inevitable by the tension in the bond markets, not as an avenue to growth. Throughout the reports, BdE also insisted on a rapid and comprehensive deregulation of the labor market and the IMF, staff noting in all their consultation reports that this institution's views were closely aligned to the Fund's, while the government's were not.

In addition to the central bank, in the fall of 2008 the cabinet already faced internal resistance from the very architects of embedded neoliberalism. The spearhead was finance minister Pedro Solbes, an orthodox economist and career civil servant who used the revolving doors between EU institutions and the summits of the Spanish economic ministries. Solbes's team at the ministry gave Zapatero the fiscal space for the stimulus, but he was also its earliest critic. In late 2008, at a time when the European Commission was effectively clamoring for holding the EU deficit rules in abeyance, Solbes demanded instead that the cabinet unflinchingly respect them (Solbes 2013, 394). In making this argument Solbes restated not only conventionally pragmatic fears about the consequence of deficit violations for spreads on Spanish sovereign debt, but also classic neoliberal arguments that a larger stimulus could crowd out private investment (Solbes 2013, 395). This was the Stability and Growth Pact on steroids.

At first, Zapatero was conciliatory and responded to the objections raised by the BdE–Ministry of Finance coalition by reducing the overall level of spending in the plan. When Solbes and BdE scaled up their objections in sync with the ballooning deficit, Zapatero resorted to his executive primacy privileges to terminate this criticism.

In early 2009, the prime minister used a G-20 meeting favorable to a coordinated global stimulus to degrade Solbes's critiques and push through further expansionary fiscal measures executed via municipal public works (Solbes 2014,

396–397). When Solbes persisted, the prime minister transferred the authority over the management of the stimulus from the finance ministry to the Ministry of Public Administration, then headed by Elena Salgado, a loyal civil servant with little economic policy expertise. When in May 2009 Pedro Solbes asked Zapatero to cut spending, he declared the request "unacceptable," leading to the minister's resignation (Solbes 2014, 408–414). To lock in further support from PSOE's left, Zapatero appointed as minister for investments a PSOE leader (José Blanco) who would become known for his insistence that fiscal expansions and retrenchments should pass the costs on to the wealthy and to corporate sectors making large profits, such as banking and energy.[16]

Meanwhile, the worsening of Spain's banking crisis (and especially the disaster of the *cajas*) and reports that at no point before 2008 had the Research Service worried about the real estate bubble eventually put the policy authority of the central bank under the hammer. For the first time in the history of the BdE the central bank governor set himself up to be effectively pushed out of his post. The de facto demotion of the Ministry of Finance and the diminution of the central bank's expertise firepower was a real institutional coup de grâce, the first ever in the history of the Spanish economic policy process.

The economic revisionism of Zapatero's economic policy team did not expand in other areas, however. This was particularly the case regarding labor market institutions. There was a virtual consensus among the most influential economic experts that the labor unions had too much power in collective bargaining. In September 2009, finance minister Salgado incorporated in her team Ángel Estrada, a Research Service economist who had authored a BdE report demanding an extensive deregulation of the labor market in line with the demands made by the employers' association.[17] Nevertheless, the prime minister decided that such radical reforms would further complicate the party's electoral future, and he did not move against the labor unions until late 2011, under external duress. The prime minister continued to believe that growth is the determining factor in creating employment and that in the worst-case scenario one should stick to the principle that "one should not weaken workers' rights to the point that one obliterates the basic pillars of collective bargaining and the guaranteeing of a basic balance between employers and workers" (Zapatero 2013, 372).

Although the cabinet's most able and influential critics were defeated, the end of Spain's own translation of revisionism was near. As the analytical framework of this book has proposed, domestic translators' freedom is externally constrained when the very core of neoliberal theory is challenged. When Zapatero and his team pushed for fiscal expansion even as the deficit and the public debt continued to grow, they challenged the goal of fiscal credibility achieved through orthodox means.

The Retrenchment of European Embedded Neoliberalism

Austere Times in Brussels

By mid-2009, the "Keynesian" window began to close rapidly in the European Commission. In its June 2009 *Quarterly Report*, the EC asked all EU governments to "prepare a credible strategy for fiscal policy so as to be able gradually to withdraw the stimulus," stressing, however, that the withdrawal should take place only gradually, once the recovery takes hold, and avoid "excessively tight budgetary policies choking the nascent recovery" (25). In October, the call to withdraw the stimulus grew a bit louder, but it was only in the March 2010, after the EU heads of state meetings in the European Council failed to produce a strong response to the Greek debt crisis, that the EC argued austerity should be pursued "urgently." It was also in the March report that the EC defined its solution to the predicted increase in unemployment in countries showing high current account deficits: harsh and immediate "internal devaluation" packages executed through extensive spending cuts and structural reforms.

The doctrinal turn to austerity was translated into practice via a combination of nudging, legalistic, and coercive governance modes of governance. The coercive mode was first activated when the Commission embedded its ideas in bailout agreements concluded in 2008 and 2009 with the crisis-ridden countries in the eastern "periphery" (Lütz and Kranke 2014). The legalistic mode kicked into gear in 2010, when the Commission pushed for the adoption of an even stricter set of fiscal rules than the Stability and Growth Pact that essentially outlawed discretionary fiscal policy by shifting compliance with an enhanced SGP away from peer pressure and toward outright sanctions and fines for public debt and deficits out of line with new, more demanding numerical targets (Hodson 2011, 242). The stress on rules-based and eventually constitutionally hamstrung fiscal policy was unprecedented and was steeped in the Commission's own research apparatus (Deroose et al. 2008; Iara and Wolff 2010).

In 2010 the Commission published a research paper based on a "unique data set," which found that "stronger fiscal rules in euro area member states reduce sovereign risk" (2010 EC Economic Paper 433, 1) and "the legal base turns out to be the most important dimension for the perceived effectiveness of the rules" (1). In the same year, the Commission also initiated the European Semester, a framework that combined nudging and coercion. Every year since 2011, the Commission has written a report for each member state detailing its position on domestic macroeconomic and structural reforms to be adopted, naming and shaming rule-breakers along the way and applying sanctions on member states found in violation of deficit targets. The European Council then writes the fine print, detailing the points made by the Commission (Crespy and Menz 2015; Scharpf 2015).

Austere Times in Frankfurt

If the EC had a relatively gradual transition from stimulus to austerity, the ECB went for austerity early on. An overarching picture of the European Central Bank's fiscal policy standpoint between 2009 and 2012 can be pieced together by looking at the views expressed in the ECB *Monthly Bulletin* reports. A year before the Greek fiscal scandal erupted and the Commission's about-face, the ECB was already on offensive against expansionary fiscal policy. Indeed, as early as January 2009, the ECB's Governing Council demanded the reversal of the fiscal stimulus measures adopted by EU member states in the fall of 2008, arguing that "if not reversed in due time, this will negatively affect in particular the younger and the future generations" (ECB 2009, 7).

By September, the ECB asked for "a swift return to sound and sustainable public finances." This entailed higher-than-usual fiscal consolidation efforts that would "exceed significantly the benchmark of 0.5 percent of GDP per annum set in the Stability and Growth Pact" (ECB 2009, 7). Removing any doubt as to who should pay for all this, the ECB stated clearly that "the focus of the structural measures should lie on the expenditure side, as in most euro area countries tax and social contribution rates are already high" (ECB 2009, 7).

The justification for this stance was anchored in the New Classical argument that places a heavy reliance on rules-based fiscal consolidation to be introduced immediately and paired with structural reforms to reign in public spending and reduce labor costs. To the extent that countries are judged to have "fiscal space" (no one other than Germany and Sweden was judged to have it), the ECB Governing Board encouraged them to allow existing levels of automatic stabilizers (mostly welfare payments) and new targeted reductions in corporate income taxes and in labor taxes to take effect. But even for these countries, the ECB cautioned against more "Keynesian" options such as government purchase of goods and services, public investment, and increased social transfers to credit-constrained households. In the view of the ECB, such measures were deemed to have rapidly fading impacts on economic growth. Even if one lived in the best of all fiscal worlds, what one should aspire to were Reagan-style tax cuts and the same levels of social spending, with the private sector remaining the hero of recovery.

Beyond doctrine, the ECB made politicized policy choices that made austerity its default position. As a member of the Troika it told governments what reforms they should conduct and how deep austerity should be. These reforms had important distributive consequences within those societies (Blyth 2013; Kentikelenis et al. 2014).

The ECB claimed that fiscal retrenchment was unavoidable given market pressures. Yet back in 2010 the ECB had the choice to ease sovereign bond markets pressure by using a robustly expansionary monetary policy to act as a lender of last resort, an action that would have been in line with orthodox macroeconomic theory. In practice the ECB yielded to the monetary policy ideas of some core eurozone member states, taking three years to adopt the Outright Monetary Transactions program, which calmed the sovereign bond markets, and adopting quantitative easing seven years after the Fed (Wyplosz 2015). Moreover, rather than being a neutral actor following the rules of a central bank, the ECB acted as the enforcer of austerity. In 2010 and 2011 the Spanish government experienced this coercive and politicized technology of rule and caved.

Structural Reforms for the End of Fiscal Policy

The push for austerity came in the same package with structural reforms, or measures that the European Commission saw as adequate to "address impediments to the fundamental drivers of growth by unshackling labor, product and service markets to foster job creation, investment, and productivity . . . and to enhance an economy's competitiveness, growth potential and adjustment capacity."[18] Increasing competition in product and labor markets, with a bow to innovation, had been a critical aspect of the EU Lisbon Agenda, but structural reform gained even greater importance when it became obvious that austerity ended up increasing, rather than decreasing, public debt levels and, with them, the sought-after investor confidence.[19]

With fiscal policy essentially outlawed, structural reforms became the only growth agenda. Consequently, they became embedded in the main coercive devices of the EU: bailouts, ECB threats of discontinuing sovereign bond market interventions, "excessive deficit procedures" and exposure to name-and-shame processes within the so-called European Semester (de la Porte and Heins 2016).

The rationale for structural reforms has been that increased competition in labor and product markets would reduce the macroeconomic imbalances between the periphery and the core of the EU because these reforms would trigger a "real devaluation" of peripheral economies chock-full of institutional rigidities, thus shrinking their competitiveness gap (Blyth 2013; Armingeon and Baccaro 2012). By increasing external aggregate demand, internal devaluation acts as an external demand-side stimulus. Moreover, echoing rational expectation theory, it was argued that such reforms would also boost expectations about future growth prospects, while stimulating current demand through wealth effects (Eggertson et al. 2014). As a research team headed by the IMF chief economist made clear (Blanchard, Jaumotte, and Loungani 2014), internal devaluation was in fact mostly about wage cuts, a point reinforced in the case of Spain by star economist Jordi Galí (2010).

How to Kill a Stimulus: Coercion and Collateral Damage

Caja Blues

In 2009 the Zapatero government already faced the retrenchment of European neoliberalism from a position of structural weakness. The Achilles heel of its economic model was its wobbly financial sector, hooked on ECB liquidity, and the extreme vulnerability of the Spanish sovereign to financial turbulence in a new world of European finance ushered by the euro. It is through this twin channel that overwhelming external coercion terminated Madrid's editing of fiscal orthodoxy with Keynesian ideas.

The massive post-Lehman financial deleveraging of large European banks that had financed Spanish banks before the crisis meant that these banks saw increasingly restricted access to wholesale funding after October 2008. By the spring of 2009, wholesale market liquidity for these banks began to dry up. While Spain's large multinational banks weathered this crisis well because they could appeal to their booming Latin American subsidiaries, the *cajas* were not in the position to do so because their balance sheets had been particularly damaged by the bursts of the real estate bubble (Royo 2013). The crisis came to a head in April and May 2010. At that point the interbank payments system of the Eurosystem (TARGET 2) showed that Spain experienced the greatest capital outflows of all the periphery countries (around 100 billion euros). The Spanish financial sector was in fact going through a slow-motion financial stop; to top it off, most *cajas* effectively lost affordable access to the international wholesale markets, making exorbitant demands on government fiscal resources.

In effect, a substantial part of the Spanish financial sector now depended on the policy decisions of the ECB, an institution that began to withdraw liquidity from the market in the aftermath of the Greek fiscal scandal. Critically, far from being a simple monetary policy body, by the spring of 2010 the ECB had become deeply involved in coordinating austerity and structural reform surveillance systems and bailouts, making politicians in Madrid extremely nervous about the fate of their attempt to defend embedded neoliberalism (Zapatero 2013, 35–36).

Paying for Financializing the State

The second channel through which the government was vulnerable to coercion was the link between its banks and the sovereign bond market analyzed in chapter 2. This "great transformation" of European finance and state debt enabled banks to multiply their business several times over before the crisis, but its downside was that the whole scaffolding was based on the heroic assumption that all government bonds used as collateral would keep their value as long as they were used in these transactions, an assumption that was clearly proven wrong following the Greek crisis. Since the entire system depended upon all eurozone bonds having the same value as collateral, in 2010 the dubious value of Greek bonds triggered a fire sale of periphery bonds, including Spanish bonds. As a result, collateral managers in Spanish banks were compelled to reduce exposure to lower-value bonds, even if they belonged to their own government, a trend that intensified in April and May 2010.[20] In this way, domestic banks' loyalty toward their government became closely tied to the collateral qualities of government debt, and in the spring of 2010 this quality was low (Gabor and Ban 2015).

As a result, Spain had to address the disruption of collateral markets for fear that bank runs would ruin its banking system and, with it, its prospects to have local buyers for its bonds.[21] Since in the view of the reigning orthodoxy the attempt to absorb these costs through expansionary fiscal policy could only make the problem worse (leading to further downgrades), the onus fell upon the Spanish government to pay the price of stabilizing collateral markets. Ultimately, the collateral damage of collateralization was austerity and "structural reforms" (Gabor and Ban 2013; Blyth 2013). The consolidation state kicked in, shifting an increasing share of society's resources from citizens to creditors while shrinking the total sum of available resources, as Streeck (2013) predicted.

In this kind of crisis, there were three ways to reassure bond investors: solidarity among the members of the monetary union, the intervention of the central bank as a lender of last resort, or austerity. The solidarity campaign could have been credible only if led by Germany (Matthijs and Blyth 2011), but Germany refused to write the Kindlebergian hegemon's checks, as some suggested (Paterson 2011) because of its domestic capacities, domestic political constraints, and entrenched ideational hostility to moral hazard (Mabbett and Schelke 2015). In these conditions, the eurobond option went nowhere (Bulmer and Johnson 2013; Berghahn and Young 2013; Crespy and Schmidt 2014). As a result, the ensemble of EU crisis management acquired a distinct ordoliberal face (Nedergaard and Snaith 2015), and until the Draghi moment the euro became a currency for which no one was responsible (Marsh 2013).

Moreover, instead of solidarity, the EU member states went into a phase of "culturalization" of the crisis, replete with morality tales and even blatant prejudice (Blyth 2013; Fourcade et al. 2013; Mylonas 2012; Streeck 2013; Matthias and Blyth 2015; Mathijs and Namara 2015).

This situation left the ECB's function as a lender of last resort the second-best option. Unfortunately, when the sovereign bond crisis started in the spring of 2010, the European Central Bank declined to repair the damaged collateral function of "peripheral" sovereign bonds (Gabor 2013). Moreover, the ECB became the enforcer of austerity on nonprogram periphery countries like Spain or Italy by using its bond purchases as leverage.

The End of Spain's Keynesian Revival

According to the memoirs of the Spanish prime minister (Zapatero 2013, 52–107), his minister of finance Pedro Solbes (Solbes 2013, 402–408, 424), and his main economic advisers interviewed by this author (Carlos Mulas Granados and Miguel Sebastián), Spain's fiscal stimulus was terminated not by the reassertion of fiscal orthodoxy in the cabinet, but by external political and economic coercion enforced via financial channels.

Indeed, Madrid's resistance proved to be no match for the combined coercion deployed by the bond markets and the EU, which reached new heights in May 2010, after a spring made "hot" by the Greek fiscal scandal. Between January and May, Zapatero watched, appalled, as the EU summits began to narrate the Greek crisis as symptomatic of a broader European debt crisis. In the process, he became convinced that the only way in which Spain could avoid losing sovereignty and a massive destruction of its public services and labor institutions through a Greek-style bailout was to acquiesce to the demands of the most powerful EU governments and the ECB. As one of his advisers put it, "He became convinced that if you give the blood of your own people, the markets will calm down." This point was driven home in conversations with EU heads of state (Zapatero 2013, 68–107) and bond investors, whose short-term views and limited knowledge about Spain were striking, with their views shaped exclusively by international financial media (212–214).

Zapatero also became particularly terrified by a conversation he had in the spring of 2010 with US vice president Joe Biden, who "with a cruelty that I've never encountered said that the only way to get market confidence is to take decisions that make you suffer really hard . . . that you are credible in a given set of circumstances if you subject your citizens to difficult tests and if unions openly reject your policies—in brief, if there are tears and suffering" (Zapatero 2013, 102).

By early May, with the *cajas* cut adrift from international liquidity and its commercial banks dumping Spanish bonds, the Zapatero government faced the demands of the EU heads of state and finance ministers that it make an explicit, immediate, and public statement to the effect that Spain would adopt significant deficit reductions to the tune of 3 percent of GDP (a level that was eventually bargained down to 1.5 percent), plus labor market deregulation. Acceptance of the deal would be followed by ECB bond purchases that would ease pressures on the Spanish state and, with it, on its private sector. Rejection would have meant financial collapse and a more invasive and drastic austerity carried out by the Troika. Given the power concentrated in his hands, Zapatero sealed the deal over the phone with his finance minister and, under the threat of early elections, had an austerity package focused on expenditure cuts passed in parliament after a dramatic debate, with 169 votes for the package and 168 votes against it (Zapatero 2013, 103–105, 115–116). A labor deregulation reform followed a month later.

In May 2010, Spain's own translation of fiscal policy revisionism came to an end. Nevertheless, the extraordinary mechanisms of coercion that started to operate then did not nullify the entrenched tradition of Spanish Socialists and their economic experts: to negotiate a middle ground between neoliberalism and social equity.

The Retrenchment of Spain's Embedded Neoliberalism (2010–2011)
Lines in the Sand

As the delayed, economically counterproductive, and piecemeal response of the EU crisis resolution regime failed to sustainably reassure the sovereign bond markets (Marsh 2013; Blyth 2013), the Zapatero cabinet spent the remaining eighteen months of PSOE's term trying to salvage the Socialist legacy, thus avoiding shifting their policy paradigm into disembedded neoliberal mode.

Critically, when designing the 2010 fiscal consolidation package, his policy team never bought the argument popular among EU elites that austerity leads to growth. Rather, in interviews and memoirs they made it clear that austerity was damaging and was adopted only out of fear that a bailout would induce even harsher austerity. Critically, Zapatero and his team stood by three main criteria for distributing the weight of adjustment. First, the pillars of social cohesion (unemployment benefits, education, student fellowships, universal and free access to healthcare, medicine subsidies) were declared "untouchable" (Zapatero 2013, 31). As such, they were barely shifted by austerity until external coercion tightened and a conservative government came to power.

Second, in line with social democratic considerations about equity, public sector wages should be cut in a steeply progressive way, a decision adopted in the May 2010 austerity package (Zapatero 2013, 33–35). Moreover, cuts to public sector wages did not average more than 7 percent in total even at the peak of the conservative government's austerity drive. Indeed, Spanish governments hesitated to cut unemployment benefits until 2012, and the healthcare system executed spending cuts mainly through pricing pressure on drug suppliers and the introduction of a nominal copayment.

Third, faced with demands for adopting a drastic deregulation of the labor market through decree laws, the cabinet adopted much milder reforms meant to reduce firing costs and offer opt-outs from collective bargaining (IMF 2010, 63–72). The same happened to pension reforms over the course of the following year.

Critically, the Zapatero government tried to defend embedded neoliberalism through labor market reforms that balanced security and flexibility by incentivizing firms to provide more permanent contracts and explicitly constraining the use of short-term contracts while also easing the conditions under which firms experiencing difficulties could opt out of the wage levels decided in collective bargaining. The reform was consistent with the embedded neoliberal principle of negotiating a compromise between credibility with the markets and society's demand from protection against the market.

Governing by Correspondence

The defense of the legacy of embedded neoliberalism in Spain became harder still in the summer of 2011, when sovereign bond investors unimpressed by the EU governance of the crisis launched fresh attacks. This time, the European Central Bank introduced a new coercive mechanism in its relationship with countries experiencing stress in the markets: letters to their heads of state stating what reforms were needed in exchange for the ECB buying their sovereign bonds on the open market (thus enabling local banks to buy their sovereign's bonds). The tactic had been tested in November 2010 when the ECB president wrote to the Irish government that the ECB would stop emergency lending to the Irish banks if the government would not adopt the fiscal and structural reforms demanded by the ECB.[22]

As the risk premiums on Spanish and Italian bonds went up dramatically yet again in August 2011, the ECB chairman, Jean-Claude Trichet, went as far as sending Zapatero a confidential letter (later published by Zapatero in his memoirs) containing a complete list of specific measures the government should adopt (Zapatero 2013, 237–268). Soon afterward, the government rushed through the parliament a constitutional amendment inspired by the German template that mandated structural surpluses. In effect, this constitutionalization of sound finance thus made fiscal revisionism illegal. This was the only time Spain had modified its constitution since the transition to democracy and the "return to Europe," and it was no small irony that it was an unelected EU institution that cast a shadow over Spanish democracy in this way.[23]

In response to market and ECB pressures that conjured up to the prime minister the specter of national humiliation represented by a bailout, the cabinet also adopted a raft of market liberalization measures. In line with the state-coordinated logic of Spanish embedded neoliberalism, after organized labor and capital failed to agree on further reform, the government adopted a raft of measures that encouraged firm-level bargaining and promoted arbitration as an alternative to labor conflicts.

Nevertheless, Zapatero's government was not a free marketer on labor reform, and the corporatist institutions and proworker courts were left to handle the details. As Hopkin and Dubin showed, the devil was in the details because "the reform either delegated the development of the proposed measures to the social partners or else left the sectoral bargaining partners with the ability to limit the development of questions like firm-level opt-outs" (2013, 37). Similarly, the IMF complained that "while these reforms are positive, they fall short of the necessary 'regime change' and, crucially, do not address the wage bargaining system. . . . The government should thus follow up on its commitment to take action itself and introduce a more fundamental reform, including of the wage bargaining system" (IMF 2014, 20).

Most certainly, the Zapatero government could have done more to shield society against the collateral damage of the European financial crisis turned sovereign debt crisis. There were no explicit objections in the recalibrated neoliberalism of the EU institutions against making large fortunes, and the most profitable sectors (banks and energy) shielded more of the fiscal burden of the adjustment. The EU orthodoxy was all about spending-based consolidation, yet in practice it never went beyond rhetorical discomfort when the Hungarian government imposed extra levies on banks even while it found itself under a Troika bailout (Johnson and Barnes 2014). Some economists pointed out that more revenue could have come from the reinstatement of the wealth taxes Zapatero eliminated in his first mandate, the reversal of all cuts in the inheritance tax adopted during the same term, and the reversal of the tax cuts he granted to individuals making more than 120,000 euros per year. His cabinet did little to tackle tax loopholes used to shelter large private fortunes and corporate profits accounting for almost two-thirds of tax avoidance in Spain (Navarro, Torres Lopez, and Garzon Espinosa 2011).

In 2010, bold ideas about more redistributive taxation were advocated by some in the Economic Bureau based on emerging research disproving the conventional wisdom that spending cuts are less damaging to growth than revenue increases. José Blanco, a prominent member of the PSOE hierarchy and a cabinet member, added to this choir, stressing that not taxing energy companies further was incompatible with the green jobs agenda and pushing for capping bankers' wages and for increasing the capital gains tax. Yet these voices faced strong opposition from the prime minister and his closest adviser (Miguel Sebastián), who feared that even a one-off levy on the banks would have further complicated the government's capacity to roll over its rapidly rising debt. Moreover, the prime minister himself also clarified that "his progressive views did not include being excessively interventionist when it came to taxing corporations."[24] Such nondecisions highlight the fact that at the end of the day, even a government as progressive and experiment-prone as Zapatero's was too shy to push the limits of neoliberal ideas about taxation.

In the end, external coercion channeled through the bond markets and the ECB forced PSOE to renege on fundamental aspects of its economic doctrine weeks before the 2011 elections. Averse to the perspective of a bailout, Zapatero fell on his sword and took the party down with him, ushering the conservative PP and its leader Mariano Rajoy into power.

The End of Embedded Neoliberalism? (2011–)
"Prussia of the South"

> Once an economic basket-case that came within a hair's breadth of a bailout, Spain now thinks of itself as the Prussia of the South—austere, disciplined and ready to absorb short-term economic pain for longer-term gains in competitiveness.
>
> —*Financial Times*, February 3, 2015

The body of ideas and policies that constituted Spain's precrisis neoliberalism experienced a drastic retrenchment after late 2011. Certainly the international coercive apparatus identified in the previous sections was still active, but this time its representatives were speaking to the converted. The economists who shaped the policy thinking of the Rajoy government (2011–2015) came from professional domains that had planned a greater disembeddedness of neoliberalism than the Socialists' experts ever had. While Zapatero's experts were drawn from a network of economists who were deeply steeped in international research on macroeconomics and, therefore, more open to the Keynesian openings in the mainstream, the economists of the Partido Popular came largely from the world of private finance, conservative think tanks, and the party's own technocracy. In these professional universes, fiscal hawkishness was hardly troubled by counterevidence unearthed by the latest IMF or academic research.

The experts and politicians clustered around the Spanish Right had been critical of Zapatero's stimulus, as well as of his cabinet's reluctance to decentralize collective bargaining institutions and drastically loosen hire-and-fire labor laws.[25] Experts like ex-Lehman CEO Luis de Guindos; the PP's former minister of finance, professor of macroeconomics, and adviser to the employers' association CEOE Cristobal Montoro; or Harvard-trained PP economist and *tecnico commercial* Álvaro Nadal saw in fiscal consolidation and extensive labor market deregulation the right responses to Spain's fiscal and competitiveness crisis. Indeed, they had espoused such ideas well before the crisis (Montoro 1995; 1997; 1998) and after 2008 they became the local spokesmen for the post-2010 Brussels-Frankfurt Consensus (Montoro and Nadal 2009; Montoro 2011a; 2011b) while attacking the spending-based stimulus of the government with New Classical arguments (Montoro and Nadal 2011).

These men drafted the PP's economic policy agenda, and when the party came to power in late 2011, Guindos became minister of the economy, Montoro became the finance minister, and Nadal headed the prime minister's Economic Bureau. Perceived in the PP as "man with firm liberal ideas who will take his theoretical idea to the very limit,"[26] Nadal, for example, was the protégé of Vice Premier Soraya Sáenz de Santamaría and was called "the most German of Spaniards" by the German press for his admiration for German policy and high-level contacts in Angela Merkel's entourage.[27] The PP and the cabinet incorporated professionals with more radical neoliberal views, such as the former director of conservative think tank FAES Jaime García-Legaz, who in the mid-2000s went as far as critiquing the Commission for proposing a relaxation of the fiscal framework of the euro (García-Legaz 2005). However, his institutional position (minister of commerce) did not put him and his team at the center of the debate on fiscal consolidation and internal devaluation.

Given their control over the policy process, the Rajoy policy team implemented a deep austerity package in 2012 and 2013 that shrunk public spending by 4 percent, bringing Spain below the EU-15 public spending average threshold, with the finance minister bragging, "We did the largest reduction of public spending in Spanish history."[28] Rajoy's top experts also subscribed to the main growth strategies advocated by the Brussels-Frankfurt Consensus under conditions of austerity: labor and product market deregulation plus bank reforms that made banks restart credit.[29] Of these, labor market reforms mattered the most, as they were seen in Madrid as the main device for lowering unit labor costs and, through the ensuing internal devaluation effect, increasing the country's competitiveness (Hopkin 2015, 177–178).

Decentralizing collective bargaining at the firm level was the main axis of Luis de Guindos's thinking before the elections. Taking Germany's Harz IV reforms of 2003 as a model, he stressed that decentralization was a necessary instrument of adjusting corporate costs and, with it, improving the economy's competitive position. In a bow to local concerns, his espousal of firm-level collective bargaining edited the neoliberal message about reducing corporate costs with the more "social" argument that decentralization would give firms incentives to lay off temporary workers because of the lower labor standards of firm-level contracts.[30] All these ideas became law in Spain in 2012.

The EC and ECB pressures locked in these policies. In 2012, Spain experienced the largest capital outflows in the "periphery" (as measured by TARGET 2), a situation that enabled the ECB to keep Madrid on a tight leash, should its fiscal orthodoxy or structural reforms flag. Meanwhile, the EC shamed Spain with its Excessive Deficit Procedure. In response to the 2012 country-specific recommendations of the EC in the European Semester, the Rajoy government launched a comprehensive plan covering fiscal, labor market, education, and product market reforms, as well as measures to improve the business environment. In response to the same demands, the cabinet adopted measures that had not been advocated by its experts, such as the establishment of an independent fiscal council to review fiscal policy decisions and the adoption of measures to increase the cost-effectiveness of the healthcare sector by reducing hospital pharmaceutical spending.

But while it was critical of the Socialists' version of embedded neoliberalism, on balance Rajoy's policy team was not prepared to go all the way down into the disembedded neoliberalism defended in East European member states like Romania. On fiscal policy, the PP technocrats never agreed with the expansionary austerity thesis popular in Brussels and Frankfurt between 2010 and 2013. Instead, they defended the weaker version of the austerity thesis, advocated by the IMF: austerity is a contractionary policy that works like a reassuring device for sovereign bond investors. They also disagreed with the pace of fiscal consolidation requested by Brussels and even pushed the European Commission to recalculate Spain's structural deficit so that the spending cuts could be stopped (Schmidt 2015).

Most importantly, in 2012 these economists balanced spending cuts with revenue increases that reflected the old progressive tax philosophy of Spain's embedded neoliberalism. They increased capital taxation from 19–21 percent to 21–27 percent and introduced an additional tax bracket for the wealthiest (54 percent rate for incomes over three hundred thousand euros), while increasing rates progressively for all other income groups. In effect, while the lowest incomes saw a tax rise of 0.7 percent, top incomes saw a rise of 7 percent. While dented, the welfare state was not ravaged. Both the duration and the size of the safety net for the unemployed are slightly higher on average than the EU-28 average, albeit not of the "old" EU. Faced with the persistence of long-term unemployment, in 2014 the government and the unions designed a support package that granted an additional six months of benefits to the half a million unemployed who had used up all their entitlements. Finally, wage deflation was not pushed as strongly as the IMF and the EC demanded (IMF 2014; EC 2015).

In terms of framing austerity, there were no morality tales about the parasitic nature of social benefit recipients and public sector workers or the inexorably rent-seeking core of state bureaucracy. Instead, the reformers framed spending cuts as technical and targeted measures meant to shield public education and health as much as possible.[31] Moreover, despite his reputation as a fiscal hawk who in 2014 received Merkel's support to head the Eurogroup (an informal and powerful club of finance ministers from the eurozone), de Guindos was an advocate of public debt restructuring as a means to create fiscal space for eurozone members who had difficulty financing themselves. In his view, this made not only economic sense, but was also the only way to guarantee that reformist governments would politically survive the reforms.[32] Although the PP operated Spain's largest labor market liberalization whereby the bargaining power of labor was dramatically scaled back (Dubin and Hopkin 2013, 41), the PP's labor market reforms were criticized for the IMF for not representing a rupture with the past (IMF 2015c, 3–5) and were certainly not as extreme as in Romania.

Whither Embedded Neoliberalism?

By mid-2015, the advocates of this stripped-down version of embedded neoliberalism claimed that they have been vindicated. "The crisis is over," said Rajoy, pointing to the beginning of a recovery (2.8 percent growth in GDP), one of the fastest-growing economies in the eurozone. There were also growing exports, and, critically, unemployment went down from 26 percent in 2012 to 23 percent by the end of 2015. De Guindos outbid his prime minister and predicted five years of uninterrupted growth. The international financial media highlighted Spain as a kind of anti-Greece, the country that did its homework and was now ready to reap the benefits. As a *Foreign Affairs* article quipped, it was time to be "bullish on Spain" (Encarnación 2015). Time will tell if these predictions turn out to be justified.

What is clear, however, is that the price tag was very high and difficult to reduce: imploding wages, ten million people on precarious labor contracts, 90 percent of the new jobs on short-term contracts (a fourth of them for less than a week), a dramatic collapse in collective bargaining agreements, and the deepest wage cut in OECD after Greece. The number of Spaniards who had been unemployed for longer than three years grew exponentially, reaching 1.2 million people in 2014, a 500 percent increase relative to the precrisis peak. In 2014, a Council of Europe report found that Spain's minimum wage was insufficient for a dignified life (Council of Europe 2014). The Spanish National Institute of Statistics found that a third of Spanish citizens were socially excluded or "at risk of poverty" status in 2014. Spain's medium-skill, medium-value-added growth model was further weakened by cuts in research and development, a poorly reformed banking sector, and extreme dependence on keeping wages low (Fishman 2014). Wage cuts and the second-highest level of unemployment after Greece make a large part of the private debt uncollectable, worsening the problems of the country's financial institutions (Fishman 2012). Critically, the central bank pointed out that the recovery had to do more with external factors (ECB monetary policy, lower oil prices, a devalued euro) and the end of austerity measures in 2014 than with the persistent deflationary bias and internal devaluation obtained via labor market deregulation and extensive public sector cuts (Banco de España 2015).

The political project aimed at the disembedding of neoliberalism in Spain seems to have important political limits. By 2014, political forces that challenge embedded neoliberalism from the left threatened the country's political status quo with political and economic ideas linked to Latin America's "pink tide." The Spanish electorate's support for Podemos and the victory of the new Left in the municipalities of Madrid and Barcelona showed that the public will not vote for the social costs of unending fiscal austerity twice when there is no light at the end of the tunnel. When this book went to press, it was not clear how prepared Podemos was to address the social deficit of Spain's neoliberalism. But the Rubicon has been crossed. Although the Greek crisis showed the extremely resilient limits to the left project inside the eurozone, for a while at least, the rise of Podemos vindicated those who argued that "if all that seems possible is the lengthening of the tunnel, then either democracy refuses the policy menu or the enforcers of the policy menu ignore democracy" (Matthijs and Blyth 2015, 266).

Conclusions

Albeit partisan politics moved successive Spanish governments in different directions, the ideas of embedded neoliberalism proved to be remarkably resilient after the Lehman crisis. At first, the crisis ushered in a recalibration of neoliberal fiscal theories with bold Keynesian ideas that pushed the limits of mainstream fiscal policy. This approach was owed to the prominent positions in the state held by Spanish economists who had been at the forefront of major intellectual shift in global macroeconomics. Given that the Spanish policy process was highly centralized and the prime minister's transnationalized economic advisers socialized him into this synthesis of neoliberal and Keynesian ideas, between

2008 and 2010 Spain met the crisis with the largest expenditure-based stimulus in Europe.

However, when the sovereign bond market crisis that struck the "periphery" of the eurozone in the spring of 2010 brought the Spanish financial system and the fiscal position of the Spanish government to the edge of the precipice, EU-level coercive mechanisms kicked into gear, terminating this Spanish experiment. As the solutions provided by the European governance of the crisis failed to stabilize the bond markets in the "periphery" and with the ECB acting as the enforcer of fiscal orthodoxy, Spain came under extreme pressure to dismantle parts of the embedded neoliberal legacy, eliminating further disembedded neoliberalism from societal demands. Even so, the Zapatero government tried to defend core public services and make the wealthy pay for a greater share of the tax end of the fiscal adjustment, testimony for the resilience of local translation processes of ruling economic ideas. It was only with the arrival of conservatives to power in 2011 and the large capital outflows of 2012 that a more drastic retrenchment of embedded neoliberalism took place.

Domestic translations of neoliberalism matter, but they face strong and increasingly constraining external coercive structures if they challenge the "consolidation state," an institution whose main job is simply "to credibly restore its long-term capacity to provide safe investment opportunities to holders of financial assets and reassure them that their claims will take precedence over the social claims made by citizens" (Streeck 2013, 155).

The Resilience of Disembedded Neoliberalism in Romania

Radicalizing Neoliberalism

It is not every day that one hears the managing director of the IMF charged with being an ideologue of the left[1] and a proponent of "state capitalism" whose fondness for it was deemed traceable to his communist youth.[2] Yet this is exactly what happened in Romania in 2010, after Dominique Strauss Kahn asked the Romanian government to spread the costs of austerity more equitably[3] and the IMF team designing the austerity package asked for more reliance on revenue measures at the expense of regressive spending cuts.[4]

The main reason for such striking positions in one of Europe's most volatile economies was that, unlike in Spain, local decision-makers and their policy intellectuals had recalibrated disembedded neoliberalism via an even greater expansion of the role of markets and an even greater redistribution of resources away from labor and toward capital. In this context, the fiscal consolidation and structural reforms exacted by the IMF-led loan packages of 2009 and 2010 provided a supportive environment in which the Romanian version of disembedded neoliberalism could be deepened in thought and in practice.

Indeed, while the economic thinking of Zapatero's cabinet was shaped by economists with high-prestige international credentials who represented the cutting edge of Keynesian calibrations of existing neoliberal theories, the economic thinking of the Romanian authorities was shaped by professional and amateur economists with local degrees and loose connections to the changes taking place in mainstream economic thinking since 2008. External coercion and competition for capital locked some of these ideas into policies, but, as the next sections explain, they do not provide complete explanations of the resilience and further radicalization of Romania's disembedded neoliberalism.

This chapter attempts to account for the resilience of neoliberal ideas and policies in Romania throughout phases of radicalization (2008–2012) and moderation

(2012–2015). It focuses on critical juncture of the crisis (2009–2011) and then examines the long-run implications of neoliberal resilience through 2015, spanning the tenure of both center-right and center-left governments. It begins by exploring the explanatory potential of conventional hypotheses such as international coercion and interest group politics and then highlights the value added of an explanation that compares the ideas and power of local translators of neoliberalism relative to that of their challengers. The chapter concludes by identifying the limits to the further radicalization of neoliberalism in Romania.

Resilience through International Coercion
The Power of Coercion

As the most traditional form for ensuring the spread and resilience of neoliberalism, coercion has not lost its punch. The previous chapter and much of the existing literature on crisis management in Eastern Europe sees international coercion via IFIs and international banks as a powerful explanatory mechanism for policy outcomes in Europe during the crisis (Gabor 2010a; Lütz and Kranke 2010; Kudrna and Gabor 2013; Jacoby 2014).

In 2009 and 2010, Romania was an easy target for international disciplining. The procyclical fiscal policies of populist neoliberalism (low flat taxes, generous real estate and corporate tax breaks, opportunist—as opposed to coordinated— wage and pension rises) and the procyclical nature of the country's transnationalized and loosely regulated banking system dragged Romania into a financial crisis and a sovereign crisis at the same time. This forced the government to ask for a bailout by the East European version of the Troika (the IMF, the European Commission, and the World Bank), with the IMF as the most important lender (Pisani-Ferry, Sapir, and Wolff 2013, 18, 82). With the risk of an impending balance-of-payments crisis, even the government's left-leaning critics agreed that any government would have been compelled to implement the IMF's standard package of fiscal consolidation and structural reforms.[5]

Chapter 3 found that the populist neoliberalism (low flat taxes and pre-election spending) left the government's finances and external position severely exposed to downturns. Chapter 7 showed that the fragmentation of the policy sphere between 2005 and 2008 created a macroeconomic toxic brew through a combination of neoliberal tax policies, clientelist public sector employment, and the replacement of redistributive social safety nets with ad hoc pension and wage increases right before the elections. Consequently, when the crisis struck, there was no surplus to spend, and a gaping current account deficit exposed the country to bond market pressures and international policy conditionality (Voinea 2009; Ban 2013a; 2014). Indeed, the government's coffers were so depleted that it was hard to even make copayments on the only countercyclical buffer available: the EU "structural funds," a form of development aid that provided over one-third of public capital investment in the new EU member states (European Commission 2013, 4; see also Jacoby 2014, 65–67). To make matters worse, between the Lehman crisis and March 2009, Eastern Europe became the "subprime region" (Gabor 2010a), as global deleveraging and currency speculation pushed currencies sharply lower, with the Romanian leu receiving the worst of the beating.

This vulnerability to external pressures became manifest in the spring of 2009, when the country's financing needs were estimated to range between ten and twenty billion euros, depending on the policy scenario used (Voinea 2009, 136–137). In February 2009, the country's gross international reserves were depleted by a currency attack and covered only 75 percent of the short-term debt, with foreign bank subsidiaries threatening not to roll over short-term debt (Gabor 2010a). As a result, had it not been for the Troika loans, the government would have been unable to service its deficit and sustain basic capital investments or pay wages, pensions, and benefits.[6]

The Limits of Coercion

International conditionality is a powerful, yet incomplete, account of what happened. As in other countries with no "fiscal space" for a stimulus, the Troika demanded harsh fiscal consolidation and structural reforms, ranging from cutting debt and deficits to liberalizing the labor and energy markets, pension reform, reducing state ownership in the railways and terminating a part of rail-based public transport.[7] Overall, the Romanian government delivered on these promises.[8]

But, upon closer examination, the Troika also tried to curb the radicalism of local neoliberalism and left significant policy room for local decision-makers to decide how to distribute the ensuing pain. The main memorandum from 2009 and the supplemental ones from the 2010–2012 period pushed the Romanian authorities to strengthen financial regulation and supervision, increase public research funding and constrain informality in the labor market via beefed up government inspections. On the other hand, within the terms of the bailout, the Romanian authorities could have balanced revenue and spending measures and distribute the costs of spending cuts more progressively, or at least refrain from adopting labor laws that were in violation of ILO conventions. While the Troika demanded limits on general government spending, it did not ask for cuts in automatic stabilizers; those cuts were left to the national government, which chose to do them. With the usual caveats, these requests were not a lot more constraining and specific than those faced by Spain, especially after the ECB's letter to Zapatero in 2010–2011.

International coercion also does not explain why fiscal consolidation in Romania was largely a "flat tax" on incomes rather than the kind of progressive distribution of the burden of adjustment across different income groups allowed by the IMF and EU policy frameworks. Even though the international coercion represented by the IMF-led bailout of Romania from 2009 onward constrained the space for action, there was enough space for policy discretion left to at least make the adjustment less procyclical and spread the costs more evenly throughout society. Instead, the government attempted to meet deficit and debt reduction targets by hiking the VAT from 19 to 24 percent, cutting public sector wages by 25 percent across all income categories, and slashing 15 percent from all social assistance payments (handicap benefits, unemployment benefits, child allowances, etc.). These were not Troika requirements. The chief IMF negotiator Jeffrey Franks publicly confirmed that they would have preferred a fiscal consolidation that was less contractionary and socially regressive:

IMF SURVEY: The government has just announced new austerity measures, including a 25 percent cut in public sector wages. Was that really necessary?

FRANKS: Well, the government found itself in a difficult situation because the revised forecast for the deficit for 2010 with no action would have put the deficit at about 9 percent of GDP. So serious action was required. There were a number of possibilities that policymakers could have chosen—different mixes of revenue and expenditure measures—but their decision was to rely almost entirely on public expenditure cuts. IMF Survey: What was the IMF's recommendation?

FRANKS: We had looked at a number of different options, and most of our proposals were more balanced between revenues and expenditures. We discussed a number of different scenarios with policymakers during our mission, which just wrapped up. The government—the president, the prime minister, and the minister of finance supported by the entire cabinet—made the decision to go ahead with this particular approach.[9]

Franks's position reflected a revisionist fiscal doctrine at the IMF. If Romanian policymakers had not been radical neoliberals, they could have capitalized on the IMF's perestroika moment (Ban and Gallagher 2015) in order to negotiate more room for maneuvering, especially given the fact that the more "Keynesian" changes in the doctrine were advocated at the very top of the Fund after 2008 (Clift 2015; Ban 2015). Indeed, senior staff called for large and coordinated fiscal stimulus programs in countries with fiscal space (low deficits and low debt), and, against the Fund's pre-2008 policy line, the authors stressed the role of public investments and downplayed the expansionary virtues of tax cuts.

In previous research I showed that IMF's Keynesian calibrations on fiscal policy also concerned countries with little fiscal space, such as Romania.[10] When the Fund's official fiscal policy pronouncements (*World Economic Outlook* and *Global Fiscal Monitor*) were published in 2009, evidence of the origins of doctrinal change and continuity in staff research was there for all to see. The *GFM* insists that in the context of the lower tax collection rates in a crisis-ridden environment, governments should strengthen tax institutions rather than cut taxes. The reports also renounce the claim that policies that make income taxes more progressive lead to a decline in revenues.

In 2010, the *WEO* asked countries to refrain from frontloading consolidation based on IMF research that finds high risks of deflation. The studies cited in the *GFM* find that, beyond a certain threshold of adjustment spending, cuts are no longer effective. Critically, the *WEO* debunks an iconic study of the austerity camp (Alesina and Perotti 1997) and shows that fiscal stimulus packages have higher multipliers than consolidation and that the latter is contractionary and increases unemployment during recessions. The 2010 *GFM's* citations echo the December 28, 2008, paper (Spilimbergo et al. 2008) and suggest that financial transaction taxes are an appropriate contribution to the fiscal sustainability effort.

The 2011 *WEO* inveighs—yet again—against the expansionary austerity thesis of Alberto Alesina and colleagues and endorses IMF research that calls for a more progressive distribution of income and reproduces research that indicates that financialization boosts inequality and inequality contributes to unsustainable growth trends such as those that predated the Great Recession. By 2012 warnings about the risk of deflation emerged, but what is particularly striking is that two new lines of attack appear, and the self-defeating effects of austerity take center stage. The most important is the finding that since 2008 the economic slack was so large, the interest rates so low, and fiscal adjustment so synchronized that fiscal multipliers were constantly well over one. This finding implies that the IMF underestimated the negative effects austerity had on output because it assumed values of the fiscal multiplier that were too low. The same finding is echoed in studies cited in *GFM* that argue that consolidation when the multiplier is high erodes some of the gains in market credibility as a result of a higher debt ratio and lower short-term growth, which causes an increase in borrowing costs.

The network visualization presented in figure 9.1 suggests that the IMF's revisionism came largely from within its own ranks, and therefore was highly usable in negotiations.[11] In addition to the Centre for Economic Policy Research, for the IMF the network analysis suggests that the providers of orthodox economists came largely from central banks and universities. The inner circle of exclusive supporters of revisionism came from three elite US academic departments (UC Berkeley, UC San Diego, Northwestern University), the Institute for New

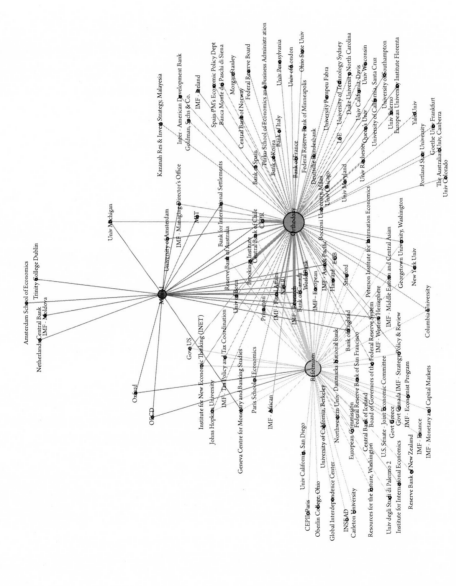

Figure 9.1 Professional affiliations of economists cited in the IMF's *World Economic Outlook* (2008–2013).

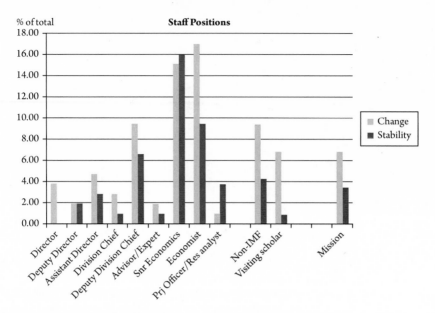

Figure 9.2 Positions of staff involved in the revisionist-orthodox debate.

Economic Thinking (INET), the Paris School of Economics, and, contrary to conventional wisdom, from several central banks (the Board of Governors of the Fed and the central banks of Denmark, Iceland, and England). In short, revisionist neoliberal fiscal policy was not only respectable. It was a high-status resource up for grabs.

Moreover, within the Fund, of the 144 economists involved in the debate (figure 9.2),[12] revisionism had the support of the top brass, not only of the "young Turks" (Ban 2015).[13]

In short, the twin financial and sovereign debt crises compelled the adoption of fiscal consolidation and structural reforms, but did not explicitly determine how the costs of adjustment would be distributed. Indeed, the IMF's ideas appeared to be to the left of the government's. To understand these critical aspects of the politics of distribution, it is first necessary to better understand the domestic politics of economic ideas that explain the resilience of radical neoliberalism in Romania.

Resilience through Competition

The previous chapters showed how disembedded neoliberalism put multinational capital at the heart of the country's industrial and service sectors. Against the background of deindustrialization, the low domestic savings and the low competitiveness of domestic capitalists, a combination of market-maximizing and pro-FDI interventionist state policies turned Romania into a semiperipheral dependent market economy where multinational capital created an export boom while exercised great leverage over local policymakers. This finding chimes with the literature that highlights the role of competitive signaling as the dominant economic strategy among most East European members of the EU (Nölke and Vliegenthart 2009; Bohle and Greskovits 2012; Hancké 2012; Appel and Orenstein 2015).

Indeed, by 2009 multinational capital was responsible for the country's export sector, so that export-based adjustment strategies would make it a particularly relevant force in the policy process (Ban 2013b). The Great Recession led to a collapse of FDI and remittance flows in 2009–2010, a development that threatened Romania with even higher current account deficits. For these multinational business interests, the recipe was their own version of embeddedness: defend the balance sheets of the local subsidiaries of multinational banks, keep wages as low as possible while deregulating the labor market, encourage state subsidies for new private investments, and reduce the tax burden on capital.

Multinational capital's sources of leverage were twofold: the financial sector and the "real economy," particularly the export sector. The financial sector constrained the policy space through its role in rolling over state debt after the deep financial crisis that came to a head in the spring of 2009 and affected most Eastern European countries (Blyth 2013, 216–225; Gabor 2013). Since 2008, this current account deficit had been harder to close than in the past (IMF 2009c). Remittance flows had been almost as important as FDI throughout the 2000s, but the countries where most Romanian remittances originated (Italy, Spain, and Ireland) faced a dramatic surge in unemployment, leading to the halving of remittance flows between 2008 and 2010 (Stanculescu et al. 2011, 18–21).

Worse still, throughout late 2008 and 2009, there was a distinct danger that the European banks that owned the bulk of the country's money supply could begin to pull out capital from their Romanian subsidiaries to supply funds to mother banks hit by the Lehman crisis, just as the West European crisis abruptly cut further investment flows into Romania. As Rachel Epstein showed, in 2008–2009 "west European states and even the European Commission tried to limit western banks' operations in CEE in favour of home market stimulus" (Epstein 2014, 869). Moreover, as panic about foreign banks in Eastern Europe set in credit rating agencies and financial media, the international counterparts of the foreign banks based in eastern Europe "either had or were threatening to cut their credit lines" to the latter (Epstein 2014, 855). Faced with this crisis, throughout 2009 central banks in Hungary, Poland, and Romania tried to convince the ECB to broaden the list of eligible collateral for its monetary operations by including government bonds issued in local currency in exchange for haircuts to these noneuro government bonds. The ECB rejected these suggestions, and, as a result, between October 2009 and February 2009, Hungary, Latvia, and Romania were effectively priced out of sovereign bond markets.[14] Only the simultaneous deployment of massive balance of payments support and an international commitment to firewall the business model of foreign banks could prevent an economic catastrophe. As an IMF official put it:

> If the banks weren't willing to roll over their loans, recapitalize their subsidiaries and more generally maintain their exposure to the region, it would have been difficult to avert a systemic crisis, even with the loans provided by the IMF, the European Union. . . .. In fact, those funds would have served only to bail out the private sector, replacing private debt by public sector debt, and done little to help the countries back on their feet, if we hadn't acted. (IMF 2009a)

The foreign banks' subsidiaries' interest to reassure their international counterparts, of national governments to roll over their debt and of international financial institutions to prevent serially correlated sovereign bankruptcies and a financial market epidemic were thus closely aligned. Ironically, it was in Vienna, the starting point of the Great Depression, where an agreement between private banks, the European Central Bank, the European Commission, the EBRD, the IMF, and the states in question was signed in 2009. In early 2009 the Vienna Agreement and the Troika bailout jointly established an international financial regime in which the IMF, the EU, and the banks exercised a form of shared control over fundamental aspects Romania's economic policy decisions. In exchange, the Romanian authorities received balance of payments support from the Troika while the Vienna Initiative signatories committed to "preventing a large-scale and uncoordinated withdrawal of cross-border bank groups from the region, which could have triggered systemic bank crises not only in individual countries but in the region as a whole; ensuring that parent bank groups maintain their exposures and recapitalise their subsidiaries in emerging Europe and ensuring that national support packages of cross-border bank groups benefited their subsidiaries in emerging Europe and thus avoided a "home bias."[15]

As in Hungary and Latvia (Mabbett and Schelke 2014), this agreement reassured banks to maintain their exposure and kept the government afloat. The banks would borrow from the central bank at 9.5 percent and lend to the government at 11.5 percent, a lucrative business in times of massive deleveraging and collapsing domestic demand (Voinea 2009, 138–139). Since the government had few international buyers for its bonds, its solvability depended on the continued willingness of local banks to buy Romanian government debt. Reassured in Vienna, these banks agreed to roll over short-term debt (BNR 2009). This willingness was in turn to be maintained by the commitment of the Romanian government to the austerity and structural reforms promised in the Troika loans. The bailout money transferred to the central bank's accounts enabled the BNR to reduce reserve requirements and increase the level of liquidity available to commercial banks. Nevertheless, the Vienna Agreement of 2009 did not survive the Greek crisis that began during the spring of 2010, and the best financing the government could get was at 12 percent rate for three months, an unsustainable rate that opened the doors to the deeper austerity and structural reforms adopted in 2010, while another collective commitment in Vienna in 2012 ensured that the foreign banks won't cut and run. In this way, neoliberal capitalism in the region could continue to operate firewalled by this evolving international institutional framework lubricated by public international liquidity.

The leverage of the multinational sector worked through the "real economy" as well. The application of disembedded neoliberalism quickly transformed Romania into a "production platform" for multinationals, from large automotive operations to the software industry, via pro-FDI policies ranging from low taxes to state aid, with questionable effects on the level of fiscal revenues for the state budget. Moreover, this approach made the Romanian economy completely dependent on the export capacities of developed countries and their inherent cyclical dynamics (Mereuță 2012). Indeed, by 2009, Austrian, German, French, and Italian firms (in this order) accounted for two-thirds of Romania's exports. Of the top one hundred exporters in 2011 (covering half of all exports), ninety-six were subsidiaries of multinationals. In 2011, out of the top one hundred Romanian firms, seventy-four were multinational (most of them West European), accounting for 82 percent of total business rollover and 86 percent of total gross profits (Mereuță 2012). This meant that, given the institutional complementarities of Eastern Europe's dependent market economies (Nölke and Vliegenthart 2009; Ban 2013), the competitive signaling to foreign capital they engaged in (Appel and Orenstein 2015) and the fact that FDI inflows were consistently procyclical during the first four year of crisis,[16] foreign entities held a great deal of leverage over the Romanian government.

In its policy documents issued during the crisis, the Foreign Investors Council (FIC, the organization representing the bulk of foreign investors, most of them European firms) demanded a raft of neoliberal policies (CIS 2010). These included public sector layoff targets, the closing down of all loss-making state firms, extensive privatization (as a way to reinvigorate the capital market, among other benefits), the outsourcing of parts of social services to private organizations, the elimination of taxes on reinvested profits, the tightening of insolvency procedures for debtors, full liberalization of the energy and gas markets, the full privatization of the energy grid, extensive tightening of the eligibility conditions for the already meager unemployment benefits, and the comprehensive deregulation of the labor market. Echoing the calls of the central bank's radical neoliberals, FIC also proposed that the government increase land taxation for small farms so that labor could be reallocated from farming to industry and services while land could be consolidated for more market-oriented use (CIS 2010; 2011).[17] Pro-FDI state supports are there too. FIC advocated the subsidization of large-scale investments aimed at building long-term growth potential (e.g., energy, infrastructure, agriculture logistics), tax incentives for new start-ups in high-value-added sectors, lowered thresholds for state aid to benefit SMEs, incentives for companies to keep the complete chain of production in Romania (including R & D), and emphasis on competitive rather than comparative advantage to help develop a "country brand." Together with the local SMEs and chapters of German, British, Dutch and American capital, GIC demanded the continuing application of the flat tax regime together with further cuts in capital gains.[18]

Given the leverage produced by their sheer weight within the economy, their high-level access to the presidency, and the executive and the overlap between their agenda and that of the IFIs, it is not surprising that the government fulfilled the key demands of organized foreign capital. The government completed drastic layoffs in the public sector, tightened unemployment benefits, and directed more than 90 percent of state aid given to new industrial projects to foreign multinationals operating in the middle-skill manufacturing sector (auto, white goods, chemicals, rail transport equipment).[19] Most importantly, in 2011 collective bargaining, the right to strike, hire-and-fire regulations, and the institutional basis of labor unions all experienced major onslaughts via a string of reforms adopted by emergency procedure and without labor union amendments (Trif 2013), in line with the FIC and American Chamber of Commerce (AmCham) demands.[20] Passed with the support of President Băsescu and Prime Minister Emil Boc, the whole legislative package, it is widely assumed, was drafted within the FIC and AmCham.[21] The extremely close fit between multinational capital's pre- and postcrisis proposals (CIS 2005; AmCham 2008; 2010) and the outcome of the 2011 reforms strengthens this argument. Strikingly, domestic employer organizations were against the reforms (Varga and Freyberg-Inan 2014).

Adopted through emergency procedure by the cabinet, the 2011 labor reforms created a probusiness liberal model of industrial relations that deregulated the labor market far more than even the IMF standards allow (Blanchard, Jaumotte, and Loungani 2014), going as far as breaking several ILO conventions ratified by Romania.[22]

Unlike in 2005, labor was unable to mobilize effectively. As chapter 3 showed, in 2005, multinational business and capital had less leverage because labor turmoil had brought down governments in the past, and the last thing Romania's weak EU accession dossier needed was social unrest. Moreover, during the boom years, lack of an agreement with the IMF labor shortages had strengthened the hand of labor. This time, labor had none of these sources of leverage. All confederations grew complacent in the shade of the progressive 2003 code and counted more on their connections with politicians than on their work to unionize more of the private sector and maintain a mobilized base.[23] Excluded from centralized collective bargaining (because of local representativeness criteria), multinational capital mobilized outside the existing corporatist institutions and resolved to take them down at the first opportunity.[24] To ensure that the labor unions would go down without a strong fight, an anticorruption agency launched an investigation into newly introduced corruption charges against fifteen trade union leaders, just as consultations and protests against the reforms were taking place (Varga and Freyberg-Inan 2014, 16–17).[25]

The labor reforms drastically unbalanced the employee-employer relation, leading to a massive drop in the number of employees covered by collective agreements (Guga and Constantin 2015). In just four years under the new legislation, the share of wages as a percentage of Romanian GDP fell to the lowest level in the EU (at roughly 30 percent) while, at the same time, the share of capital has skyrocketed to more than 60 percent (Georgescu 2015).

However, the critical role of the FIC and AmCham in the policy process does not explain all of the reforms that further disembedded neoliberalism from society. Crucially, foreign employers were not on board with fundamental fiscal policy reforms. They also proposed a slew of industrial policy reforms that grafted neodevelopmentalist ideas onto the very core of the neoliberal paradigm. In this regard, the European corporate lobby challenged both the neoliberalism of the Troika and its more radical local version.

Specifically, the FIC's *White Book* reports viewed fiscal consolidation as contractionary and criticized the agreement with the IMF as excessively deleterious to the country's short- and long-term growth prospects, going as far as to demand a renegotiation that would allow a higher deficit target and the establishment of larger infrastructure funds. To buffer the extreme contraction in domestic demand, the FIC also demanded the reversal of the VAT increase included in the IMF agreement and the reduction of the VAT for food from 23 percent to 9 percent. More striking still was the FIC's demand that the government establish financial institutions able to fulfill industrial policy objectives. First, the FIC requested the formation of a public development bank to boost lending to SMEs using the German KfW as a model, a proposition ignored by Romanian policy elites. Finally, the FIC demanded larger state aid schemes for what it thought were competitive sectors (e.g., energy and agriculture), while also challenging the corporate flat-tax regime by requesting lower tax brackets for research-and-development activities. More reliably pro-market than FIC, even the American Chamber of Commerce pushed for industrial policy and tax-finance German-style vocational training.[26]

As the next sections show, the reason why Romanian policy elites did not have to be convinced by the IMF and multinational business organizations regarding key neoliberal reforms, and why they in fact often challenged these organizations from the right, had do with the institutional cohesion and radical ideas of a policy coalition that had aligned all of its component parts by late 2009.

Radicals for Neoliberalism

Two and a half years of institutional cohesion between 2010 and 2012 enabled the transformation of radical neoliberal ideas into policies. This was not the case at the beginning of the crisis, however. Although they were the most determined advocates of radicalization, the Democrat-Liberals (PDL), the center-right party that had won the 2008 elections, did not have enough votes to form a majority government and only survived thanks to the temporary support of the Social Democrats (PSD). Since the Social Democrats had their own candidate in the presidential race of 2009, they had no incentive to support a harsh fiscal adjustment.[27] While the presidential elections of November 2009 had little economic policy substance, they did give conservative president Traian Băsescu a second term. With their leader in the presidential palace and their parliamentary support boosted by defectors from the ranks of the Liberals and the Social Democrats, the conservative PDL was finally able to form a solid majority.[28] Thus, the neoliberal coalition between the PDL and smaller conservative parties could count on having a cohesive policy process.

Romania is a semipresidential republic in which the president is directly elected and therefore plays a leading role in policy. Although the presidency has a stronger mandate in defense and foreign policy, this institutional guideline was most creatively interpreted during Băsescu's terms, with this former ship captain cavalierly pushing the limits of the presidential mandate to include socio-economic policy. Băsescu was the uncontested informal leader of the PDL and, from the very beginning, made it clear that he would control the main economic policy decisions of the cabinet, a task facilitated by the impeccable loyalty of Prime Minister Boc. To ensure the coherence of the economic ideas of the policy team at the top, one of Băsescu's former economic policy advisers (Andrea Paul Vass) was posted to serve the prime minister—a lawyer by training—in the same capacity.

This solid political coalition could count on the central bank (BNR) for support, expertise and reserve cadre. Respected, untainted by corruption scandals, and one of the few public institutions known for being meritocratic, BNR had spent a decade at the pinnacle of economic policy influence in the country.[29] As the next section shows, from the very onset of the crisis, BNR emerged as the most articulate advocate for radicalizing neoliberalism, and, therefore, from their perspective, this new government was an "unreserved blessing."[30] The central bank's top economists gave interviews and made regular public statements defending the government's reform ideas. Moreover, although the central bank boasted about its independence, its links with the presidency's and ruling party's economic team were deep. In 2008, Lucian Croitoru, the governor's main adviser and a passionate advocate of an original mix of New Classical macroeconomics and Hayekian political theory (see next section), coauthored PDL's party program together with the economic advisers of the president and prime minister. In the same year, the president even proposed that Croitoru become the new prime minister.[31]

The policy alliance between central bankers, the cabinet, the main ruling party, and the presidency was strengthened by the work of new independent agencies and policy think tanks strongly supported by the IMF and the EU. The think tanks were steeped in the early advocacy for neoliberal theories and policies that emerged during the 1990s and early 2000s. Through its regular reports, between 2009 and 2010, Societatea Academică din România (SAR), the pioneer of the policy think tank form in Romania, continued to play an important role in the continuing translation of "source" neoliberalism and the reproduction of its local "edits," albeit with less of the market radicalism it was known for before the crisis. The radical agenda was now advanced by think-tanks more embedded in the governing party and closer to libertarian radicalism (CADI, KAS). In between were two think tanks (Expert Forum and Center for European Public Policies) that had been established during the crisis by some of the most entrepreneurial and pro-market members of the SAR staff (Sorin Ioniță and Cristian Ghinea).[32]

Funded by the EC, the World Bank, UNDP, and the local corporate sector, Expert Forum (EFOR) quickly became an effective contributor to Romania's increasingly privatized knowledge regime and an important clearinghouse for debates on public finance, social policy, and energy, in addition to a host of classic issues pertaining to political liberalism and state capacity. Like SAR back in the late 1990s, this was not your typical probusiness think tank; instead, it was a hybrid between a business-friendly organization and a civil society activist dealing in "good governance" and institutional capacity contracts.

The same was true of the Romanian Center for European Policies (CRPE). Established by the LSE-trained SAR expert Cristian Ghinea in 2009, CRPE was a member of the Stockholm Network, the most organized effort to date to create a transnational community of radical neoliberal liberal think tanks in Europe.

Ghinea turned CRPE into one of the key civil society partners for the European Commission, and even became an exporter of EU-sanctioned expertise in EU's "near abroad."

Finally, the Romanian chapter of the Konrad Adenauer Stiftung (KAS), the foundation of Germany's main conservative party (the Christian Democratic Union, CDU) and PDL's own Institute for Conservative Studies (ISP) challenged the party and the cabinet to take neoliberal reforms further still by advocating a local adaptation of ordoliberalism that was in fact closer to Austrian economics than to anything resembling CDU policies, let alone Germany's coordinated market economy.[33] In contrast, the German Social Democrats' foundation (Ebert Stiftung) whose reading of the "social market economy" concept was distinctly more left-leaning social democratic, maintained a policy of not getting closely involved in the policy process beyond publishing independent research.[34] To date, its connections with the Romanian Social Democrats remain underdeveloped.[35] As a result, the local translation of German influence via think-tanks pointed a more libertarian reading of neoliberalism.

As in the past, the high status awarded by working directly with EU institutions heightened the relevance of think tanks in the policy process. EFOR and CRPE experts became Brussels regulars, and whenever European Commission representatives in Romania organized big debates on important issues such as the management of the sovereign debt crisis, the evolution of EU economic policy templates, or the enlargement of the eurozone, they partnered with CRPE to organize events bringing together EU officials and senior staff from the Romanian presidential administration, the central bank, the fiscal council, Ministry of Finance, and employer associations.[36] By choosing CRPE as its privileged partner, the EC made a statement about who was credible and about which ideas were normatively appropriate at a time when the SAR expert elite had become an essential component of the country's knowledge regime. As CRPE's Cristian Ghinea wryly observed in a Facebook post from 2015, "At the end of the day, folks who fourteen years ago fit in a small room at SAR have spread all over the place: in the cabinet, in the Competition Council, think-tanks, parties, the lot. We could start a mafia organization if we wanted."

The central bank and executive think tank chorus was further reinforced by the IMF's establishment of a fiscal council, a putatively independent institution tasked with evaluating the government's fiscal policy decisions, publicizing the results and regularly reporting its findings to the Troika (see Hagemann 2010 for an overview of pro-fiscal council arguments). In Romania, this agency proved to be an external-yet-internal anchor for austerity and structural reforms. By law, the parliament's draft bills could not be adopted without first consulting the Fiscal Council. Like central bank independence two decades ago, the argument that such an institution was necessary to enhance the credibility of macroeconomic policy was an extension of the neoliberal drive to insulate more economic policy issues from the democratic process. In reality, the fiscal council has acted as little more than an extension of the revolving door between the IMF, central bank, and the presidency.

External empowerment was critical in shoring up the council's authority. In the summer of 2010, weeks after the Fiscal Council was established, the Senate decided to vote on the bill without bothering to consult the new institution. In response, the Fiscal Council and the IMF staged a public intervention reaffirming the authority of the Council, and the bill was stopped in its tracks following the IMF's unveiled threats that its passage could result in trouble for the continuation of the loan agreement.[37] Furthermore, the Fiscal Council's voice in the policy sphere quickly grew thanks to the unqualified support it received from the European Commission. However, it was the IMF whose explicit demands led to the establishment of the Council in 2010 and, from the very beginning, the Fund gave weight to the Council's analysis by staging coordinated IMF–Fiscal Council interventions in which the IMF used the power of the purse to enforce the Council's prescriptions.

When "source" neoliberalism in the West came under fire after the Lehman crisis, the resilience of disembedded neoliberalism was ensured by the same network of professional and amateur economists who used the revolving doors between the central bank, the state (the executive power and political parties), the think tanks, and the private sector (consultancies and employer organizations). But instead of merely playing a defensive role, these actors went further, radicalizing old ideas and rejecting attempts made by the IMF and European Commission to recalibrate some aspects of neoliberal thinking and deflect some of the most extreme forms of dislocation produced by the crisis.

Manning the Ramparts

Throughout late 2008 and 2009, neoliberal theories faced formidable Keynesian critiques from bastions of orthodoxy such as the IMF, the G-20, the European Commission, the international financial press, and many mainstream economists (Blyth 2013; Ban 2015). Indeed, these theories were humbled by the multibillion-dollar government rescues of "too big to fail" financial institutions, large fiscal and monetary stimulus packages, the redefinition of fiscal consolidation, and the introduction of barriers to cross-border flows of financial capital (Blyth 2013; Moschella 2014; Grabel 2015; Chwieroth 2014; Ban and Gallagher 2015; Gallagher 2015; Gabor 2015). After decades of neglect, talk about the scourge of income inequality became mainstream, even in such bastions of neoliberalism as the IMF (Ban 2015).[38] The world, it seemed, was ripe for new economic thinking, and multibillionaire investor George Soros bankrolled a whole institute (INET) seeking such a change.

No such angst and soul-searching haunted Romanian defenders of neoliberalism, who closed ranks and struck back, forgoing the chance to make the most of the doctrinal and policy relaxation brought about by these events. Instead of being perceived as coercion, as in Spain, the policy agenda of the Troika was understood as a structural enabler for a local version of disembedded neoliberalism that, for reasons explained in chapter 7, could not be fulfilled before 2008. Even as mainstream economists in the West made tactical concessions, the majority of Romanian counterparts ignored arguments about the role of the deregulation of finance, the supervision-finance revolving door, the systemic risk posed by transnational banking, the importance of fiscal multipliers, let alone the perils of inequality and quasi-privatized public services. Rather, they portrayed the crisis as a result of too much state intervention, corruption, and the combination between social expectations and democracy.

In line with the findings of the previous chapters, some of the most radical views came from policymakers with fast-track transnationalization experiences or, in some cases, no economic training at all. Andrea Paul Vass was a professional researcher in economics at one of the institutes of Academia Română, but she could not boast more than a few short-run training programs and research trips at a few West European universities. Between 2009 and 2012, the president's economic advisers had similar experiences, and one of the most determined advocates of drastic labor market deregulation were known libertarian sociologists (Marian Preda, Sebastian Lazaroiu). Neither one of the ministers of finance (Sebastian Vlădescu and Gheorghe Ialomiţeanu) had gone through more than a few short courses abroad that awarded them skill-specific certificates. The labor minister who presided over the destruction of collective bargaining and the drastic deregulation of hire-and-fire rules in 2011 (Ioan Botiş) had no economic training and his family owned of a firm specializing in recruiting local workers for the West European labor market.

Professional transnationalization served as a conduit for diffusing neoliberal ideas, but in peripheral policy contexts low-intensity professional transnationalization tends to radicalize the policy implications of neoliberal theories. There was no awareness in these circles of the intellectual opening in mainstream economics and the IMF regarding fiscal policy, for example, as their thinking was shaped more by local conventional wisdom than by high-status international knowledge.

Replete with contradictions, this ideological project was radical for two main reasons. First, it defended the innovations of the 2000s (flat taxes, pension privatization), despite the potential fiscal benefits of their reversal. Second, local policymakers willingly exceeded the demands of IFIs and foreign capital by espousing and translating into practice a recalibrated form of monetary ortho-doxy that privileged exchange rate policy and the defense of a transnational-ized banking model. This minimalist form of monetary orthodoxy, stripped of the recalibrations ushered in by the crisis, called for swift structural reforms and a supply-side public investment policy with low fiscal and employment multipliers.

Monetary Policy as Pulp Orthodoxy

Since Lehman, the widespread deviations from the conservative mandate of central banking in developed countries were assessed with scorn by Romanian neoliberals. The use of New Keynesian economic models that factored in the output gap was deemed symptomatic of the "populist" drive in Western central banking, a mistake that meant that central bankers should be held responsible for the eruption of crises in the future.[39] New monetary policy instruments such as quantitative easing and Forward Guidance were similarly dismissed as hubris-tic forms of interventionism whose deployment was purely inflationary.

For the central bank's governor, the deep causes of the crises were the cheap liquidity of systemic central banks and the savings glut in Asia, with securitiza-tion, deregulation, and other market-maximizing policies relegated to "aggravated circumstances" status (Isărescu 2009, 2). One senior central banker outbid the governor and opined that quantitative easing was a clear example of a democratic pathology and, citing Tocqueville, argued that QE was the expression of the fact that, in a democracy, the lay public always prefers ideas that promise a maximum of comfort and a minimum of sacrifice. In his view, central banks had gone "pop-ulist."[40] Accordingly, senior Romanian central bankers deplored the ECB's shift from Trichet's pure orthodoxy to Draghi's innovations and called for even deeper structural reforms than those proposed within mainstream Western circles.

Another senior central bank economist expressed disappointment at the betrayal of orthodoxy by Western central banks, a fact he attributed to the social pathologies left behind by postwar Keynesianism:

> Those of us who come from former socialist states expected that devel-oped states who had taught us the lessons of the market economy would cease to intervene beyond TBTF institutions; but it seems that between them and their citizens there exists a special relationship that favors large-scale interventions. This special relationship did not exist before Keynesian views of the role of the state in the economy emerged, creating expectations about interventions and guiding action in hard times. (Croitoru 2012, 35)

If these statements are indicative of the intellectual atmosphere at the top of the BNR, it is unsurprising that this central bank's monetary policy theories remained closed to the unorthodox experiments adopted by many of its peers in the aftermath of the Lehman crisis. While central banks outside the euro-zone rushed to ease financing conditions for the sovereigns, the Romanian central bank did not. Daniela Gabor (2010a) showed that, in a replay of the 1999 crisis, in 2009 and 2010 the BNR refused to countenance direct moneti-zation of government debt by easing liquidity access for domestic commercial banks who bought sovereign bonds. Moreover, she shows that the central bank successfully demanded the transfer of the bulk of the Troika forex financing into its coffers (rather than turn it into leu liquidity), thus refusing to act as the government's forex agent. The ensuing liquidity crunch increased yields on these bonds above the central bank's policy rate, quickly reaching unsustainable levels (9 percent for three-month T-bills). It was a replay of the BNR's policy actions during the 1999 crisis, which had almost plunged the government into bankruptcy.

These policy actions were not unavoidable. A strong counterfactual is sup-plied by Gabor's analysis of the monetary policy of the central bank of Hungary, a country engaged in a similar bailout agreement with the Troika in 2009 and whose government had much higher levels of public debt. Gabor found that, in contrast to the BNR, the Hungarian central bank embraced the unorthodox ideas ushered in by the crisis and practiced an accommodative policy that kept yields below the policy rate, let the bulk of IMF financing reach the Treasury, and acted as the government's foreign exchange agent by turning all its forex into foreign liquidity. This enabled the Hungarian government to avoid a bailout in 2010.

Gabor attributes this decision to three normative positions that remained sacrosanct in the Romanian central bank: a narrow interpretation of its man-date as to not include debt sustainability considerations, a strong preference for exchange rate stability, and the radical neoliberal theory that central banks should not bother with coordinating monetary and fiscal policy in countercycli-cal ways.

Moreover, the central bankers interviewed by this author indicated that the central bank chose to prioritize foreign exchange rigor over accommodating the government's funding needs, not only because of the trauma left behind by a currency run in late 2008 (see Gabor 2010a), but also because it did not trust politicians to pursue fiscal rigor and adopt liberalizing structural reforms. The reason for this distrust of politicians was not the latter's ideology. Rather, it was the economic pitfalls of democracy.[41]

The crisis was an opportunity to build momentum for the ascent of domestic and external forces that would end previous deviations from fiscal orthodoxy by constitutionalizing it, in ordoliberal fashion. For a senior Romanian central banker, the crisis was a chance that was too big to be wasted by neoliberals worldwide: "The sovereign debt crisis is the greatest opportunity for progress. It can help us complete the reform began in the 1970s as long as it will diffuse across the world the idea that fiscal policy should be rules-based, the only protection against discretionary interventions" (Croitoru 2012, 37).

The neoliberal radicalism of the central bank was not airtight. Vice governor Florin Georgescu, for example, is known for his left-leaning New Keynesian views.[42] Moreover, on one key aspect of monetary policy (the exchange rate), the BNR as a whole did not embrace radical ideas about the irrelevance of accommodative currency devaluation in times of recession. The 15 percent devaluation of the leu during the crisis buffered some of the shocks suffered by the economy and contributed to the country's improved export competitiveness.

Fiscal Amputation
Outliberalizing the Troika

The parameters of the fiscal consolidation demanded by the Troika in 2010 were harsh, but they left room for maneuvering on two fronts: the balance between spending cuts and revenue increases, and the distribution of the costs of expenditure cuts. On both counts, the government did not use the available policy space.

The IMF's fiscal doctrine (since 2008) encouraged more taxation at the top of the income distribution through wealth, property, and capital gains taxes. This meant that, before cutting automatic stabilizers to balance the budget, the government would be advised to trim other forms of spending or opt for revenue-increasing measures (Ban 2015).

Romanian officials rejected revenue increases on the basis of two theories. The first was the familiar austerity theory—refuted by the IMF's own research (Ban 2015a)—that revenue increases are more damaging to growth rates than spending cuts because, while the former discourage investment, the latter encourage it. In a position note, the PM advisor Andreea Vass even used the classic research study of Harvard economist Alberto Alesina on "expansionary fiscal consolidation," arguing that spending-based fiscal adjustments benefit the economy in two ways: they reassure investors, and they spur growth faster than alternative strategies do (Vass 2010). By 2010, this argument had been rejected by IMF headquarters, and this author's interviews with the IMF staff involved suggest that the Fund did not condone the expansionary austerity thesis in its negotiations with the Romanian government that took place in the spring of 2010.

The second theory had more to do with particular local translations that reflected versions of neoliberalism that were no longer mainstream after 2008. For a senior central banker, government spending always confuses microeconomic expectations and reduces competition, thereby contributing to a decline in output. Moreover, it perpetuates bad cultural practices that sap the energies of the capitalist economy by encouraging the public's loss of confidence in the free market, stimulating sloth by "paying workers not to work" and creating new bonds between the state and society that favor large-scale government interventions in the economy even after a crisis is over (Croitoru 2012, 33–37). Also, for the chief economist of the BNR, activist fiscal policy was by definition undermined by the moral hazard of current generations passing the costs of adjustment onto future ones, while the idea of an alternative adjustment strategy based around progressive income taxes and differentiated VAT rates risked worsening the deficit. In effect, Romania's radical neoliberal flat-tax regime was deemed as the only conducive instruments of macroeconomic stabilization.[43]

Even an institution as loyal to the IMF as the Fiscal Council did not refrain from layering its sponsor's ideas with local content. Going against the IMF's new fiscal theory that fiscal consolidation focused mostly on the expenditure side stands to deepen the effects of recessions, the Council went as far as to define the very term "fiscal adjustment" as a strategy based almost exclusively on expenditure cuts (Consiliul Fiscal 2010, 1–2).

In its dealings with Romania, the Troika also left room for some flexibility in the distribution of the social costs of spending cuts. Author interviews with IMF economists involved in the negotiations suggest that the flat cut of 25 percent in all public wages was not an IMF demand. This makes sense, since the Fund's own fiscal policy doctrine emphasizes spreading the social costs of spending cuts equally and letting automatic stabilizers operate in full (Ban 2015a, b), which in this context would have meant wage cuts that cut more from the top than from the bottom of what was one of the most unequal public wage pyramids in the EU (Domnişoru 2014).

Graduated cuts were rejected by the Romanian authorities with the argument that a progressive cut would have required more staff and time to administer the cuts (an outcome opposed by the IMF).[44] Moreover, progressive cuts were deemed inconsistent with the philosophy of the flat-tax system. Ministry of Finance staff interviewed by this author confirmed that, since the public service payroll was entirely formal, progressive cuts would have been easily implemented. As for the second argument, it was little more than an innovative extension of the libertarian flat-tax philosophy that had framed progressive taxation as "socialist" for more than a decade. In the view of the prime minister's economic counsel, the flat tax represented an identity marker of the Romanian policy regime, a form of asserting personal freedom against the government and a "growth accelerator" for investors that no amount of government investment could compensate for.[45] Local commitment to this principle was so strong that, in the summer of 2010, PDL pushed a tax reform bill through the Senate that reduced the flat income tax from 16 to 10 percent. The bill was derailed only after the IMF issued threats that its pursuance could result in trouble for the continuation of the loan agreement.

Such interpretations of the economy make even more sense if we take a closer look at how local technocrats understood the shift in macroeconomics in the world. The chief economist of the central bank saw the crisis resolution mechanisms put in place as a betrayal of the principle of thrift, prudence, and market discipline : low interest rates in the EU and the United States that rewarded debtors and punished savers, loose fiscal policies in the EU that rewarded the current generation at the expense of future generations, bank bailouts without tax settlements, quantitative easing.[46] For the same senior central banker, US Keynesians' views about how to get out of the crisis should be ignored not only because they were based in US exceptionalism, but also because they spelled doom for the future of US public finance, an argument defended by citing two nonexpert neoliberals: a journalist (Thomas Friedman) and a political scientist (Michael Mandelbaum).[47]

The SAR, EFOR, and CRPE think tanks bolstered the government and central bank's efforts to "circle the wagons" around disembedded neoliberalism, while also engaging in the equivalent of corporate "greenwashing" by advocating progressive liberal reforms on gender issues, administrative reform, the functioning of democratic institutions, and the plight of people with disabilities. Think tankers worked to sustain this radical form of fiscal consolidation by generating new forms of expert knowledge that defended the core of local libertarian achievements (the flat tax) and experimental neoliberalism (pension privatization), in addition to the scripted ideas of mainline neoliberal orthodoxy (sound finance, labor market deregulation, social policy targeting, and privatization of all public companies). They published policy analyses defending the complete removal of fiscal policy from the realm of politics via the constitutionalization of fiscal rules at the EU level, thus paving the way for the local acceptance of this EU policy two years later by using language, concrete examples, and local data to add flesh to the Fund's dry, technical arguments.

Ordnungspolitik without *Vitalpolitik*

Ordoliberalism is about "policy activism that begins from the premise that markets and competition are not 'naturally' grounded in society but instead require a kind of 'positive liberalism' in order to continually promote and stimulate them."

The main pillars of this positive liberalism are "legal and regulatory frameworks that act to promote competition, rather than control its adverse effects" (Flew 2012, 56). But unlike in 1970s Spain, in Romania ordoliberalism was not understood as including *Vitalpolitik* or downward distribution via a progressive "social market economy," but as a form of market fundamentalism that further strengthened the radical reading of local neoliberalism.

Given the extensive corruption plaguing the Romanian state (Mungiu 2015), the use of *Ordnungspolitik* as an ideological basis for asserting the rule of law and the authority of state authority over rent-seeking networks was generally uncontroversial. Moreover, its implementation in the form of televised arrests of political and business elites by a special anticorruption body was popular, albeit increasingly controversial because the judicial branch did less about corporate graft, worked closely with national intelligence services (Rogozanu 2013) and according to a UN report, "even in successful anti-corruption contexts, the amount recovered from the proceeds of corrupt conduct is estimated at only 5–15 percent of the assets subject to a court order."[48]

The local translators deviated from the ordoliberal script in several ways. For President Băsescu, *Ordnungspolitik* was also the basis for rolling back the responsibilities of the state in remedying the dislocations produced by the market. His reasoning combined elitist anticommunism, libertarianism, and *Ordnungspolitik* ideas into a hybridized yet cohesive argument. He alleged that the bad work ethic and dependency on the state brought about by communism still plagued the mentality of large swaths of the low-income strata, and that their demands on the wealth produced by the emerging middle class were supported by corrupt politicians. Further, he posited a moral equivalence between corrupt politicians and the corrupted "mentalities" of the losers of transition. Therefore, by cracking down on politicians via anticorruption campaigns and stamping out a bad work ethic and welfare dependency through austerity, a strong but minimal state could simultaneously indict political fraudsters and dissembled the noncompetitive dynamics weighing down Romania's economic potential. Thus, the "reform of the state," a key term in presidential speeches, meant anticorruption and continuous adjustment of the state to respond to market needs.[49]

In a speech given at the LSE during the heat of the crisis, President Băsescu argued that "the global crisis has shown how vulnerable those states that interfere too much in the workings of the free market really are; that includes the labor market and social programs that are often unnecessary."[50] Prime Minister Boc told this author that "if we want to redistribute more than we do, we should wait until we reach German output levels and civil service quality."[51]

These statements were not rhetorical accidents. Their political party, the Democratic Liberal Party (PDL), went into the 2008 elections with a program that entailed paring down social programs to a minimum and focusing on a minimalist, indeed "Hayekian" safety net: minimum pension programs, better child benefits, and a partnership between the church and the state on social programs that would transfer some of the government's functions to parishes. As the president put it in his address to the parliament:

> For Romania, this crisis has been an opportunity. It exposed our vulnerabilities. All we need is the courage and the determination needed to fix them. . . . A careful analysis shows that Romania struggles more with sloth and welfare abuse than it does with poverty.[52]

The prime minister soon endorsed an economic strategy report drafted by the party's official think tank (Institutul de Studii Populare or ISP) in partnership with the Konrad Adenauer Stiftung, the official foundation of the German conservative party CDU, which defined "Romanian ordoliberalism" as representing nothing less than the elimination of the minimum wage and the complete privatization of the pension system, the public health insurance system, and public hospitals. This dramatic cutback of government support was seen as a way to stimulate the moral virtues absent among the Romanian population: saving, prudence, and the exercise of rational anticipations (ISP 2012, 27–28).

While state-provided protections were minimized for lower-income groups, state-provided support for reshaping the economy to the interests of the higher-income groups and corporations was maximized. The ISP-Adenauer report also paralleled the economic doctrine of the president's and prime minister's economic teams when it argued that the savings gained from social spending cuts should be channeled toward the highway projects demanded by foreign investors, to entrepreneurship education, microcredit, industrial clusters, and the dissemination of R & D among entrepreneurs. In other words, income redistribution through the state was to become self-financing through waged work, entrepreneurship, and the rule of law. As for the rural poor, who were unlikely to benefit from such infrastructures, the chief economist of the central bank proposed a decisive solution: punitive taxes to throw them off the land and into industrial or service sector employment.[53]

A book published in the heat of the 2010 austerity with the support of Adenauer Stiftung and authored by a government minister and high-profile intellectual of the center-right went further even, demanding the shrinking of government functions to defense, coin minting, diplomacy and public justice. According to the author, this entailed replacing welfare spending with a private Christian philanthropic system based around workfare conditionalities (10–11, 154) meant to turn them "from slaves into relatively free people" (Baconschi 2010, 150).

De-Europeanizing Redistribution

The other pillar of radicalized neoliberalism was a specific theory of redistribution. While most ordoliberals would agree that redistribution is necessary to
ensure social cohesion and/or provide a cushion of demand in times of recession,
their Romanian counterparts expressed unvarnished hostility toward attempts to
find value in automatic stabilizers and social investment. Such ideas were spurned
in the corridors of power in Romania. Prime Minister Emil Boc saw all forms of
redistribution that exceeded basic safety nets as net costs to the economy that
were inconsistent with the country's development stage.[54] President Basescu
argued that, even if Romania were as wealthy as the EU average, its social safety
nets should not be shaped by "Social Europe" because it was citizens' entitlement
to the economic rights embedded in Social Europe that created the crisis in the
first place.[55] He divided society into risk-takers (the private sector) and aging and
uncompetitive rent-seekers (the public sector), with the latter preying upon the
resources of the former through public services and welfare schemes. The president mixed (paleo)conservative political ideas about the "undeserving poor"
with neoliberal ideas about the virtues of having a labor market made competitive
by the widespread use of short-term contracts, the removal of seniority benefits,
and the drastic lowering of unemployment benefits.

This political theory of redistribution was rooted in a particular moral theory
of market-society relations. Its main claim was that Western-style social spending was indicative of the flagging moral fiber of West European nations, which,
in the view of the chief economist of the Romanian central bank, were cultur-
ally "spoilt by the welfare state," making them unable to take a more detached
view of austerity: "Estonian GDP dropped by 9.2 percent and Slovenia GDP
shrunk by 8.3 percent between 2007 and 2011. Despite this, no one heard of
protests in Tallin and Ljubliana on a scale close to that of Italian protests, where
GDP contracted by 4.6 percent during the same period."[56] Blending economic
libertarianism and peculiar readings of Eastern Orthodox theology, a number of
high-profile officials and supporters of the president insisted that the emphasis
on saving social services reflected the West's spiritual crisis (Neamțu 2009).

Chiding Western democrats for losing their "sense of historical mission,"
President Băsescu argued that prevailing concerns about minimizing the effects
of austerity on welfare systems reflected nothing less than a "crisis of values."
In a widely celebrated speech at the LSE, Basescu tied consumerism and social
protection into the same toxic package, calling for a return to the fundamentals
of liberal economic freedom:

> The disproportionate focus on the politics of welfare can be approached
> from another angle, that of a crisis of values. There is a temptation to

focus inwards on a limited sphere of consumption and benefits and to support different variants of protectionism or isolationism. Yet modern democracies have had a sense of their historical mission. By favouring peace rather than war and trade rather than isolation, democracies have created an expanding space, where freedom and individual rights have become key values for millions of people.[57]

Indeed, like the cultural neoliberals of the early 1990s, these actors saw continental Europe as a social-economic system doomed by "socialist" regulations, social security systems, and labor unions. In contrast, they cited research by private consultancies that pitted Western Europe against the United States—which was held up as an example of the reasserted vigor of "untainted" capitalism—and argued that Western Europe should emulate the United States if its leaders wanted their economies to remain competitive.[58] In such a way, they saw the radicalization of neoliberalism as a strategy that deepened competitiveness and democracy at the same time.

Senior central banker and top candidate for the prime ministership Lucian Croitoru upheld similar theories. The idea that the government should provide universal social rights, he insisted, was rooted in the utopian ideology of socialism. He argued that the very idea of not cutting social welfare spending first when fiscal consolidation was necessary meant that one had to rely on tax increases, thereby limiting the liberal right of private property that constitutes the core of capitalism. Or, undermining capitalism was tantamount to undermining liberal democracy, since capitalism constituted the very "microfoundations" of this political system. This was true because capitalism's fostering of private ownership and competition increases labor productivity and, with it, the sustainable resources of democracy. Should democracy break down, capitalism will eventually bring it back in the long run. In turn, democracy guarantees capitalism because, by changing political leaders, it ensures that politicians won't go too far in messing with self-adjusting market mechanisms (Croitoru 2012, 41).[59] Otherwise put, slashing welfare was an insurance policy for democracy.

The end of the Băsescu era did not coincide with the end of the attempt to radicalize neoliberalism in the presidency. The economic adviser of Klaus Johannis, the new president elected in 2014, is a committed Austrian school economist (Marinescu 2012) who initiated the first official class in Austrian economics at ASE. He has unabashedly advocated for fiscal competitiveness and for the complete destruction of labor market institutions as sources of comparative advantage in middle-income countries like Romania, leading him to warn against adopting Western European ideas on this front. A critic of neoclassical economics, he believed the 2008 crisis had nothing to do with capitalism and everything to do with state intervention.

In closing, it is important to stress that this author's interviews with Ministry of Finance staff in June 2014 confirm the Troika did not use its leverage to coerce the Romanian government into renouncing such policies that further radicalized Romania's disembedded neoliberalism while clashing with the IMF's post-2008 policy doctrine. Indeed, as the next section shows, while the Troika's governance of the crisis exercised its structural power over domestic actors intent on rolling back some of the elements of disembedded neoliberalism, it refrained from using its power to prevent the radicalization of the neoliberal policy regime.

Moderating Neoliberalism?
The Limits of Radicalization

One of the insights of this book is that the untidy mechanisms of neoliberalism's ascendance entail temporary accommodations with countervailing ideas. This is also true in the case of its mechanisms of resilience in Romania. Disembedded neoliberalism reached a moment of crisis in the winter of 2011–2012. The attempted privatization of the ambulance system and the more extensive privatization of health services triggered the biggest antiausterity protests in the region, leading to the collapse of the Boc cabinet and, soon afterward, of its successor. Between 2012 and 2015, Victor Ponta, the young leader of the Social Democrats, took the helm of two governments, one in a coalition with the Liberals (2012–2014) and the other as a minority government, with constitutional controversies marking his early months in office (Iusmen 2015).[60] The economic ideas and policies of these governments highlighted both the limits and the power of disembedded neoliberalism, bolstering the argument of the previous chapter that substantial forms of professional transnationalization are necessary to craft and negotiate more embedded forms of neoliberalism under external duress.

While in opposition, Ponta and the Social Democrats had been critical of the economic policies of the Băsescu administration and, once in government, they made appointments to key posts that seemed to suggest disembedded neoliberalism was not a one-way street. Critically, key players in the economic ministries of the new government were plucked from the ranks of the few economists who had survived the advance of radical neoliberal ideas in academia and policy institutions, but whose international credentials and technical skills made them the most credible appointments for senior jobs.[61] These economists had openly critiqued the macro- and microeconomic theories of neoliberalism in their work, using the authority conferred to them by virtue of their international graduate degrees and professional experience. Once in office, they moved beyond critiques and tried to create the conditions necessary for a more embedded form of neoliberalism to take root, within constraints imposed by bond markets and the Troika (which carefully monitored the more unorthodox views they had espoused as professors at the country's elite economics departments).

This was especially true in the cases of Minister of Finance Florin Georgescu and Minister of the Budget Liviu Voinea. The former came from the old-school neodevelopmentalist elite of the 1990s (he was minister of finance between 1992 and 1996). A quiet member of the central bank board and a respected US-trained macroeconomics professor at ASE, Georgescu holds personal views that are closer to fiscally activist New Keynesianism and for years has been firmly on the left regarding taxation, wage policy, and the need for better safety nets.[62]

Similarly, Swedish-educated budget Minister Liviu Voinea conducts research that is a mix of post-Keynesian finance economics and neo-Keynesian macro-economics. A research partner for Blocul Național Sindica (BNS), a left labor union confederation, he holds views of structural reforms that blend the Brussels Consensus and strongly progressive views on taxation and labor issues. Cristian Socol, a lecturer in economics at the same economics department and economic adviser to the prime minister, has expressed similar views, albeit from a more traditional New Keynesian perspective, placing a stronger emphasis on heterodox industrial policy theories in the Myrdal-Kindleberger tradition (Dinu, Socol, and Niculescu 2005, 308–309). Although, like neoliberals, these technocrats were not keen on highlighting the value of labor unions and coordinated indus-trial relations, they were among the few policymakers who lambasted the fact that capital's share of the value added produced in Romania during the crisis was Europe's largest, while labor's share was among the lowest (Georgescu 2015)

Since Voinea served in the cabinet for the longest time and also held the power of the purse as budget minister, his views deserve special consideration. Quoting directly from Keynes, Minsky, Rodrik, and ILO reports, he argues that only high levels of employment can substantially increase the growth rate and that, for this objective to be met, Romania needs to adopt sharply countercyclical fiscal and monetary policies, reunionization, public employment programs, and targeted industrial policies (Voinea 2009, 164–172). His writings also suggest that he finds the principle of tax neutrality to be deceptive at best and identifies the flat tax as a source of deplorable economic inequality and current account deficits (Voinea and Mihăescu 2009). Such positions have led him to suggest that genu-ine fiscal policy in Romania should start with a progressive tax reform based on solidarity and the defense of automatic stabilizers, shifting the tax burden from low- to high-income groups via the reintroduction of progressive income, wealth, and real estate property taxes, and the introduction of solidarity taxes on the exceptional profits of large companies (Voinea 2009, 170–172; 2013). Citing Minsky, he showed that such a progressive system could also reduce infla-tionary pressures by acting as an automatic stabilizer for price levels, thus creat-ing policy space for the central bank to adopt more expansionary policies (2009,

170–171). In short, Voinea was not one of the usual suspects of East European neoliberalism.

From Antiausterity to "High-Quality Fiscal Consolidation"

The profile of top cabinet technocrats thus suggests that it was not for lack of ideas that Romania failed to experience a dramatic reversal of disembedded neoliberalism. Indeed, as a neo-Keynesian who flirted with heterodox ideas, Voinea was intellectually to the left of Zapatero's economic advisers. At the same time, like Carlos Mulas Granados and Javier Vallés, Voinea and Socol had no illusions about the narrow policy space within which they could act. Fifteen years of neoliberal reforms had transformed the economy beyond recognition, and the most important decisions about investment and consumption were now undertaken abroad, making Romania look more like a dependent market economy (Ban 2013). In interviews and correspondence with this author, all three technocrats indicated the vulnerability of the Romanian government's finances and policy autonomy to external constraints. The signing of the Fiscal Compact by the previous government, the demonstration effects of the ordoliberal management of the Greek crisis, and the procyclical nature of Romania's financial system gave them no alternative but to advise the prime minister that, for all their contractionary effects, fiscal consolidation, structural reforms, and the agreements with the Troika should continue. They were also aware that the agenda of the multinational capital controlling the country's export sector limited the reach of their ideas for ambitious prolabor tax reforms and the rolling back of labor market deregulation. The interventions associated with disembedded neoliberalism had in-built material irreversibilities that drastically constrained the space for action.

Consequently, the intellectual critique of austerity was scaled down in practice to what the prime-minister's economic advisor termed "high quality fiscal consolidation," meaning an emphasis on curbing tax evasion, securing more EU structural funds, trimming public investments with low fiscal multipliers, and, after EC approval, rechanneling public investment into high-value-added sectors. The liberalization of energy prices, a measure demanded by the Troika and transnational capital, was adopted even though the government's key economists did not buy into the neoclassical logic behind it. Initial support for rolling back some of the labor market deregulation of 2011 waned after the IMF and the European Commission made their adamant opposition clear (Adăscăliţei and Guga 2015).

Tellingly, the critiques of the inequality-increasing taxation were replaced with a reluctant acquiescence to organized capital's views of growth, a transition that begs for further research. As a result, the second Ponta government adopted a tax reform that was largely in favor of capital: a 5 percent cut in social security taxes paid by employers (rather than those paid by workers), the slashing of the dividend tax from 16 percent to 5 percent, and a 3 percent profit tax for the self-employed. The prime minister even rejected higher royalty taxes for the oil industry, using supply-side arguments that such taxes would diminish investment.

But, again, external coercion did not mean one could *not* negotiate at the margins of the ruling ideas. By 2012, the IMF's recalibration of fiscal neoliberalism had gone quite far (Ban 2015a, b), and these three economists made the most of this opening. By using the studies of IMF chief economist Olivier Blanchard acknowledging the contractionary effects of fiscal consolidation, they engaged in four waves of minimum wage increases, narrowing the gap between the minimum and median wage to an extent present only in top-tier European economies. In so doing, they tried to reduce one of the most important sources of economic inequality while also increasing aggregate demand in a country with the highest share of minimum wage labor in the EU. Accordingly, public sector wage cuts were reversed, and the government adopted substantially lower VATs on food, both of which were measures that benefited lower-income groups. Voinea also proposed mortgage relief measures aimed at low- and median-income households and, because of Socol's industrial policy ideas, the government steered one hundred million euros of state aid toward the high-technology sector while simultaneously offering higher tax deductions for firms' R & D investments. To sum up, the policy regime shifted in a direction that gave greater importance to demand-side factors and the even neo-structuralist policy instruments.

Other, more ambitiously progressive policy ides that had the consent of the Troika did not go through because of the institutional fragmentation of the policy team. One notable casualty of this fragmentation was Voinea's Keynesian theory that domestic demand can be increased and stabilized through better distribution in taxation and spending schemes. Similarly, ideas such as progressive taxation and wealth taxes were discussed and vetoed by actors within the coalition and the Social Democratic Party itself. Between 2012 and 2014, the PSD was forced to govern with the Liberals, a solidly neoliberal party whose minister of finance employed a notorious Austrian school academic economist (Cosmin Marinescu) as his right-hand secretary of state. But even though the Liberals left the coalition in 2014, the Ponta government has not, as of yet, made decisive moves to buffer the social dislocations produced by disembedded neoliberalism. In late 2014, Ponta lost the presidential elections to a Liberal (Klaus Iohannis), whose appointment of Austrian school economist Cosmin Marinescu as presidential councilor was a telling indication of where the presidency stood on economic policy.

Most importantly, however, opposition within the PSD to Keynesian tax policies was significant and organized. Even by the standards of contemporary social democracy, the critical mass of the PSD elite and Ponta personally have very modest credentials. In addition to looking more like a conservative party on issues such as gay rights and church-state relations, most of the central and provincial party leadership is composed of wealthy professionals and business-persons whose interest in redistribution is hard to detect even in the midst of electoral campaigns.

Ponta himself is a well-off lawyer who frequently boasts about his promar-ket views and gave the Third Way a new lease on life when he invited Anthony Giddens to Bucharest, treating him as a source of ideological inspiration. Praising the labor deregulations of the German Social Democrats during the early 2000s, he opposed the rollback of the labor market deregulation reforms adopted in 2011.[63] By 2015 the government's mode shifted into aggressiveness with labor unions, aware that they lost most of their leverage. Indeed, the PM allowed the minister of labor to threaten public sector workers who went on strike that they would be forced to pay damages for every day of work lost.[64] Moreover, when workers at Renault, the largest auto plant, demanded higher wages, the prime minster was openly on the side of their employer, telling work-ers, "If you keep spending your time on strikes rather than work the company will move to Morocco."[65]

In contrast, when the government created a Coalition for Growth with the multinational capital (effectively a state-corporate policy design body), labor unions were left out of the equation, and no attempts have been made to resur-rect social pacts.[66] Indeed, the 2011 labor market reforms reconfigured the very nature of the policy apparatus regarding labor issues, so that from then onward knowledge input into the government on this topic was strictly limited to the two organizations of multinational capital and their supporters in the world of think tanks and consultancies.[67]

MPs who moved to the left since the crisis have been forced to keep a low profile. Even the party's youth wing, traditionally quite leftist among Western social democratic parties, shows little interest in such affairs.[68] This means that those who espouse more moderate forms of neoliberalism or disembedded neo-liberalism face an uphill battle within the party. Tellingly, in 2014, Voinea joined his mentor, Florin Georgescu, on the board of the central bank.[69]

Whither Disembedded Neoliberalism?

By mid-2015 the Romanian government could boast the second-highest growth rate in the EU, bringing GDP levels back to the peak precrisis levels. While the

Spanish government bragged about growth rates slightly below 1 percent beginning in 2013, Romania's were four times larger. The gross net value added of manufacturing increased from 28 percent of GDP in 2008 to 34 percent in 2015, a development that owed to a boom in manufacturing FDI, by far the largest share of multinational investment in the Romanian economy. These investments continued to flow increasingly toward medium-high technology, so that by 2015 industrial output in low-technology intensity sectors was smaller than in sectors with medium and high technology intensity. In 2015, FDI increased by 25 percent and by 2015 most areas with a significant export-oriented manufacturing presence did so well in terms of employment growth that employers struggled to find enough workers and began attracting labor from Moldova and Serbia. By bringing in new technologies and using wind power subsidy schemes, multinationals helped reduce energy intensity, thus helping with the effort to reduce the current account deficit. Even as the share of agriculture in total output decreased, multinational investments in large farms and warehousing capacity increased agricultural profits and exports.

This performance was not achieved at the expense of "sound finances." Indeed, the IMF deemed Romania's monetary and fiscal policies to have been "prudent" during the Ponta government.[70] Foreign debt began to shrink, inflation and deficits were some of Europe's lowest, forex reserves were above fiscal sustainability thresholds, tax arrears were cut, and the country borrowed easily at very favorable rates on international markets in the midst of the worst crisis in the Eurozone. Inflation was close to zero, and there was a primary budget surplus. According to the IMF, the recovery was driven by consumption, investment, and exports (IMF 2015a; 2015b) and according to Ministry of Finance officials, domestic demand was also supported by minimum wage increases and the rollback of public sector wage cuts.

Radical neoliberals attributed this robust recovery to the deepening of disembedded neoliberalism during the early phases of the crisis, via the confidence effects and increasing competitiveness of the economy.[71] Their critics argued that recovery came despite austerity, pointing to the reversal of wage cuts, minimum wage increases,[72] a tax collection reformed that raked in 25 percent more revenue[73] and higher EU structural fund inflows that provided a strong demand-side stimulus.[74] They also pointed at market appetite for emerging markets and frontier economies and higher external demand in Germany's industrial clusters, the main customers of the Romanian industry.[75]

A critical voice in the board of the central bank showed that in terms of distribution, workers paid the cost of recovery while capital increased its gains. Specifically, BNR deputy governor Florin Georgescu showed that the recovery was of a jobless kind (of 637,000 jobs lost since 2008, only 321,000 had come back by 2015) and that labor's share of GDP decreased from 39.3 percent in

2008 to 31.0 percent in 2014 (the EU average is 48.0 percent); in contrast, the share of capital grew from 50.2 percent in 2008 to 57.0 percent in 2014.[76] The IMF also indicated that the unemployed youth and the low-skilled were another large category of losers (IMF 2015b).

The jury is not in, and future research will parse out the contribution of these different factors. What is clear, however, is that disembedded neoliberalism faces important challenges. Despite tax cuts for capital, fiscal rigor came at the expense of a collapse of 45 percent in public and private investments.[77] Low public and private R & D investments bode ill for improving the local value added of local goods. Access to finance remains difficult, particularly for small and medium-sized enterprises. The 2010 wage cuts and the uninterrupted decrease in capital investments in public services demoralized staff in education and health, leading to insufficient quality and deteriorating access. This stands to reduce the supply of semiskilled labor for the export sector and hamper competitive advantage aspirations. The damaged public services, creaking public transport, poor safety nets, and expensive housing damage the skill pool of the labor force and reduce its mobility from pockets of poverty to booming manufacturing zones. The demographic crisis looms large. Romania is the EU member state that lost the largest share of its population (11 percent), mostly via emigration. The problem is compounded by the fact that the migrants are not just construction workers, truck drivers, and fruit pickers but also large numbers of physicians, engineers, and researchers.

The increase in the share of manufacturing in gross value added was accompanied by the continuous shrinking of the industrial labor force from 24 percent in 2008 to 22 percent in 2013, a phenomenon linked to the continuing increase in labor productivity and capital intensity in manufacturing, even as productivity plateaued in the rest of the economy.[78] The share of foreign investment in information and communications technology was roughly the same between 2005 and 2013, and the share of industries with high technological intensity in total industrial output remained small. The sluggish development of transport infrastructure reduced growth potential, as investment clustered in areas closer to the capital and the Western border, which quickly reached full employment, while the labor force in the more disconnected parts of the country continued to be decimated by the largest intra-EU emigration wave. In 2015, Romania had one of the highest demographic declines in the EU.

Conclusions

Like their translation, the resilience of neoliberal policies in Romania was reinforced by hierarchical pressures from multilateral institutions and regional competition for capital. At the same time, the resilience of neoliberal policies and institutions became actionable through the crisis-driven readaptation of neoliberal ideas at the hands of powerful local agents and institutions. Indeed, coercion and competition explain a lot but they do not explain critical aspects of the radicalization of disembedded neoliberalism between 2008 and 2012, or its attempted moderation between 2012 and 2015. The evidence suggests that the answer to these developments can be found in the interplay of external structural constraints, domestic institutional constraints, and ideational agency.

Beginning in 2009, IFI conditionality and the domestic leverage of transnational financial and nonfinancial firms controlled most of the economic agenda in Romania during the crisis. Their demands, far from facing opposition, knocked on an open door. Rather than enforce these foreign agendas reluctantly, domestic policymakers were determined to use the crisis and external conditionality to enact economic theories whose political consequences had been deemed too costly before the crisis.

Moreover, policy leaders at the highest levels outbid the Troika's neoliberalism with a blend of libertarian, conservative, and ordoliberal theories about the state and society. Central bank theories untouched by the unorthodox currents unleashed by the crisis worsened the government's fiscal problems by not facilitating debt monetization and access to foreign exchange. Fiscal policy ideas edited with local economic, political, and moral theories foreclosed the choice of a fiscal consolidation that would have sheltered more low-income groups and the public supply of common goods. Indeed, libertarian tax theories, political theories of the state, and moral panics about benefit fraud and work ethic had more local currency than high-prestige economic research, including the IMF's own.

The same interplay of forces also explains the moderation of disembedded neoliberalism after 2012. Although technocrats with Keynesian leanings took top posts in a new cabinet, their ideas had a limited reach in the policy process because of the constitutionalization of fiscal policy by the EU, the reverberations of the Greek crisis, the conditionalities of the Troika, the pressures of foreign capital, the institutional fragmentation of the policy process, and resistance from their own party. Critically, their own prime minister was a lot less ideologically committed to basic social democratic principles than his Spanish counterpart had been. Finally, their own reluctance to value the role of labor unions offered them little political leverage on the left. At a result, the slight moderation observed during the post-2012 centrist governments was more a case of plus ça change than anything else. Given the compulsion of Europeanized competitive as well as coercive pressures and the structural weakness of postneoliberal movements, forces, and interests in this country, the long-run prospects of neoliberalism's continuing resilience appear as robust as ever.

Conclusions

Localization and Resilience

When neoliberal ideas emerge from their "labs" and find new homes, they "go local." Through translation, a form of bounded innovation occurs whereby the meanings of the source paradigm are reinvented. The results of this translation span the spectrum between replication and systemic alteration. This should be familiar knowledge. What is less known is how the politics of these translation processes work and impact real-world policy decisions and survive adversity. If we don't understand this particular form of politics, we miss important aspects of how national policy regimes resolve the tension between building/maintaining market mechanisms and preserving social cohesion.

This book took up this task and made two main contributions to the literature on the global dissemination of neoliberalism. First, it showed that different translation outcomes depend on what competing ideas are locally available and on the kinds of relations that the domestic translators develop over time with the global purveyors of "source" neoliberalism. The content of these local translations of neoliberalism matters because they inform critical decisions about how policy elites think about distributing their societies' resources. The book highlighted the fact that neoliberalism is not necessarily more moderate (or "embedded") in some societies because they are wealthier and have better institutions, as one would expect from reading much of the literature on tis topic. Instead, this book invites scholars to examine the role of domestic intellectual legacies, the timing of incorporation into the transnational diffusion of neoliberalism via political and/or professional channels as well as the institutional cohesion of the leading policy team.

The second contribution is to theorize the ways in which local neoliberal hybrids survive crises that challenge their relevance or their validity. When communism collapsed in Eastern Europe, there was no neoliberal "transition economics" available. Two decades later, the global financial crisis and the Great Recession questioned fundamental neoliberal tenets, opening up a crisis of disconfirmation. The evidence presented in the book suggests that the resilience of Spanish and Romanian neoliberal hybrids was a function of institutional cohesion and the extent of exposure of domestic policy elites to forms of international coercion that stabilize neoliberal ideas, policies, and their supporters, while disciplining their adversaries.

Neoliberalism in Translation

Embedded Neoliberalism

Beginning in the 1970s, a group of Spanish economists who regularly switched hats between their roles as central bankers, academic mandarins, and government bureaucrats acted as the translators of neoliberal theories about fiscal, monetary, and labor market policy. But rather than replicate these ideas in whole cloth, they edited them with select Keynesian ideas about the distribution of the tax burden in society, ordoliberal ideas about the "social market economy," and structuralist ideas about "industrial champions."

Indeed, some of the most radical propositions of the neoliberal revolution were edited out. Most importantly, Spain's most influential translators of neoliberalism never embraced the New Classical thesis on the irrelevance of all countercyclical macroeconomic interventions. Several years before the new neoclassical synthesis sealed the compromise between New Keynesians and New Classicals, leading neoliberals sought a synthesis between Keynesianism, monetarism, and New Classical macroeconomics.

Moreover, the same academic mandarins and policy gurus who proclaimed the end of neo-Keynesianism also made the case for tax policies that were more an extension of the ideational consensus of "embedded liberalism" than they were reverberations of the supply-side tax theory du jour. There is no doubt that orthodox neoliberals would raise eyebrows at the argument that since market mechanisms alone are unable to deliver a robust catch-up economic performance, the state has to step in to invest in social services and social dialogue institutions, while also sheltering competitive domestic industries and banks deemed able to take Spain into the "First World." Yet this was precisely the view that local policy economists endowed with impeccable neoliberal credentials when it was proposed (and implemented). Neoliberalism indeed "went native" in Spain, and not always in ways in which most neoliberal economists would have approved at the critical juncture when this event took place during the late 1970s and through the 1980s.

Disembedded Neoliberalism

Neoliberal ideas also went local in Romania, but not before they were subject to a near-death experience. Unlike in Spain, after the end of authoritarianism there were few sophisticated translators of neoliberal ideas in early 1990s Romania. As a result, the dominant voice in the corridors of power was that of elites who tried to graft select neoliberal ideas onto a robust local developmentalist one. The result was two varieties of neodevelopmentalism, one that was more open to the "core" of neoliberal transition economics and which shaped policy between 1990 and 1992, and another (in power between 1992 and 1996) that was more skeptical of neoliberalism and more invested in statist logics. The first postcommunist government grafted the orthodox goal of macroeconomic stabilization onto a developmentalist one: state-led industrial recovery. The second espoused ideas that entailed a set of arguments that endorsed such non-neoliberal ideas as the doubling of public investment, public purchases of domestic industrial goods, subsidized credit to industry, the defense of sectors considered strategic for industrial policy, capital controls to manage a dual exchange rate, and so on. When the IMF or the central bank pushed the neodevelopmentalists to decide between these two goals, they chose the developmentalist one. In effect, it was as if the neodevelopmentalists let unorthodox ideas devour the orthodox ones in the hybrid they created.

In 1996, the neodevelopmentalists left the political scene for good, ushering in a generation of neoliberals. By the late 1990s and early 2000s, IOs, transnational research programs, and access to Western-licensed graduate programs provided the cause of neoliberalism in Romania with a critical mass of translators of neoliberal theories. These economists quickly took much of the neoliberal model as "fact," but they also scrutinized some of its implications and wove together a network of conceptual relations between neoliberalism and other schools of thought (institutionalism, structuralism). The EU accession process from the early 2000s generally strengthened this neoliberal hybrid despite the purported "embedded" nature of neoliberalism at the EU level.

Unlike in Spain, however, the result was a variant of neoliberalism that was much less concerned with balancing marketization and social protection than it was with maximizing the space for market mechanisms, with a smattering of state-protected corporate rents on the side. Its advocates radicalized some of the "classic" neoliberal positions on taxation, income redistribution, and industrial policy while facing no opposition from the EU. The structuralist tradition, for example, was used to bolster calls for a local version of neoliberal shock therapy that left very little space for protecting the economically disenfranchised. Also unlike Spain, where economists retained skepticism toward market-fundamentalist ideas culled from the margins of the international economics profession, in Romania such ideas were incorporated into mainstream economics as uncontested scientific facts, enabling the adoption of a very regressive tax regime.

The Weight of the Past

The fact that the Spanish translation of neoliberalism was faster and avoided radicalization had little to do with the state of the country's economy and a lot to do with the condition of the country's economics profession during the authoritarian regime of Francisco Franco and Spain's geopolitical position during that period. Indeed, neoclassical economics and strands of economic libertarianism were kept alive and even thrived because of the public servants and academic economists who took advantage of domestic institutions and geopolitical opportunities that allowed a considerable degree of intellectual diversity and professional transnationalization.

A strong dose of ordoliberalism injected into local economics by a German economist with an intriguing Nazi past made the Spanish interpretation of neoclassical economics more skeptical of "small state" theories and more open to the virtues of progressive social redistribution. When the regime ended, taking down with it the developmentalists in charge of economic policy, it paved the way for the promulgators of the neoclassical-ordoliberal synthesis that had developed under Franco. As a result, the normative universe of Spain's economic transition during the 1970s and 1980s inherited from the liberal elites of the Franco era a strong preference for a rule-bound and market-oriented policy regime while endorsing a predisposition toward relatively bold income and wealth redistribution programs.

As in Spain, the geopolitical opening in Romanian-US relations during the communist regime allowed local economists to make research trips to American and British universities and facilitated the training of local technocrats at the IMF. Also, in both countries, interested economists were able to keep up to date with Western economics in the libraries and discussion groups of elite academic institutions, government think tanks, foreign trade institutions, and the planning bureaucracy itself. But while in Spain neoclassical economics grew to become an important part of mainstream economics, in Romania the intellectual bedrock of neoliberalism was never explored systematically (let alone publicly espoused), being relegated to a handful of entrepreneurial economists.[1] The main reason for this was that opportunities for professional transnationalization did not pave the way for the dissemination of neoclassical economics in Romania. A handful of local economists studied in the United States and Britain at the graduate level for relatively short periods, in contrast to dozens of economists from Spain. While the Romanians studied for an academic year at most, their Spanish counterparts earned PhDs in top Western universities. While the Romanians studied with heterodox Western economists, many of their most prominent Spanish counterparts completed their PhDs alongside orthodox neoclassical economists, some of them showing outsight aversion to Keynesian insights. Additionally,

Romanian economists did not have the possibility of being trained at home for several years by one of the luminaries of German ordoliberal economics, as their Spanish counterparts did.

The relationship between the authoritarian state and the economics profession was also significant in both countries. Franco's regime allowed a much more extensive degree of intellectual pluralism in the profession than Ceauşescu's regime did, thus enabling neoclassical economists to espouse their views relatively unimpeded in areas as different as the central bank, economic ministries and academia. In contrast, in Romania one faced severe professional (and even penal) punishment for much more modest deviations from the official economics of the state. While in Spain the regime did not change the professional norm that awarded high professional status to local economists with Western training and networks, the opposite was true in Romania. Finally, while engagement with the Western profession flourished in late Francoism, in pre-1989 Romania the (re)tightening of the authoritarian regime after the 1981 debt crisis effectively terminated almost all opportunities for engagement with Western economics.

These intellectual legacies of the authoritarian era quickened the pace of translation of neoliberalism in Spain and slowed it considerably in Romania. However, the intensity of transnational professionalization shaped the results of translation in different ways.

Translation and Transnational Socialization

When policy intellectuals' training and work entails regular contact with peers or superiors in the "labs" of neoliberalism, translation is more likely to lead to closer approximations of the source paradigm. Into this category fall domestic civil servants who have regular contacts with the IMF and foreign peers (central bankers, fiscal council economists), policy-oriented economists whose careers depend on publishing in mainstream economic journals, and nongovernmental sector economists whose jobs depend on grants extended by donors invested in neoliberal ideas. By contrast, hybrids are more likely where translators are more loosely connected to transnational neoliberal networks and are more exposed to swings in domestic political and professional ideas.

In both Romania and Spain central bankers stayed within the boundaries of the "source" neoliberal paradigm. When central bankers were also embedded in international academic networks by virtue of their graduate education (Spain), they were even more loyal to the source. This was less true when their education was done on the cheap, in domestic graduate programs or short-term courses in international economic organizations and universities (Romania). Spain's British-trained central bankers who were pivotal to the policymaking process stuck close to mainstream macroeconomics. When these bankers did venture to edit it, they did so by moderating neoliberalism's market-disciplinary core. In contrast, their more parochial Romanian counterparts were more likely to edit source neoliberalism by radicalizing its core tenets. Nevertheless, when domestic translators were closely linked with the "left" of the global macroeconomic orthodoxy and served political offices with center-left views (the case of the advisers to the Socialist government during the Great Recession), the result was a more unorthodox reading of mainstream views on fiscal policy.

One of the most striking findings of this book is that the noneconomists who became involved in the Romanian translation of neoliberal ideas were the authors of some of the boldest reinventions of neoliberalism. In Spain, the existence of a robust network of credentialed economists with neoliberal ideas obviated the need to allow think tanks as members of the neoliberal coalition in their own right. In contrast, in Romania, when the supply of qualified neoliberal economists proved to be too low, Western funding enabled amateur economists (political scientists, sociologists, and philosophers) to enter the jurisdictional space of the economics profession via "dual use" civil society organizations that were half prodemocracy NGOs and half economic think tanks. The entry of these think tanks onto the scene in Romania added to the radicalization of local neoliberalism and was an important variable in the defense of neoliberal ideas during the Great Recession and its aftermath.

Neoliberalism in Power

Institutional Cohesion

Domestically translated economic ideas do not travel freely into the policy sphere. Instead, their translators can alter the menu of policy choices if they occupy strategic sites in centralized policy processes. Thus, the relatively smooth institutionalization of embedded neoliberal ideas in Spain was facilitated by the formation of a cohesive policy team composed of the central bank and the economic ministries in the cabinet. In effect, the translators of neoliberal theories were able to take the helm of the most strategic decision-making institutions in the state. Specifically, central bankers and economists connected to the central bank who became ministers of finance ensured consistent advice to the prime minister, crowding out alternative economic ideas.

The maintenance of this coherence owed itself to inherited institutions and current institutional strategies. First, the Socialists inherited a highly centralized policy sphere that revolved around the prime minister, the Ministry of Finance, and the central bank. Given Spain's "pacted transition," this institutional configuration survived, reinforced by informal linkages between central bankers and the cabinet's economic policy elite. Second, haunted by the memory of internal factionalism during the time of the Second Republic leading up to the civil war of 1936–1938, PSOE leaders built a highly centralized and authoritarian party structure, making the party unaccountable to its base and suppressing ideological dissent. In this way, they further centralized the policy process by suppressing party democracy and eventually cutting the Socialist labor union loose from the party executive. These institutional features made PSOE a highly disciplined political machine, enabling Prime Minister González to rule with a tight network of young "pragmatic" social democrats holding a central banker's view of the world. The same dynamic was also evident within the PSOE government during the Great Recession.

In contrast, although a strong coalition of neoliberal policy intellectuals was increasingly visible and politically astute in early 1990s Romania, it was not until they became policymakers after 1996 that they were able to translate their ideas into policy. However, unlike in Spain, they did not always benefit from the same degree of cohesion and centralization in government. Conflict prone relations between the executive and the ruling party in Romania between 1996 and 2000 and then again between 2007 and 2009 thwarted many of the efforts of neoliberal translators to make their imprint on policy. These efforts were more successful during periods of greater centralization and cohesion between 2000 and 2004 and between 2009 and 2012. The same institutional dynamic disabled the efforts of Romanian neodevelopmentalists between 1990 and 1992, but enabled them between 1992 and 1996.

The Power of Coercion

Not all translations of global economic paradigms get to shape policy realities. One of the hypotheses proposed by this book is that the translators' freedom to turn their ideas into policies is likely to be coercively contained by their exposure to international actors invested in the replication of the source paradigm. The degree of transnational coercion present—in the form of international policy conditionality or financial market disciplining—is an important factor in calculating how much space exists for actual policy hybridity.

The evidence in favor of this argument is also quite strong. Between 1992 and 1996, leading Romanian policymakers designed a policy program that grafted neoliberal and neodevelopmentalist ideas. However, when the grafting exercise proved to be more about neodevelopmentalism than about neoliberalism, international policy conditionality kicked in. Given the fact that the neodevelopmentalist cabinets faced recurrent balance of payment crises, the neodevelopmentalists were unable to fully translate their ideas into policy because of the conditions set by the IMF's loan programs. Even though none of the IMF loans were fully completed, they severely damaged the capacity for implementation of unorthodox monetary, fiscal, and industrial policies in Romania during this period.

International coercion also impinged upon the deep editing of orthodox fiscal policy in Spain between 2008 and 2009. Transnational market-based and collateral intensive finance turned Spanish banks against their sovereign once the sovereign bonds issued by "peripheral" eurozone countries were downgraded. As a result, the Zapatero government was obliged to address the disruption of collateral markets for fear that bank runs would ruin Spain's banking system and lead to the sovereign's bankruptcy. Since European solidarity was in short supply and the ECB refused to act as a lender of last resort, the onus fell upon the Spanish government to pay the price of stabilizing collateral markets. Compounding these pressures in the bond market was the coercive power of the EU ministers of finance, heads of state, and the ECB. Beginning in 2010, they used both moral suasion and the power of the purse to push the Spanish government to abjure its unorthodox ideas and implement several rounds of austerity and labor market deregulation that chipped away at the country's embedded neoliberalism.

Finally, the two European countries analyzed in this book have been remarkably consistent, as evidenced by the persistent moderating tendencies of the Spanish translators and the radicalizing ones characteristic of their Romanian counterparts. This helps explain why Spanish elites made the most of opportunities for maximizing the space for maintaining social cohesion, whereas their Romanian counterparts did not.

Indeed, even after they were forced to abandon expansionary demand-side policies and adopt austerity, Spanish policymakers tried to defend the welfare state and make the wealthy pay for a greater share of the tax-based portion of the fiscal adjustment. Certainly, partisanship made a big difference in this regard and the price paid by Spanish society was high. Yet, overall, the bulk of these changes were done by policymakers who remained unconvinced about the virtues of austerity and deepening the realm of the market in general. In contrast, in Romania pivotal policymakers construed the crisis as an opportunity to deepen the reach of disembedded neoliberalism, leading to more marketization and less social cohesion. Certainly, international policy coercion deployed by IFIs and the regional competition for international investment flows have remained important mechanisms for ensuring the resilience of neoliberalism. Yet the evidence suggests that the economic ideas shared by Romanian authorities explain, not only why they did not resist the policy package demanded by the creditors in the first place, but also why they pushed the reforms in a direction that further disembedded neoliberalism. Finally, although a political shift to the left catapulted to the helm of critical policy bureaucracies several economists with a history of editing the conventional economic wisdom of their age with Keynesian ideas, like their Spanish counterparts they also found their room for maneuvering sharply curtailed by the structural power of external coercion and concerns about international competition specific to dependent market economies such as Romania's.

Neoliberalism has been disseminated so widely and has survived crises not because it is an antistate, market fundamentalist paradigm, nor because it is a rigid "dogma." It has survived because both the advocates of the "source" neoliberal texts and their creative translators have been flexible, coopting select ideas of oppositional social forces and recasting the state into their image. The results included recalibrations, accommodations and reversals the cycle completed with yet another roadshow for an improved version (Peck and Theodore 2012).

Economic schools of thought as different as developmental state structuralism and various strands of Keynesianism have had parts of their intellectual scaffolding integrated into the localized transmogrifications of the neoliberal master script. The same happened to various strands of political ideologies as different as Islamism (Bozkurt 2013) and environmentalism (Bakker 2005). While this book showed how this played out at the macro levels of economic decision-making and across long periods of time, future research could establish how neoliberalism goes local in everyday politics of the world economy.

Looking at the post-Lehman crisis, the book bolsters the argument that far from announcing paradigm shifts (Blyth 2013; Hall 2013) or even "gestalt flips" (Baker 2012), neoliberalism's openness to hybridity, coexistence with incongruous ideas, incompleteness, and even temporary breakdowns seem more likely to lead to adaptive recalibrations and incremental transformations that seem to ensure its constant rebirth (Peck 2010; Mirowski 2013).

Ruling Ideas also shows that the protean nature of neoliberalism cannot be fully understood as a simple matter of intellectual history. Instead, we also have to examine the heaving waves of economic turbulence and international coercion, the meticulous rebuilding of domestic policy spheres through material and professional status transfers from abroad, and the institutional politics of who gets to have a say in the local economic policy regime.

ACKNOWLEDGMENTS

With a long gestation, the book accumulated a pile of debts that are impossible to settle adequately.

My special thanks go to Mark Blyth, whose brilliance, intellectual irreverence, high-octane brainstorming sessions, and invaluable friendship accompanied me for more than ten years. A man of unassailable pedagogical commitment, rare wit, and immense, unclassifiable intelligence, Mark was and remains my mentor and maestro. He is the only person who has seen this project go from preliminary thoughts in 2005 to its revise-and-resubmit stage in 2015. Words are truly inadequate to fully express my gratitude to him.

The crisp, brilliant, and structured intellect of Oddny Helgadottir is behind several critical junctures in the development of this book from 2010 onward. I am particularly grateful for her enormous patience, for not letting me take the argument in potentially interesting but inelegant directions and for constantly providing alternative pathways to my argument. Oddny helped me navigate the baroque complexities of the post-2008 crisis and translate my analysis into a more focused form of writing than I am generally capable of.

I remain enormously indebted to David McBride, the editor of Oxford University Press and two anonymous reviewers for their earnest support, constructive challenges, and professional rigor. They played a key role in helping me use a (post)doctoral project as the basis for a new book spanning Spain's and Romania's postwar crises and their experience with the Great Recession.

The beginnings of this book date back to 2005–2006 and a series of conversations I had with the late Anca Romantan, loved partner and friend, at the University of Pennsylvania, where she was pursuing a postdoctoral stint. Fascinated with Southern Europe and continental intellectual history, Anca also pushed me to assume the potential costs of breaking out of the Eastern European universe of cases that absorbed my library time and undertake a comparative study between carefully selected countries from the Southern and the Eastern periphery.

My PhD committee, Mark Blyth, Ken Conca, Mark Lichback, and Vladimir Tismaneanu, offered immensely valuable advice and support as some of the ideas behind this book emerged in my doctoral training at University of Maryland. During my three and a half years at Brown University's Watson Institute for International Studies, Gianpaolo Baiocchi, Nitsan Chorev, Patrick Heller, Jose Itzigsohn, Jazmin Sierra, Alex Gourevitch, Dietrich Rueschemeyer, and Richard Snyder helped me explore new theoretical and empirical ramifications of the arguments that went into the final manuscript.

Since I joined Boston University, Jeremy Menchik, Sofia Perez, Cathie Jo Martin, and John Gerring offered feedback on individual chapters as they received their final shape. Kevin Gallagher and Vivien Schmidt should be singled out for mobilizing their crisp analytical thinking, warm support, and scholarly erudition to help me overcome the birth pangs of this book. Jermemy Menchik's brilliance was a critical companion on several winter evenings in 2013, as the book's theoretical framework was being polished. William Grimes and Strom Thacker supported a workshop on the IMF during the Great Recession that helped me sharpen critical arguments in the concluding chapters. I would also like to thank Adil Najam, Erik Goldstein, Igor Lukes, Susan Eckstein, Taylor Boas, Joseph Fewsmith, Renata Keller, William Keylor, Andrew Bacevich, Manjari Miller, and Min Ye for engaging conversations that helped a great deal with polishing the overall argument.

The wordsmithing that went into critical parts of this book benefited from long walks with great novelist and friend Allen Kurzweil on the magic side-walks of Benefit Street, Providence, Rhode Island. With his many lives spanning Viennese *Hochkultur*, Florentine *sarcasmo*, and lightning speed Greenwich Village wit, Allen read my arguments as a novelist, pushing me to think about narrative structure and style more than I would have been tempted to do by virtue of my training.

Numerous country experts have been generous with their time and engaged with my Romania and Spain chapters. In addition to teaching me a thing or two about economics, Daniela Gabor did numerous strafing rounds on my arguments about neoliberalism in Romania. She also did the most to shape the thinking behind these chapters. Stefan Guga's critical eye and his expertise on labor issues helped me refine the arguments in three chapters on Romania as I was closing the manuscript. I am extremely thankful to Wade Jacoby, Rachel Epstein, Juliet Johnson, Mitchell Orenstein, Liliana Pop, Narcis Tulbure, and Besnik Pula for providing substantial and critical feedback on select aspects of the chapters on Romania. Juliet Johnson's comments during a long van ride between Kosovo and Albania, across the breathtaking Cursed Mountains, helped me rethink my discussion of central banks. Andrei State, Daniel Daianu, Gheorghe Zaman, Stefan Guga, Sorin Ionita, Gabriel Badescu, and Victoria Stoiciu have also made useful critical comments on select sections of this book.

I also remain heavily indebted to Ken Dubin, Sofia Perez, Jonathan Hopkin, Matthias Matthijs, Federico Steinberg, Aitor Erce, Jorge Tamames, and Miguel Otero for their insightful feedback on the Spain chapters. My special thanks go to Sofia Perez, whose work inspired me to pick Spain as a case study and whose advice during the last stages of writing was critical. A most unconventional-looking and unconventional-sounding central bank economist, Aitor Erce, spotted the weakest part of my initial reading of the Spanish crisis and reconstructed it with gusto over copious portions of *txangurro* rigorously cooked in the darkest belly of Malasaña. Jefferey Milley provided me with invaluable support during the early stages of my fieldwork in Madrid, and Sebastian Royo challenged me to sharpen my argument regarding Spain during the 1980s economic transition before I sat down to turn this project into a book.

Since 2012, a significant part of the theoretical apparatus of this book has benefited from Leonard Seabrooke's generous and uniquely reflexive feedback during the past three years of workshops, fine dinners, and long-range fieldwork trips through the Balkans. At Copenhagen Business School (CBS), Len has played a critical role in shaping one of the world's premier political economy milieus. During my frequent visits there, I benefited both from funding support for my work on the role of central banks in the story (PIPES project) and from the input of the intellectual hive swirling around Len, Eleni Tsingou, Martin Carstensen, Duncan Wigan, Lasse Folke Henriksen, and Andre Broome. It was also at the CBS that I put the finishing touches on the manuscript in the summer of 2015.

The ambitions of this project would not have been fulfilled without the assistance of my smart, creative, and industrious research assistants. I take this opportunity to thank Chantel Pfeiffer, Bryan Patenaude, Akanksha Patnaik, Adriana Romantan, Charlott Johansen, Jesse Turiel, and William Murphy for their excellent work. Daniela Baches, Sorana Constantinescu, and Jorge Tamames assisted me with critical fact-checking work. My special thanks go to Adriana Romantan and Bryan Patenaude for their technical support and building the data sets. Careful editing of select chapters by Brooke Lamperd, Karyn Marcus, Sam Franklin, and Jesse Turiel got the manuscript ready for review.

The generous research support offered by Boston University and particularly by the Stuart and Elisabeth Pratt Career Development Professorship made this extensive research support possible. Boston University has been an incredibly supportive environment in which this book could be completed. I take this opportunity to thank Christian Esterella for managing the complex administration of these research funds. Similarly, the fieldwork for the research presented in chapter 3 has been supported by the European Research Council's Professions in International Political Economies (#263741-PIPES) project led by Leonard Seabrooke, which provided an original framework to understand how professions and professionals shape transnational governance. Funding from European Legitimacy in Governing Through Hard Times (#649456-ENLIGHTEN), a collaborative research project coordinated at the Copenhagen Business School and funded by the European Commission's Horizon 2020 research program, proved critical for research needed to address the first round of reviews for chapters 8 and 9.

When putting this book together I was lucky to have the intellectual friendship of Kostis Kornetis. My favorite flâneur and young historian of Europe, Kostis seduced me into making the book speak to a broader interest in the intellectual history story of peripheral Europe. Kostis's tours de force of European history and particularly of our fascination with 1968 during our long walks in Providence, New York, Madrid, and Athens always brought about swarms of original, irreverent thoughts about individual chapters. Unfairly, this book manages to honor only a small fraction of them.

Finally, I would like to thank my parents for their endless affection, their support, and especially their commitment to my education. I am particularly grateful to my mother for her excitement over intellectual pursuits denied to her by the socioeconomic status of her family.

NOTES

Chapter 1

1. See Nelson and Katzenstein 2014 for a recent review of this literature.
2. See Czarniqwska (2008) for an overview of Gabriel Tarde's contemporary implications.
3. See Schmidt 1996; 1998; Campbell and Pedersen 2001; Harvey 2005; Lindvall 2004; Maes 2008; Silva 1991; 1993; Markoff and Montecinos 1993; Montecinos 1997; Teichman 2001; Babb 2004; Dezalay and Garth 2002; Biglaiser 2002; MacPherson 2006.
4. In contrast, postwar Keynesianism's goals were full employment, the stabilization of demand across economic cycles, and the regulatory stabilization of finance.
5. This insight is based on some of the existing theorizing of neoliberalism (Blyth 2002; 2013; Peck 2010; Brenner, Peck, and Theodore 2010a), as well on economic theory and intellectual history (Robinson 1975; Crotty 1980; Davidson 1992; Skidelsky 2010; 2011; Mirowski 2013; Woodford 2009; Linnemann and Schabert 2003; Aghion et al. 1990; Lucas 1990; Canto, Joines, and Laffer 2014).
6. I do not understand this disembeddedness as a teleological story, in which regardless of the different paces and pathways, a fully disembedded liberalism is sooner or later the outcome. As the following chapters show, I see it as a historically contingent one.
7. State-mediated forms of social-protection need not be necessarily progressive or social-democratic. Rather, they can be regressive, such as protections targeted at insider elites, specific ethnic groups or sections of the middle class, and criminal networks. As such, they can be instrumentalized by the far-right, oligarchic regimes or ethnocratic sectarianism. This view is consistent with Polanyi's non-directional take on embeddedness.
8. This term was used to refer to a foil of embedded liberalism in the context of global financial debates but was not distinguished very clearly from general neoliberalism (Best 2003, 372).
9. The book uses embedded and disembedded neoliberalism as ideal types, not pure theoretical and policy constructs. For example, the dominant economic thinking in Romania may be a good representative of European disembedded neoliberalism today, but this does not mean that Romanian neoliberals with real influence in the policy sphere are actually against all forms of embeddedness. It only means that, unlike the advocates of embedded neoliberalism, their concern with most forms of downward redistribution is either entirely marginal to their thinking or is the extension of ad hoc electoral strategies.
10. As such the book speaks to the insight of Culpepper and Reinke (2014) that structural power is not just the capacity of finance to force "automatic adjustment of policy to the possibility of disinvestment" (428) but also a strategy of disciplining government action in ways that differ from its instrumental power based on lobbying and campaign finance.
11. Author correspondence with Venelin Ganev, December 2015.

Chapter 2

1. Charles Boix cites Boyer 1983; 1984; Boix 1998, 108.
2. In his memoirs, Joaquín Almunia acknowledges that as a minister of labor he agreed with the substance of the economic policy designed by Miguel Boyer (Almunia 2001, 170).
3. Solchaga confirmed his ex ante opposition in an interview with this author, July 6, 2012.
4. Author interview with Joaquín Almunia, April 2015.
5. Ernest Lluch, "Banco de Espana," *Cinco Dias*, November 7, 1990, 3.
6. Interviewed in Aceña 2001, 545.
7. *El País*, November 11, 1996.
8. Author interview with Joaquín Almunia, April 2015.
9. Jaime Garcia Anoveros, former UCD minister, cited in Gutiérrez 1991, 192–193.
10. "Las fugas del Banco de España," *El País*, October 30, 1988, 52.
11. Author interview with Carlos Solchaga, July 2012.
12. Author interview with Joaquín Almunia, April 2015.
13. Author interview with Carlos Solchaga, July 2012.
14. Constantino Lluch was a PSOE MP and Spain's leading economic historian. A professor at Essex and Louvain, Lluch had also worked as the chief of the World Bank's Labor Market Research Department.
15. *Libro blanco sobre el paro*, cited in *El Pais*, June 1988.
16. See Bentolila et al. 1994; Dolado and López-Salido 1996; and Dolado and Jimeno 1997.
17. "Nueve años como 'hombre de la Ebert' en España," *El País*, January 17, 1985.
18. Author interview with former MEH civil servant, July 7, 2012.
19. The high levels of centralization within PSOE were achieved during the two PSOE congresses in 1979 (Share 1998; Gillespie 1989).
20. Author interview with Joaquín Almunia, April 2015.
21. Author interview with Joaquín Almunia, April 2015.
22. Author interview with Carlos Solchaga, July 2012.
23. "El Pleno del Senado ratifica el Tratado de Maastricht sin ningún voto en contra," *El País*, November 27, 1992.
24. Author interview with senior PP economist, July 10, 2013.
25. Statement cited in Solbes 2013, 334.
26. "Aznar capitaliza la entrada en el euro y ofrece a la oposición un pacto de Estado," *El País*, May 13, 1998.
27. Miguel Sebastian, "El tipo único es más justo y eficiente," *El País*, November 3, 2007.
28. Author interview with Miguel Sebastián, June 2012.
29. Author interview with Joaquín Almunia, April 2015.
30. Author interview with Carlos Mulas Granados, June 2012.

Chapter 3

1. See more at: http://www.ohchr.org/EN/NewsEvents/Pages/DisplayNews.aspx?NewsID=16 737&LangID=E#sthash.GUVL7xHt.dpuf.
2. "Raport de conjunctură," firm survey of the German-Romanian Industry Chamber, August 1, 2015.
3. UniCredit Group, "CEE Banking—Still the Right Bet," July 2008, www.bankaustria.at/en/index.html.
4. After the 2008 crisis the median Romanian hourly wage was lower than the minimum wage in China's wealthier regions.
5. Cited in *Gandul*, November, 2013.
6. Some of the arguments presented in some of the following sections were more extensively presented in select chapters of my economic history of Romania published in the Romanian language in 2014 and entitled *Dependent and developing. The Political Economy of Romanian Capitalism/Dependență și dezvoltare. Economia politică a capitalismului românesc)* and published by the Cluj-based Tact publishing house. The analysis done here benefited extensively from the thorough reviews received by that book.

7. United Nations Human Rights Office of the High Commissioner, "Is Romania in denial about poverty and discrimination against the poor?" UN, 2015.
8. Interview with Petre Roman, *Adevărul*, November, 1990.
9. Author interview with Petre Roman, July, 2006.
10. Interview with Alexandru Bârlădeanu, *Adevărul*, January, 1990.
11. Interview with Ion Iliescu, *Adevărul*, March, 1991.
12. I use a non-normative definition of populism as in Etchemendy et al. (2011) and Remmer (2012).
13. Interview with President Iliescu in *Adevărul*, September 1992.
14. Government report, *Adevărul*, October 1992.
15. Statement by Mişu Negriţoiu in *Adevărul*, August 1993.
16. Author interview with Prime Minister Nicolae Văcăroiu, January 2013.
17. Author interview with Nicolae Văcăroiu, January 2009.
18. Author interview with Prime Minister Nicolae Văcăroiu, January 2013.
19. Government report, *Adevărul*, October, 1992.
20. Interview with Nicolae Văcăroiu, Academia Caţavencu, October 27, 2009.
21. Author interview with PSD MP, June 2006.
22. Memoirs of Iosif Boda, one of Iliescu's advisers (Boda 1999, 57).
23. OMRI Daily Digest, July 1995.
24. Author interview with Nicolae Văcăroiu, January 2009.
25. Author interview with former Ministry of Industry economist, January 2009.
26. Author interview with Ministry of Finance personnel expert, July 2006; January 2009.
27. Iliescu 1994; author interview with Nicolae Văcăroiu, January 2009.
28. Author interviews with BNR Research Service economists, January 2009.
29. In accordance with transition economics, an appropriate spectrum of inflation ranged between 20 and 30 percent (Croitoru 1993, 161).
30. This evaluation is based on my doctoral fieldwork (Ban 2011).
31. In 1991 the IMF's technical assistance in Romania demanded (and obtained) the adoption of a steeply progressive income and corporate taxation system (Pop 2006).
32. Author interview with IMF economist in Bucharest, January, 2009.
33. Economist Intelligence Unit, Romania, Country Report, 1997.
34. See Daniel Dăianu, "Argentina: o lecţie pentru România," *Revista 22*, January 21, 2002.
35. For example, Nicolae Filipescu, « *Politica şi succesul economic* » , *Revista22*, May 26, 2003; Daniel Vighi, « Capitalismul Românesc între integrame şi apariţii OZN, » *Revista 22*, April 21–27, 1998, p.11.
36. H. R. Patapievici, « Cine guvernează cu adevărat România, » *Revista 22*, March 17–23, p.7; Dan Pavel, « Capitalism şi neocorporatism românesc, » *Revista 22*, February 24–March 2, p.3.
37. Andrei Cornea, « Dincoace şi dincolo de reformă, » *Revista 22*, June 2–8, 1998, p. 3.
38. Dan Petrescu "Ciobănizare sau Europenizare?" *Revista 22*, April 15–22, p.12.
39. Şerban Orescu, « Câteva reflexii despre mentalitatea germană, » *Revista 22*, June 16–22, 1998, p. 8.
40. Author interview with Horia Terpe, July 2006.
41. "Isărescu: Taxa unică îşi arată efectele," *Ziarul financiar*, August 16, 2006.
42. Author interview with Gabriel Biriş, July 2006.
43. Author interviews with Anca Harasim, January 2009; Bogdan Hossu, December 2013; Ovidiu Jurca, January 2009; Cătălin Păuna, January 2009.
44. Author interview with Luminiţa Dima, January, 2009.
45. Author interview with Luminiţa Dima, January 2009.
46. Author interviews with Richard Georgescu, January 2009.
47. Author interviews with Suzana Dobre, January 2009; Ruxandra Băndilă, January 2009.
48. Finance Minister Varujan Vosganian cited in *Ziarul Financiar*, May, 2008.
49. BNR chief economist Cristian Popa, cited in *Ghişeul Bancar*, January, 2008.
50. Author interview with Florin Georgescu, January 2009; June 2014.
51. Author interviews with Florin Abraham, July 2006; Bogdan Hossu, December 2013; Ovidiu Jurcă, January 2009; Ion Iliescu, July 2006; Sorin Ioniţă, January 2009.

52. Author interview with Richard Florescu, January 2009.
53. Romanian National Institute of Statistics (INS) data and analysis by Ziarul Financiar; available at http://www.zf.ro/analiza/ce-spun-despre-romania-14-indicatori-economici-la-14-ani-de-la-lansarea-zf-10335623/poze/?p=11.
54. Author interview with Ovidiu Jurcă, January 2009; Bogdan Hossu, December 2013.

Chapter 4

1. Based on Lukauskas 1997 and Pérez 1997.
2. Neohistoricism was a school of thought that defined itself against neoclassical economics (Velarde 2001, 350). The main policy implications of the neohistoricism were protectionism and the state-managed cartelization of select industries.
3. The main limit of tolerance was involvement in antiregime student movements or political organizations. For example, in August 1965 several professors lost tenure for siding with protesting students. "Five Professors Dismissed," *Minerva* 4 (1) (1965): 135–145.
4. Author interview with Joaquín Almunia, April 2015; Fernando Fernandez, June 2012.
5. Author interview with Spanish economist Joaquín Almunia, April, 2015.
6. These were *Información Comercial Española* and *Hacienda Pública Española*.
7. As an economist working for the Venezuelan central bank (1949–1956), he developed close contacts with Latin American economists working for the IMF and the World Bank. This enabled him to supply his collaborators in Spain with up-to-date Western economic literature and IMF and World Bank research (Estapé 1999).
8. This section was more extensively covered in my article on von Stackelberg (Ban 2013c).
9. A Nazi Party member since 1931, in 1933 had he joined the SS, the elite paramilitary organization of the Nazis. After 1936, however, he became gradually estranged from the regime, and during the war he refused a request to join the armed wing of the SS (Waffen SS), preferring instead to serve in the interpreting service. By the early 1940s he was definitively disillusioned with Nazism and was active in some dissident circles. "It is important to stress at this point that his (temporary) Nazi sympathies had no resonance among the Freiburg (later Ordo) group. On the contrary, he was not among the group's founding members and the classics of this school of thought, Walter Eucken in particular, delivered unambiguous and harsh critiques of the politics and economics of the Nazi regime. Indeed, much of their political legitimacy in postwar Germany came from their impeccable anti-Nazi past. Von Stackelberg's intriguing Nazi past should not be used to sully the credentials of this school of thought of democratic Germany." I thank Peter Nedergaard for this qualification.
10. According to Senn (1996, 2012), the economist's distance from Hitler's regime began in 1936, and turned into an active estrangement in 1942 when two of von Stackelberg's friends and fellow professors at the University of Berlin who had been part of the antiregime "Beck-Goerdeler" opposition group were executed. By going to Spain, von Stackelberg was probably saving his own life.
11. There were many Freiburg Circles at the time Stackelberg left Germany. The one he participated in was called the Beckerath Circle (named after Stackelberg's adviser). The circles had a different genesis than the Freiburg School.
12. Julio Segura Sánchez (2002) and Juan Velarde Fuertes (1999) identified six major publications during Stackelberg's three-year stay in Madrid.
13. Sarda extensively and relatively positively reviewed the classical Ordo volumes of 1948 and 1949 in a 1949 issue of *Anales de Economía* (Lissen n.d., 15).

Chapter 5

1. Author interview with Valentin Cojanu, January 2012. See also Kirițescu 1992.
2. Author interview with Gheorghe Zaman, June 2015 (via Elena Baches).
3. Author interview with Valentin Cojanu, January 2009.

4. Author interview with Moisa Altar, January 2009.
5. Author interview with Moisa Altar, January 2009.
6. Author's correspondence with Johanna Bockman, August 2010.
7. A "political dossier" could block such international scholarly opportunities even if one had publications in Western journals, a rare performance in those years (Bălaş 2000, 415, 436).
8. Academia Română, "Aurel Iancu, la 80 de ani," http://www.ince.ro/iancu-eng-2.pdf.
9. Aurel Iancu, "Nicholas Georgescu-Roegen, întemeietor de şcoală economică," Academia Română, 2007.
10. Author interview with Gheorghe Zaman, June 2015 (via Elena Baches).
11. At this seminar, the leading representatives of America's postwar "embedded liberalism" (Daniel Bell, Margaret Mead, Talcott Parsons) presented their ideas to East European scholars.
12. IMF Institute Archives, Box 3, File 3, RM 1987-0150, INSAI Course Files, Immediate Office Sous-Fonds; Box 3, File 4-5, Insai Course Files.
13. Memorandum, Gerard M. Teyssier, Director of the IMF Institute, to the Deputy Managing Director, Per Jacobsson Foundation, Romania, 1974-77.
14. Author interview with Gheorghe Zaman, June 2015 (via Elena Baches).
15. Author interview with Gheorghe Zaman, June 2015 (via Elena Baches).
16. Interview with Ştefan Andrei, former foreign trade official during the 1980s (Betea 2011, 412–413).
17. IMF Institute Report on the IMF Institute Seminar in Hungary, March 18–29, 1985, Box 12, File 1, RM 1990-0271
18. Letter from Teyssier to central bank chairman Cristian Dumitrescu, September 3, 1986, Box 11, File 5.
19. This information was traced in the IMF Institute files with the following identification: Box 3, Files 8, 10–13; Box 5, File 15.
20. Daniel Dăianu, "Să scrii (critici) înainte de 1989," in *Jurnalul Naţional*, October 9, 2007.
21. Author interview with Valentin Cojanu. January, 2009.
22. Author interview with Adrian Severin. July 2006.
23. Author interview with Moisa Altar. January 2009.
24. Author interview with Moisa Altar. January 2009.
25. Author interview with Moisa Altar, January 2009.
26. Daniel Dăianu, "Să scrii (critici) înainte de 1989," *Jurnalul Naţional*, February 10, 2007.
27. Author interviews with President Ion Iliescu (1990–1996; 2000–2004), July 2006; Prime Ministers Petre Roman (1990–1991) July 2006; and Nicolae Văcăroiu (1992–1996) January 2009, and Minister of Finance Florin Georgescu (1992–1996), January 2009; June 2015.
28. Author interview with Adrian Severin, July 2006.
29. Author interview with Ion Iliescu, July 2006; author interview with Valeriu Ioan-Franc, June 2015.
30. This is manifest in the list of authors of the Commission (*Schiţă*, annex 3, 59–70).
31. Author interview with Nicolae Văcăroiu, January 2009.
32. Author interview with Valeriu Ioan-Franc, a close collaborator of Postolache, June 2015.
33. Author interview with Valeriu Ioan-Franc, June 2015.
34. Author interview with Nicolae Văcăroiu, January 2009.
35. Author interview with Valeriu Ioan-Franc, June 2015 (via Elena Baches).
36. See Dobrescu and Postolache 1990 and Gheorghe Zaman, "Planificarea indicativă şi rigorile pieţei," *Tribuna Economica* 14 (1990).
37. Given the social disruptions unleashed by milder forms of liberalization this expectation strikes one as a sample of wishful thinking, yet what matters is that this vision was very different from dominant transition economics.
38. Author interview with Valeriu Ioan-Franc, June, 2015 (via Elena Baches).
39. The authors propose also minimalist one that suggests making unprivatizable only public services, energy firms and extractive firms.

Chapter 6

1. For Johnson's influence in Esteve's work on monetary policy see Esteve Serrano 1968; 1980.
2. Author interview with Spanish economist Fernando Fernandez, June 19, 2012.
3. Manuel Sánchez Ayuso, "La estrategia económica, alternativa de los laboristas británicos," *El País*, August 7, 1981. For a more systematic perspective on his political views, see Ayuso 1981a; 1981b.
4. A banking family, the Villalongas had been invested significant amounts fighting interventionist economic ideas and the advocacy of free-market ones (Huerta de Soto 2005, 390–391).
5. The possibility that the PCE could emerge as the strongest challenger to the establishment was real, as suggested by the PCE's control over the labor union Comissiones Obreras, the most active force of resistance against the Franco regime (Diamandouros 1986, 552–553).
6. According to PSOE historian Juan Marichal, PSOE never had a Marxist ideology per se. Interview with Marichal in Maranon (1996, 30–42).
7. "Nueve años como 'hombre de la Ebert' en España," *El País*, January 17, 1985.
8. "Fundacion Ebert: 30 años an Espana" (on file with the author).
9. Author interview with Joaquín Almunia, April 29 2015.

Chapter 7

1. Some of the arguments presented in select sections of this chapter were more extensively presented in my work published in Romanian (Ban 2014). This version incorporates the extensive feedback received on that book after its publication.
2. Author interview with Nicolae Văcăroiu, January 2009; author interview with Constantin Gheorghe, July 2006, adviser to the presidency.
3. This evaluation is based on the central bank governor's own survey of BNR policies during the 1990s (Isarescu 2006, particularly on pages 18–36).
4. Author interview with former Treasury official, January 2009; June 2014.
5. In contrast, as evidenced in chapter 3, the central-bank economists treated arrears as a pathology of neodevelopmentalism and as the basis for demanding faster and deeper structural reforms.
6. Cited in *Economistul*, issue 707, 1005.
7. Author interview with IMF and World Bank experts based in Bucharest, January 2009.
8. In contrast, the World Bank nevertheless continued to lend and provide technical assistance, a decision that met with harsh criticism later on inside the Bank (World Bank 2005, 28–29).
9. Author interview with Ovidiu Jurca, January 2009; Dumitru Hossu, December 2013.
10. See Spendzharova 2003, Papadimitriou and Phinnemore 2008, and Gabor 2010a for extensive overviews of EU-IMF-World Bank conditionality in Romania.
11. An IMF officials interviewed by this author in January 2009 felt that the EC delegated most of these policy areas to the Bretton Woods institutions because they were judged to have more experience in this regard.
12. Author interview with Ovidiu Jurca, January 2009.
13. Author interview with Romano Prodi, March 2009.
14. Author interview with Florin Abraham, July 2006.
15. Author interview with Ion Iliescu, July 2006.
16. Author interview with Adrian Severin, July 2006.
17. Author interview with Romani Prodi, March 2009.
18. Author interview with Ion Iliescu, July 2006; Florin Abraham, July 2006.
19. "Adrian Năstase meets Tony Blair in Budapest before Progressive Governance Summit," Romanian Ministry of Foreign Affairs Newsletter, October 15, 2004; "Proiectul programuluii participării primului ministru Adrian Năstase, la conferința și summitul 'Progressive governance'" (Londra, 12–14 iulie 2003).
20. Author interview with Alfred Gusenbauer, former social democratic prime minister of Austria, April 2009.

21. Author interview with Mugur Tolici, December 2013.
22. Statement by IMF managing director Michel Camdessus, cited in Broome 2010, 616.
23. JVI Macroeconomic policy course description, 1996 (on file with the author).
24. See the position of Michel Camdessus, the IMF managing director at the time: http://www.brettonwoodsproject.org/2000/06/art-16159/.
25. Author interview with Romanian central bank and Ministry of Finance experts who studied at JVI, October, 2013; June, 2014.
26. Author interview with Romanian central bank economist, June 2014.
27. Author interview with Bogdan Moinescu, BNR economist, January, 2009.
28. Author interview with Romanian central bank and Ministry of Finance experts who studied at JVI, June 2014.
29. Author interview with Gabriel Biriş, July 2006.
30. Focus group with Ministry of Finance staff, June, 2014.
31. Author interview with Narcis Tulbure, January 2009.
32. Author interview with Valentin Cojanu, January 2009.
33. This analysis is based on Phillips and Kaser 1992; Pleskovic et al. 2000; Svejnar 2000; Kraft and Vodapoviec 2003; Earle 2007.
34. Author interview with Mugur Tolici, December 2013; author interview with Horia Braun, January 2009.
35. Beginning with 1998, DOFIN received financing from the World Bank for paying expenses associated with doctoral conferences and lectures delivered by Western academic economists as well as for fellowships at partner universities for DOFIN's PhD and MSc students.
36. After finishing his PhD at the European University Institute, Bilbiie won a prize research fellowship at Oxford and then a professorship at the Sorbonne and Paris School of Economics, a joint institute of France's *écoles*. Interview with Florin Bilbiie, *Hotnews*, March 29, 2010.
37. Interview with Moisa Altar, *Hotnews*, March 17, 2010.
38. Statement by Carol Alexander on DOFIN website http://dofin.ase.ro/different.php.
39. While most DOFIN graduates chose careers in private finance, almost 20 percent went to work for the central bank and 15 percent in academia. 2010 DOFIN survey, http://www.dofin.ase.ro/.
40. Interview with Daniel Dăianu, *Revista 22*, May 12–18, pp. 7–8.
41. World Bank, *Socialist Economies in Transition* 1 (9) (April 1990).
42. Author interviews with IMF and World Bank delegates in Bucharest, January 2009.
43. The central bank team was represented at the highest level (Mugur Isărescu, Lucian Croitoru, Daniel Dăianu), as were ASE (Cornel Târhoacă) and the Economic Prognosis Institute of the Academy (Lucian Albu).
44. Author interview with Ministry of Finance economists, January 2009; July 2014.
45. Author interview with Daniel Dăianu, December 2013.
46. Excerpt from the CPP mission statement available at www.ong.ro/ong/sar/center.htm.
47. Initially senior staff in the Romanian central bank were against the flat tax. Author interview with Sorin Ioniţă, January 2009; Valentin Lazea, January 2009.
48. Author interview with Anca Harasim, January 2009; Suzana Dobre, January 2009.
49. Author interview with Anca Harasim, January 2009.
50. Author interview with Sorin Ioniţă, January 2009.
51. Author interview with Sorin Ioniţă, January 2009.
52. Author interviews with Vlad Topan, January 2009; Horia Terpe, July 2006.
53. Author interview with Octavian Dragomir Jora, December 2013.
54. Author interview with Vlad Topan, January 2009.
55. Foreign and domestic partnerships are listed in the CADI archives: http://archive-ro.com/ro/c/cadi.ro/2013-04-29_1968970_45/CADI_RO/.
56. Author interview with Horia Terpe, July 2006.
57. The list of guests and partners is available at http://www.cadi.ro/index.php/vizualizare/articol/multimedia/167.
58. Author interview with Mihai Zulean, January 2009.
59. Author interview with Horia Terpe, July 2006; Mihai Zulean, January 2009.
60. Author interview with Octavian Dragomir Jora, December 2013.

Chapter 8

1. Stimulus Packages," rodrik.typepad.com.
2. *El País*, November 28, 2008; Plan E's official page is available at http://www.plane.gob.es/.
3. *El País*, August 30, 2009; for a critique of its effectiveness see the report of the Spanish Court of Public Accounts (Tribunal de Cuentas), *El País*, December 18, 2012. The report is available at http://boe.es/boe/dias/2013/04/30/pdfs/BOE-A-2013-4558.pdf.
4. Author interview with Carlos Mulas Granados, Zapatero's economic adviser, June 27, 2012.
5. See statement by the International Trade Union Confederation, November 21, 2012. Available at http://www.ituc-csi.org/imf-and-ec-apply-behind-the-scenes?lang=en.
6. See Ban 2015 for an overview.
7. Author interview with Research Service economist, July 20, 2009.
8. Author interview with Carlos Mulas Granados, June 27, 2012.
9. Author interview with Miguel Sebastián, June 26, 2012.
10. Author interview with Carlos Mulas-Granados, June 27, 2012.
11. Interview with Joseph Stiglitz in *ABC*, May 6, 2009.
12. Author interview with Carlos Mulas Granados, June 27, 2012; phone interview with Javier Vallés. July 26, 2013.
13. Author interview with Carlos Mulas Granados.
14. Author interview with Fernando Fernandez, CEMFI, June 19, 2012.
15. Author interview with Economic Bureau expert, June 29, 2013.
16. Statement for *Europapress*, September 27, 2011.
17. *Expansion*, September 2, 2009.
18. ECFIN Economic Briefs 34, June 2014, Brussels.
19. This focus is clear in the Troika-designed loan agreements as well as in the Commission's policy surveillance apparatus (annual growth surveys, country-specific policy recommendations to member states in the framework of the European Semester, the EU's annual cycle of economic policy coordination).
20. Author interview with Spanish Treasury official, July 3, 2012.
21. Author interview with Spanish central bank economist, June 25, 2012; author interview with Spanish Treasury official, July 3, 2012.
22. "ECB Threatened to End Funding Unless Ireland Sought Bailout," *Financial Times*, November 6, 2014.
23. "Who's in Charge in Spain?" *El País*, December 2, 2013.
24. Author interview with Economic Bureau economist, July 10, 2013.
25. Author interview with Economic Bureau economist, July 10, 2013.
26. "Meet the Euro-sherpas," *Guardian*, October 17, 2012.
27. "Alvaro Nadal ist Heimlicher Wirtschaftminister," *Suddeutsche Zeitung*, October 20, 2012.
28. Statement for *ABC*, http://www.abc.es/videos-espana/20131218/montoro-17000-millones-euros-2947411158001.html.
29. Author interview with economic counsel to the Spanish prime minister, July 2, 2013; interview with Luis de Guindos in *El País*, January 27, 2012.
30. Luis de Guindos, interview in *ABC*, July 11, 2011.
31. Luis de Guindos, interview in *ABC*.
32. "Más Allá de la Austeridad," *El Mundo*, April 3, 2011.

Chapter 9

1. Statement by presidential adviser Sebastian Lăzăroiu, *Mediafax*, May 25, 2010.
2. Tom Gallagher, "Grija domnului Strauss-Kahn față de România," *Romania liberă*, June 6, 2010. Tom Gallagher sat on the board of Institutul de Studii Populare, the think tank of the ruling party.
3. "If you have to save, increase taxes, and especially taxes on the richest people." The Romanian government responded, "No, the decision is ours." Statement by Dominique Strauss Kahn on French TV channel France 2, cited in *Liberation*, June 10, 2010.

4. https://www.imf.org/external/np/tr/2010/tr052010.htm.

5. Author interview with Liviu Voinea, June 2015; author correspondence with Cristian Socol, February 2015.

6. Author interview with Ministry of Finance staff, January, 2009; June 2015.

7. The relevant Troika memoranda, supplemental memoranda and public notices are available at http://www.imf.org/external/country/ROU/index.htm and http://ec.europa.eu/economy_finance/assistance_eu_ms/romania/index_en.htm.

8. IMF, EC, World Bank, "Statement by the IMF, EC and WB on the Review of Romania's Economic Program," Press Release No. 12/292, 2012.

9. Interview with the IMF's mission chief for Romania, Jeffrey Franks, in *IMF Survey Magazine*, May 11, 2010.

10. This analysis draws on Ban (2015a; 2015b).

11. See online methodological appendix.

12. Figure first published in Ban (2015a, 177–180).

13. For a more elaborated argument see Ban 2015a; see online appendix for data set https://fundprofessionaldataset2013.wordpress.com/.

14. "And Justice for All: In Emerging Europe," *Financial Times*, November 7, 2011.

15. Vienna Initiative 1.0, http://vienna-initiative.com/vienna-initiative-part-1/overview/.

16. *Ziarul Financiar*, September 17, 2003.

17. See also *Ziarul Financiar*, November 8, 2010.

18. This joint position paper is available at http://www.amcham.ro/UserFiles/committeePaper/FISCAL%20STRATEGY%20RECOMMENDATIONS,%20Feb%202010_01061702.pdf.

19. Author interviews with Liviu Voinea, August, 2010; June 2015.

20. Author interview with Anca Harasim, January 2009.

21. Author interview with Bogdan Hossu, December 2013.

22. See statement by the International Trade Union Confederation, November 21, 2012. Available at http://www.ituc-csi.org/imf-and-ec-apply-behind-the-scenes?lang=en.

23. Author correspondence with Stefan Guga, July, 2015.

24. Author interview with Anca Harasim, January 2009.

25. Author interview with Bogdan Hossu, December 2013.

26. Position paper on energy industry is available at http://www.amcham.ro/UserFiles/committeePaper/OBSERVATII%20PNAER_01061318.pdf, while on ICT is available at http://www.amcham.ro/UserFiles/committeePaper/ICT%20position%20paper_October%202010_EN_12151457.pdf.

27. Author interview with Social Democratic presidential candidate Mircea Geoană, January 2010.

28. http://adevarul.ro/news/politica/componenta-actuala-parlamentului-instala-cristian-diaconescu-demisia-psdp-1_50acd76a7c42d5a6638a8347/index.html.

29. BNR staff interviewed by the author strongly suggested that they perceived BNR as a meritocratic employer (author interviews, May 28–30, 2014).

30. Author interview with BNR economist, January, 2009.

31. Feeling that he did not have enough political support, Croitoru eventually backed off.

32. Incidentally, their departure was associated with SAR's economic policy agenda moving more toward the center.

33. Certainly since the 1990s the ideas behind Germany's "social market economy" had been supportive of more liberal industrial relations and liberalized social protections in the name of external competitiveness (Armingeon and Baccaro 2015). Nevertheless, they did not morph into another brand of the Austrian school.

34. Author interview with Victoria Stoiciu, December 2013; June 2015.

35. Author interview with Victoria Stoiciu, December 2013; June 2015.

36. Such events included CRPE "Zece ani de azi înainte" 2010; CRPE "Adoptarea Euro in 2015: cum am ajuns la această data și ce șanse avem?" 2010.

37. Author interview with Fiscal Council economist, June 3, 2014.

38. http://www.imf.org/external/pubs/ft/fandd/2014/06/books.htm.

39. Valentin Lazea, "A Crisis Too Good to Be Wasted: What Economists Have Learned from the Current Recession," September 12, 2013.

40. Lazea, "Crisis Too Good to Be Wasted."
41. Author interview with central bank economists, June 2014.
42. Author interview with Florin Georgescu, June 2014.
43. Valentin Lazea, "Dilema zilei," *Curs de Guvernare*, May 13, 2012.
44. Author interviews with ministry of finance staff, June, 2015.
45. Andreea Vass blog post, July 21, 2010.
46. Valentin Lazea, "Lumea post-criza," *Curs de Guvernare*, May 5, 2011.
47. Valentin Lazea, "Pactul fiscal," *Curs de Guvernare*, February 29, 2012.
48. End-of-mission statement on Romania, by Professor Philip Alston, United Nations Human Rights Council Special Rapporteur on extreme poverty and human rights. http://www.ohchr.org/EN/NewsEvents/Pages/DisplayNews.aspx?NewsID=16737&LangID=E.
49. Speech at joint ISP-KAS workshop, January 18, 2011; ANEIR Jubilee, December 19, 2011.
50. Traian Băsescu, "Politics and the Pursuit of Welfare," LSEE Ghiță Ionescu Memorial lecture, London School of Economics, June 6, 2011.
51. Intermediated author correspondence with Emil Boc (July 2012).
52. Statement by Traian Băsescu, September 21, 2010.
53. Interview with Valentin Lazea, Recolta.eu, October 25, 2012.
54. Author correspondence with Emil Boc, August 2012.
55. Presidential statement, November 11, 2011.
56. Valentin Lazea, *Curs de Guvernare*, June 5, 2012.
57. Traian Băsescu, "Politics and the Pursuit of Welfare," speech at London School of Economics, http://www.lse.ac.uk/assets/richmedia/channels/publicLecturesAndEvents/transcripts/20110606_1715_aLectureByTraianBasescu_tr.pdf.
58. Andreea Paul Vass, economic counsel to the PM, blog post.
59. Intermediated author correspondence with Emil Boc (July 2012).
60. The beginnings of the 2012 government were mired in a constitutional controversy solved via the intervention of the EU.
61. Author interview with Mircea Geoană, December 2014.
62. Author interviews with Florin Georgescu (January 2009; June 2015).
63. Victor Ponta, interview with Costi Rogozanu, Realitatea TV, December 7, 2014.
64. Statement by minister Liviu Pop, *Hotnews*, April 29, 2015.
65. Victor Ponta, *Mediafax*, April 16, 2015.
66. Author correspondence with Florentin Iancu, July 2015.
67. Author correspondence with Florentin Iancu, July 2015.
68. Author interview with Ebert Stiftung expert, September, 2014; participant observation at PSD training sessions, Sibiu, September 2014.
69. Author correspondence with PSD MP, July 2015.
70. Transcript of a Conference Call on the 2015 Article IV Consultation with Romania, Washington, DC, Friday, March 27, 2015
71. Lucian Croitoru, "Un deceniu înainte și cinci ani după tăierea salariilor cu 25 la sută în 2010," *Curs de Guvernare*, July 17, 2015.
72. Author interview with Cristian Socol, August 2013.
73. Central bank data at http://www.bnr.ro/page.aspx?prid=11236.
74. Author interview with senior Budget Ministry economists, June , 2014.
75. Author interview with Liviu Voinea, June 2014.
76. Florin Georgescu, "Growth, Ageing and Income Distribution in Romania," presentation at the IMF–World Bank Constituency workshop, Sofia (Bulgaria), May 29–31, 2015.
77. Daniel Daianu, "Steroizii: Ciclul economic si dezechilibrele," *Curs de guvernare*, August 21, 2015.
78. Florin Georgescu, "Growth, Ageing and Income Distribution in Romania."

Conclusions

1. In this respect Romanian economists differed from their peers in the region who had explored the uses of neoclassical economics in the reform of socialism for decades (Bockman 2011).

BIBLIOGRAPHY

Abraham, Florin. 2006. *România de la Comunism la Capitalism, 1989–2004: Sistemul Politic*. Bucharest: Tritonic.

Aceña, Pablo Martín. 1999. "Los Estudios de Macroeconomía en España: Las Enseñanzas del Profesor Rojo." In E. Fuentes Quintana, ed., *Economía y Economistas Españoles*. Barcelona: Galaxia Gutenberg and Círculo de Lectores. Vol. 7: 525–550.

———. 2000. *El Servicio de Estudios del Banco de España: 1930/2000*. http://dialnet.unirioja.es/servlet/libro?codigo=268306.

———. 2001. "El Banco de España entre Dos Siglos: De Banquero del Estado a Prestamista en Última Instancia." In Antonio Morales Moya, ed., *Las claves de la España del siglo XX*. Sociedad Estatal España Nuevo Milenio. Vol. 7: 95–139.

Acharya, Amitav. 2004. "How Ideas Spread: Whose Norms Matter? Norm Localization and Institutional Change in Asian Regionalism." *International Organization* 58.2: 239–275.

———. 2009. *Whose Ideas Matter? Agency and Power in Asian Regionalism*. Ithaca, NY: Cornell University Press.

Adăscăliței, Dragoș, and Ștefan Guga. 2015. "Negotiating Agency and Structure: Trade Union Organizing Strategies in a Hostile Environment." *Economic and Industrial Democracy*, ahead of print.

Aghion, Philippe, et al. 1998. *Endogenous Growth Theory*. MIT Press.

Aligică, P. D., and H. Terpe. 2007. "Economie, Epistemologie si Previziune." Bucharest: Editura Triton.

Albu, Lucian Liviu. 2001. "Tax Evasion and the Size of Underground Economy: A Theoretical and Empirical Investigation." *Journal for Economic Forecasting* 1: 16–31.

Albu, Lucian Liviu, and Elena Pelinescu. 2000. "Sustainability of Public Debt: A Theoretical and Empirical Investigation." *Revue Roumaine des Sciences Economiques* 45.1: 101–127.

Almenar Palau, Salvador. 2002. "La Recepción e Influencia de Keynes y del Keynesianismo en España: Después de la *Teoria General*." In E. Fuentes Quintana, dir., *Economía y economistas españoles*. Barcelona: Galaxia Gutenberg and Círculo de Lectores. Vol. 7: 409–523.

Almunia, Joaquín. 2001. *Memorias Políticas*. Madrid: Aguilar.

Alvarez, Corugedo J. 2001. "Valentin Andrés Álvarez: Ciencia y Humanism." In E. Fuentes Quintana, dir., *Economía y economistas españoles*. Barcelona: Galazia Gutenberg-Círculo de Lectores. Vol. 7: 223–242.

Amable, Bruno. 2011. "Morals and Politics in the Ideology of Neo-liberalism." *Socio-economic Review* 9.1: 3–30.

AmCham. 2008. "Proposed Amendments to the Labor and Social Security Legislation." Position Paper.

———. 2010. "Proposed Labor Code Amendments." Position Paper.

Andrés, Javier, J. David López-Salido, and Javier Vallés. 2001. *Money in an Estimated Business Cycle Model of the Euro Area*. Madrid: Banco de España.

Appel, Hilary, and Mitchell A. Orenstein. 2013. "Ideas versus Resources Explaining the Flat Tax and Pension Privatization Revolutions in Eastern Europe and the Former Soviet Union." *Comparative Political Studies* 46.2: 123–152.

———. 2015. "Duda's Economic Populism." *Foreign Affairs*, June 1.

Arestis, Philip, ed. *Is There a New Consensus in Macroeconomics?*. Basingstoke: Palgrave Macmillan, 2007.

Armingeon, Klaus, and Lucio Baccaro. 2012. "Political Economy of the Sovereign Debt Crisis: The Limits of Internal Devaluation." *Industrial Law Journal* 41.3: 254–275.

Arocena, Pablo, Ignacio Contín, and Emilio Huerta. 2002. "Price Regulation in the Spanish Energy Sectors: Who Benefits?" *Energy Policy* 30.10: 885–895.

Arocena, Pablo, M. Köthenbürger, H. Sinn, and J. Walley. 2006. "Privatisation Policy in Spain: Stuck between Liberalisation and the Protection of Nationals' Interest." In Marko Köthenbürger, Hans-Werner Sinn, and John Whalley, eds., *Privatization Experiences in the European Union.* Cambridge, MA: MIT Press, 339–364.

Aslund, Anders, ed. 1992. *Market Socialism or the Restoration of Capitalism?* New York: Cambridge University Press.

Babb, Sarah. 2003. "The IMF in Sociological Perspective: A Tale of Organizational Slippage." *Studies in Comparative International Development* 38.2: 3–27.

———. 2004. *Managing Mexico: Economists from Nationalism to Neoliberalism.* Princeton, NJ: Princeton University Press.

———. 2012. "The Washington Consensus as Transnational Policy Paradigm: Its Origins, Trajectory and Likely Successor." *Review of International Political Economy* 20.2: 268–297.

Backhaus, J. G. 1996. "Stackelberg's Concept of the Post-war Economic Order." *Journal of Economic Studies* 23.5–6: 141–148.

Bajgar, Matej, and Beata Javorcik. 2015. "Climbing the Rungs of the Quality Ladder: FDI and Domestic Exporters in Romania." Unpublished manuscript.

Baker, Andrew. 2013. "The Gradual Transformation? The Incremental Dynamics of Macroprudential Regulation." *Regulation and Governance* 7.4: 417–434.

Bălaş, Egon. 2000. *Will to Freedom: A Perilous Journey through Fascism and Communism.* Syracuse, NY: Syracuse University Press.

Baldacci, Emanuele, Carlos Mulas-Granados, and Sanjeev Gupta. 2009. *How Effective Is Fiscal Policy Response in Systemic Banking Crises?* Washington, DC: International Monetary Fund.

Baldwin, Richard, Pertti Haapararanta, and Jaakko Kiander. 1995. *Expanding Membership of the European Union.* New York: Cambridge University Press.

Balmaseda, Manuel, Miguel Sebastián, and Patry Tello. 2002. "Spain Accession to the EMU: A Long and Hilly Road." *Economic and Social Review* 33.2: 195–222.

Ban, Cornel. 2011. "Neoliberalism in Translation: Economic Ideas and Reforms in Spain and Romania." College Park: Digital Repository at University of Maryland, http://drum.lib.umd.edu/handle/1903/11456.

———. 2012. "Sovereign Debt, Austerity, and Regime Change: The Case of Nicolae Ceauşescu's Romania." *East European Politics and Societies* 26.4: 743–776.

———. 2013a. "Brazil's Liberal Neo-developmentalism: New Paradigm or Edited Orthodoxy?" *Review of International Political Economy* 20.2: 298–331.

———. 2013b. "From Cocktail to Dependence: Revisiting the Foundations of Dependent Market Economies." Available at SSRN 2233056.

———. 2013c. "Heinrich von Stackelberg and the Diffusion of Ordoliberal Economics in Franco's Spain." *History of Economic Ideas* 20.3: 85–104.

———. 2014. *Dependenţă şi dezvoltare. Economia politică a capitalismului românesc*, Cluj, Editura Tact.

———. 2015a. "Austerity versus Stimulus? Understanding Fiscal Policy Change at the International Monetary Fund since the Great Recession." *Governance* 28.2: 167–183.

———. 2015b. "From Designers to Doctrinaires: Staff Research and Fiscal Policy Change at the IMF." *Elites on Trial.* Bingley, UK: Emerald Group Publishing, 337–369.

Ban, Cornel, and Mark Blyth. 2013. "The BRICs and the Washington Consensus: An Introduction." *Review of International Political Economy* 20.2: 241–255.

Ban, Cornel, and Kevin Gallagher. 2015. "Recalibrating Policy Orthodoxy: The IMF since the Great Recession." *Governance* 28.2: 131–146.

Banca Națională a României (BNR). 2009. *Annual Report.*

Banco de España (BdE), 2009. *Annual Report.*

———. 2010. *Annual Report.* Banco de Espana.

———. 2015. *Annual Report.* Madrid: Banco de España.

Barnett, Michael, and Martha Finnemore. 2004. *Rules for the World: International Organizations in Global Politics.* Ithaca, NY: Cornell University Press.

Baturo, Alexander, and Julia Gray. 2009. "Flatliners: Ideology and Rational Learning in the Adoption of the Flat Tax." *European Journal of Political Research* 48.1: 130–159.

Baunsgaard, Thomas, and Steven Symansky. 2009. "Automatic Stabilizers." IMF Staff Position Note 09/23.

Bentolila, Samuel. 1991a. "Analisis de las modalidades de contratacion en Espana (with J. Segura, F. Duran and L. Toharia). Madrid, Ministerio de Trabajo y Seguridad Social.

Bentolila, Samuel. 1991b. Estudios de economìa del trabajo en Espana, III: El problema del paro. (editor, with L. Toharia). Madrid, Ministerio de Trabajo y Seguridad Social.

Bentolila, Samuel, Juan J. Dolado, Wolfgang Franz, and Christopher Pissarides. 1994. "Labour Flexibility and Wages: Lessons from Spain." *Economic Policy* 9.18: 53–99.

Berg, Andrew, and Jonathan Ostry. 2011. "Inequality and Unsustainable Growth: Two Sides of the Same Coin?" IMF Staff Discussion Note No. 11/08.

Berghahn, Volker, and Brigitte Young. 2013. "Reflections on Werner Bonefeld's 'Freedom and the Strong State: On German Ordoliberalism' and the Continuing Importance of the Ideas of Ordoliberalism to Understand Germany's (Contested) Role in Resolving the Eurozone Crisis." *New Political Economy* 18.5: 768–778.

Bermeo, Nancy. 1994. "Sacrifice, Sequence, and Strength in Successful Dual Transitions: Lessons from Spain." *Journal of Politics* 56.3: 601–627.

Bermeo, Nancy, and Jonas Pontusson. 2012. *Coping with Crisis.* New York: Russell Sage Foundation.

Best, Jacqueline. 2003. "From the Top–Down: The New Financial Architecture and the Re-Embedding of Global Finance." *New Political Economy* 8.3: 363–384.

Betea, Lavinia. 2008. *Partea Lor de Adevăr.* Bucharest: Adevarul Holding.

———. 2011. *I se Spunea Machiavelli. Stefan Andrei in dialog cu Lavinia Betea.* Bucharest: Adevarul Holding.

Biezen, Ingrid van. 2003. *Political Parties in New Democracies.* New York: Macmillan.

Biglaiser, Glen. 2002. "The Internationalization of Chicago's Economics in Latin America." *Economic Development and Cultural Change* 50.2: 269–286.

Blanchard, Olivier J., Florence Jaumotte, and Prakash Loungani. 2014. "Labor Market Policies and IMF Advice in Advanced Economies during the Great Recession." *IZA Journal of Labor Policy* 3.1: 1–23.

Blanchard, Olivier J., and Juan F. Jimeno. 1995. "Structural Unemployment: Spain versus Portugal." *American Economic Review* 85.2: 212–218.

Blanchard, Olivier, Giovanni Dell'Ariccia, and Paolo Mauro. 2010. "Rethinking Macroeconomic Policy." *Journal of Money, Credit and Banking* 42.s1: 199–215.

Blanchard, Olivier J., and Daniel Leigh. 2013. "Growth Forecast Errors and Fiscal Multipliers." IMF Working Paper No. 13/1.

Blaug, Mark. 1990. "Comment on O'Brien's 'Lionel Robbins and the Austrian Connection.'" In B. J. Caldwell, *Carl Menger and His Legacy in Economics.* Durham, NC: Duke University Press, 185–188.

Block, Fred, and Margaret R. Somers. 2014. *The Power of Market Fundamentalism: Karl Polanyi's Critique.* Cambridge, MA: Harvard University Press.

Blustein, Paul. 2015. "Laid Low: The IMF, the Eurozone and the First Rescue of Greece." CIGI Papers No. 61.

Blyth, Mark. 2002. *Great Transformations: Economic Ideas and Institutional Change in the Twentieth Century*. New York: Cambridge University Press.

——. 2013. *Austerity: The History of a Dangerous Idea*. New York: Oxford University Press.

Boas, Taylor C., and Jordan Gans-Morse. 2009. "Neoliberalism: From New Liberal Philosophy to Anti-liberal Slogan." *Studies in Comparative International Development* 44.2: 137–161.

Bockman, Johanna. 2011. *Markets in the Name of Socialism: The Left-Wing Origins of Neoliberalism*. Stanford, CA: Stanford University Press.

Bockman, Johanna, and Gil Eyal. 2002. "Eastern Europe as a Laboratory for Economic Knowledge: The Transnational Roots of Neoliberalism." *American Journal of Sociology* 108.2: 310–352.

Boda, Iosig. 1999. *Cinci ani la Cotroceni*. Bucharest: Ev Românesc.

Bodea, Gabriela, and Emilia Herman. 2014. "A World of Poverty?" *Procedia Economics and Finance* 15: 643–653.

Bohle, Dorothee. 2006. "Neoliberal Hegemony, Transnational Capital and the Terms of the EU's Eastward Expansion." *Capital and Class* 30.1: 57–86.

Bohle, Dorothee, and Béla Greskovits. 2007. "Neoliberalism, Embedded Neoliberalism and Neocorporatism: Towards Transnational Capitalism in Central-Eastern Europe." *West European Politics* 30.3: 443–466.

——. 2012. *Capitalist Diversity on Europe's Periphery*. Ithaca, NY: Cornell University Press.

Bohle, Dorothee, and Gisela Neunhöffer. 2009. "Why Is There No Third Way." In Dariusz Aleksandrowicz, Stefani Sonntag, and Wielgohs Jan, eds., *The Polish Solidarity Movement in Retrospect. A Story of Failure or Success*. Berlin: Berliner Debatte, 66–87.

Boix, Carles. 1998. *Political Parties, Growth and Equality: Conservative and Social Democratic Economic Strategies in the World Economy*. New York: Cambridge University Press.

Boughton, James M. 2004. *The IMF and the Force of History: Ten Events and Ten Ideas That Have Shaped the Institution*. Washington, DC: International Monetary Fund.

Bourdieu, Pierre. 1998. "L'essence du Néolibéralisme." *Le Monde Diplomatique*: 3–7.

Boyer, Miguel. 1983. "Opiniones." *Papeles de Economía Española* 16: 366–368.

——. 1984. "Características de los Presupuestos Generales del Estado para 1984." *Hacienda Pública Española* 85: 145–151.

Brake, Benjamin, and Peter J. Katzenstein. 2013. "Lost in Translation? Nonstate Actors and the Transnational Movement of Procedural Law." *International Organization* 67.04: 725–757.

Brenner, Neil, Jamie Peck, and Nik Theodore. 2010a. "Variegated Neoliberalization: Geographies, Modalities, Pathways." *Global Networks* 10.2: 182–222.

——. 2010b. "Postneoliberalism and Its Malcontents." *Antipode* 41.s1: 94–116.

Brenner, Neil, and Nik Theodore. 2002. "Cities and the Geographies of 'Actually Existing Neoliberalism.'" *Antipode* 34: 349–379.

Brettschneider, Antonio. 2008. "On the Way to Social Investment? The Normative Recalibration of the German Welfare State." *German Policy Studies* 4.2: 19–66.

Broome, André. 2010. "The Joint Vienna Institute." *New Political Economy* 15.4: 609–624.

Broome, André, and Leonard Seabrooke. 2015. "Shaping Policy Curves: Cognitive Authority in Transnational Capacity Building." *Public Administration* 93.4: 956–972.

Brondolo, John. 2009. "Collecting Taxes during and Economic Crisis." IMF Staff Position Note 09/23.

Buesa, Mikel, and José Molero. 1998. *Economía Industrial de España: Organización, Tecnología e Internacionalización*. Madrid: Civitas.

Buiter, Willem H. 1980. "The Macroeconomics of Dr. Pangloss: A Critical Survey of the New Classical Macroeconomics." *Economic Journal*, 90.357: 34–50.

Cahill, Damien. 2013. "Ideas-Centred Explanations of the Rise of Neoliberalism: A Critique." *Australian Journal of Political Science* 48.1: 71–84.

Calvo, Manuel Jesús Lagares. 2004. "La Modernización del Sistema Fiscal Español durante la Democracia." In E. Fuentes Quintana, dir., *Economía y Economistas Españoles*. Barcelona: Galaxia Gutenberg and Círculo de Lectores.

Cammack, Paul. 2004. "What the World Bank Means by Poverty Reduction, and Why It Matters." *New Political Economy* 9.2: 189–211.

Campbell, John L. 2009. "What Do Sociologists Bring to International Political Economy?" In Mark Blyth, ed., *Routledge Handbook of International Political Economy (IPE): IPE as a Global Conversation*. New York: Routledge, 266–279.

Campbell, John L., and Ove Kaj Pedersen, eds. 1996. *Legacies of Change: Transformations of Postcommunist European Economies*. New York: Aldine de Gruyter.

———. 2001a. *The Rise of Neoliberalism and Institutional Analysis*. Princeton, NJ: Princeton University Press.

———. 2001b. "The Second Movement in Institutional Analysis." In John L. Campbell and Ove Kaj Pedersen, eds., *The Rise of Neoliberalism and Institutional Analysis*. Princeton, NJ: Princeton University Press, 249–274.

———. 2014. *The National Origins of Policy Ideas: Knowledge Regimes in the United States, France, Germany, and Denmark*. Princeton, NJ: Princeton University Press.

Canto, Victor A., Douglas H. Joines, and Arthur B. Laffer. 2014. *Foundations of Supply-Side Economics: Theory and Evidence*. Academic Press.

Caporaso, James A., and Sidney Tarrow. 2009. "Polanyi in Brussels: Supranational Institutions and the Transnational Embedding of Markets." *International Organization* 63.4: 593–620.

Caraway, Teri L., Stephanie J. Rickard, and Mark S. Anner. 2012. "International Negotiations and Domestic Politics: The Case of IMF Labor Market Conditionality." *International Organization* 66.1: 27.

Cavalieri, Elena. 2014. "España y el FMI: La integración de la economía española en el Sistema Monetario Internacional, 1943–1959." *Estudios de Historia Económica* 65. Madrid: Banco de Espana.

Carothers, Thomas. 1996. *Assessing Democracy Assistance: The Case of Romania*. Washington, DC: Carnegie Endowment for International Peace.

Carstensen, Martin B. 2011a. "Ideas Are Not as Stable as Political Scientists Want Them to Be: A Theory of Incremental Ideational Change." *Political Studies* 59.3: 596–615.

———. 2011b. "Paradigm Man vs. the Bricoleur: Bricolage as an Alternative Vision of Agency in Ideational Change." *European Political Science Review* 3.1: 147–167.

Cencini, Alvaro, and Sergio Rossi. 2015. "From Monetarism to the New Classical Synthesis." In *Economic and Financial Crises*. Basingstoke: Palgrave Macmillan, 83–105.

Centeno, Miguel A., and Joseph N. Cohen. 2012. "The Arc of Neoliberalism." *Annual Review of Sociology* 38.1: 317–340.

Centrul Român de Politici Europene (CRPE). 2010. "Să nu ne fie frică de Fondul Monetar European." Policy Memo 9.

Cerna, Silviu. 2011. "Gândirea Economică Românească în Perioada Postcomunistă." *Academica* 4–5: 44–56.

Cernat, Lucian. 2006. *Europeanization, Varieties of Capitalism and Economic Performance in Central and Eastern Europe*. Basingstoke: Palgrave Macmillan.

Chari, Raj, and Paul M. Heywood. 2009. "Analysing the Policy Process in Democratic Spain." *West European Politics* 32.1: 26–54.

Chuliá, Elisa. 2006. "Spain: Between Majority Rule and Incrementalism." In Ellen M. Immergut, Karen M. Anderson, and Isabelle Schulze, eds., *Oxford Handbook of West European Pension Policies*. Oxford: Oxford University Press, 499–554.

Chwieroth, Jeffrey M. 2007. "Neoliberal Economists and Capital Account Liberalization in Emerging Markets." *International Organization* 61.2: 443–463.

———. 2010. *Shrinking the State: Neoliberal Economists and Social Spending in Latin America*. Ithaca, NY: Cornell University Press.

———. 2014. "Controlling Capital: The International Monetary Fund and Transformative Incremental Change from within International Organisations." *New Political Economy* 19.3: 445–469.

Cogan, John F., et al. 2010. "New Keynesian versus Old Keynesian Government Spending Multipliers." *Journal of Economic Dynamics and Control* 34.3: 281–295.

Consiliul Fiscal. 2010. "Opinia Consiliului Fiscal Privind Strategia Fiscal Bugetară pe Perioada 2011–2013." September 23.

Consiliul Investitorilor Străini (CIS). 2005. *Cartea Alba*.

———. 2009. *Cartea Alba*.

———. 2010. *Cartea Alba*.

———. 2011. *Cartea Alba*.

Constantinescu, N. N. 1991. *Acumularea primitivă a Capitalului în România*. Bucharest: Editura Academiei Române.

Copeland, Paul. 2014. *EU Enlargement, the Clash of Capitalisms and the European Social Dimension*. Manchester: Manchester University Press.

Council of Europe. 2014. European Social Charter: European Committee of Social Rights Conclusions XX-3 Spain.

Crespy, Amandine. 2010. "When 'Bolkestein' Is Trapped by the French Anti-liberal Discourse: A Discursive-Institutionalist Account of Preference Formation in the Realm of European Union Multi-level Politics." *Journal of European Public Policy* 17.8: 1253–1270.

Crespy, Amandine, and Georg Menz. 2015. "Commission Entrepreneurship and the Debasing of Social Europe before and after the Eurocrisis." *Journal of Common Market Studies* 53.4: 753–768.

Crespy, Amandine, and Vivien Schmidt. 2014. "The Clash of Titans: France, Germany and the Discursive Double Game of EMU Reform." *Journal of European Public Policy* 21.8: 1085–1101.

Croitoru, Lucian. 1993. *Macrostabilizare și Tranziție*. Bucharest: Editura Expert.

———. 1994. "Politica de Stabilizare Și Impunerea Restricțiilor Financiare Tari Într-O Economie În Tranziție."

———. 2012. *In apararea pietelor*. Bucharest: Curtea Veche.

Croitoru, Lucian, C. Dolțu, and Cornel Târhoacă. 2001. "Gap-ul Produsului Intern Brut și Inflația: Cazul României." *Oeconomica, IRLI* 2: 5–10.

Croitoru, Lucian, and Mark Edwin Schaffer. 2002. "Measurement and Assessment of Soft Budget Constraints in Romania." National Bank of Romania Occasional Paper 2.

Croitoru, Lucian, and Cornel Tarhoaca. 1999. "Fiscal Policy in Romania." CEROPE, Bucharest.

Crotty, James R. 1980. "Post-Keynesian Economic Theory: An Overview and Evaluation." *American Economic Review* 70.2: 20–25.

Crouch, Colin. 2011. *The Strange Non-death of Neo-Liberalism*. Cambridge: Polity.

Culpepper, Pepper D. 2010. *Quiet Politics and Business Power: Corporate Control in Europe and Japan*. New York: Cambridge University Press.

———. 2014. "The Political Economy of Unmediated Democracy: Italian Austerity under Mario Monti." *West European Politics* 37.6: 1264–1281.

Czarniawska, Barbara, and Guje Sevón, eds. 1996. *Translating Organizational Change*. New York: Walter de Gruyter.

Dăianu, Daniel. 1994a. *Inter-enterprise Arrears in a Post-command Economy: Thoughts from a Romanian Perspective*. EPub. International Monetary Fund.

———. 1994b. *The Changing Mix of Disequilibria during Transition: A Romanian Background*. EPub. International Monetary Fund.

———. 1996. "Stabilization and Exchange Rate Policy in Romania." *Economics of Transition* 4.1: 229–248.

———. 1998. *Transformation of Economy as a Real Process: An Insider's Perspective*. Brookfield, VT: Ashgate.

———. 2000. "Structure, Strain and Macroeconomic Dynamic in Romania." *Economic Transition in Romania, CEROPE and the World Bank*. Bucharest: Arta Grafica, 5–35.

Dăianu, Daniel, and Lucian-Liviu Albu. 1996. "Strain and the Inflation-Unemployment Relationship: A Conceptual and Empirical Investigation." University of Leicester Research Memorandum 96/15: 1–40.

Dăianu, Daniel, and Radu Vrânceanu. 2002. "Opening the Capital Account of Transition Economies: How Much and How Fast." William Davidson Working Paper No. 511.

Davidson, Paul. 1992. "Would Keynes Be a New Keynesian?" *Eastern Economic Journal* 8.4: 449–463.

Deacon, Bob. 2000. "Eastern European Welfare States: The Impact of the Politics of Globalization." *Journal of European Social Policy* 10.2: 146–161.

Deacon, Bob, and Michelle Hulse. "The Making of Post-Communist Social Policy: The Role of International Agencies." *Journal of Social Policy* 26.01: 43–62.

De Castro, Francisco. 2007. "The Macroeconomic Effects of Fiscal Policy in Spain." *Applied Economics* 38.8: 912–924.

De Castro, Francisco, and Pablo Hernández de Cos. 2008. "The Economic Effects of Fiscal Policy: The Case of Spain." *Journal of Macroeconomics* 30.3: 1005–1028.

Decressin, Jörg, and Douglas Laxton. 2009. "Gauging Risks for Deflation." IMF Staff Position Note 09/01.

De Grauwe, Paul. 2011. "Managing a Fragile Eurozone." VoxEU.org. May 10.

de Guindos Jurado, Luis. 2005. "La Política Económica Española en la Zona Euro: La Importancia de las Reformas Económicas." *Información Comercial Española, ICE: Revista de Economía* 826: 115–123.

De La Fuente, Angel, and Rafael Doménech. 2009. *Convergencia Real y Envejecimiento: Retos y Propuestas*. Universitat Autònoma de Barcelona, Departament d'Economia i d'Història Econòmica, Unitat Fonaments de l'Anàlisi Econòmica.

de la Porte, Caroline, and Elke Heins. 2014. "Game Change in EU Social Policy: Towards More European Integration." *The Eurozone Crisis and the Transformation of EU Governance*: 157–171.

DeLong, J. Bradford. 2000. "The Triumph of Monetarism?" *Journal of Economic Perspectives* 14.1: 83–94.

Demekas, Dimitri G., and Mohsin S. Khan. 1991. *The Romanian Economic Reform Program*. Washington, DC: International Monetary Fund.

Deroose, Servaas, Martin Larch, and Andrea Schaechter. *Constricted, Lame and Pro-Cyclical? Fiscal Policy in the Euro Area Revisited*. No. 353. Directorate General Economic and Monetary Affairs (DG ECFIN), European Commission, 2008.

Dezalay, Yves, and Bryant G. Garth. 2002. *The Internationalization of Palace Wars: Lawyers, Economists, and the Contest to Transform Latin American States*. Chicago: University of Chicago Press.

Dinu, Marin, Cristian Socol, and Aura Niculescu. 2005. *Economia României: O Viziune Asupra Tranziției Postcomuniste*. Bucharest: Editura Economica.

Djelic, Marie-Laure. 1998. *Exporting the American Model: The Post-war Transformation of European Business*. New York: Oxford University Press.

———. 2008. "Sociological Studies of Diffusion: Is History Relevant?" *Socio-economic Review* 6.3: 538–557.

Dobbin, Frank, Beth Simmons, and Geoffrey Garrett. 2007. "The Global Diffusion of Public Policies: Social Construction, Coercion, Competition, or Learning?" *Annual Review of Sociology* 33: 449–472.

Dolado, Juan. 1983. "Contrastación de Hipótesis no Anidadas en el caso de la Demanda de Dinero en España." *Cuadernos Económicos de ICE* 24: 119–139.

———. 1984. "Neutralidad Monetaria y Expectativas Racionales: Alguna Evidencia en el Caso de España." *Revista Española de Economía* 1.1: 77–98.

———. 1986. "La Estabilidad de la Demanda de Dinero en España." *Boletín Económico*, issue 9 40–49. Banco de España.

Dolado, Juan J., and J. David López-Salido. 1996. "Hysteresis and Economic Fluctuations (Spain, 1970–94)." CEPR Discussion Papers No. 1334: 3–43.

Dolado, Juan J., and Juan F. Jimeno. 1997. "The Causes of Spanish Unemployment: A Structural VAR Approach." *European Economic Review* 41.7: 1281–1307.

Dolado, Juan José, Miguel Sebastián, and Javier Vallés. 1993. "Cyclical Patterns of the Spanish Economy." Banco de España, Servicio de Estudios.

Domenech, Rafael, Ángel Estrada, and Luis González-Calbet. 2007. "Potential Growth and Business Cycle in the Spanish Economy: Implications for Fiscal Policy." International Economics Institute, University of Valencia Working Paper No. 0705.

Domnișoru, Ciprian. 2012. "Decent Work Policy Options for the Romanian Economy." Working Paper No. 105, Policy Integration Department, International Labour Office.

———. 2014. "The Largest Drop in Income Inequality in the European Union during the Great Recession: Romania's Puzzling Case." Conditions of Work and Employment Series No. 51, International Labour Office.

Dornbusch, Rudiger. 1990a. "The New Classical Macroeconomics and Stabilization Policy." *American Economic Review* 80.2: 143–147.

———. 1990b. "From Stabilization to Growth." Working Paper No. 3302, National Bureau of Economic Research.

Dornescu, Valeriu, and Teodora Manea. 2013. "The Migration of the Romanian Physicians: Sociodemographic and Economical Dimensions." *Revista de Economie Socială* 3.1: 139–156.

Drăgulin, Ion, and Eugen Rădulescu. 2000. "Monetary Policy in Romania: Challenges and Options." *Economic Transition in Romania, CEROPE and the World Bank.* Bucharest: Arta Grafica, 457–476.

Dubin, Ken, and Jonathan Hopkin. 2013. "Flexibility for Some, Security for Others: The Politics of Welfare and Employment in Spain." In Daniel Clegg and Paolo Graziano, eds., *The Politics of Flexicurity in Europe: Labor Market Reform in Hostile Climes and Tough Times.* Basingstoke: Palgrave Macmillan. http://personal.lse.ac.uk/HOPKIN/DubinHopkinFinal2013.pdf.

———. 2014. "A Crucial Case for Flexicurity: The Politics of Welfare and Employment in Spain." In Daniel Clegg and Paolo Graziano, eds., *The Politics of Flexicurity in Europe: Labour Market Reform in Hostile Climes and Tough Times.* Basingstoke: Palgrave Macmillan. http://personal.lse.ac.uk/HOPKIN/DubinHopkinFinal2013.pdf.

Duménil, Gérard, and Dominique Lévy. 2011. *The Crisis of Neoliberalism.* Cambridge, MA: Harvard University Press.

Dumitrescu, F. 1993. *Caĭle stabilitaţii monetare.* Bucharest: Editura Academiei Române.

Duncan, Fraser. 2006. "A Decade of Christian Democratic Decline: The Dilemmas of the CDU, ÖVP and CDA in the 1990s." *Government and Opposition* 41.4: 469–490.

Earle, John S. 2007. "Developing Graduate Economics Education from Scratch." In François Bourguignon, Yehuda Elkana, and Boris Pleskovic, eds., *Capacity Building in Economics Education and Research.* Washington, DC: The World Bank, 277–299.

Eggertsson, Gauti, Andrea Ferrero, and Andrea Raffo. 2014. "Can Structural Reforms Help Europe?." *Journal of Monetary Economics* 61: 2–22.

Elkins, Zachary, and Beth Simmons. 2005. "On Waves, Clusters, and Diffusion: A Conceptual Framework." *Annals of the American Academy of Political and Social Science* 598.1: 33–51.

Encarnación, Omar G. 1997. "Social Concentration in Democratic and Market Transitions: Comparative Lessons from Spain." *Comparative Political Studies* 30.4: 387–419.

———. 2009. "Spain's New Left Turn: Society Driven or Party Instigated?" *South European Society and Politics* 14.4: 399–415.

———. 2015. "Bullish on Spain: Why the Country Is Faring Better Than Greece." *Foreign Affairs,* July 14.

Epstein, Rachel A. 2008a. "The Social Context in Conditionality: Internationalizing Finance in Post-communist Europe." *Journal of European Public Policy* 15.6: 880–898.

———. 2008b. *In Pursuit of Liberalism: International Institutions in Postcommunist Europe.* Baltimore: Johns Hopkins University Press.

———. 2014. "When Do Foreign Banks 'Cut and Run'? Evidence from West European Bailouts and East European Markets." *Review of International Political Economy* 21.4: 847–877.

Estapé, Fabian R. 1999. "Joan Sardá Dexeus y sus Aportaciones a los Estudios Económicos y a la Economía Español." In E. Fuentes Quintana, dir., *Economía y Economistas Españoles.* Barcelona: Galaxia Gutenberg and Círculo de Lectores. Vol. 7: 367–380.

Estapé, Fabián. 2000. *Sin acuse de recibo: Las estraordinarias memorias de un gran economista.* Vol. 40. Plaza & Janés Editores.

Estrada García, Angel, Álex Pons, and Javier Vallés. 2006. "La Productividad de la Economía Española: Una Perspectiva Internacional." *Información Comercial Española, ICE: Revista de economía* 829: 7–25.

Estrin, Saul, and Milica Uvalic. 2014. "FDI into Transition Economies." *Economics of Transition* 22.2: 281–312.

Etchemendy, Sebastián. 2004a. "Repression, Exclusion, and Inclusion: Government-Union Relations and Patterns of Labor Reform in Liberalizing Economies." *Comparative Politics* 36.3: 273–290.

———. 2004b. "Revamping the Weak, Protecting the Strong, and Managing Privatization Governing Globalization in the Spanish Takeoff." *Comparative Political Studies* 37.6: 623–651.

———. 2011. *Models of Economic Liberalization: Business, Workers, and Compensation in Latin America, Spain, and Portugal.* New York: Cambridge University Press, 283–306.

Etchemendy, Sebastián, Candelaria Garay, Steven Levitsky, and Kenneth Roberts. 2011. "Argentina: Left Populism in Comparative Perspective, 2003–2009." In Steven Levitsky and Kenneth M. Roberts, eds., *The Resurgence of the Latin American Left.* Baltimore: John Hopkins University Press.

Eucken, Walter, and G. Schmölders. 1948. "Obituary: Heinrick von Stackelberg." *Economic Journal* 58.229: 132–134.

European Central Bank. 2009. "Monthly Bulletin," ECB Publications, January.

European Commission. 2013. "Cohesion Policy: Strategic Report, 2013." April 18. COM 210.

———. 2015. Spain: European Semester, COM 259 final, Brussels.

Evans, Anthony J. 2006. "The Spread of Economic Theology: The Flat Tax in Romania." *Romanian Economics and Business Review* 1.1: 41–53.

Evans, Anthony J., and Paul Dragos Aligică. 2008. "The Spread of the Flat Tax in Eastern Europe: A Comparative Study." *Eastern European Economics* 46.3: 49–67.

Farrell, Mary. 2001. *Spain in the EU: The Road to Economic Convergence.* Basingstoke: Palgrave.

Fernández, María José Aracil. 2001. "El Papel del Profesor Fuentes Quintana en el Avance de los Estudios de Hacienda Pública en España." *Documentos—Instituto de Estudios Fiscales* 17: 1–58.

Fernandez-Villaverde, Jesus, Luis Garicano, and Tano Santos. 2013. "Political Credit Cycles: The Case of the Euro Zone." Working Paper No. w18899, National Bureau of Economic Research.

Ferrera, Maurizio, ed. 2005. *Welfare State Reform in Southern Europe: Fighting Poverty and Social Exclusion in Greece, Italy, Spain and Portugal.* New York: Routledge.

Field, Bonnie N. 2009. "Minority Government and Legislative Politics in a Multilevel State: Spain under Zapatero." *South European Society and Politics* 14.4: 417–434.

———. 2011. "Interparty Consensus and Intraparty Discipline in Spain's Transition to Democracy." In Gregorio Alonso and Diego Muro, eds., *The Politics and Memory of Democratic Transition: The Spanish Model.* New York: Routledge, 71–91.

———. 2013. *Spain's Second Transition? The Socialist Government of José Luis Rodríguez Zapatero.* New York: Routledge.

Fina, Luis, and Luis Toharia. 1987. *Las Causas del Paro en España: Un Punto de Vista Estructural.* Madrid: Fundación IESA.

Fischer, Stanley, and Ratna Sahay. 2000. "The Transition Economies after Ten Years." Working Paper No. 7664, National Bureau of Economic Research.

Fishman, Robert. 1989. *Labor and the Return of Democracy to Spain.* Notre Dame, IN: Helen Kellogg Institute for International Studies.

———. 1990. *Working Class Organization and the Return to Democracy in Spain.* Ithaca, NY: Cornell University Press.

———. 2010. "Rethinking the Iberian Transformations: How Democratization Scenarios Shaped Labor Market Outcomes." *Studies in Comparative International Development* 45.3: 281–310.

———. 2012. "Anomalies of Spain's Economy and Economic Policy-Making." *Contributions to Political Economy* 31.1: 67–76.

Flew, Terry. 2012. "Michel Foucault's *The Birth of Biopolitics* and Contemporary Neo-liberalism Debates." *Thesis Eleven* 108.1: 44–65.

Foreign Investors Council. N.d. "The Foreign Investors Council and the Labour Code." Press release.

Fourcade, Marion. 2006. "The Construction of a Global Profession: The Transnationalization of Economics." *American Journal of Sociology* 112.1: 145–194.

———. 2009. *Economists and Societies: Discipline and Profession in the United States, Britain, and France, 1890s to 1990s.* Princeton, NJ: Princeton University Press.

Fourcade, Marion, and Joachim J. Savelsberg. 2006. "Introduction: Global Processes, National Institutions, Local Bricolage: Shaping Law in an Era of Globalization." *Law and Social Inquiry* 31.3: 513–519.

Fourcade, Marion, Philippe Steiner, Wolfgang Streeck, and Cornelia Woll. 2013. "Moral Categories in the Financial Crisis." *Socio-economic Review* 11.3: 601–627.

Fradejas, Fernando Hernandez. 2015. "Liberal Economics in Spain." *Econ Journal Watch* 12.2: 221–232.

Freeman, Richard. 2009. "What Is 'Translation'?" *Evidence and Policy* 5.4: 429–447.

Friedman, Milton, and Richard Musgrave. 1972. *Problemas económicos actuales. Política monetaria versus política fiscal. Cuestiones españolas.* II Semana económica internacional organizada por el semanario Mundo. Barcelona: Dopesa, 141–159.

Fuentes Quintana, Enrique. 2002. In E. Fuentes Quintana, dir., "La Consolidación Académica de la Economía Española." *Economía y economistas españoles.* Barcelona: Galaxia Gutenberg and Círculo de Lectores. Vol. 7: 7–145.

Fuertes, Juan Velarde. 2001. "Una nota sobre los setenta años del Servicio de Estudios del Banco de España." *Revista de Historia Económica/Journal of Iberian and Latin American Economic History (Second Series)* 19.01: 173–185.

Fuest, Clemens, Andreas Peichl, and Thilo Schaefer. 2008. "Is a Flat Tax Reform Feasible in a Grown-Up Democracy of Western Europe? A Simulation Study for Germany." *International Tax and Public Finance* 15.5: 620–636.

Gabor, Daniela. 2010a. *Central Banking and Financialization. A Romanian Account of How Eastern Europe Became Subprime.* Basingstoke: Palgrave Macmillan.

———. 2010b. "The International Monetary Fund and Its New Economics." *Development and Change* 41.5: 805–830.

———. 2012. "The Road to Financialization in Central and Eastern Europe: The Early Policies and Politics of Stabilizing Transition." *Review of Political Economy* 24.2: 227–249.

———. 2013. "The Financialisation of the Romanian Economy: From Central Bank-Led to Dependent Financialization." Study No. 05, Financialisation, Economy, Society and Sustainable Development (FESSUD) Project.

———. 2015. "The IMF's Rethink of Global Banks: Critical in Theory, Orthodox in Practice." *Governance* 28.2: 199–218.

Gabor, Daniela, and Cornel Ban. 2013. "Fiscal Policy in Financialized Times: Investor Loyalty, Financialization and the Varieties of Capitalism." *Financialization and the Varieties of Capitalism*, January 16.

———. 2015. "Banking on Bonds: The New Links Between States and Markets." *Journal of Common Market Studies* (first online).

Galí, Jordi, J. David López-Salido, and Javier Vallés. 2005. "Understanding the Effects of Government Spending on Consumption." Working Paper No. 11578, National Bureau of Economic Research.

———. 2007. "Understanding the Effects of Government Spending on Consumption." *Journal of the European Economic Association* 5.1: 227–270.

Gallagher, Kevin P. 2015. "Contesting the Governance of Capital Flows at the IMF." *Governance* 28.2: 185–198.

Gallagher, Tom. 2005. *Theft of a Nation: Romania since Communism.* London: C. Hurst.

García-Legaz, Jaime. 2005. "La Reforma del Pacto de Estabilidad y Crecimiento: Un Error Histórica." *Cuadernos de Pensamiento Político*, March issue, 79–96.

Genschel, P. 2002. "Globalization, Tax Competition, and the Welfare State." *Politics & Society*, 30.2: 245–275.

Genschel, Philipp, Achim Kemmerling, and Eric Seils. 2011. "Accelerating Downhill: How the EU Shapes Corporate Tax Competition in the Single Market." *Journal of Common Market Studies* 49.3: 585–606.

Georgescu, Florin. 2002. *L'état Économique et Social de la Roumanie en 2000*. Bucharest: Expert.

Georgescu, Florin. 2015. "Capitalul în România anului 2015." *Economistul*, issue 49–50, December 14, 2015.

Germann, Julian. 2014. "German 'Grand Strategy' and the Rise of Neoliberalism." *International Studies Quarterly* 58.4: 706–716.

Gillespie, Richard. 1989. *The Spanish Socialist Party: A History of Factionalism*. Oxford: Clarendon Press.

Glyn, Andrew. 2001. *Social Democracy in Neoliberal Times: The Left and Economic Policy since 1980*. New York: Oxford University Press.

Goddard, Stacie E., and Daniel H. Nexon. 2005. "Paradigm Lost? Reassessing Theory of International Politics." *European Journal of International Relations* 11.1: 9–61.

González-Fernández, M., and González-Velasco, C. 2014. "Shadow Economy, Corruption and Public Debt in Spain." *Journal of Policy Modeling* 36.6: 1101–1117.

Grabel, Ilene. 2015. "The Rebranding of Capital Controls in an Era of Productive Incoherence." *Review of International Political Economy* 22.1: 7–43.

Grecu, Andrei. 2004. *Flat Tax: The British Case*. London: Adam Smith Institute.

Guga, Stefana, and Camelia Constantin. 2015. "Analiza impactului noii legislatii a dialogului social adoptate in 2011." Bucharest: Swiss-Romanian Cooperation Programme.

Guillén, Ana M., and Manos Matsaganis. 2000. "Testing the 'Social Dumping' Hypothesis in Southern Europe: Welfare Policies in Greece and Spain during the Last 20 Years." *Journal of European Social Policy* 10.2: 120–145.

Gunther, Richard. 1980. *Public Policy in a No-Party State: Spanish Planning and Budgeting in the Twilight of the Franquist Era*. Berkeley: University of California Press.

———. 1996. "The Impact of Regime Change on Public Policy: The Case of Spain." *Journal of Public Policy* 16.2: 157–201.

Gunther, Richard, José R. Montero, and Juan Botella. 2004. *Democracy in Modern Spain*. New Haven, CT: Yale University Press.

Gutiérrez, José Luis. 1991. *Miguel Boyer: El Hombre Que Sabía Demasiado*. Madrid: Ediciones Temas de Hoy.

Gutiérrez, Rodolfo, and Ana M. Guillén. 2000. "Protecting the Long-Term Unemployed." *European Societies* 2.2: 195–216.

Hagemann, Robert P. 2010. "Improving Fiscal Performance through Fiscal Councils." OECD Economics Department Working Paper No. 829.

Hall, Peter A. 1989. "The Political Power of Economic Ideas: Keynesianism across Nations." Princeton University Press.

Hall, Peter A. 1993. "Policy Paradigms, Social Learning, and the State: The Case of Economic Policymaking in Britain." *Comparative Politics* 25.3: 275–296.

Hall, Peter A., and Michèle Lamont. 2013. *Social Resilience in the Neoliberal Era*. New York: Cambridge University Press.

Hall, Peter A., and David Soskice. 2001. "An Introduction to Varieties of Capitalism." In Peter A. Hall and David Soskice, eds., *Varieties of Capitalism: The Institutional Foundations of Comparative Advantage*. New York: Oxford University Press, 43–76.

Hamann, Kerstin. 1998. "Spanish Unions: Institutional Legacy and Responsiveness to Economic and Industrial Change." *Industrial and Labor Relations Review* 51.3: 424–444.

———. 2011. *The Politics of Industrial Relations: Labor Unions in Spain*. Vol. 24. New York: Routledge.

Hancké, Bob. 2012. "Multinational Companies and the Production of Collective Goods in Central and Eastern Europe." In Heidenreich, Martin, ed. *Innovation and Institutional Embeddedness of Multinational Companies*. Northampton: Edward Elgar Publishing, 295–311.

Hardie, Iain, and David Howarth. 2013. *Market-Based Banking and the International Financial Crisis*. New York: Oxford University Press.

Hardiman, Niamh, and Aidan Regan. 2013. "The Politics of Austerity in Ireland." *Intereconomics* 48.1: 4–32.

Harvey, David. 2005. *A Brief History of Neoliberalism*. New York: Oxford University Press.

Hay, Colin. 2010. "Chronicles of a Death Foretold: The Winter of Discontent and Construction of the Crisis of British Keynesianism." *Parliamentary Affairs* 63.3: 446–470.

Hein, Michael. 2015. "The Fight Against Government Corruption in Romania: Irreversible Results or Sisyphean Challenge?." *Europe-Asia Studies* 67.5: 747–776.

Hemment, Julie D. 2004. "The Riddle of the Third Sector: Civil Society, Western Aid and NGOs in Russia." *Anthropological Quarterly* 77.2: 215–241.

Henry, John F. 2010. "The Historic Roots of the Neoliberal Program." *Journal of Economic Issues* 44.2: 543–550.

Heywood, Paul. 1998. "Power Diffusion or Concentration? In Search of the Spanish Policy Process." *West European Politics* 21.4: 103–123.

Hicks, Alexander M. 1999. *Social Democracy and Welfare Capitalism: A Century of Income Security Politics*. Ithaca, NY: Cornell University Press.

Hilgers, Mathieu. 2013. "Embodying Neoliberalism: Thoughts and Responses to Critics." *Social Anthropology* 21.1: 75–89.

Hirschman, Albert O. 1989. "How the Keynesian Revolution Was Exported from the United States, and Other Comments." In Peter A. Hall, ed., *The Political Power of Economic Ideas: Keynesianism across Nations*. Princeton, NJ: Princeton University Press, 347–360.

Hirschman, Daniel, and Elizabeth Popp Berman. 2014. "Do Economists Make Policies? On the Political Effects of Economics." *Socio-Economic Review*, doi:10.1093/ser/mwu017.

Hix, Simon, Abdul Noury, and Gérard Roland. 2005. 'Power to the Parties: Cohesion and Competition in the European Parliament, 1979–2001." *British Journal of Political Science* 35.02: 209–234.

Holman, Otto. 1993. "Transnationalism in Spain." In Henk Overbeek, *Restructuring Hegemony in the Global Political Economy: The Rise of Transnational Neo-Liberalism in the 1980s*. New York: Routledge, 134–161.

———. 1996. *Integrating Southern Europe*. New York: Routledge.

Hopkin, Jonathan. 2001. "A 'Southern Model' of Electoral Mobilisation? Clientelism and Electoral Politics in Spain." *Western European Politics* 24.1: 115–136.

———. 2001. "Bringing the Members Back In? Democratizing Candidate Selection in Britain and Spain." *Party Politics* 7.3: 343–361.

Hopkin, Jonathan, and Mark Blyth. 2012. "What Can Okun Teach Polanyi? Efficiency, Regulation and Equality in the OECD." *Review of International Political Economy* 19.1: 1–33.

Huerta de Soto, Jesús. 2007. "Lucas Beltrán Flórez: Semblanza de un economista." In *Nuevos estudios de economía política*, 321–378. Madrid: Unión Editorial.

Iara, Anna, and Guntram Wolff. 2010. *Rules and Risk in the Euro Area: Does Rules-Based National Fiscal Governance Contain Sovereign Bond Spreads?*. No. 433. Directorate General Economic and Monetary Affairs (DG ECFIN), European Commission.

Iglesias, María Antonia, and Felipe González Márquez. 2003. *La Memoria Recuperada: Lo Que Nunca Han Contado Felipe González y los Dirigentes Socialistas de Sus Años de Gobierno*. Madrid: Aguilar.

Iliescu, Ion. 1994. *Revoluție Și Reformă*. Bucharest: Editura Enciclopedică.

Institutul de Studjii Populare (ISP). 2012. "Ordoliberalism si Economie Sociale de Piata." June 4, 2012.

International Monetary Fund (IMF). 1991. Romania: Article IV Consultations.

———. 1992. Romania: Article IV Consultations 1992.

———. 1994. Romania: Article IV Consultations 1994.

———. 1995. Romania: Article IV Consultations 1995.

———. 1996. Romania: Article IV Consultations 1996.

———. 2000. Romania: Article IV Consultations 2000.

———. 2009a. "Agreement with Banks Limits Crisis in Emerging Europe," IMF Survey Online, 28 October.

———. 2009b. Romania: Article IV Report 2009.

———. 2009c. "Romania: Request for Stand-By Arrangement - Staff Report;" June 10.

———. 2010. Romania: Article IV Report 2010.

———. 2014. Spain: Article IV Consultation. IMF country report 14/192, DC.

———. 2015a. "Statement at the Conclusion of an IMF Staff Visit to Romania." Press Release No. 15/474, October 22.

———. 2015b. "Romania: Article IV Consultation" IMF, March 27.

———. 2015c. "Spain: Article IV Consultation" IMF country report 15/232, March 27.

Ionete, Constantin. 1993. *Criza de Sistem a Economiei de Comandă Și Etapa Sa Explozivă.* Bucharest: Editura Expert.

Isărescu, Mugur. 1990. "Recent Developments in Romania." In *Proceedings: Economic Policy Symposium–Jackson Hole.* Federal Reserve Bank of Kansas City.

———. 1992. "Romania's Economic Reform." In Daniel N. Nelson, ed., *Romania after Tyranny.* Boulder, CO: Westview, 149–165.

———. 1996. "Inflația și Echilibrele Fundamentale ale Economiei Românești." Caiete de studii, issue 3/1996, 1–37.

———. 2003. "Spre o Nouă Strategie de Politică Monetară: Țintirea Directă a Inflației." Craiova: Editura Universitaria. http://www.ucv.ro/pdf/international/informatii_generale/doctor_ honoris/77.pdf.

———. 2005. "New and Future Member States: Romania's Role in the EU-27." *Romanian Journal of European Affairs* 5.3: 9–12.

———. 2006. *Reflecții Economice.* Bucharest: Expert.

Isărescu, Mugur, Lucian Croitoru, and Cornel Tarhoaca. 2003. "Politica Monetara, Inflatia si Sectorul Real." In Lucian Croitoru, Daniel Daianu, George de Menil, and Cornel Tarhoaca, eds., *Cadrul Macroeconomic si Ajustarea Structurala.* Bucharest: CEROPE, 47–71.

Iusmen, Ingi. 2015. "EU Leverage and Democratic Backsliding in Central and Eastern Europe: The Case of Romania." *JCMS: Journal of Common Market Studies* 53.3: 593–608.

Jabko, Nicolas. 2006. *Playing the Market: A Political Strategy for Uniting Europe, 1985–2005.* Ithaca, NY: Cornell University Press.

———. 2013. "The Political Appeal of Austerity." *Comparative European Politics* 11.6: 705–712.

Jacoby, Wade. 2014. "The EU Factor in Fat Times and in Lean: Did the EU Amplify the Boom and Soften the Bust?" In Rachel Epstein and Wade Jacoby, eds., "Eastern Enlargement Ten Years On: Transcending the East-West Divide?" *Journal of Common Market Studies* 52.1: 52–70.

Javorcik, Beata S. 2014. "Does FDI Bring Good Jobs to Host Countries?" *World Bank Research Observer* 30.1: 74–94.

Jessop, Bob. 2001. "Path Contingency in Postcommunist Transformations." *Comparative Politics* 33.3: 253–274.

———. 2013. "Putting Neoliberalism in Its Time and Place: A Response to the Debate." *Social Anthropology* 21.1: 65–74.

Johnson, Juliet, and Andrew Barnes. 2014. "Financial Nationalism and its International Enablers: The Hungarian Experience." *Review of International Political Economy*, ahead of print.

Jones, Erik. 2013. "The Collapse of the Brussels-Frankfurt Consensus and the Future of the Euro." In Vivien Schmidt and Mark Thatcher, eds., *Resilient Liberalism in Europe's Political Economy.* New York: Cambridge University Press, 145–170.

Keen, Michael, Yitae Kim, and Ricardo Varsano. 2006. "The 'Flat Tax(es)': Principles and Experiences." *International Tax and Public Finance* 15.6: 712–751.

Kentikelenis, Alexander, et al. 2014. "Greece's Health Crisis: From Austerity to Denialism." *The Lancet* 383.9918: 748–753.

Kideckel, David A. 2002. "The Unmaking of an East-Central European Working Class." In C. M. Haan, ed., *Postsocialism: Ideals, Ideologies and Practices in Eurasia*. New York: Routledge, 114–132.

———. 2008. *Getting by in Postsocialist Romania: Labor, the Body, and Working-Class Culture*. Bloomington: Indiana University Press.

Kinsella, Stephen. 2011. "Is Ireland Really the Role Model for Austerity?" *Cambridge Journal of Economics* 36.1: 223–235.

Kirițescu, Costin C. 1991. *Tezaur 1991*. Vol. 8. Institutul Național de Cercetări Economice, Academia Română.

———. 1992. *Călător Prin Secolul XX. Memoriile Unui Bancher Fără Bani*. Bucharest: Enciclopedica.

Kitschelt, Herbert, and Regina Smyth. 2002. "Programmatic Party Cohesion in Emerging Postcommunist Democracies Russia in Comparative Context." *Comparative Political Studies* 35.10: 1228–1256.

Kjær, Peter, and Ove Pedersen. 2001. "Translating Liberalization." In John L. Campbell and Ove K. Pedersen, eds., *The Rise of Neoliberalism and Institutional Analysis*. Princeton, NJ: Princeton University Press, 219–248.

Kogut, Bruce, and J. Muir MacPherson. 2008. "The Decision to Privatize: Economists and the Construction of Ideas and Policies." In Beth A. Simmons, Frank Dobbin, and Geoffrey Garrett, eds., *The Global Diffusion of Markets and Democracy*. New York: Cambridge University Press, 104–141.

Kornetis, Kostis. 2014. ""Is there a Future in this Past?" Analyzing 15M's Intricate Relation to the Transición." *Journal of Spanish Cultural Studies* 15.1–2: 83–98.

Kraft, Evan, and Milan Vodopoviec. 2003. "The New Kids on the Block: The Entry of Private Business Schools in Transition Economies." *Education Economics* 11.3: 239–257.

Kudrna, Zdenek, and Daniela Gabor. 2013. "The Return of Political Risk: Foreign-Owned Banks in Emerging Europe." *Europe-Asia Studies* 65.3: 548–566.

Kurz, Marcus J., and Sarah M. Brooks. 2008. "Embedding Neoliberal Reform in Latin America." *World Politics* 60.2: 231–280.

Lankowski, Carl F. 1982. *Germany and the European Communities: Anatomy of a Hegemonial Relation*. New York: Columbia University Press.

Latour, Bruno. 1987. *Science in Action: How to Follow Scientists and Engineers through Society*. Cambridge, MA: Harvard University Press.

LeBaron, Genevieve. 2010. "The Political Economy of the Household: Neoliberal Restructuring, Enclosures, and Daily Life." *Review of International Political Economy* 17.5: 889–912.

Lee, Chang Kil, and David Strang. 2006. "The International Diffusion of Public-Sector Downsizing: Network Emulation and Theory-Driven Learning." *International Organization* 60.4: 883–909.

Lierse, Hanna, and Laura Seelkopf. 2016. "Room to Manoeuvre? International Financial Markets and the National Tax State." *New Political Economy* 21.1: 145–165.

Lindvall, Johannes. 2004. "The Politics of Purpose: Swedish Macroeconomic Policy after the Golden Age." PhD diss., Statsvetenskapliga Institutionen, Göteborgs Universitet.

———. 2009. "The Real but Limited Influence of Expert Ideas." *World Politics* 61.4: 703–730.

Linnemann, Ludger, and Andreas Schabert. 2003. "Fiscal Policy in the New Neoclassical Synthesis." *Journal of Money, Credit and Banking*, 911–929.

Linz, Juan J., and Alfred Stepan. 1996. *Problems of Democratic Transition and Consolidation: Southern Europe, South America, and Post-communist Europe*. Baltimore: Johns Hopkins University Press.

Lipton, David, Jeffrey Sachs, Stanley Fischer, and Janos Kornai. 1990. "Creating a Market Economy in Eastern Europe: The Case of Poland." *Brookings Papers on Economic Activity*, issue 1, 75–147.

Lipton, David, Jeffrey Sachs, and Lawrence H. Summers. 1990. "Privatization in Eastern Europe: The Case of Poland." *Brookings Papers on Economic Activity*, issue 2, 293–341.

Lissen, R. S. N.d. "Juan Sarda y la Politica Monetaria del Plan de Estabilizacion." Unpublished manuscript.

Love, Joseph L. R. 1996. *Crafting the Third World: Theorizing Underdevelopment in Rumania and Brazil*. Stanford, CA: Stanford University Press.

———. 2004. "Structuralism and Dependency in Peripheral Europe: Latin American Ideas in Spain and Portugal." *Latin American Research Review* 39.2: 114–140.

Lucas, Robert E. 1990. "Supply-Side Economics: An Analytical Review." *Oxford Economic Papers* 42.2: 293–316.

Lukauskas, Arvid John. 1997. *Regulating Finance: The Political Economy of Spanish Financial Policy from Franco to Democracy*. Ann Arbor: University of Michigan Press.

Lütz, Susanne, and Matthias Kranke. 2010. "The European Rescue of the Washington Consensus? EU and IMF Lending to Central and Eastern European Countries." LEQS Paper No. 22/2010.

Mabbett, Deborah, and Waltraud Schelkle. 2014. "What Difference Does Euro Membership Make to Stabilization? The Political Economy of International Monetary Systems Revisited." *Review of International Political Economy*, ahead of print.

Macpherson, J. Muir. 2006. "Palace Wars and Privatization: Did Chicago Beat Cambridge in Influencing Economic Policies?" *European Management Review* 3.3: 190–198.

Maes, Ivo. 2008. "The Spread of Keynesian Economics: A Comparison of the Belgian and Italian Experiences (1945–1970)." *Journal of the History of Economic Thought* 30.4: 491–509.

Mahoney, James, and Kathleen Thelen. 2010. "A Theory of Gradual Institutional Change." In James Mahoney and Kathleen Thelen, eds., *Explaining Institutional Change: Ambiguity, Agency, and Power*. New York: Cambridge University Press, 1–37.

Mandelkern, Ronen, and Michael Shalev. 2010. "Power and the Ascendance of New Economic Policy Ideas: Lessons from the 1980s Crisis in Israel." *World Politics* 62.3: 459–495.

Manolescu, G. 1995. *Procese și Politici Macroeconomice de Tranziție*. Bucharest: Editura Economica.

Maravall, Jose Maria. 1991. "From Opposition to Government: The Politics and Policies of the PSOE." In *Socialist Parties in Europe*. Barcelona: Institute de Ciènces Politíques y Sociales.

———. 1993. "Politics and Policy: Economic Reforms in Southern Europe." In Luiz Carlos Bresser Pereira, José María Maravall, and Adam Przeworski, *Economic Reforms in New Democracies: A Social-Democratic Approach*. New York: Cambridge University Press, 77–131.

Marinescu, Cosmin. 2012. "Transaction Costs and Institutions' Efficiency: A Critical Approach." *American Journal of Economics and Sociology* 71.2: 254–276.

Markoff, John, and Verónica Montecinos. 1993. "The Ubiquitous Rise of Economists." *Journal of Public Policy* 13.1: 37–68.

Marks, Michael P. 1997. *The Formation of European Policy in Post-Franco Spain: The Role of Ideas, Interests, and Knowledge*. Brookfield, VT: Avebury.

Martin, Andrew, and George Ross. 2004. *Euros and Europeans: Monetary Integration and the European Model of Society*. New York: Cambridge University Press.

Martin, Cathie Jo, and Duane Swank. 2012. *The Political Construction of Business Interests: Coordination, Growth, and Equality*. New York: Cambridge University Press.

Mas-Colell, Andreu. 1983. "Teoría del Desempleo en Keynes y en la Actualidad." *Información Comercial Española* 593: 68.

Matthijs, Matthias. 2011. *Ideas and Economic Crises in Britain from Attlee to Blair (1945–2005)*. New York: Routledge.

Matthijs, Matthias, and Mark Blyth. 2015. *The Future of the Euro*. New York: Oxford University Press.

McCombie, John, and Maureen Pike. 2013. "No End to the Consensus in Macroeconomic Theory? A Methodological Inquiry." *American Journal of Economics and Sociology* 72.2: 497–528.

McNamara, Kathleen R. 1998. *The Currency of Ideas: Monetary Politics in the European Union*. New York: Cambridge University Press.

Medve-Bálint, Gergö. 2014. "The Role of the EU in Shaping FDI Flows to East Central Europe." *JCMS: Journal of Common Market Studies* 52.1: 35–51.

Meeus, Bruno. 2013. "Welfare Through Migrant Work: What If the Romanian 'Safety Valve'Closes?." *Southeast European and Black Sea Studies* 13.2: 175–194.

Mereuță, Cezar. 2012. "The Classes of Economic Concentration and the 80 Percent Factor." *Economics Books* 1.

Milanović, Branko. 1999. "Explaining the Increase in Inequality during Transition." *Economics of Transition* 7.2: 299–341.

Miley, Thomas Jeffrey. 2011. "Franquism as Authoritarianism: Juan Linz and His Critics." *Politics, Religion and Ideology* 12.1: 27–50.

Mirowski, Philip. 2013. *Never Let a Serious Crisis Go to Waste: How Neoliberalism Survived the Financial Meltdown.* New York: Verso Books.

Mitchell, Daniel. 2007a. "Iceland Joins the Flat Tax Club." *Romania* 16: 16–20.

Molina, Oscar, and Martin Rhodes. 2007. "The Political Economy of Adjustment in Mixed Market Economies: A Study of Spain and Italy." In Bob Hancké, Martin Rhodes, and Mark Thatcher, eds., *Beyond Varieties of Capitalism: Conflict, Contradictions and Complementarities in the European Economy.* New York: Oxford University Press, 223–252.

Montecinos, Verónica. 1997. "Economists in Political and Policy Elites in Latin America." *History of Political Economy* 28: 279–300.

Montecinos, Verónica, and John Markoff, eds. 2010. *Economists in the Americas.* Northampton, MA: Edward Elgar.

Montero, Alfred P. *Shifting States in Global Markets: Subnational Industrial Policy in Contemporary Brazil and Spain.* University Park: Pennsylvania State University Press.

Montero, José R., Francisco J. Llera, and Mariano Torcal. 1992. "Sistemas Electorales en España: Una Recapitulación." *Reís,* April issue, 7–56.

Montoro Romero, Cristóbal. 1995. "Reactivación Económica, Crisis Política y Ausencia de Reformas Estructurales." *Economistas* 13.64: 89–91.

———. 1997. "La Política Económica Española y la Unión Económica y Monetaria Europea." *Información Comercial Española* 767: 15–22.

———. 1998. "Un Nuevo Modelo de Crecimiento Económico." *Anuario El País:* 336.

———. 2011a. *Hacia una Nueva Política Económica Española: Diagnóstico, Desafíos, Estrategias.* Madrid: Alianza Editorial.

———. 2011b. "La Crisis del Estado de Bienestar." In Fernando Jáuregui and Manuel Ángel Menéndez, eds., *La España que necesitamos, del 20-N a 2020.* Córdoba: Editorial Almuzara, 301–304.

Montoro Romero, Cristóbal, and Álvaro Nadal. 2009. "La Crisis del Paro, de las Empresas y de las Finanzas Públicas." *Economistas* 119: 34–37.

———. 2011. "El Ajuste Incompleto." *Economistas* 126: 16–19.

Moreno, Luis. 2013. "Spain's Catch up with the EU Core: The Implausible Quest of a 'Flying Pig'?." *South European Society and Politics* 18.2: 217–236.

Moschella, Manuela. 2014. "The Institutional Roots of Incremental Ideational Change: The IMF and Capital Controls after the Global Financial Crisis." *British Journal of Politics and International Relations* 17.3: 442–460.

Mosley, Layna. 2003. *Global Capital and National Governments.* New York: Cambridge University Press.

Moya, Angel R. Zapata, Maria Carmen Navarro Solano, and Olga Soto Peña. 2013. "The Politics of Poverty in Spain." *Social Alternatives* 32.1: 36.

Mulas-Granados, Carlos. 2003. "The Political and Economic Determinants of Fiscal Adjustments in Europe." *European Political Economy Review* 1.1: 33–64.

———. 2005. "Fiscal Adjustments and the Short-term Trade-off between Economic Growth and Equality." *Hacienda Pública Española/Revista de Economia Pública* 172.1: 61–92.

———. 2006. *Economics, Politics and Budgets: The Political Economy of Fiscal Consolidations in Europe.* Basingstoke: Palgrave Macmillan.

———. 2010. *El estado dinamizador: nuevos riesgos, nuevas políticas y la reforma del estado de bienestar en Europa.* Editorial Complutense.

Mulas-Granados, Carlos, and Ismael Sanz. 2008. "The Dispersion of Technology and Income in Europe: Evolution and Mutual Relationship across Regions." *Research Policy* 37.5: 836–848.

Mungiu-Pippidi, Alina. 2002. "Politica după comunism." *Bucharest: Humanitas.*

———. 2015. *The Quest for Good Governance: How Societies Develop Control of Corruption.* New York: Cambridge University Press.

Muns, Joaquín. 1986. *Historia de las Relaciones entre España y el Fondo Monetario Internacional 1958–1982: Veinticinco años de Economía Española.* Madrid: Alianza Editorial.

———. 1980. "La Economía Española en el Contexto Económico Internacional." *Papeles de Economía Española* 4: 94–101.

Murgescu, Costin. 1990. *Mersul Ideilor Economice la Români: Epoca Modernă.* Vol. 2. Bucharest: Editura Științifică și Enciclopedică.

Mylonas, Yiannis. 2012. "Media and the Economic Crisis of the EU: The 'Culturalization' of a Systemic Crisis and Bild-Zeitung's Framing of Greece." *Communication, Capitalism and Critique* 10.2: 646–671.

Nadal, Álvaro. 2006. "Por una Verdadera Reforma Fiscal: Menos Impuestos, Más Ahorro y Más Competitividad." May 3. Papeles FAES No. 29, Fundación Para el Analísis y los Estudios Sociales.

Năstase, Adrian. 2004. *De La Karl Marx La Coca Cola: Dialog Deschis Cu Alin Teodorescu.* Bucharest: Nemira.

———. 2007. *România Europeană.* Ovidiu Șincai.

Navarro, Vicenç, Julian Torres López, and Alberto Garzón Espinosa. 2011. "Hay Alternativas: Propuestas para Crear Empleo y Bienestar Social en Espana." ATTAC.

Neamțu, Mihail. 2009. *Elegii Conservatoare: Reflecții Est-Europene Despre Religie și Societate.* Cluj-Napoca: Editura Eikon.

Nedergaard, Peter, and Holly Snaith. 2015. "'As I Drifted on a River I Could Not Control': The Unintended Ordoliberal Consequences of the Eurozone Crisis." *JCMS: Journal of Common Market Studies* 53.4: 1094–1109.

Nelson, Edward. 2013. "Friedman's Monetary Economics in Practice." *Journal of International Money and Finance* 38: 59–83.

Nelson, Stephen C. 2014. "Playing Favorites: How Shared Beliefs Shape the IMF's Lending Decisions." *International Organization* 68.2: 297–328.

Nölke, Andreas, and Arjan Vliegenthart. 2009. "Enlarging the Varieties of Capitalism: The Emergence of Dependent Market Economies in East Central Europe." *World Politics* 61.4: 670–702.

O'Dwyer, Conor, and Branislav Kovalčík. 2007. "And the Last Shall Be First: Party System Institutionalization and Second-Generation Economic Reform in Postcommunist Europe." *Studies in Comparative International Development* 41.4: 3–26.

Orenstein, Mitchell A. 2008a. "Out-Liberalizing the EU: Pension Privatization in Central and Eastern Europe." *Journal of European Public Policy* 15.6: 899–917.

———. 2008b. "Postcommunist Welfare States." *Journal of Democracy* 19.4: 80–94.

———. 2008c. *Privatizing Pensions: The Transnational Campaign for Social Security Reform.* Princeton, NJ: Princeton University Press.

Ortuño Anaya, Pilar. 2005. *Los Socialistas Europeos y la Transición Española.* Madrid: Marcial Pons.

Owens, John E. 2003. "Part 1: Cohesion: Explaining Party Cohesion and Discipline in Democratic Legislatures: Purposiveness and Contexts." *The Journal of Legislative Studies* 9.4: 12–40.

Papadimitriou, Dimitris, and David Phinnemore. 2004. "Europeanization, Conditionality and Domestic Change: The Twinning Exercise and Administrative Reform in Romania." *Journal of Common Market Studies* 42.3: 619–639.

———. 2008. *Romania and the European Union: From Marginalisation to Membership?* New York: Routledge.

Patapievici, Horia-Roman. 2002. *Omul recent.* Humanitas.

Paterson, William, and James Sloam. 2006. "Is the Left Alright? The SPD and the Renewal of European Social Democracy." *German Politics* 15.3: 233–248.

Peck, Jamie. 2010. *Constructions of Neoliberal Reason.* New York: Oxford University Press.

Peck, Jamie, and Nik Theodore. 2012. "Reanimating Neoliberalism: Process Geographies of Neoliberalisation." *Social Anthropology* 20.2: 177–185.

Pedersen, Lene Holm. 2007. "Ideas Are Transformed as They Transfer: A Comparative Study of Eco-taxation in Scandinavia." *Journal of European Public Policy* 14.1: 59–77.

Pérez, Sofía A. 1997. *Banking on Privilege: The Politics of Spanish Financial Reform*. Ithaca, NY: Cornell University Press.

———. 1998. "Systemic Explanations, Divergent Outcomes: The Politics of Financial Liberalization in France and Spain." *International Studies Quarterly* 42.4: 755–784.

———. 1999. "From Labor to Finance Understanding the Failure of Socialist Economic Policies in Spain." *Comparative Political Studies* 32.6: 659–689.

———. 2002. "Monetary Union and Wage Bargaining Institutions in the EU Extrapolating from Some Member State Experiences." *Comparative Political Studies* 35.10: 1198–1227.

Perez-Diaz, Victor. 1990. "Governability and the Scale of Governance: Meso Governments in Spain." Estudios / Working Papers No. 6:1, Centro de Estudios Avanzados en Ciencias Sociales.

Phillips, David, and Michael Kaser. 1992. *Education and Economic Change in Eastern Europe and the Former Soviet Union*. Wallingford: Triangle Books.

Phinnemore, David. 2010. "And We'd Like to Thank . . . Romania's Integration into the European Union, 1989–2007." *Journal of European Integration* 32.3: 291–308.

Pilat, Vasile, and Daniel Dăianu. 1984. "Some Problems of the Development of European Socialist Economies." *Revue Roumaine d'Etudes Internationales* 18.3: 245–261.

Pisani-Ferry, Jean, André Sapir, and Guntram Wolff. 2013. "EU-IMF Assistance to Euro-Area Countries: An Early Assessment." *Bruegel Blueprint* 19: Q46.

Pleskovic, Boris, et al. 2000. "State of the Art in Economics Education and Research in Transition Economies." *Comparative Economic Studies* 42.2: 65–108.

Pop, Liliana. 2006. *Democratising Capitalism? The Political Economy of Post-communist Transformations in Romania, 1989–2001*. Manchester: Manchester University Press.

Pop, Liliana. 2007. "Time and Crisis: Framing Success and Failure in Romania's Post-Communist Transformations." *Review of International Studies* 33.03: 395–413.

Pop-Elecheș, Grigore. 2001. "Romania's Politics of Dejection." *Journal of Democracy* 12.3: 156–169.

———. 2008a. "A Party for All Seasons: Electoral Adaptation of Romanian Communist Successor Parties." *Communist and Post-communist Studies* 41.4: 465–479.

———. 2008b. *From Economic Crisis to Reform: IMF Programs in Latin America and Eastern Europe*. Princeton, NJ: Princeton University Press.

Popa, Ana-Maria. 2012. "The Impact of Social Factors on Economic Growth: Empirical Evidence for Romania and European Union Countries." *Romanian Journal of Fiscal Policy* 3.2: 1–16.

Popa, Cristian. 1998. "Nominal-Real Tradeoffs and the Effects of Monetary Policy: The Romanian Experience." Paper presented at Davidson Institute, University of Michigan.

Powell, Charles. 2003. "Spanish Membership of the European Union Revisited." *South European Society and Politics* 8.1–2: 147–168.

Pridham, Geoffrey. 1990. *Securing Democracy: Political Parties and Democratic Consolidation in Southern Europe*. New York: Routledge.

———. 2007. "The Scope and Limitations of Political Conditionality: Romania's Accession to the European Union." *Comparative European Politics* 5.4: 347–376.

Ptak, Ralf. 2009. *Vom Ordoliberalismus zur Sozialen Marktwirtschaft: Stationen des Neoliberalismus in Deutschland*. Opladen: Laske-Budrich.

Quaglia, Lucia. 2005. "Civil Servants, Economic Ideas, and Economic Policies: Lessons from Italy." *Governance* 18.4: 545–566.

Quaglia, Lucia, and Sebastián Royo. 2013. "Banks and the Political Economy of the Sovereign Debt Crisis in Italy and Spain." Center for European Studies Working Paper Series.

Rabushka, Alvin. 2003. "The Flat Tax in Russia and the New Europe." National Center for Policy Analysis Brief Analysis No. 452.

Recio, Albert, and Jordi Roca. 1998. "The Spanish Socialists in Power: Thirteen Years of Economic Policy." *Oxford Review of Economic Policy* 14.1: 139–158.

Remmer, Karen L. 2012. "The Rise of Leftist-Populist Governance in Latin America: The Roots of Electoral Change." *Comparative Political Studies* 45.8: 947–972.

Rhodes, Martin. 2000. "Desperately Seeking a Solution: Social Democracy, Thatcherism and the 'Third Way' in British Welfare." *West European Politics* 23.2: 161–186.

Rivasés, Jesús. 1991. *Mariano Rubio: Los Secretos del Banco de España*. Madrid: Ediciones Temas de Hoy.

Robbins, Geraldine, and Irvine Lapsley. 2014. "The Success Story of the Eurozone Crisis? Ireland's Austerity Measures." *Public Money and Management* 34.2: 91–98.

Robinson, Joan. 1975. "The Unimportance of Reswitching." *Quarterly Journal of Economics* 89.1: 32–39.

Rodó, Laureano López. 1992. *Memorias: El Principio del Fin*, Barcelona: Plaza & Janés / Cambio 16.

Rogozanu, Costi. 2013. *Carte de Muncă*. Cluz-Napoca: Editura Tact.

Rojo Duque, Luis Ángel. 1965. *Keynes y el Pensamiento Macroeconómico Actual*. Madrid: Tecnos.

———. 1976. *Inflación y Crisis en la Economía Mundial: (Hechos y Teorías)*. Madrid: Alianza Editorial.

———. 1980. "Keynes y los Problemas de Hoy." *Papeles de Economía Española* 2: 268–283.

———. 1982. "Sobre el Estado Actual de la Macroeconomía." *Pensamiento Iberoamericano* 1: 45–70.

———. 1984. *Keynes: Su Tiempo y el Nuestro*. Madrid: Alianza.

———. 1993. "Desempleo y Factores Reales." In *Diez Ensayos sobre Economía Española*. Madrid: Eudema Universidad.

———. 2002a. "Las Fluctuaciones Financieras y la Política Monetaria." *Anales de la Real Academia de Ciencias Morales y Políticas*. No. 79. Academia de Ciencias Morales y Políticas.

———. 2002b. *Veinticinco años de la Economía Española, 1977–2002*. Madrid: Círculo de Empresarios.

Rojo Duque, Luis Ángel, and José Castañeda Chornet. 1984. *JM Keynes*. Stanford, CA: Stanford University Press.

Rojo Duque, Luis Ángel, and José Pérez. 1977. *La Política Monetaria en España: Objetivos e Instrumentos*. Madrid: Banco de España, Servicio de Estudios.

Roland, Gérard. 2001. "Ten Years after ... Transition and Economics." *IMF Staff Papers* 48: 29–52.

Roman, Petre. 1994. *Libertatea ca Datorie*. Cluj-Napoca: Editura Dacia.

Røvik, Kjell Arne. 2011. "From Fashion to Virus: An Alternative Theory of Organizations' Handling of Management Ideas." *Organization Studies* 32.5: 631–653.

Royo, Sebastián. 2000. *From Social Democracy to Neoliberalism: The Consequences of Party Hegemony in Spain, 1982–1996*. New York: Macmillan.

———. 2001. "The Collapse of Social Concertation and the Failure of Socialist Economic Policies in Spain." *South European Society and Politics* 6.1: 27–50.

———. 2008. *Varieties of Capitalism in Spain: Remaking the Spanish Economy for the New Century*. Basingstoke: Palgrave Macmillan.

———. 2009. "Reforms Betrayed? Zapatero and Continuities in Economic Policy." *South European Society and Politics* 14.4: 435–451.

———. 2013. "How Did the Spanish Financial System Survive the First Stage of the Global Crisis?" *Governance* 26.4: 631–656.

Sachs, Jeffrey, and David Lipton. 1990. "Poland's Economic Reform." *Foreign Affairs* 69.3: 47–66.

Sahlin, Kerstin, and Linda Wedlin. 2008. "Circulating Ideas: Imitation, Translation and Editing." In Royston Greenwood, Christine Oliver, Kerstin Sahlin, and Roy Suddaby, eds., *The Sage Handbook of Organizational Institutionalism*. Thousand Oaks, CA: Sage, 218–242.

Sahlin-Andersson, Kerstin. 2000. *National, International and Transnational Constructions of New Public Management*. Stockholm: SCORE (Stockholm Center for Organizational Research), Univ.

Sampson, Steven. 2005. "Integrity Warriors: Global Morality and the Anti-corruption Movement in the Balkans." In Dieter Haller and Cris Shore, eds., *Corruption: Anthropological Perspectives*. London: Pluto, 103–130.

Sánchez, Antonio Muñoz. 2008. "La Fundación Ebert y el Socialismo Español de la Dictadura a la Democracia." *Cuadernos de Historia Contemporánea* 29: 257–278.

Sánchez, D. Julio Segura. 1996. "Sobre la introducción y asimilación del análisis neoclásico marginalista en España." *Anales de la Real Academia de Ciencias Morales y Políticas*. No. 73. Academia de Ciencias Morales y Políticas.

Sánchez Hormigo, Alfonso. 2002. "El Pensamiento Económico de Valentín Andrés Álvarez." In E. Fuentes Quintana, dir., *Economía y Economistas Españoles*. Barcelona: Galaxia Gutenberg and Círculo de Lectores. Vol. 7: 162–222.

Scharpf, Fritz W. 2009. "The Asymmetry of European Integration, or Why the EU Cannot Be a 'Social Market Economy.'" *Socio-Economic Review* 8.2: 211–250.

———. 2015. "After the Crash: A Perspective on Multilevel European Democracy." *European Law Journal* 21.3: 384–405.

Schiță Privind Strategia Înfăptuirii Economiei de Piață in România. 1990. Comisia Guvernamentală Pentru Elaborarea Programului de Tranziție la Economia de Piață.

Schmidt, Vivien A. 1996a. "Industrial Policy and Policies of Industry in Advanced Industrialized Nations." *Comparative Politics* 28.2: 225–248.

———.1996b. *From State to Market? The Transformation of French Business and Government*. New York: Cambridge University Press.

———. 2009. "Putting the Political Back into Political Economy by Bringing the State Back in Yet Again." *World Politics* 61.3: 516–546.

———. 2014. "Speaking to the Markets or to the People? A Discursive Institutionalist Analysis of the EU's Sovereign Debt Crisis." *British Journal of Politics and International Relations* 16.1: 188–209.

Schmidt, Vivien A., and Mark Thatcher, eds. 2013. *Resilient Liberalism in Europe's Political Economy*. New York: Cambridge University Press.

Schmidt, Vivien A., and Cornelia Woll. 2013. "The State: The Bête Noire of Neo-liberalism or Its Greatest Conquest?" In Vivien A. Schmidt and Mark Thatcher, eds., *Resilient Liberalism in Europe's Political Economy*. New York: Cambridge University Press, 112–145.

Schmitter, Philippe. 1978. "Reflections on Mihail Manoilescu and the National Consequences of Delayed Dependent Development on the Periphery of Western Europe." In Kenneth Jowitt, ed., *Social Change in Romania, 1860–1940: A Debate on Development in a European Nation*. Berkeley: Institute of International Studies, University of California, 117–173.

Schwartz, Pedro. 1998. *Nuevos Ensayos Liberales*. Madrid: Espasa Calpe.

Seabrooke, Leonard. 2014. "Epistemic Arbitrage: Transnational Professional Knowledge in Action." *Journal of Professions and Organization* 1.1: 49–64.

Seabrooke, Leonard, and Eleni Tsingou. 2009. "Revolving Doors and Linked Ecologies in the World Economy: Policy Locations and the Practice of International Financial Reform." http://wrap.warwick.ac.uk/1849.

———. 2014. "Distinctions, Affiliations, and Professional Knowledge in Financial Reform Expert Groups." *Journal of European Public Policy* 21.3: 389–407.

Seabrooke, Leonard. 2014. "Epistemic Arbitrage: Transnational Professional Knowledge in Action." *Journal of Professions and Organization* 1.1: 49–64.

Seabrooke, Leonard, and Duncan Wigan. 2014. "Global Wealth Chains in the International Political Economy." *Review of International Political Economy* 21.1: 257–263.

Segura, Julio. 2001. "La Reforma del Mercado de Trabajo Español: Un Panorama." *Revista de Economía Aplicada* 25.9: 157–190.

Segura Sánchez, Julio. 2002. "Una Nota sobre la Historia de la Introducción y Asimilación del Análisis Microeconómico Moderno en España." In E. Fuentes Quintana, dir., *Economía y Economistas Español*. Barcelona: Galaxia Gutenberg and Círculo de Lectores. Vol. 7: 385–407.

Senn, Peter S. 1996. "Heinrich von Stackelberg in the History of Economic Ideas." *Journal of Economic Studies* 23.5–6: 15–39.

———. 2012. "The Scientific Contributions of Heinrich von Stackelberg." In J. G. Backhaus, ed., *Handbook of the History of Economic Thought*. New York: Springer, 565–581.

Severin, Adrian. 1995. *Lacrimile Dimineții: Slăbiciunile Guvernului Roman*. Bucharest: Scripta.

———. 2000. *Locurile unde se Construieste Europa*. Bucharest: Polirom.

Share, Donald. 1999. "From Policy-Seeking to Office-Seeking: The Metamorphosis of the Spanish Socialist Workers Party." In Wolfgang C. Müller and Kaare Strøm, eds., *Policy, Office, or Votes? How Political Parties in Western Europe Make Hard Decisions*. New York: Cambridge University Press, 89–111.

Siani-Davies, Peter. 2007. *The Romanian Revolution of December 1989*. Ithaca, NY: Cornell University Press.

Silva, Eduardo. 1993. "Capitalist Coalitions, the State, and Neoliberal Economic Restructuring: Chile, 1973–88." *World Politics* 45.4: 526–559.

Simmons, Beth A., Frank Dobbin, and Geoffrey Garrett. 2006. "Introduction: The International Diffusion of Liberalism." *International Organization* 60.4: 781–810.

Simmons, Beth A., Frank Dobbin, and Geoffrey Garrett, eds. 2008. *The Global Diffusion of Markets and Democracy*. New York: Cambridge University Press.

Simmons, Beth A., and Zachary Elkins. 2004. "The Globalization of Liberalization: Policy Diffusion in the International Political Economy." *American Political Science Review* 98.1: 171–189.

Skidelsky, Robert. 2010. *Keynes: The Return of the Master*. New York: PublicAffairs.

———. 2011. "The Relevance of Keynes." *Cambridge Journal of Economics* 35.1: 1–13.

Snagov Declaration. 1995. Din lucrările Comisiei de la Snagov: Declarația de la Snagov. www.cdep.ro/pdfs/snagov95.pdf.

Solbes, Pedro. 2002. "Budgetary Challenges in the Euro Area." *Communication, SEC* 1009.3: 24.

———. 2013. *Recuerdos: 40 Años de Servicio Público*. Barcelona: Deusto.

Solchaga, Carlos. 1997. *El Final de La Edad Dorada*. Madrid: Taurus.

Sommers, Jeffrey, and Charles Woolfson. 2014. *The Contradictions of Austerity: The Socio-economic Costs of the Neoliberal Baltic Model*. New York: Routledge.

Spendzharova, Aneta B. 2003. "Bringing Europe in? The Impact of EU Conditionality on Bulgarian and Romanian Politics." *Southeast European Politics* 4.2–3: 141–156.

Spendzharova, Aneta B., and Milada Anna Vachudova. 2012. "Catching Up? Consolidating Liberal Democracy in Bulgaria and Romania after EU Accession." *West European Politics* 35.1: 39–58.

Spengel, Christoph, Sebastian Lazar, Lisa Evers, and Benedikt Zinn. 2012. "Reduction of the Effective Corporate Tax Burden in Romania 1992–2012 and Romania's Current Ranking among the Central and Eastern European EU Member States." *Post-communist Economies* 24.4: 477–502.

Spilimbergo, Antonio, Steve Symansky, Olivier Blanchard, and Carlo Cottarelli. 2008. "Fiscal Policy for the Crisis." IMF Staff Position Note, December 29.

Stark, David. 1994. "Path Dependence and Privatization Strategies in East Central Europe." *Transition to Capitalism*: 63–101.

Stark, David, and Laszlo Bruszt. 1998. *Postsocialist Pathways: Transforming Politics and Property in East Central Europe*. New York: Cambridge University Press.

Stănculescu, Manuela Sofia, and Georgiana Neculau. 2014. *The Performance of Public Health-Care Systems in South-East Europe*. Belgrade: Friedrich-Ebert-Stiftung.

Stănculescu, M., V. Stoiciu, I. Alexe, and L. Motoc. 2011. "Impactul crizei economice asupra migrației forței de muncă românești." București: Friedrich Ebert Stiftung.

Stiglitz, Joseph E. 1996. *Whither Socialism?* Cambridge, MA: MIT Press.

Stoenescu, Virgil. 1998. "Costin Kirițescu—un neoclasic bine temperat." *Oeconomica* 3–4.

Stoica, Cătălin Augustin. 2004. "From Good Communists to Even Better Capitalists? Entrepreneurial Pathways in Post-socialist Romania." *East European Politics and Societies* 18.2: 236–277.

Stone, Diane. 2001. "Think Tanks, Global Lesson-Drawing and Networking Social Policy Ideas." *Global Social Policy* 1.3: 338–360.

———. 2003. "Knowledge Bank and the Global Development Network, The." *Global Governance* 9: 43.

Streeck, Wolfgang. 2013. "The Crisis in Context: Democratic Capitalism and Its Contradictions." In Armin Schäfer and Wolfgang Streeck, eds., *Politics in the Age of Austerity*. Cambridge: Polity, 262–286.

Svejnar, Jan. 2000. "Economics Ph. D. Education in Central and Eastern Europe." *Comparative Economic Studies* 42.2: 37–50.

Swank, D. and Steinmo, S. 2002. "The New Political Economy of Taxation in Advanced Capitalist Democracies." *American Journal of Political Science* 46.3: 642–655.

Tănăsoiu, Cosmina. 2008. "Intellectuals and Post-communist Politics in Romania: An Analysis of Public Discourse, 1990—2000." *East European Politics and Societies* 22.1: 80–113.

Tarde, Gabriel. 1890/1903. *The Laws of Imitation*. New York: Henry Holt.

Teichman, Judith A. 2001. *The Politics of Freeing Markets in Latin America: Chile, Argentina, and Mexico*. Chapel Hill: University of North Carolina Press.

Tesliuc, Emil, Lucian Pop, and Filofteia Panduru. 2003. "Poverty in Romania: Profile and Trends during the 1995–2002." *Romania: Poverty Assessment*. Report 26169-RO.

Tismăneanu, Vladimir. 2003. *Stalinism for All Seasons: A Political History of Romanian Communism*. Berkeley: University of California Press.

Toharia, Luis. 1983. *El Mercado de Trabajo: Teorías y Aplicaciones*. Madrid: Alianza Editorial.

Trif, Aurora. 2007. "Collective Bargaining in Eastern Europe: Case Study Evidence from Romania." *European Journal of Industrial Relations* 13.2: 237–256.

———. 2008. "Opportunities and Challenges of EU Accession: Industrial Relations in Romania." *European Journal of Industrial Relations* 14.4: 461–478.

———. 2013. "Romania Collective Bargaining Institutions under Attack." *Transfer: European Review of Labour and Research* 19.2: 227–237.

Văcăroiu, Nicolae. 1998. *România, Jocuri de Interese: Carte Interviu de Gheorghe Smeoreanu*. Bucharest: Editura Intact.

Vachudova, Milada Anna. 2005. *European Undivided: Democracy, Leverage and Integration after Communism*. New York: Oxford University Press.

Vanberg, Viktor J. 2011. "The Freiburg School: Walter Eucken and Ordoliberalism." Freiburg Discussion Papers on Constitutional Economics 4.

Van Apeldoorn, Bastiaan. 2009. "The Contradictions of 'Embedded Neoliberalism'and Europe's Multi-Level Legitimacy Crisis: The European Project and its Limits." In Van Apeldoorn, Bastiaan, Jan Drahokoupil, and Laura Horn, eds., *Contradictions and Limits of Neoliberal European Governance*. Basingstoke: Palgrave Macmillan, 21–43.

Van Apeldoorn, Bastiaan. 2003. *Transnational Capitalism and the Struggle over European Integration*. New York: Routledge.

Van Apeldoorn, Bastiaan. 2001. "The Struggle over European Order: Transnational Class Agency in the Making of 'Embedded Neo-liberalism.'" In Bieler, Andreas, and Adam Morton, eds., *Social Forces in the Making of the New Europe*. Basingstoke: Palgrave Macmillan, 70–89.

Van Apeldoorn, Bastiaan, and Henk Overbeek. 2012. "Introduction: The Life Course of the Neoliberal Project and the Global Crisis." In Overbeek, Henk, and Bastiaan Van Apeldoorn, eds., *Neoliberalism in Crisis*. Basingstoke: Palgrave Macmillan, 1–20.

Varga, Mihai, and Annette Freyberg-Inan. 2014. "Post-communist State Measures to Thwart Organized Labor: The Case of Romania." *Economic and Industrial Democracy* 35, doi:10.1177/0143831X14548770.

Vasi, Ion Bogdan. 2004. "The Fist of the Working Class: The Social Movements of Jiu Valley Miners in Post-socialist Romania." *East European Politics and Societies* 18.1: 132–157.

Vasile, Radu. 2002. *Curspe Contrasens: Amintirile unui Prim-Ministru*. Bucharest: Humanitas.

Vass, Andreea. 2010. "Experienta europeana in ajustarile fiscale de amploare." *Economistul*, July 13.

Velarde Fuertes, Juan. 1996. "Stackelberg and His Role in the Change in Spanish Economic Policy." *Journal of Economic Studies* 23: 128–140.

———. 2001. "Una Nota sobre los Setenta Años del Servicio de Estudios del Banco de España." Madrid: Centro de Estudios Constitucionales: Fundación Fomento de la Historia Económica.

———. 2002. "Stackelberg y su Papel en el Cambio de la Política Económica Española." In E. Fuentes Quintana, dir., *Economía y Economistas Españoles*. Barcelona: Galaxia Gutenberg and Círculo de Lectores. Vol. 7: 349–366.

Villoria, Manuel, Gregg G. Van Ryzin, and Cecilia F. Lavena. 2013. "Social and Political Consequences of Administrative Corruption: A Study of Public Perceptions in Spain." *Public Administration Review* 73.1: 85–94.

Vinze, Enikō, and Cristina Raţ. 2013. "Spatialization and Racialization of Social Exclusion: The Social and Cultural Formation of 'Gypsy Ghettos' in Romania in a European Context." *Studia Universitatis Babes Bolyai-Sociologia* 2: 5–21.

Vliegenthart, Arjan, and Henk Overbeek. 2009. "Corporate Tax Reform in Neoliberal Europe: Central and Eastern Europe as a Template for Deepening the Neoliberal European Integration Project?" In Bastiaan van Apeldoorn, Jan Drahokoupil, and Laura Horn, eds., *Contradiction and Limits of Neoliberal European Governance.* London: Palgrave Macmillan, 143–163.

Voinea, Liviu. 2009. *Sfârşitul Economiei Iluziei, Criză Şi Anticriză: O Abordare Heterodoxă.* Bucharest: Editura Publică.

———. 2013. "Revisiting Crisis Generators in Romania and Other New EU Member States." *Review of International Political Economy* 20.4: 979–1008.

Voinea, Liviu, and Flaviu Mihăescu. 2009. "The Impact of the Flat Tax Reform on Inequality. The Case of Romania." *Romanian Journal of Economic Forecasting* 4: 19–41.

———. 2012. "A Contribution to the Public-Private Wage Inequality Debate." *Economics of Transition* 20.2: 315–337.

Vrânceanu, R. P., and D. Dăianu. 2001. "Pitfalls of Taxation Policy in Transition Economies." *Acta Oeconomica* 51.1: 3–15.

———. 2003. "What Strategies Are Viable for Developing Countries Today? The World Trade Organization and the Shrinking of 'Development Space.'" *Review of International Political Economy* 10.4: 621–644.

Watrin, Christian. 1979. "The Principles of the Social Market Economy: Its Origins and Early History." *Journal of Institutional and Theoretical Economics* 135: 405–425.

Widmaier, Wesley W. 2003. "Constructing Monetary Crises: New Keynesian Understandings and Monetary Cooperation in the 1990s." *Review of International Studies* 29.01: 61–77.

Woodford, Michael. 2009. "Convergence in Macroeconomics: Elements of the New Synthesis." *American Economic Journal: Macroeconomics* 1.1: 267–279.

Woods, Ngaire. 2006. *The Globalizers: The IMF, the World Bank, and Their Borrowers.* Ithaca, NY: Cornell University Press.

World Bank. 1991. "Romania: Staff Appraisal Report." Report no. 9652-RO, June 11.

World Bank. 2005. "Romania: Country Assistance Evaluation." Report no. 32452.

Wyplosz, Charles. 2015. "Grexit: The Staggering Cost of Central Bank Independence." *Vox,* June 29.

Zaman, Gheorghe. 1970. "L'utilisation du Modèle Input-Output dans le Calcul de l'Efficience du Commerce Extérieur." Colloque Franco-Roumain sur le Thème: Problèmes de l'Efficience Économique, France, Institut de Recherches Economiques, Institut de Science Economique Appliquée.

Zamfir, Cătălin. 2001. *Poverty in Romania.* Bucharest: CASPIS.

Zapatero, José Luis Rodríguez. 2013. *El Dilema: 600 Días de Vértigo.* Barcelona: Editorial Planeta.

Zic, Zoran. 1998. "From Lambs to Lions. The Changing Role of Bulgarian and Romanian Labor Unions in the Course of Democratic Transition." *Perspectives on Political Science* 27.3: 155–161.

INDEX

Note: page numbers followed by *f* refer to figures; those followed by n refer to notes, with note number.

Printed in the USA/Agawam, MA
March 29, 2017

649999.043